NetSuite ERP for Administrators

Learn how to install, maintain, and secure a NetSuite implementation, using the best tools and techniques

Anthony Bickof

Packt>

BIRMINGHAM - MUMBAI

NetSuite ERP for Administrators

Copyright © 2018 Packt Publishing

All rights reserved. No part of this book may be reproduced, stored in a retrieval system, or transmitted in any form or by any means, without the prior written permission of the publisher, except in the case of brief quotations embedded in critical articles or reviews.

Every effort has been made in the preparation of this book to ensure the accuracy of the information presented. However, the information contained in this book is sold without warranty, either express or implied. Neither the author, nor Packt Publishing or its dealers and distributors, will be held liable for any damages caused or alleged to have been caused directly or indirectly by this book.

Packt Publishing has endeavored to provide trademark information about all of the companies and products mentioned in this book by the appropriate use of capitals. However, Packt Publishing cannot guarantee the accuracy of this information.

Commissioning Editor: Aaron Lazar
Acquisition Editor: Aiswarya Narayanan, Chaitanya Nair
Content Development Editor: Anugraha Arunagiri
Technical Editor: Jijo Maliyekal
Copy Editor: Safis Editing
Project Coordinator: Ulhas Kambali
Proofreader: Safis Editing
Indexer: Pratik Shirodkar
Graphics: Tania Dutta
Production Coordinator: Nilesh Mohite

First published: June 2018

Production reference: 1280618

Published by Packt Publishing Ltd.
Livery Place
35 Livery Street
Birmingham
B3 2PB, UK.

ISBN 978-1-78862-887-7

www.packtpub.com

To my wife Leanne, for her love, support, and inspiration

Contributors

About the author

Anthony Bickof is an independent NetSuite consultant specializing in NetSuite consulting and training. He spent 10 years in the training department at NetSuite-Oracle, designing NetSuite Administrator and End User training courses while authoring and delivering some of the training videos used in the NetSuite Help center. He's a NetSuite Certified Administrator and Certified ERP Consultant with 13 years of experience in training and implementing NetSuite. He lives in Toronto with his wife and three children and can be reached at anthony@nofrillsnetsuitetraining.com.

About the reviewer

Gaurav Aroraa has an MPhil in computer science. He is a Microsoft MVP, lifetime member of Computer Society of India (CSI), advisory member of IndiaMentor, certified as a scrum trainer/coach, XEN for ITIL-F, and APMG for PRINCE-F and PRINCE-P. Gaurav is an open source developer, a contributor to TechNet Wiki, and the founder of Ovatic Systems Private Limited. In over 20 years of his career, he has mentored thousands of students and industry professionals. You can tweet to Gaurav on his twitter handle `@g_arora`.

> *I would like to thank my wife Shuby Arora and my angel (daughter) Aarchi Arora who permitted me to steal some time for this book that I supposed to spend with them. Also, I thank the entire PACKT Team, especially Anugraha Arunagiri and Ulhas, whose coordination and communication during the period was tremendous, and Denim, who introduced me for this book.*

Packt is searching for authors like you

If you're interested in becoming an author for Packt, please visit `authors.packtpub.com` and apply today. We have worked with thousands of developers and tech professionals, just like you, to help them share their insight with the global tech community. You can make a general application, apply for a specific hot topic that we are recruiting an author for, or submit your own idea.

Mapt

mapt.io

Mapt is an online digital library that gives you full access to over 5,000 books and videos, as well as industry leading tools to help you plan your personal development and advance your career. For more information, please visit our website.

Why subscribe?

- Spend less time learning and more time coding with practical eBooks and Videos from over 4,000 industry professionals
- Improve your learning with Skill Plans built especially for you
- Get a free eBook or video every month
- Mapt is fully searchable
- Copy and paste, print, and bookmark content

PacktPub.com

Did you know that Packt offers eBook versions of every book published, with PDF and ePub files available? You can upgrade to the eBook version at www.PacktPub.com and as a print book customer, you are entitled to a discount on the eBook copy. Get in touch with us at service@packtpub.com for more details.

At www.PacktPub.com, you can also read a collection of free technical articles, sign up for a range of free newsletters, and receive exclusive discounts and offers on Packt books and eBooks.

Table of Contents

Preface	1
Chapter 1: The Value Proposition – Doing More with Less	**7**
Value of ERP	7
The NetSuite value proposition – the whole is greater than the sum of its parts	14
Summary	16
Chapter 2: Exploring NetSuite Tools	**17**
Features that support businesses	18
Features that support administrators	24
Duplicate Detection	29
Security, from password policies to roles	30
Publishing dashboards	33
Building searches	33
Using Workflow Manager to automate tasks	35
Page loading times	36
Features that support users	36
Reminders	39
Key Performance Indicators (KPIs)	40
KPI meters	41
KPI scorecards	42
List	43
Saved Search	44
Trend graphs	45
Report snapshots	46
Pivoting data on the dashboard	47
Global search	49
Memorized transactions	50
Summary	51
Chapter 3: OneWorld	**53**
Subsidiary hierarchy	54
List records	56
Customers	56
Vendors	58
Items	59
Employees	60
Chart of accounts	60
Transactions	61

Table of Contents

Intercompany journal entries and advanced intercompany journals	62
Summary	63
Chapter 4: Implementing	**65**
Procure-to-pay process	65
Enabling the feature	66
Configuring the defaults and preferences	67
General tab – Accounts Payable	68
Items/Transactions tab	68
Order Management – Purchasing	69
Order Management – Receiving	71
Order Management – Vendor bills	72
Approval routing	72
Building blocks	72
Employees	73
Vendors	74
Item record	75
Transactions	76
Order-to-Cash	86
Enabling features	86
Configuring the defaults and preferences	89
Shipping and tax	90
Accounting Preferences – Order Management	90
Accounting Preferences – Items/ Transactions and Accounts	93
Sales & Pricing section in Accounting Preferences	94
Accounts Receivable in Accounting Preferences	94
Building blocks	95
Customer	96
Item record	97
Shipping Items	98
Transactions	100
Summary	105
Chapter 5: Security and Permissions	**107**
Authentication	107
Username and password	108
Security questions	109
IP address rules	109
Login URL	109
Roles and permissions	111
Center	112
Permissions, restrictions, and forms	112
Permissions	113
Restrictions	114
View access to specific records	116
Restrictions by segment	116
Forms	118
User Roles	119
Identifying differences between roles	120
Global permissions	121

Table of Contents

Audit Trail	122
View login Audit Trail	122
System notes	124
Audit Trail	126
Saved Search Execution Log	127
Custom reports	128
The Audience subtab	129
The Access subtab	130
File Cabinet	131
Summary	134
Chapter 6: Customization	135
Customization options	136
Tips and tricks	137
Common characteristics	141
Custom entity field	143
Employee and transaction fields use case	145
Custom records	151
Online forms	152
Custom record example	152
Reporting on custom records	160
Custom Record online form example	160
Customizing forms	165
Main screen	166
Advanced PDF/HTML layouts	170
Summary	176
Chapter 7: Imports	177
The CSV Import Assistant	178
Best practices	182
Internal IDs	182
Source data	184
Importing tips	184
Customer import	185
Example 1 – Customer import use case	185
Item import	193
Inventory import	194
Kit import	196
Transaction import	199
Edge cases	205
Change a transaction form via import	206
Extending CSV imports	208
Troubleshooting	209
Summary	211

[iii]

Chapter 8: Analytics – Searches, Reports, and the Dashboard — 213
Dashboard overview — 214
Searches versus reports — 223
Advantages — 223
Advantages of Saved Searches — 223
Advantages of Reports — 223
Saved Searches — 224
Criteria tab — 224
Formulas — 228
Standard versus summary criteria — 229
Results tab — 231
Summary column — 232
Function column — 235
Formula column — 235
Custom label and summary label columns — 235
Highlighting — 236
Available filters — 237
Audience tab — 239
Email — 240
Scheduled Emails — 241
Email alerts — 242
Roles — 243
Search settings — 244
The PUBLIC checkbox — 244
Available as List view — 244
Available as Dashboard view — 247
Available as Sublist — 247
Available for Reminders — 248
Examples — 249
Entity saved search example — 249
Transaction search example — 251
Reports — 253
Standard reports — 259
Report edit columns — 260
Report filters — 268
Report sorting — 269
Report – More options — 270
Financial Report Builder — 273
Dashboard — 277
Custom KPIs and KPI Scorecards — 278
KPI — 278
Custom KPI example — 278
KPI Scorecard — 281
KPI scorecard example — 284
Summary — 287

Chapter 9: Workflows — 289

SuiteFlow	290
Which record will be affected?	291
When will the automation be activated?	293
Initiation	294
Order	295
Triggers	296
What will be automated?	297
How do we set up a workflow?	298
Creating a new workflow	298
Creating states	300
Creating Actions	301
Troubleshooting workflows	302
Use case	304
Creating the custom field	305
Saved search	305
Workflow	305
Summary	306
Chapter 10: Integration	**307**
The suite versus best of breed	307
The suite	307
Best of breed	308
The framework	308
Lessons learned	309
Summary	310
Chapter 11: New Releases	**311**
Major releases	311
What release am I on?	312
Notifications	312
Important dates	314
Release Preview	314
Preparing for the upgrade	314
Sneak peeks and release notes	314
Training videos	315
Test plan	317
Sandbox	317
Summary	318
Chapter 12: Troubleshooting Tips	**319**
Database uptime	319
Documentation	320
Help center	321
SuiteAnswers	322
Training videos	323
NetSuite user group	324

A methodology for troubleshooting	324
Troubleshooting errors	325
New functionality	325
Enabling features	326
Accounting preferences	326
Setup manager	327
Help Center	327
A philosophical approach	328
Summary	329
Chapter 13: An Ongoing Maintenance Checklist	331
Checklist	331
Backups	331
Review administrative confirmations	334
System alerts	335
Login audit trail	336
Billing information	336
Duplicate detection	337
Summary	338
Other Books You May Enjoy	339
Index	343

Preface

Peruse the job boards and you'll find many listings for NetSuite Administrators. The job descriptions require skills such as building reports and dashboards to configuration, importing data, troubleshooting, supporting end users as well as leveraging NetSuite to improve and automate processes. In other words, be a system administrator, developer, business analyst, trainer, implementer, and strategic advisor, the point of contact for all things is NetSuite. That is a lot to expect from one person.

My objective is to teach the skills that will enable the reader to perform all those interdisciplinary tasks. This is not easy, because as you have likely seen already, NetSuite is a powerful application, rich with functionality. The administrator can be bombarded with so much information that it is impossible to retain it all. I take a different approach.

To use the analogy of a puzzle, what's the first thing we need to do when doing a puzzle? Look at the picture on the front of the box! Without that context, it's more likely that the reader will forget the details of each piece. I, therefore, start by showing them the picture on the front of the box and only then delve into the details of the individual pieces. This shows the reader how each piece contributes to the bigger picture and how and where it fits in.

We will start with an overview of ERP and NetSuite ERP, because we need to know the end goal that we are striving for and why we do it. We will then explain the built-in features to show the breadth of the product and its ease of use. This illustrates how you can easily solve complex problems and have an impact on work in the short term. In the long term, they can use this chapter to solve problems that will arise in the future.

The focus then shifts to specific skills that are required to administer any system, such as role, permissions, customization, and data imports. The administrators know the concepts as they have used them in administering other systems. I, therefore, provide tips and tricks to perform this effectively in NetSuite without having to learn all the theory that underpins it.

Preface

Now that we know where the data resides in the database and how to get it in there, we can look at mining it for business intelligence. We will look at the tools NetSuite includes to perform that data mining, namely, searches, reports, and the dashboard. I will explain when to use one tool as opposed to the others and compare the functionality to apps already used, such as Excel. I will explain how the administrator can centralize the creation of search templates and give the users the tools to pivot the data and expose it to the user in useful ways, such as on the dashboard.

The topic then shifts to the future, arming the administrator with the tools they will need to support the application through new releases and troubleshooting problems.

Finally, I will provide checklists that summarize the entire book, providing actionable steps administrators can take to do their jobs.

The value is not just in the content of each chapter but in how they impact topics in other chapters. Custom fields, for instance, are of limited use if you can't update the data easily using an import or search the field and place the results on a dashboard. It is only by cross-referencing the other chapters that the reader gains a holistic view of the NetSuite product, and I will highlight that relationship throughout the book.

Who this book is for

The book is targeted at administrators who have been employed to either maintain an existing NetSuite database or to liaise with external NetSuite consultants who are implementing the system at their employer (and then use that experience to administer NetSuite after it has been deployed). They know databases and coding but may have limited knowledge of ERP and business process.

The reader has likely some limited experience with NetSuite, has accessed it, and reviewed some of the help documentation. Administrators, however, tend to find the interface overwhelming with an unfriendly menu system and complex help knowledge base. They describe seeing all the options NetSuite offers as drinking through the proverbial fire hose and want help to make sense of all this information.

There may also be several experienced administrators reading this book. They may have been NetSuite customers for many years and want to learn about the new features that NetSuite has introduced since they were first implemented.

Administrators want to learn the tasks they need to perform on a daily basis (troubleshooting errors and setting up users) as well as monthly (such as imports and duplicate detection and merge). They also want to become expert enough to be seen as the NetSuite leader internally, being able to advise department heads on specific processes as well as on strategic decisions (such as whether to use NetSuite webstore or shopify.) They want to learn these skills quickly without having to spend weeks of time and thousands of dollars taking NetSuite corporate training.

What this book covers

Chapter 1, *The Value Proposition – Doing More with Less*, discusses the ERP Value Proposition and how NetSuite enhances the value from efficiency to automation to illustrate its strengths and how the administrator can maximize those strengths. NetSuite has solved a lot of the business challenges that companies have encountered and are yet to encounter, so there is no need to waste time and money to solve problems that have already been solved.

Chapter 2, *Exploring NetSuite Tools*, gives you because there is no need to reinvent the wheel. We shift to exploring the tools NetSuite gives you, breaking down the features that support the business, the administrator, and the user. This gives you a list of specific tools that you can use right away to make your job easier and effectively support your users.

Chapter 3, *OneWorld*, simplifies OneWorld by showing how it differs from the core NetSuite, thereby streamlining its implementation as some readers will be using NetSuite's flagship OneWorld product.

Chapter 4, *Implementing*, demonstrates NetSuite's core processes for an administrator to understand NetSuite core processes in order to support the users effectively. It will simultaneously demonstrate the tools that can be used to tweak a process.

Chapter 5, *Security and Permissions*, explores NetSuite's security options from providing access to the system and enhancing security using roles and permissions. We will also cover how NetSuite provides access to data and forms using roles and how to customize the existing role templates with specific recommendations of permissions to add and remove (such as the ability to export data).

Preface

Chapter 6, *Customization*, focuses on building fields to classify customers and vendors or specific details on invoices and Purchase Orders, whether it applies to the whole transaction or specific products purchased in the transaction. It also covers differentiating between one-to-one fields and one-to-many fields and its application in building forms that can be filled out by outsiders, such as a customer satisfaction survey.

Chapter 7, *Imports*, includes topics such as importing new leads and updating data, such as price increases. We will look at how to cleanse the source data, build an import template, and test the import. We also look at refining an existing template and troubleshoot error messages encountered in the test.

Chapter 8, *Analytics – Searches, Reports, and the Dashboard*, is devoted to Searches, Reports, and Dashboards, because analytics may be the most important task that an Administrator does. We look at best practices when using the build in the features of the dashboard and show specific dashboard tools to be used and the positive impact they can have on efficiency. NetSuite has two different reporting tools, namely Reports and Saved Searches. This can be extremely confusing for Administrators and users alike. We tackle that question head on, showing the advantages and disadvantages of each.

We look at building commonly used searches and reports demonstrating the filtering and formatting options available. After a lengthy discussion on using the filtering and formatting tools available in Reports and Saved Searches, we show how you can leverage that information by placing it on the dashboard.

Chapter 9, *Workflows*, provides an introduction to the Workflow Manager. What do you do when the built-in functions are not sufficient to automate a particular process? NetSuite includes a tool that can be used to achieve automation without the need for any coding. The Workflow Manager is a point-and-click tool that can be used to enter data and communicate with users performing actions, such as sending emails.

Chapter 10, *Integration*, outlines a framework that can be used to help make the decision on whether to use the legacy system for a module or to migrate it to NetSuite. An Administrator is often called upon to provide strategic direction on how NetSuite can automate the entire business.

Chapter 11, *New Releases*, explains the NetSuite release process and how to prepare for new releases as well as ensures that you have access to all the features that you paid for.

Chapter 12, *Troubleshooting Tips*, lists the steps to use when troubleshooting and steps to take to maintain the accuracy of the data as well as what to do when things go wrong, where to go to find answers, and a philosophy to use to find answers to these questions.

Chapter 13, *An Ongoing Maintenance Checklist*, summarizes the steps needed to be taken monthly to administer a NetSuite database.

There are many demands placed on a NetSuite Administrator, who is expected to be a product expert who can advise the management on the strategic uses of NetSuite as well as support users by training them on the tips and tricks they can use to work more effectively. Furthermore, the administrator is expected to tweak processes, automate actions, import and manipulate data, and ensure that the system is secure so that unauthorized users do not get access to sensitive data. Also, if that's not enough, the Administrator is also expected to fix anything that goes wrong in the system. That is no mean feat; however, I've designed the content in an attempt to transform a new NetSuite Administrator into someone who can tackle those tasks after reading this book.

Most of all, I want you to be excited about the challenge of administering NetSuite by seeing how you can have a huge impact on your company by leveraging NetSuite to its fullest. Armed with the knowledge in this book, you can really make a difference.

To get the most out of this book

1. Ensure that you have administrator access to a NetSuite database, preferably a sandbox or demo database.
2. Review the navigation to get familiar with the menus.

Download the color images

We also provide a PDF file that has color images of the screenshots/diagrams used in this book. You can download it from `https://www.packtpub.com/sites/default/files/downloads/NetSuiteERPforAdministrators_ColorImages.pdf`.

Conventions used

Menu paths appear in this format: **Setup** | **Company** | **Enable Features**

Warnings or important notes appear like this.

Tips and tricks appear like this.

Get in touch

Feedback from our readers is always welcome.

General feedback: Email `feedback@packtpub.com` and mention the book title in the subject of your message. If you have questions about any aspect of this book, please email us at `questions@packtpub.com`.

Errata: Although we have taken every care to ensure the accuracy of our content, mistakes do happen. If you have found a mistake in this book, we would be grateful if you would report this to us. Please visit `www.packtpub.com/submit-errata`, selecting your book, clicking on the Errata Submission Form link, and entering the details.

Piracy: If you come across any illegal copies of our works in any form on the Internet, we would be grateful if you would provide us with the location address or website name. Please contact us at `copyright@packtpub.com` with a link to the material.

If you are interested in becoming an author: If there is a topic that you have expertise in and you are interested in either writing or contributing to a book, please visit `authors.packtpub.com`.

Reviews

Please leave a review. Once you have read and used this book, why not leave a review on the site that you purchased it from? Potential readers can then see and use your unbiased opinion to make purchase decisions, we at Packt can understand what you think about our products, and our authors can see your feedback on their book. Thank you!

For more information about Packt, please visit `packtpub.com`.

The Value Proposition – Doing More with Less

Modern business is complex. There are many suppliers and even more customers transacting with our employees every day. It's difficult to collate all that information because it involves sales, fulfillment, billing, and collections, as well as ordering products to sell in quantities that keep stock at their optimal levels. In addition, an accountant requires that copies of all transactions be kept to create income statement and balance sheet.

You may ask how ERP and NetSuite, in particular, can help in running a business. In this chapter, we will focus on the value of ERP as well as the NetSuite value proposition, namely that the whole is greater than the sum of its parts.

Value of ERP

Enterprise Resource Planning (ERP). The objectives of ERP are to make operations more efficient while simultaneously building financial statements, ordering from suppliers at the right time to optimize the quantity kept in the inventory, selling and fulfilling the products, processing payments efficiently, and initiating the next step in a process, without the need for human intervention. It also enables employees to communicate without having to speak to each other, thereby optimizing customer communications and reducing internal effort by allowing customer self-service while simultaneously capturing the journal entries necessary to accurately reflect the state of the business from an accounting perspective, and to create actionable business intelligence.

The Value Proposition – Doing More with Less

Yogi Berra once quipped, *"if you don't know where you are going, you'll end up someplace else"*, which is why we start by exploring the benefits of ERP in this chapter. ERP crosses different departments in the company, requiring the administrator to take a holistic view because a process in one department has knock-on effects on processes in other departments. This also illustrates the impact a good administrator can have on the health of the company.

But that sounds more of an MBA book full of, *"low hanging fruit, with soup to nuts, where the rubber meets the road"* and not a book on software, so let's illustrate the value of ERP using a use case of a mobile phone reseller.

The analysis will use this paradigm—each step in the buying and selling process will be categorized as either a transaction, a list of reusable information, a customization, and/or as having a financial impact. Doing so will not only teach us about ERP but also about the steps we as administrators will need to take to keep the process running smoothly.

The process starts by ordering five iPhones from Apple. The phones are ordered from a supplier using a purchase order that records the quantity and cost of the items being ordered:

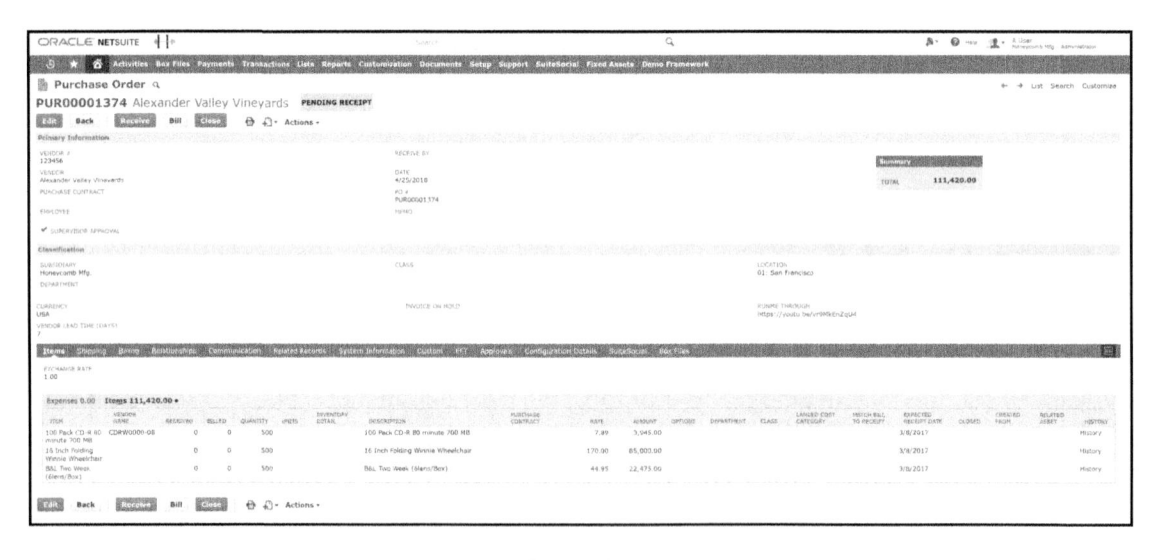

Purchase order

This will be the first of many iPhones that will be ordered, so we should probably set the iPhone up as a reusable list with the name, the cost, and all the characteristics of the product. It will also be the first of many orders sent to Apple, so Apple should also be set up in our reusable list of vendors with their details, such as phone numbers, email address, and physical address:

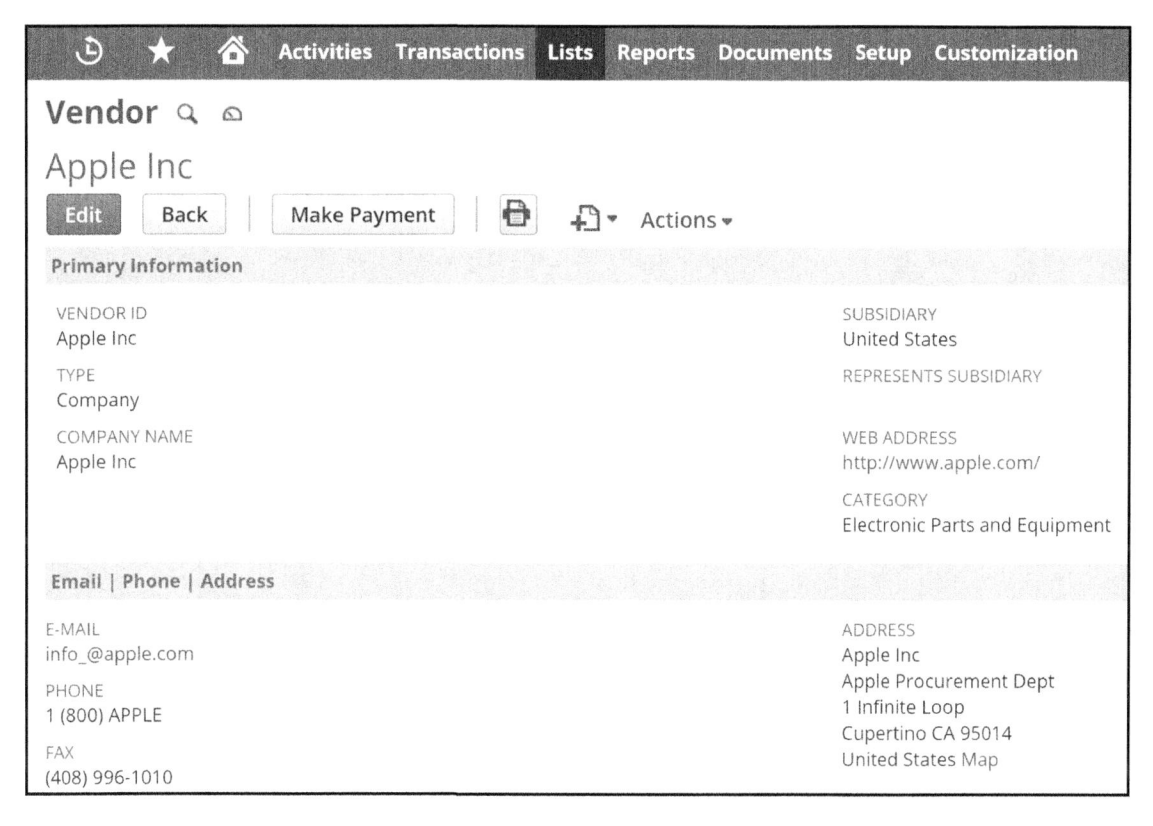

Vendor	
Apple Inc	
Edit Back Make Payment Actions ▼	
Primary Information	
VENDOR ID Apple Inc	SUBSIDIARY United States
TYPE Company	REPRESENTS SUBSIDIARY
COMPANY NAME Apple Inc	WEB ADDRESS http://www.apple.com/
	CATEGORY Electronic Parts and Equipment
Email | Phone | Address	
E-MAIL info_@apple.com	ADDRESS Apple Inc Apple Procurement Dept 1 Infinite Loop Cupertino CA 95014 United States Map
PHONE 1 (800) APPLE	
FAX (408) 996-1010	

Vendor Record

The Value Proposition – Doing More with Less

The transaction is entered into our system for historical purposes, as well as to alert the warehouse to expect to receive the iPhones; a copy of the transaction also needs to be sent to the vendor. Apple will not accept a screenshot of our system and requires a professional looking purchase order form before they will recognize this as a valid order. We will, therefore, need to customize the internal purchase order form as well as the external purchase order form:

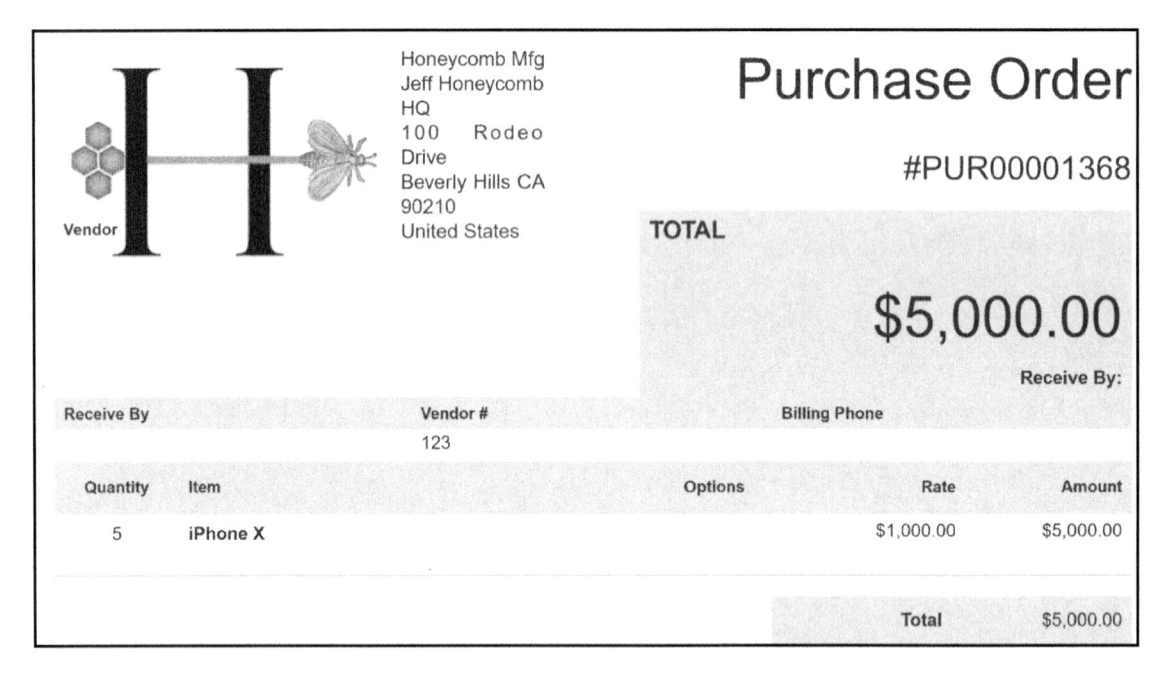

Vendor	Honeycomb Mfg Jeff Honeycomb HQ 100 Rodeo Drive Beverly Hills CA 90210 United States	**Purchase Order** #PUR00001368 **TOTAL** **$5,000.00**

Receive By:

Receive By	Vendor # 123	Billing Phone	
Quantity	Item	Options	Rate	Amount
5	iPhone X		$1,000.00	$5,000.00
			Total	$5,000.00

Purchase order to be sent to the vendor

The categories from this one transaction will look like this:

Category	Activity
Transactions	Purchase order
Lists	Item: iPhone Vendor: Apple
Customization	Purchase order internal form; Purchase order external form
Accounting impact	

When UPS delivers that inventory, the warehouse manager enters the receipt of the iPhones. To summarize, the **Transactions** category is updated with the **Item Receipt** and the **Accounting Impact** is that our inventory increases by $5,000:

Category	Activity
Transactions	Purchase order Receipt
Lists	Item: iPhone Vendor: Apple
Customization	Purchase order internal form; Purchase order external form
Accounting impact	Inventory: +$5,000

The vendor attaches an invoice to the shipment and the accountant needs to enter this transaction to reflect the indebtedness. The accountant bills the **purchase order** (**PO**), which creates the **Accounting Impacts** of adding the $5,000 to **accounts payable** (**AP**):

Category	Activity
Transactions	Purchase order Receipt Bill PO
Lists	Item: iPhone Vendor: Apple
Customization	Purchase order internal form; Purchase order external form
Accounting impact	Inventory: +$5,000 AP: +$5,000

Once Apple is paid using a **Pay Bills Transaction**, the debt is extinguished. In other words, the accounts payable entry is reversed and the bank account is decreased by $5,000:

Category	Activity
Transactions	Purchase order Receipt Bill PO Pay Bill
Lists	Item: iPhone Vendor: Apple
Customization	Purchase order internal form; Purchase order external form
Accounting impact	Inventory: +$5,000 AP: +$5,000 - $5,000 = $0 Bank: -$5,000

The Value Proposition – Doing More with Less

At the end of the process, the company is left an additional $5,000 in inventory and the bank account has decreased by $5,000.

As administrators, we can see that the reusable lists of item and vendor can make entering purchase orders more efficient in the future because, once selected, all the information about the item and vendor is automatically sourced into the purchase order. We can also start compiling our task list, as it seems we will need to customize the internal purchase order form and the external form that was sent to the vendor. Now, to relate that to NetSuite specifically, you will see that NetSuite has **Transactions**, **Lists**, and **Customization** menus, where you will find each of these records under that category. Furthermore, there is a link to the **GL Impact** on each transaction, which displays the **Accounting Impact** of that transaction:

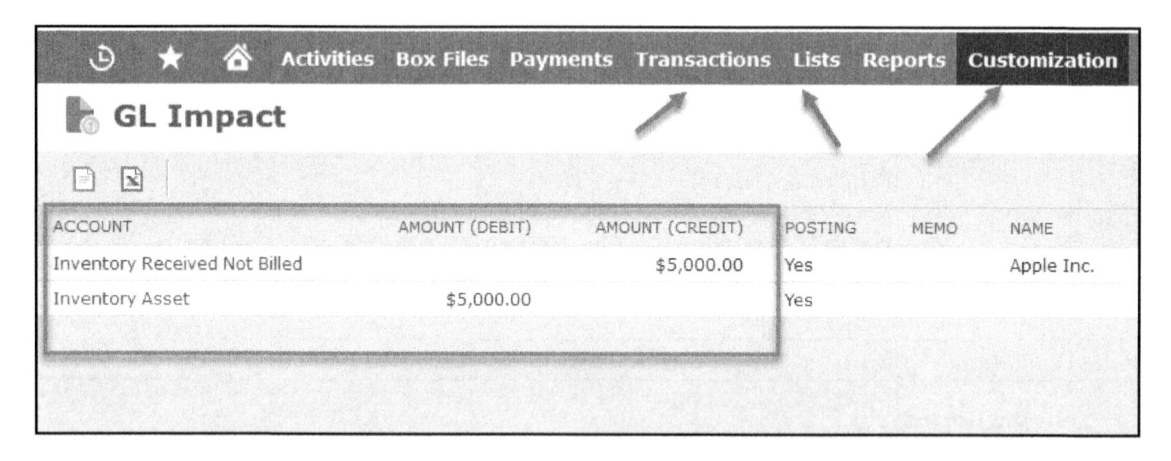

GL Impact

ACCOUNT	AMOUNT (DEBIT)	AMOUNT (CREDIT)	POSTING	MEMO	NAME
Inventory Received Not Billed		$5,000.00	Yes		Apple Inc.
Inventory Asset	$5,000.00		Yes		

GL Impact

On the sales side, the starting point is a sales order that contains the item (iPhone) and the customer. The item was already created when we used it in the purchase order, so we can simply reuse it. The customer will, however, need to be created but can be reused in future transactions. It may require a customization of the sales order form, as well as the external form that needs to be given to the customer:

Category	Activity
Transactions	Sales order
List	Item: iPhone Customer: Brad Pitt
Customization	Sales order internal form; Sales order external form
Accounting impact	

The order is then sent to the warehouse for fulfillment. The iPhone is picked from the warehouse, packed into a box, and shipped to the customer, requiring a pick ticket, packing slip, and shipping label. Shipping the order results in one less iPhone available in the inventory, so it decreases the inventory by $1,000:

Category	Activity
Transactions	Sales order Fulfillment
List	Item: iPhone Customer: Brad Pitt
Customization	Sales order internal form; Sales order external form Pick ticket, packing slip, shipping label
Accounting impact	Inventory: -$1,000

The accountant will invoice the customer as soon as the item ships, which requires an internal invoice form as well as an external professional looking invoice that is sent to the customer. It also results in an accounting impact on the **accounts receivable** (**AR**) in the amount of the sales price:

Category	Activity
Transactions	Sales order Fulfillment Invoice
List	Item: iPhone Customer: Brad Pitt
Customization	Sales order internal form; Sales order external form Pick ticket, packing slip, shipping label Invoice internal form, invoice external form
Accounting impact	Inventory: -$1,000 AR: +$1,500

Once payment is received, the accountant will bank the check, which will extinguish the customer's indebtedness; in other words, it will reverse the amount in accounts receivable:

Category	Activity
Transactions	Sales order Fulfillment Invoice Accept payment

List	Item: iPhone Customer: Brad Pitt
Customization	Sales order internal form; Sales order external form Pick ticket, packing slip, shipping label Invoice internal form, invoice external form
Accounting impact	Inventory: -$1,000 AR: +$1,500 Bank +$1,500

The accounting impact category enables the CFO to run the financial reports without having to do any further work, which is a major benefit of ERP. The **Lists** and **Customization** categories are the administrator's responsibility, to ensure the process works efficiently without the need for re-entering information. The sales rep, warehouse manager, and accountant have unwittingly created the financial statement by merely recording their work in the ERP system.

The NetSuite value proposition – the whole is greater than the sum of its parts

NetSuite takes ERP a step further. It is an ERP with a built-in CRM, all available in the cloud.

Most of the products out there are specialist products for specific areas of the business; for instance, *salesforce.com*, *ConstantContact*, or *ShipStation*. While these are excellent products with deep functionality, they are designed to automate departments whereas NetSuite automates the entire business.

NetSuite's functionality spans accounting, the warehouse, the website, marketing, sales, and customer support. This doesn't just provide efficiencies because we are administering one system instead of many. All the data is in one place for reporting and can easily be leveraged by different departments; for instance, the pricing matrix on the item master serves the website as well as the sales reps. If there is a price increase, it only needs to be changed once instead of in multiple databases.

Chapter 1

NetSuite also tracks all the transactions and interactions on aggregate—such as sales reports for the company as a whole—but also on a per customer level. The result is a complete 360° customer view showing each individual customer history on one page, capturing the historical sales and products sold with records of the calls, meetings, and emails exchanged with anyone in the company, which enables us to serve the customer more effectively and efficiently.

An employee can see the details by merely looking at subtabs on the customer card or at a summary by accessing the customer dashboard. So, the accountant can see that the sales rep is close to closing a huge opportunity with the customer prior to calling to collect a small outstanding debt, which could place the opportunity in jeopardy. The converse is also true; the sales rep can view the customer's average days to pay invoices prior to extending that customer's credit. Most importantly, it enables sales and marketing departments to access a customer's purchase history to determine which products represent good upsell opportunities—*would you like fries with that?*:

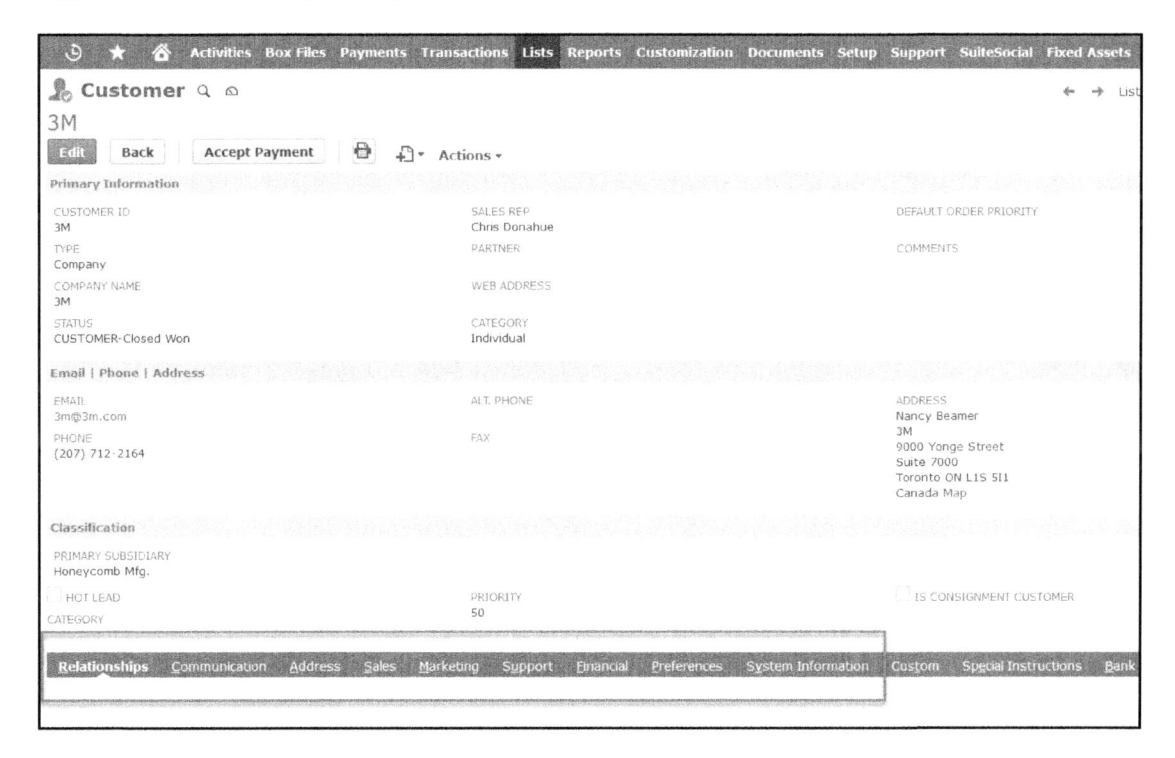

Customer record

The Value Proposition – Doing More with Less

The cloud also has implications for the business as well as administrators. The system requires minimal IT support. All you need is an internet connection and there is no need for database management, such as backups.

It also allows us to centralize administration. Do you need to implement and support a feature for the subsidiary in China? There is no need to fly there; you can simply do it all right from your office. (In my view, this shouldn't apply to subsidiaries in Hawaii, which require an onsite visit, especially if the deployment is scheduled for the winter!)

The cloud also offers opportunities for easier customer self-service by merely opening a window into the core business system. A cloud system is simply a database permanently on the web, which allows people access based on specific permissions. We typically think of employees as those users but there is no need to restrict this just to employees. We can simply allow outsiders into our system provided they have the right set of permissions, so NetSuite contains built-in customer, vendor, and partner portals, which can be made available to specific customers, vendors, and partners at no additional cost.

Summary

There is an old joke that goes: how do you know when your SAP implementation is finished? It's when you run out of money!

Companies used to have to spend millions of dollars on ERP in order to achieve the benefits of running the business in one system. The benefits of buying, selling, planning, and reporting within a single platform had to be weighed against the substantial cost of implementing and running the ERP. It required teams of consultants to gather requirements, consolidate processes between departments, and be physically present to configure the processes in the ERP system.

The internet democratized knowledge, technology, and ERP. There is no need to pay millions when you can rent a robust ERP like NetSuite for an affordable price per user per month. There is also no need to employ a team of consultants when a strong administrator can control a worldwide deployment from a home office; we will be exploring how an administrator can do so in the remaining chapters.

NetSuite has thousands of customers and has built features and processes to solve business problems you don't even know you have. Leveraging these tools is an effective way for an administrator to demonstrate value to the business, so we will start by examining them in `Chapter 2`, *Exploring NetSuite Tools*.

Exploring NetSuite Tools

NetSuite has thousands of customers, and it prioritizes new features based on the number of customer requests for each feature. As a result, NetSuite has built-in solutions for many of the business challenges that you are already experiencing, and for many more that you may not have encountered yet. There is no need to waste time and money solving problems that have already been solved; let's take a tour of NetSuite's features, so that you don't need to reinvent the wheel.

This chapter will cover:

- Features that support businesses
- Features that support users
- Features that support administrators

Features that support businesses

I've claimed that NetSuite's functionality is extensive, and now it's time for me to demonstrate that. You may not have access to all of the features that I refer to in this section. Some are advanced features that are only available for an additional fee. You can verify this by clicking on the **Setup** button on the toolbar and selecting **Setup Manager**. A search box will appear, allowing you to search through the entire **Setup** menu to look for a feature. If you don't find it, you don't have access to it and will need to speak to your NetSuite sales rep:

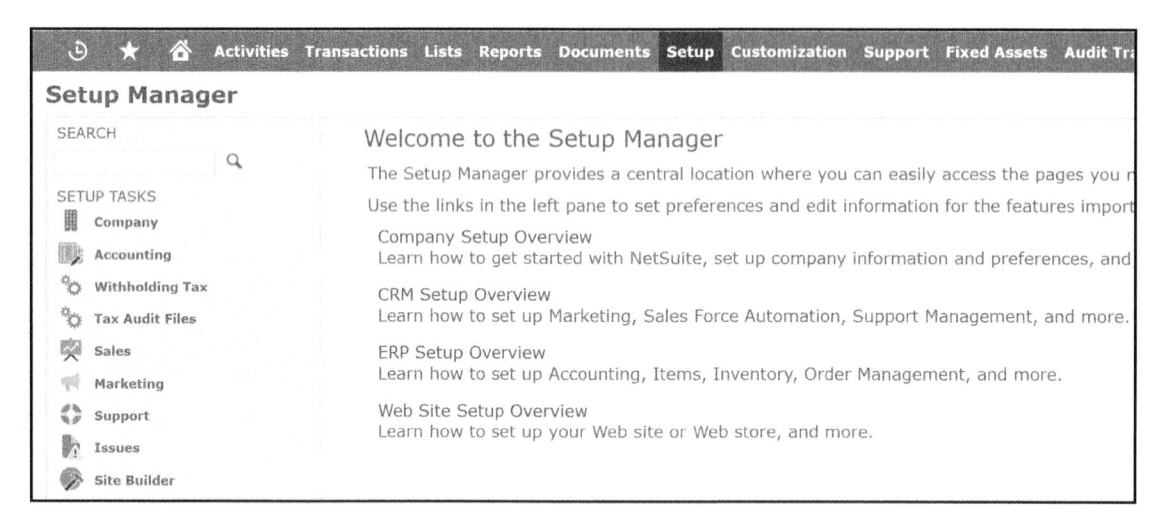

Setup Manager

If you do have access to a feature, you will find it under **Setup | Company | Enable Features**.

Some features are self-explanatory; they include the following:

- **Accounting** lets you use NetSuite as your accounting system in conjunction with **ACCOUNTING PERIODS**, enabling your company to report financial statements.
- **A/R** (Account Receivable) is used to manage customers who owe money, so that the company can properly manage its cash flow.

- Cash flow management can also be optimized by paying vendors and suppliers when the bill is finally due, which is managed by the **A/P** (Account Payable) feature:

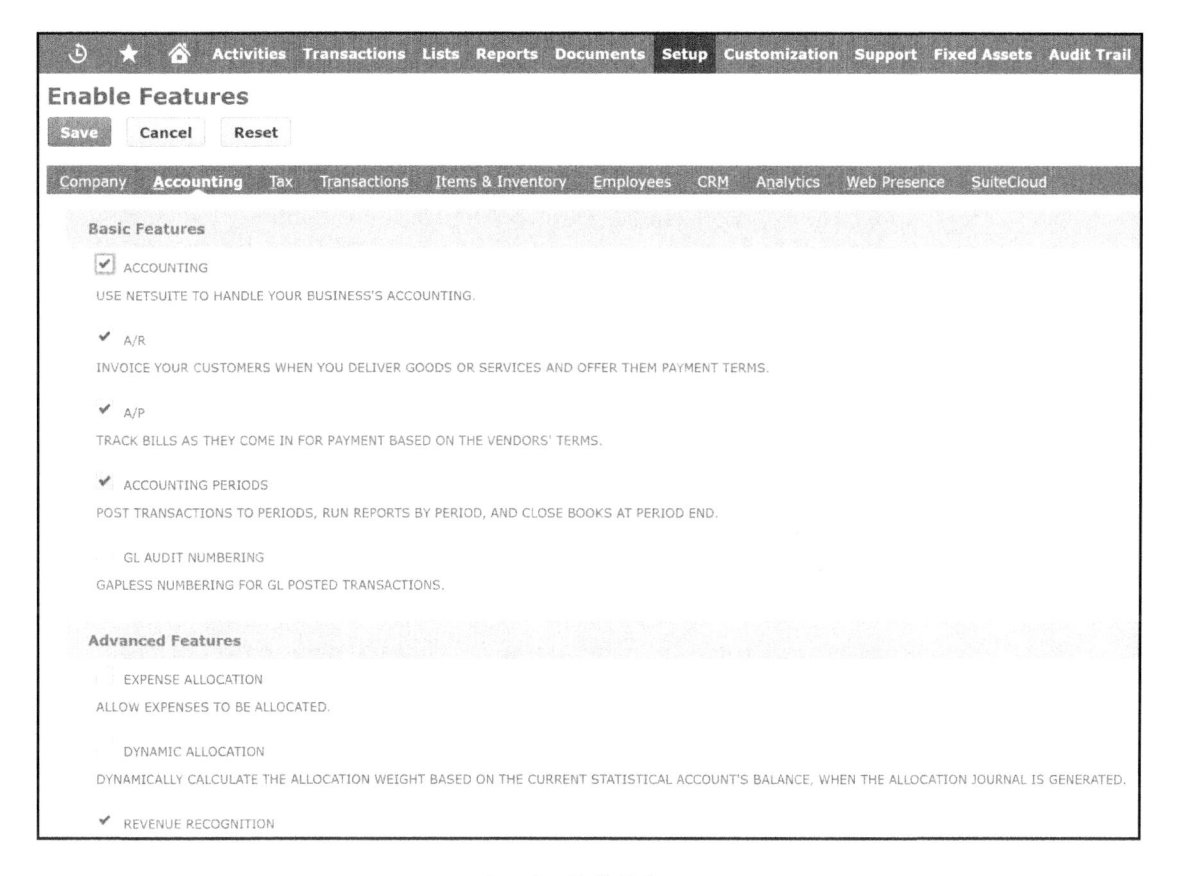

Accounting tab in Enable Features

- Companies need to know the number of items that they have in stock. This information is used for selling purposes, as well as to value the inventory on the company's balance sheet.
- For a large company, this may require tracking inventory at many different warehouses, which is achieved by using the **MULTI-LOCATION INVENTORY** feature. In addition, it may be useful to know where each item is stored within each warehouse, and the BINS feature can be used to help organize each warehouse.

Exploring NetSuite Tools

- Inventory is critical for tracking purposes, and is always changing. It is increased when items are received, based on a purchase order that is sent to the vendor; it is decreased when items are shipped to a customer, when a sale is recognized through sales order. This can be tricky when purchasing and selling items in different quantities. A restaurant, for instance, may order Pepsi in crates, stock it in cases, and sell it in individual bottles.
- Keeping track of the quantity of Pepsi in stock would require constantly converting cases and crates of Pepsi into individual bottles. Luckily, NetSuite does the math for us, using a unit-of-measure feature. In a similar vein, a company may not sell items in the same configuration in which it purchases them from the vendor. Manufacturing requires the purchase of inventory, which is then combined with other components and built into a completely new item then sold to customers.
- NetSuite uses **ASSEMBLY ITEMS** to keep track of the quantities and values of all of the items in that process. A computer manufacturer would set up RAM, hard drives, CPUs, and so on, as inventory items, and the computers as assembly items. One assembly item uses one CPU, one hard drive, and two sticks of RAM as components. The built transaction reflects that a computer has been built and is available for sale, and there are one less hard drive, one less CPU, and two fewer RAM sticks in the inventory. Many computer manufacturers build to order, so how would that be reflected in NetSuite?
- How would the warehouse manager know to build the new computer? The **WORK ORDERS** feature provides the warehouse manager with a process to accomplish this. **WORK ORDERS** can be automatically created when the sales order is entered, providing detailed instructions to build a specific assembly item consisting of specific components. Many items, such as computers, are given individual serial numbers:

Chapter 2

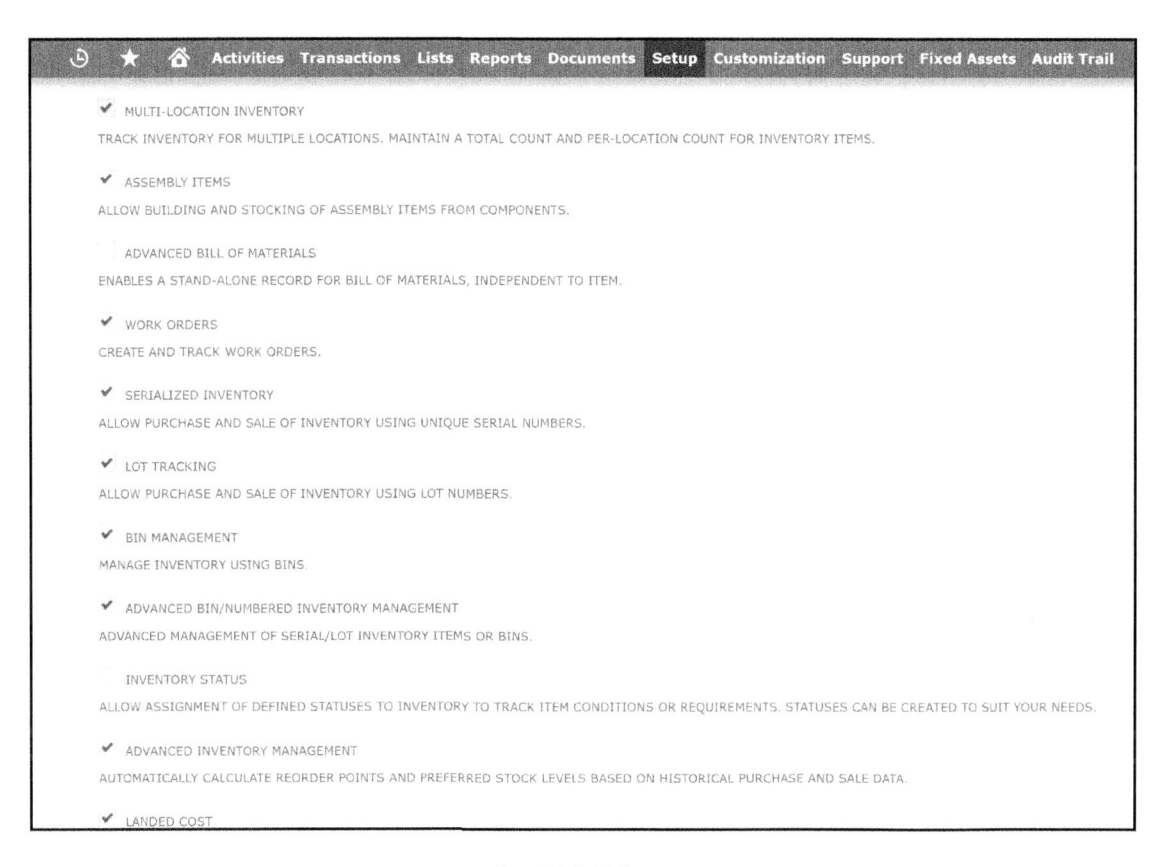

```
✓ MULTI-LOCATION INVENTORY
TRACK INVENTORY FOR MULTIPLE LOCATIONS. MAINTAIN A TOTAL COUNT AND PER-LOCATION COUNT FOR INVENTORY ITEMS.

✓ ASSEMBLY ITEMS
ALLOW BUILDING AND STOCKING OF ASSEMBLY ITEMS FROM COMPONENTS.

  ADVANCED BILL OF MATERIALS
ENABLES A STAND-ALONE RECORD FOR BILL OF MATERIALS, INDEPENDENT TO ITEM.

✓ WORK ORDERS
CREATE AND TRACK WORK ORDERS.

✓ SERIALIZED INVENTORY
ALLOW PURCHASE AND SALE OF INVENTORY USING UNIQUE SERIAL NUMBERS.

✓ LOT TRACKING
ALLOW PURCHASE AND SALE OF INVENTORY USING LOT NUMBERS.

✓ BIN MANAGEMENT
MANAGE INVENTORY USING BINS.

✓ ADVANCED BIN/NUMBERED INVENTORY MANAGEMENT
ADVANCED MANAGEMENT OF SERIAL/LOT INVENTORY ITEMS OR BINS.

  INVENTORY STATUS
ALLOW ASSIGNMENT OF DEFINED STATUSES TO INVENTORY TO TRACK ITEM CONDITIONS OR REQUIREMENTS. STATUSES CAN BE CREATED TO SUIT YOUR NEEDS.

✓ ADVANCED INVENTORY MANAGEMENT
AUTOMATICALLY CALCULATE REORDER POINTS AND PREFERRED STOCK LEVELS BASED ON HISTORICAL PURCHASE AND SALE DATA.

✓ LANDED COST
```

Setup tab in Enable Features

- The NetSuite **SERIALIZED INVENTORY** feature will require each serialized item to be identified when that item is received from a vendor, fulfilled to a customer, or transferred to another warehouse or another **BIN MANAGEMENT** within a warehouse. You may be wondering: Does that require the user to type the serial number in when entering any of the transactions? No; the barcoding feature lets you attach a scanning gun and simply scan the serial number.

- Manufacturers and suppliers of medical devices need to know which specific items were sold to which customers, in the event that there is a recall. **LOT TRACKING** provides this ability, by assigning lots to a number of items, and automatically tracking where each item is at any time. The CFO is usually reluctant to purchase too much inventory. It reduces cash flow and runs the risk of redundancy. So, how does NetSuite help ensure that the company is purchasing the right amount of inventory to meet customer demand? This can be done manually, by setting a minimum quantity and preferred stock level on each individual item. When the minimum quantity level is reached, a reminder pops up on the dashboard, warning the warehouse manager. The reminder is tied to a pro-forma purchase order, which defaults at the correct quantity to order so as to get to the preferred stock level.
- That begs the question: How do we know what values to set on the inventory record? NetSuite has two options to calculate these values automatically. **ADVANCED INVENTORY MANAGEMENT** will look at previous purchases and sales to determine the preferred stock level, taking into account the lead time to receive the items, if the vendor is based in China. It even takes seasonality into account, to ensure that a snow blower manufacturer doesn't have a glut of inventory in the summer because the calculation was performed based on purchases in the winter. Whereas advanced inventory management looks backward, demand planning is used to predict future demand, by using quotes and opportunities, as well as analyzing previous sales history.
- Warehouse distributors have defined prices for many of their customers. It is tedious and difficult to ensure that the correct price is being charged, especially since many have over 10,000 items in the inventory. NetSuite's multiple prices feature is used to set up different price levels, such as retail and wholesale. The correct price is set for each price level automatically (when it is a specific percentage of the base price), or can be imported to update the item record. Associating a specific customer with a price level ensures that the customer receives the correct price. Quantity pricing is used to entice a customer to buy more than one item, by providing a bulk discount, enabling a buy-one-get-one-free pricing scenario.

- Many customers ask for a quote prior to purchasing, so NetSuite also includes an estimate feature, which can be printed and sent to the customer for approval. Once approved, the estimate is converted to a sales order, which in turn becomes an invoice.
- NetSuite includes a number of features to optimize the fulfillment of orders. Advanced shipping splits the fulfillment and billing processes into separate functions, so that they can be managed independently by operations and accounting. Pick, pack, and ship splits the fulfillment into three separate steps, enabling multiple users to collaborate easily on the fulfillment.
- Reports are great, but wouldn't it be nice to drill-down even further, comparing sales by specific lines of business, or expenses by department? NetSuite calls these **Classifications**, and uses them to tag transactions to a particular department, class, or location, so that the transaction will show reports by that classification. Simply enable the feature and set up your list of **DEPARTMENTS, LOCATIONS, AND CLASSES**, and they are ready to be selected by your users on transactions. Speak to your department heads about what those picklist values should be, and don't be too concerned about the headings departments, classes, and location, as those can be renamed. So, you can use them for any classifications that you want to report, such as the line of business option that I mentioned earlier. In order to run reports by products versus services versus software, for example, navigate to **Reports | Sales | Sales by Customer** and change the **Column** filter from **Total** to **Class,** in order to compare the values between classes.
- Software and service companies can take advantage of a number of NetSuite features to solve their core challenges, from expense reports to time tracking to purchase requests, all of which work in conjunction with approval routing and **Projects** to be billed through to the customer.
- **Projects** enable a **PROJECT MANAGEMENT** tool, with a work breakdown structure to ensure that projects are on track and on budget.
- The **Service Resource Planning (SRP)** bundle helps you to staff projects based on each individual resource's existing project allocation.

Exploring NetSuite Tools

- Customers often pay for software and services over time, and the advanced financial's billing schedules feature can automate the creation of the bills for you. In addition, the company may not be able to recognize revenue at the time of billing when, for instance, the costs of providing the service will be incurred over a long period, such as in a support contract.
- In that case, revenue recognition can be used to automate the necessary journal entries.

In the event that there is no built-in automation for a specific process that you use, NetSuite offers a series tool that you can use to build that automation. Suiteflow is a workflow engine that enables the administrator to automate processes using point and click. If you require something more sophisticated, **Client Suitscript** and **Server Suitscript** can be used to custom-code automation, including automating addition database tables that can be set up by using custom records.

Features that support administrators

They say that the only constant is change, so how do you change data when circumstances change?

NetSuite provides you with a number of tools to do so. The import wizard is the most comprehensive tool to update data, and we cover it in depth in a later chapter. Inline editing, on the other hand, is the simplest. Once enabled, this feature turns the lists in NetSuite into quasi-Excel spreadsheets, and it can be used to edit data without having to drill-down to each individual record in the list.

Chapter 2

Inline editing is represented by an **Edit** button at the top of all lists. The list becomes editable as soon as the **Edit** button is clicked. Data in any column that contains a pencil icon in the column header can be edited simply by clicking into the column on the appropriate row and editing the data. The new data will be saved as soon as the user clicks out of that cell:

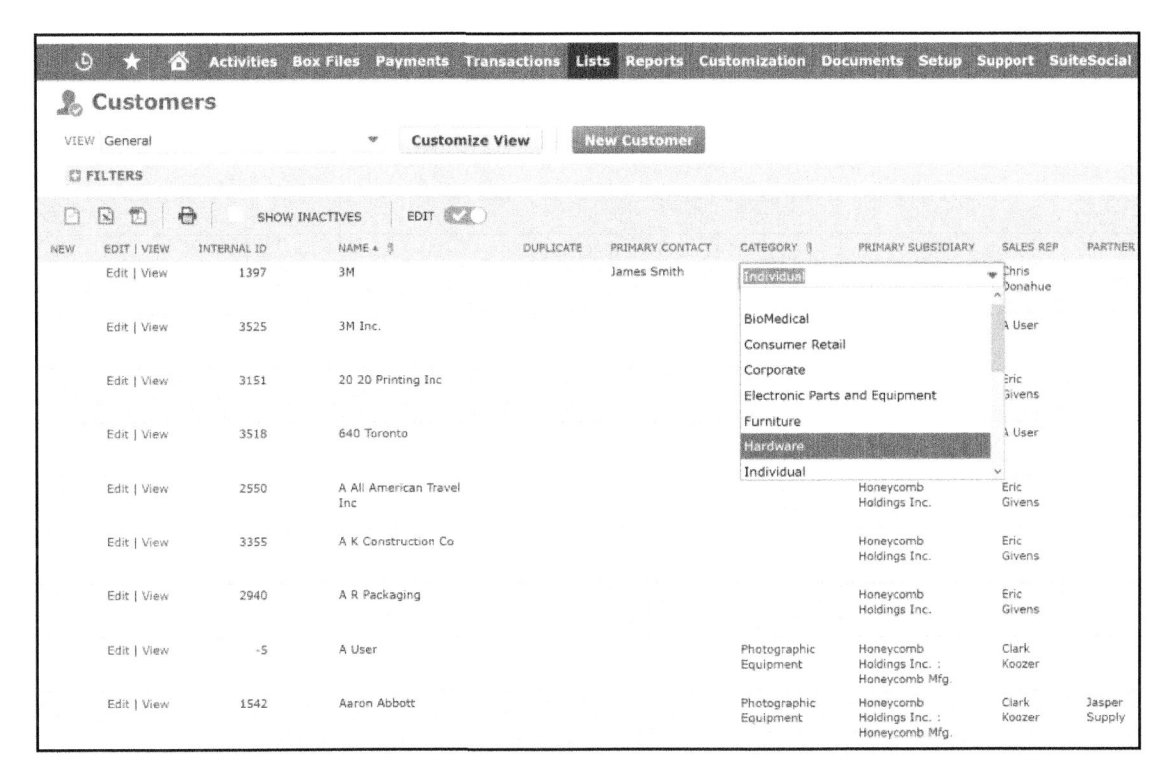

Inline editing

[25]

Exploring NetSuite Tools

An educated administrator can use inline editing to mass-update up to 999 records at a time, by using the tools we describe in `Chapter 8`, *Analytics – Searches, Reports, and the Dashboard*, in order to limit the list to records that require updating. Once the list is filtered to those records, the administrator can select the first row requiring updating, as described previously; but before making the edit, go to the bottom of the screen and select the same column in the last row, with the *Shift* key held down on the keyboard. This will select all of the rows between the two records that have been selected. Simply return to the data in the initial cell and make the data change. This will update all of the rows to the same selection that was made in the initial row:

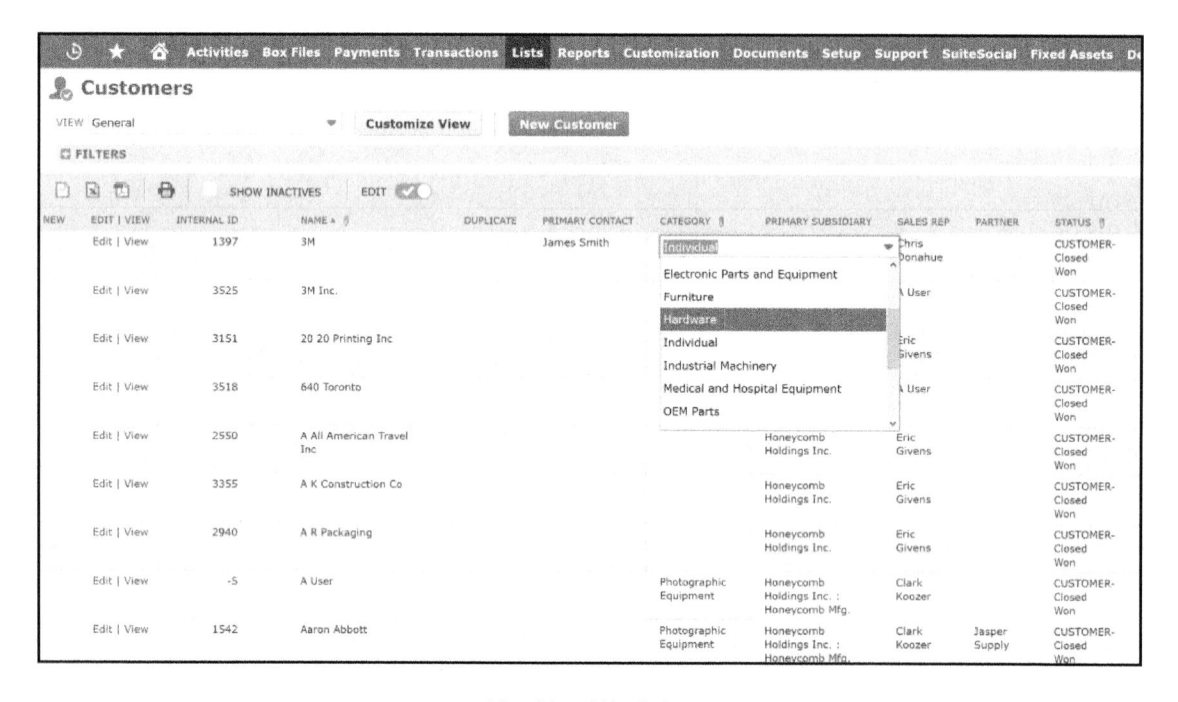

Inline editing multiple selections

The obvious question is: What do you do about columns that do not contain a pencil icon? In that case, we can use more sophisticated tools to perform the mass update. These tools are found under **Lists | Mass Update**, and can be used in a variety of ways. The **Update Prices** tool is useful when you need to make consistent updates to the prices of your items. It works with both positive and negative numbers, as well as percentages, and can update prices on all items or a subset of items. The alternative is to export your items, make the changes in Excel, and simply re-import them to update the prices in NetSuite:

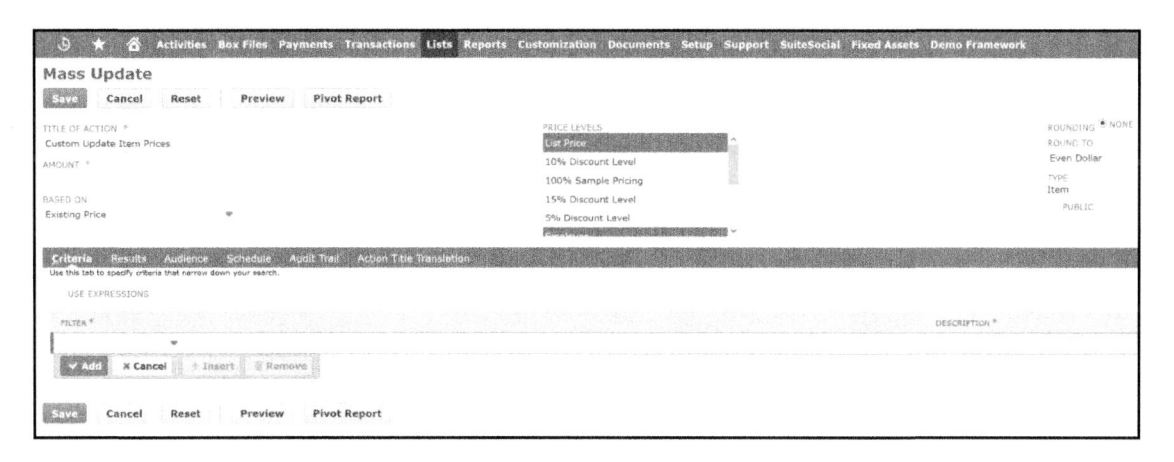

Mass Update screen

You will see additional options for updates in **Lists** | **Mass Update** | **Mass Update**, spanning most, if not all, records. Select the type of record to be taken to the update screen from the list. The first tab allows you to filter the records that will be updated, to enable you to update a subset of records. The skills necessary to use this tab are covered in `Chapter 8`, *Analytics – Searches, Reports, and the Dashboard*.

The **Schedule** tab gives you the option of executing a recurring mass update to update data in the future. It can be used to normalize data where you anticipate it may be corrupted in the future, such as sales reps who abbreviate San Francisco to SFO. The recurring mass update can be set up to automate the update to the correct spelling:

Mass Update of prices

Exploring NetSuite Tools

The **Mass Update Fields** tab is used to update the actual data. Simply select the checkbox next to the field that needs to be updated, and edit the value of that field to the correct value. Those records will be updated to the value you entered as soon as you execute the mass update. You can, however, be provided with a preview prior to execution, in order to double-check your work, and you can deselect individual records from the update on that screen:

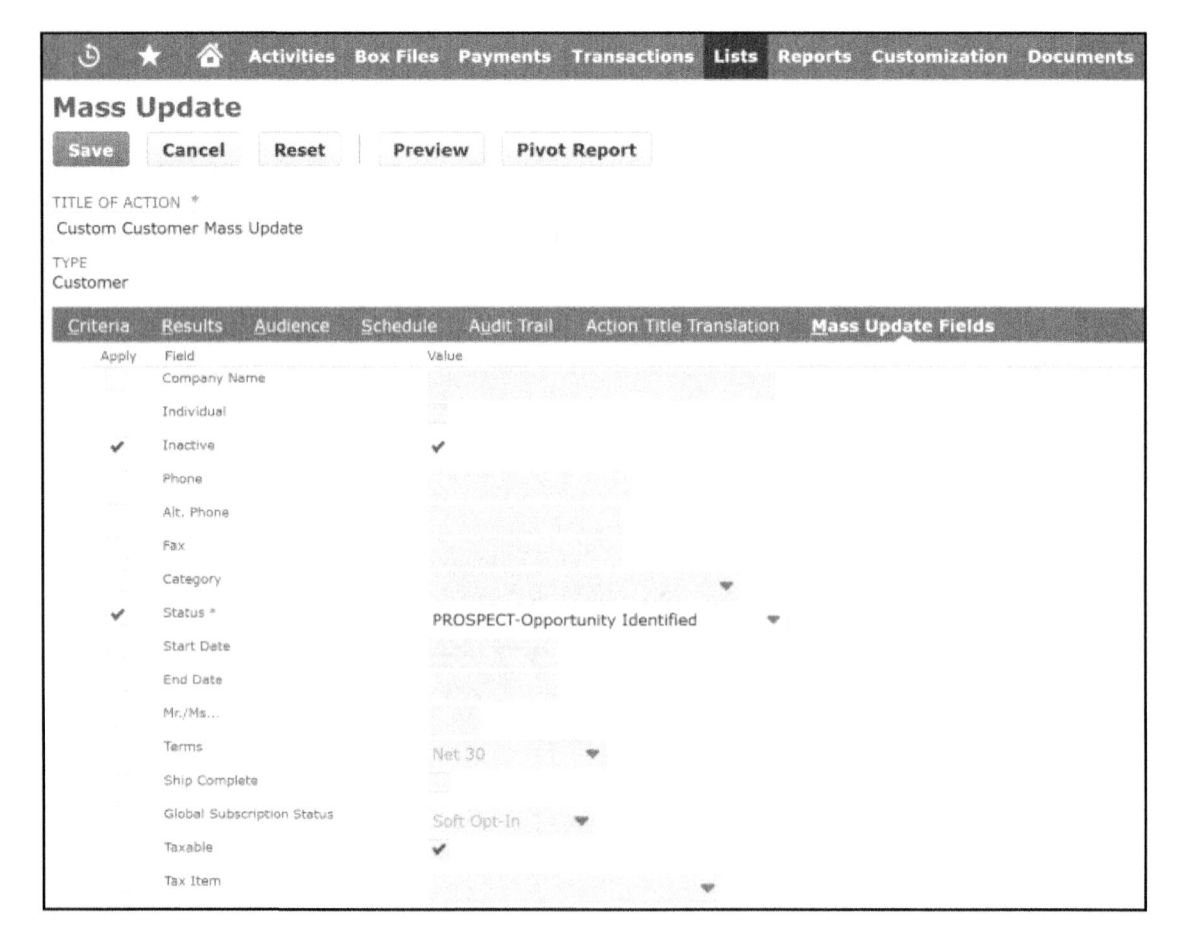

Mass Update of fields on the customer record

Mass updates can also be saved for future use. This saves the template, as opposed to running it automatically using the schedule mass update tool. Click the **Save** button on the mass update screen in order to do so.

Duplicate Detection

Duplicate Detection is another form of mass update, where NetSuite identifies duplicate customers, contacts, vendors, and/or partner records, and can merge the duplicates into a master record or delete the duplicates.

The administrator sets the criteria that NetSuite will use to search for duplicates on the **Setup | Company | Duplicate Detection** screen. One can choose an individual criterion, such as a name, or use multiple criteria simultaneously. This selection is as much an art as it is a science, and it relies on knowing the intricacies of the data. If you are too aggressive, you risk deleting non-duplicates, whereas the opposite is also true; by making the search too specific, actual duplicates will be excluded. A name is an obvious criterion to use, but it is usually not sufficient, as companies and people can have the same name. It is, therefore, useful to include a unique identifier, such as a zip code or phone number. Once you have saved the criteria, NetSuite begins to identify possible duplicates:

Duplicate Detection settings

Exploring NetSuite Tools

Duplicate records display a warning at the top of the screen, advising the user that this record may indeed be a duplicate. The warning contains a hyperlink to a list of the duplicate records for further analysis.

Administrators can view a full list of possible duplicates in **Lists** | **Mass Update** | **Entity Duplicate Resolution**. There are options to mark records as either **DUPLICATES** or **NOT DUPLICATES**. The **NOT DUPLICATES** option prevents a non-duplicate that conforms to the criteria from always appearing in the duplicate results.

The administrator can choose to delete duplicates or merge them into a master record. The best practice is to select merging and not deleting, because all of the information in the duplicate records will be lost upon deletion. A merge will preserve the history of that record and simply copy it over to the master record.

Security, from password policies to roles

There are a number of options to secure your account. Concerned about allowing your users to access the system from anywhere? Worried that a sales rep can view your customer list from his home, or during his final interview, while signing his new employment contract with your main competitor? Well, there is a feature for you, called IP address rules, which limits access to your NetSuite database to specific IP addresses. On a cautionary note, this is also the quickest way to potentially lock yourself out of your own NetSuite account, so it's best to set this up while you have NetSuite support on the line.

You can also tighten the password policy under **Setup** | **Company** | **General Preferences**, by setting the policy to **Strong** and deciding how often users will need to change their passwords:

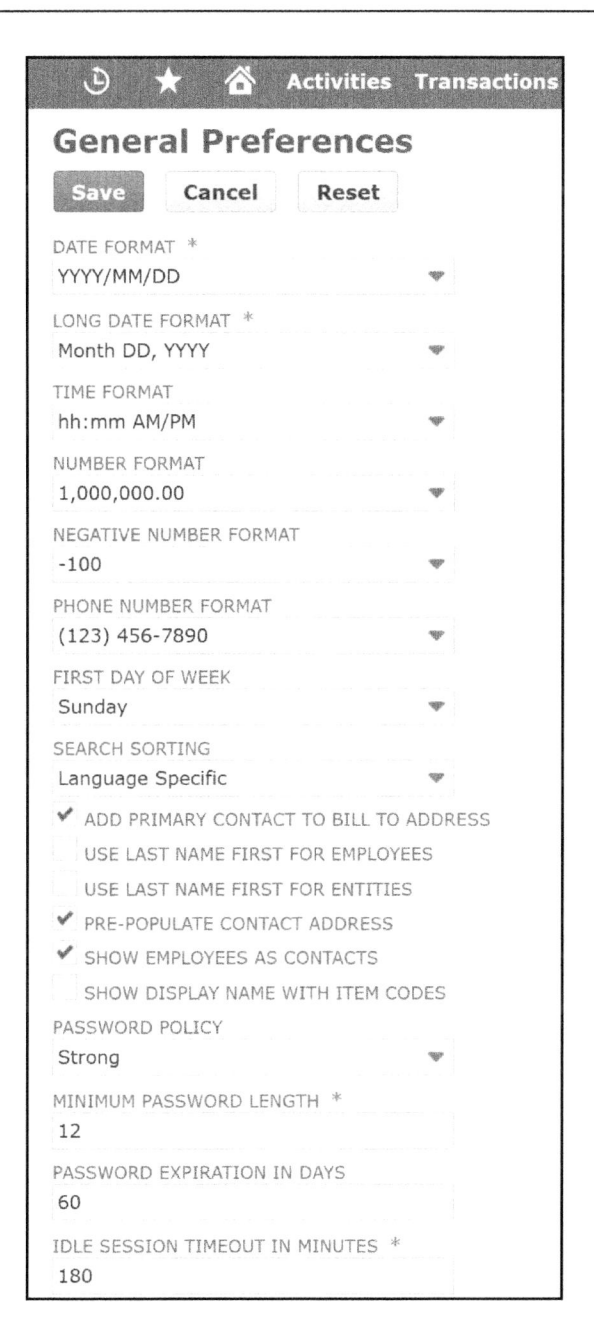

Password settings on the General Preferences screen

Exploring NetSuite Tools

These preferences (being general) will apply, unless they can be overridden by a user's personal preferences, so you can determine whether a user can override specific general preferences. One field to consider is the **Customer Credit Limit Handling** warning, which should be restricted from users; it's best to turn that off. Don't worry; users cannot override the password policy!

Setting the user's ability to override preferences

The critical security option is the ability to customize a user's roles and permissions. We cover that in `Chapter 6`, *Customization*, so let's leave it there for now. However, NetSuite gives you the ability to test roles by assigning multiple roles to yourself. You provide access to a user by going to the **Access** tab on the employee record and selecting the various roles that you wish to assign to the user. Once you have created a role, go to your own employee record and assign it to yourself. That enables you to switch your role to the custom role and test whether it is acting as designed.

Publishing dashboards

Dashboards are crucial to NetSuite users. They operate like a dashboard in a car, which summarizes all of the important information that the driver needs to see to operate the vehicle. The dashboard also happens to be a great opportunity for the administrator to shine. You can create a dashboard template and assign it to specific roles, thereby centralizing the creation of dashboards.

Building searches

Users will often ask administrators to help them execute searches and reports. NetSuite lets you build the search template, instead of just building each individual search. The user will access the search by going to the **Search** option on the menu for that record; for instance, **Lists** | **Relationships** | **Customers** | **Search**. This is a multifaceted search, giving the user the ability to run filters on one or more of the fields. The administrator can also edit the search to add fields to search on:

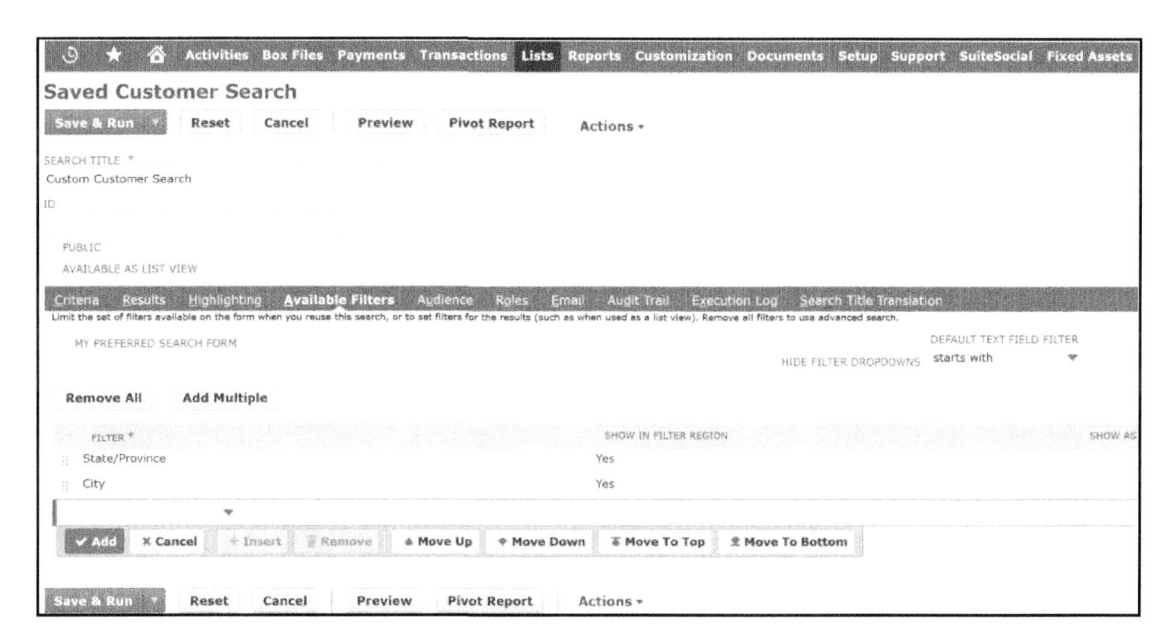

Selecting Search fields

Exploring NetSuite Tools

This configuration will be presented to the user as follows:

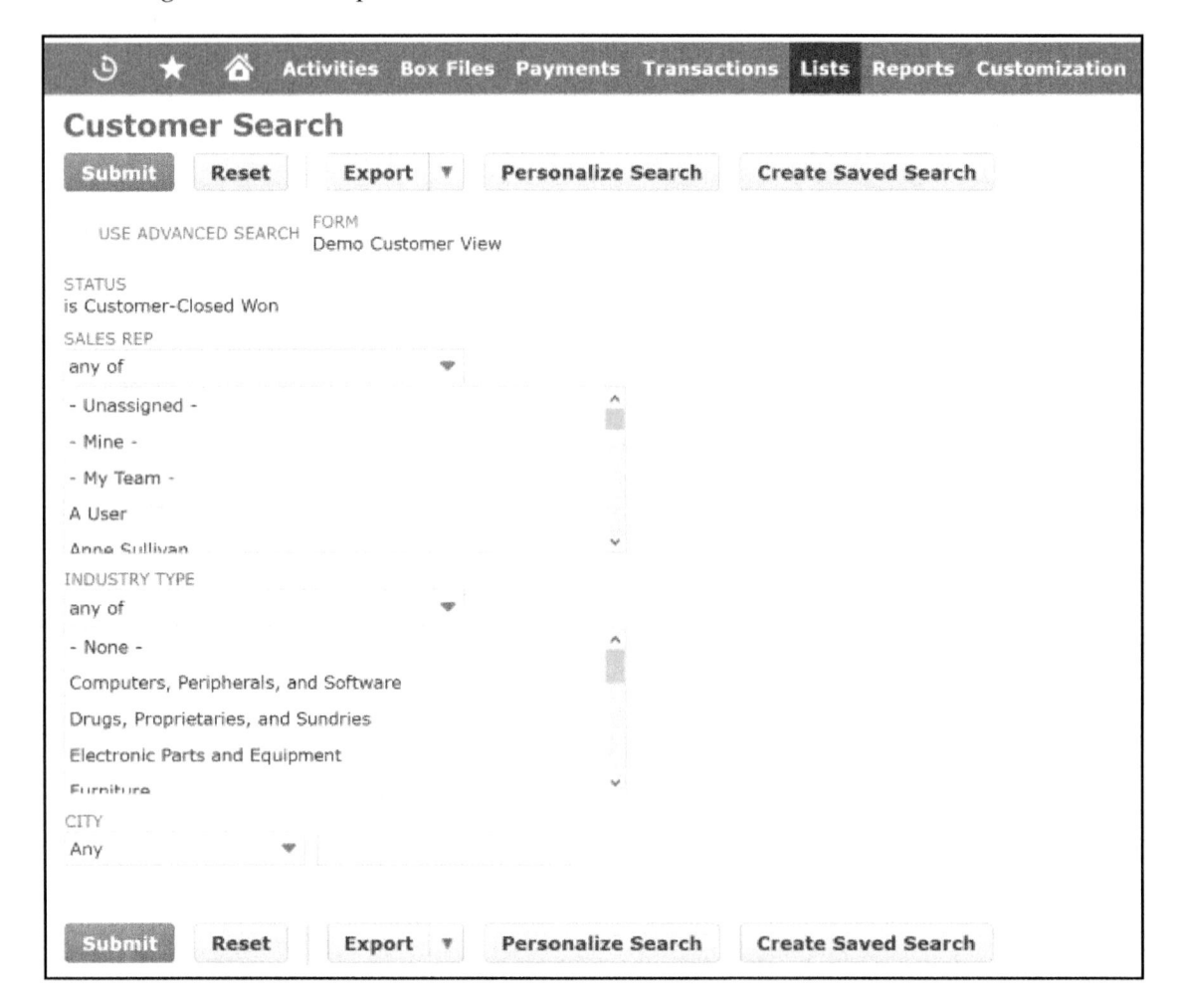

Multifaceted search screen

Click the **Create Saved Search** button and add additional fields to the **Available Filters** tab, with **SHOW IN FILTER REGION** checked. Then, go to the **Roles** tab, and make this the preferred form for the role. Give it a name, and click **Save**. The users with that role will now be able to execute searches with those additional fields when they go to **Lists | Relationships | Customers | Search**.

Using Workflow Manager to automate tasks

Want to automate a bunch of tasks that users would otherwise need to enter manually? Workflow Manager will help you do this. It has a number of cool options, including setting values, as well as routing a transaction to a specific user for approval. It even enables you to create transactions based on an existing transaction; for instance, automatically billing a sales order once it has been fulfilled. Workflow Manager is a feature that is accessible through the **Customization** menu:

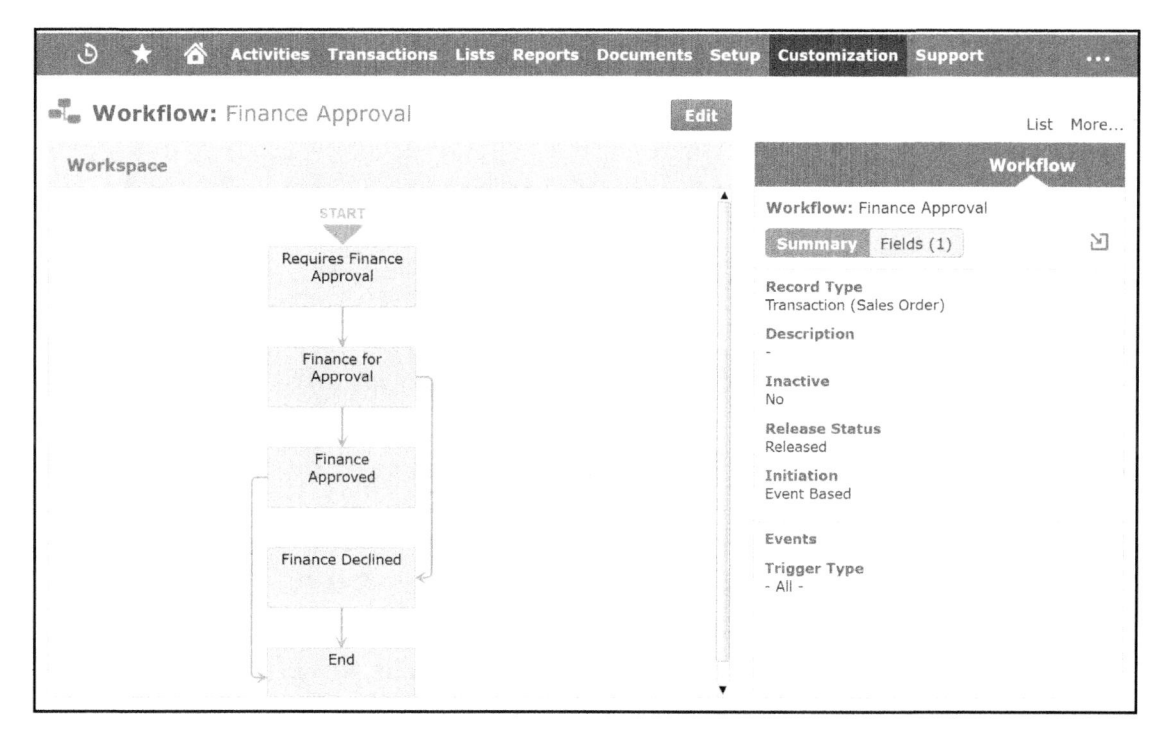

Example workflow

Exploring NetSuite Tools

Page loading times

Pages taking too long to load? Is it a server issue, or a client issue? There is no need to guess. Simply double-click on the **NetSuite** icon in the top-left corner of the screen, and a popup will show you the breakdown:

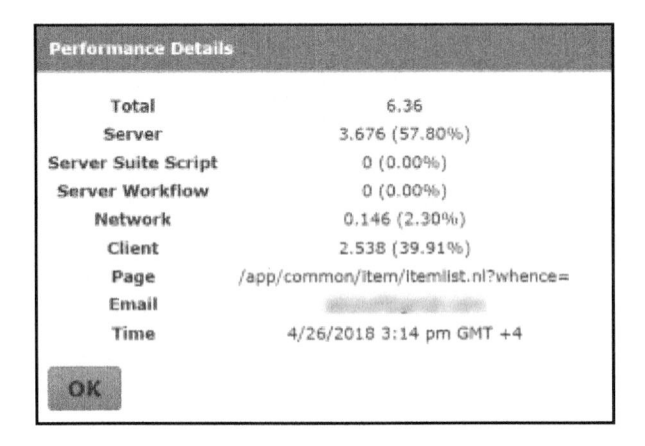

Performance Details	
Total	6.36
Server	3.676 (57.80%)
Server Suite Script	0 (0.00%)
Server Workflow	0 (0.00%)
Network	0.146 (2.30%)
Client	2.538 (39.91%)
Page	/app/common/item/itemlist.nl?whence=
Email	
Time	4/26/2018 3:14 pm GMT +4

Page loading statistics

Features that support users

User experience plays a major role in an administrator's workload. The inability to execute functions can easily result in a lot of complaints from users, including requests to automate the functions for them. So, let's focus on tools that will help them, which will, in turn, make the administrator's life easier.

The dashboard is a crucial tool for users to understand what is happening in the business and the tasks that need to be completed. Think of it as an interactive control panel to ensure that you are on track to reach your goals. You didn't need to open the gas tank of your car to see whether you have enough gas to make it to work in the morning. All you need do is check the dashboard, which summarizes important information for you.

People usually speak of the dashboard as the Home dashboard, signified by the home icon on the first tab, but in reality, there are multiple dashboards. In fact, each tab contains its own dashboard. If necessary, additional tabs can be added to the menus to add reporting functionality:

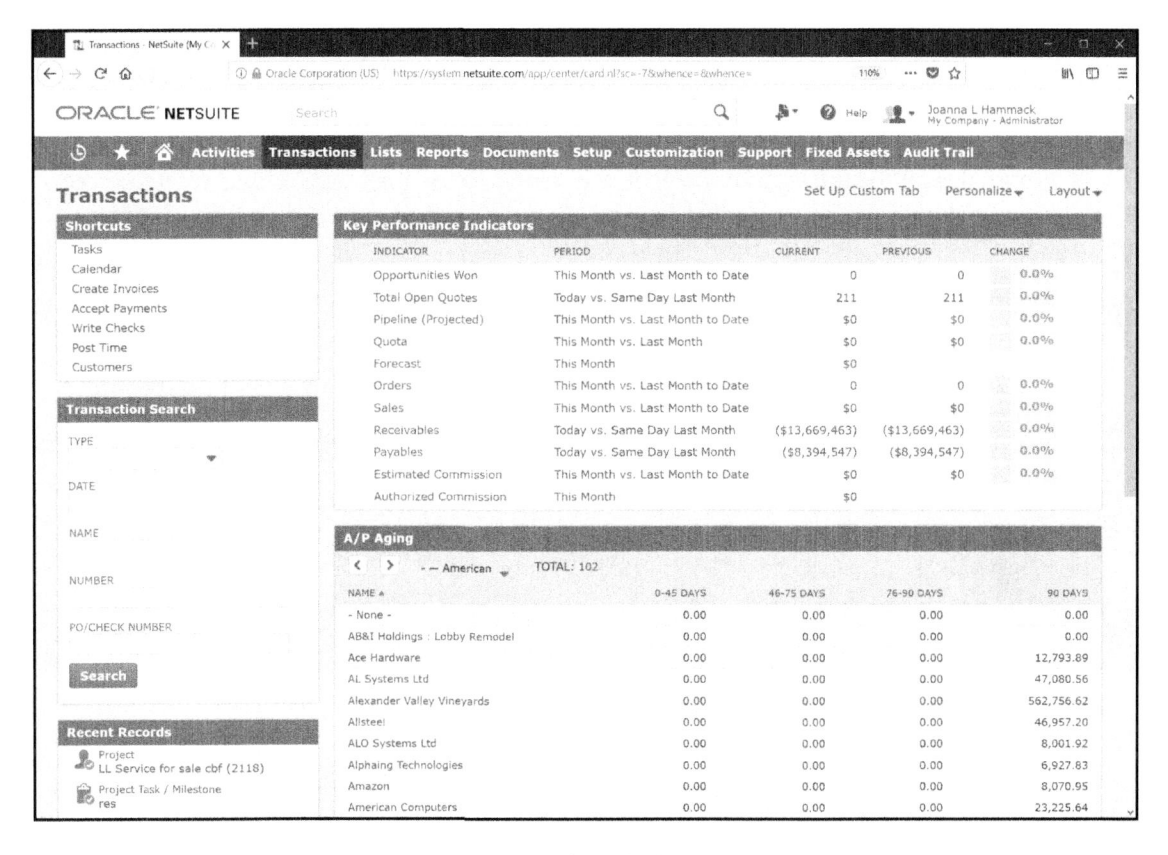

Transactions dashboard

There is a reason why we may need more than one dashboard. There is limited space on the Home dashboard. While the dashboard can theoretically accept an unlimited amount of content, chances are the user will not continually scroll down to the bottom of the dashboard; the information at the bottom will likely be lost. In addition, placing too much information on the dashboard will slow down its loading time, which can be frustrating to users, because they will spend so much time on the dashboard. Now, you can minimize each of the boxes (called **portlets**) by clicking on them. Minimized portlets do not contribute to slowing the loading of the dashboard however it hides the data returned by the portlet which defeats the purpose of placing that data on the dashboard in the first place. The reason we put information on the dashboard is to alert the user to specific events, and minimizing the portlet does the exact opposite. The lesson here is for the user to prioritize the information that they need to see on the dashboard. It is designed as a summary, and placing too much information there defeats the purpose of the summary.

Exploring NetSuite Tools

The dashboard is divided into categories of information called portlets; each portlet is defined in its own box, with its own refresh button and setup option in the top right-hand corner of the box. Portlets can be moved around the dashboard by dragging and dropping the header into a different position. They can also be disabled, by clicking in the top right-hand corner and clicking **Remove**. Portlets are added to the dashboard by clicking on the **Personalize** dashboard link at the top of the screen. Portlets perform different functions, and I'll describe the more important ones shortly:

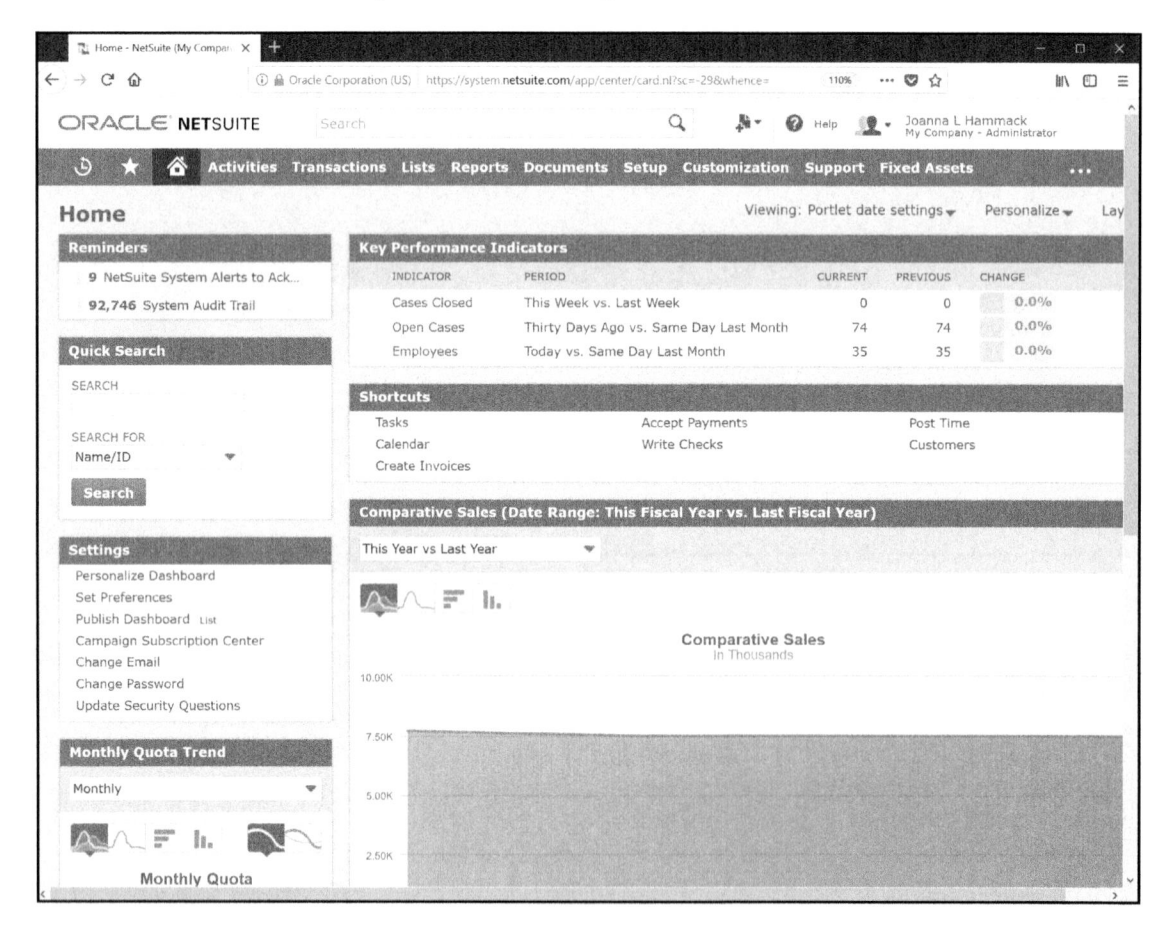

Various portlets on the Home dashboard

Reminders

Reminders serve a very important purpose: they are a to-do list of tasks a user needs to perform. There are a number of pre-built reminders, which can be accessed by clicking on the setup link and selecting them. Examples include **Orders to Invoice** and **Overdue Invoices** for accountants, and **Items to Fulfill**, **Items to Receive**, and **Items to Order** for warehouse managers. The reminder will only appear if the task is open, and it includes a hyperlink to the screen where the actual work is performed:

```
Reminders
  63  Items to Order
 285  Orders to Fulfill
 119  Orders to Receive
   6  Orders to Ship
   3  Orders to Pack
   5  Transfer Orders to Approve
   2  Memorized Transactions due
   8  Overdue Projects
```

Reminders portlet

The administrator can also create custom reminders to alert users when a standard reminder is not sufficient. We will demonstrate how to do this in `Chapter 8`, *Analytics – Searches, Reports, and the Dashboard*.

Reminders span the entire breadth of the system, so you should have the appropriate users turn on those reminders whenever a new feature is implemented; for instance, if you turn on revenue recognition, ask the accountant to set up revenue recognition journal entries to post as a reminder.

As you can see, reminders perform a valuable function, as they alert users that particular work is now required. In a sense, they allow users to communicate without speaking. Each user contributes to a process like an athlete in a relay race. The user is alerted by the reminder that their contribution is needed, and, once completed, that task falls off the user's dashboard and is passed to the next runner in the form of a reminder on his/her dashboard.

Reminders tend to be used by individual contributors; however, they can also alert managers to bottlenecks in the process. I recommend that managers turn on all reminders, because a reminder such as **438 Invoices are overdue** or **556 orders to fulfill** will alert the manager to operational difficulties.

Key Performance Indicators (KPIs)

Key Performance Indicators (**KPIs**) are text-based reports that summarize data on the dashboard, and they are mainly used by management. Note that they can be used by individual contributors, as well, but only for specific metrics that the user is interested in, as opposed to a manager, who will want to view more widespread data.

KPIs have built-in hyperlinks to the underlying reports that they summarize, so that the user is only a click away from the details. KPIs can compare each report against a previous date or date range, so that the user sees the information in context, as opposed to simply the metrics as of today's date. The change is summarized at the end of the line of each KPI, and is colored in red or green, to signify whether the metric has improved or declined since the comparative date. There is also a link to a trend graph, if users want to see more than two date ranges. Click on the icon to the left of the KPI to view the trend graph:

Key Performance Indicators

Bank Balance

0.0%

INDICATOR	PERIOD	CURRENT	PREVIOUS	CHANGE
Shipments by SFO	This Year vs. Last Year	57	8	↑ 612.5%
Cases Closed	This Year vs. Last Year	0	0	0.0%
Cases Escalated	This Year vs. Last Year	0	0	0.0%
Bank Balance	**Today vs. Yesterday**	**$4,596,749**	**$4,596,749**	0.0%
Estimated Partner Commission	This Month vs. Last Month to Date	$0	$0	0.0%
Expenses	This Month vs. Last Month to Date	$207	$78,638	↓ 99.7%
Fixed Assets	Today vs. Same Day Last Month	($798,280)	($798,280)	0.0%
Forecast	This Month vs. Last Month to Date	$13	$1,565	↓ 99.2%
Forecast Override	This Month vs. Last Month	$0	$0	0.0%
Hosted Page Hits	Today vs. Yesterday	0	0	0.0%
Open Cases	Today vs. Same Day Last Month	53	53	0.0%
Open Opportunities	This Month vs. Last Month to Date	0	0	0.0%
Open Projects	Current	12		
Open Prospects	Today vs. Same Day Last Month	138	138	0.0%

Key Performance Indicator portlet

Click the **Setup** button on the **Key Performance Indicator** portlet to add or remove reports. There are a number of standard reports available, as well as the ability for the administrator to create custom KPIs, to drill-down into specific areas pertaining to your industry.

The user can also determine the specific date range and comparative date range for each individual KPI, and can highlight that metric if it reaches a particular value, such as when the bank balance falls below $10,000.

As you can see, KPIs can be very useful for managers to keep track of many different aspects of the business.

KPI meters

Some people are more visual, and prefer to see data in the form of a graph. KPIs can be used to display the information in the form of a traffic light, where red is bad, yellow is average, and green is good. These KPI meters can be turned on in the **Personalize Dashboard** option, and require to be set up individually. They use existing KPIs and existing thresholds to determine whether the metric is red, yellow, or green. You are limited to three KPI meters on the Home dashboard:

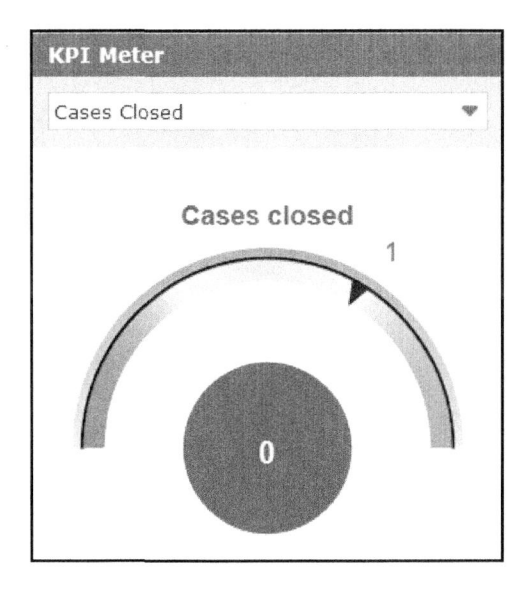

KPI Meter

Exploring NetSuite Tools

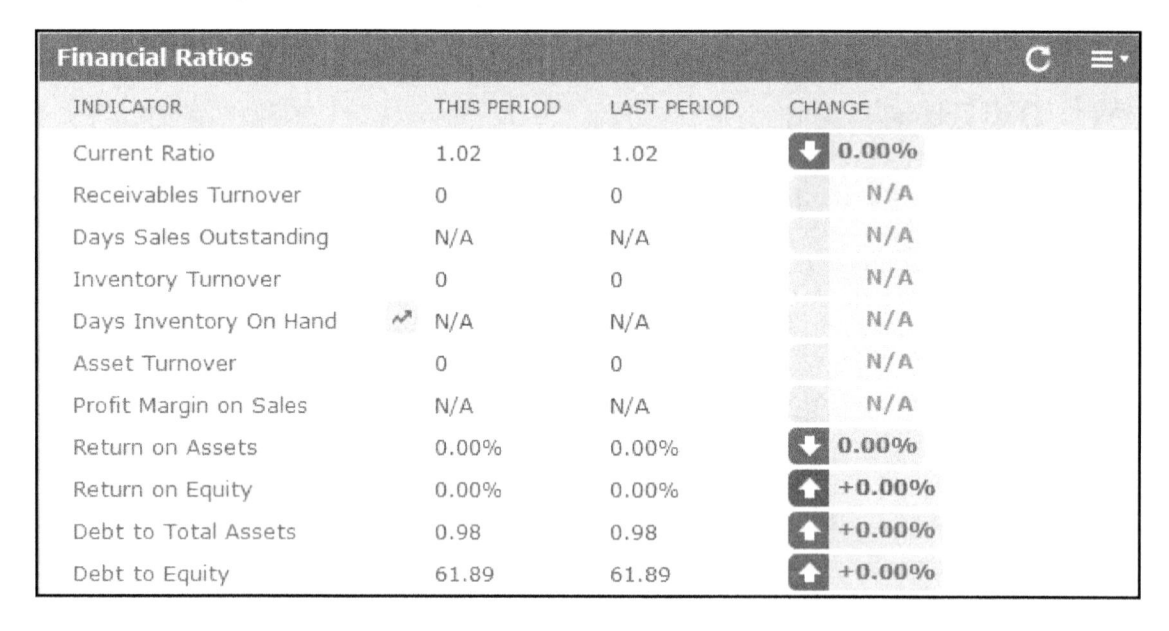

KPI scorecards

Scorecards take KPIs to a new level. Scorecards enable you to show data over multiple data ranges, unlike KPIs, which limit you to only two date ranges. Scorecards can also perform calculations; for instance, you can leverage a KPI of your total customers and a KPI of customers who canceled this month to calculate the churn rate (percentage of the customer base that has been lost). Churn is important to any business, but is of particular interest to a software company. In fact, there is a pre-built KPI scorecard showing **Financial Ratios,** which will be of particular interest to the CFO:

INDICATOR	THIS PERIOD	LAST PERIOD	CHANGE
Current Ratio	1.02	1.02	↓ 0.00%
Receivables Turnover	0	0	N/A
Days Sales Outstanding	N/A	N/A	N/A
Inventory Turnover	0	0	N/A
Days Inventory On Hand	N/A	N/A	N/A
Asset Turnover	0	0	N/A
Profit Margin on Sales	N/A	N/A	N/A
Return on Assets	0.00%	0.00%	↓ 0.00%
Return on Equity	0.00%	0.00%	↑ +0.00%
Debt to Total Assets	0.98	0.98	↑ +0.00%
Debt to Equity	61.89	61.89	↑ +0.00%

KPI scorecard

Go to **Personalize Dashboard** to turn on the KPI scorecards feature, and then set it up to select the scorecard you want to show. We will be focusing on building custom scorecards in `Chapter 8`, *Analytics – Searches, Reports, and the Dashboard*.

List

The list portlet is usually used by individual contributors, and it shows a list of specific records of transactions directly on the dashboard. An accountant, for instance, can see the actual invoices that are overdue on the dashboard by using this portlet, or a project manager can view his or her assigned projects.

Enable the portlet in the normal way, by using the **Personalize Dashboard** option and then choosing the specific list you wish to view. You can then specify the number of records that you want to see in the portlet. The list will be divided into pages, based on the total number of records divided by the number you specify for each page. This is a good tip: if the company has 10,000 invoices, then it's probably not a good idea to choose invoices in the list portlet, because there is no way 10,000 invoices can be viewed on one page. Paging through the list defeats the purpose of having the list directly available on the dashboard:

Customers list

Therefore, it is better to filter the list. For instance, filter by overdue invoices, because otherwise using this portlet for that function becomes difficult.

Exploring NetSuite Tools

Saved Search

The **Saved Search** portlet is very similar to the list portlet, as it shows the results of a saved search. In other words, it shows the specific records returned by the search criteria to summarize the record, with a link to the actual record. Once again, this portlet is often used by individual contributors, and is enabled in the same way:

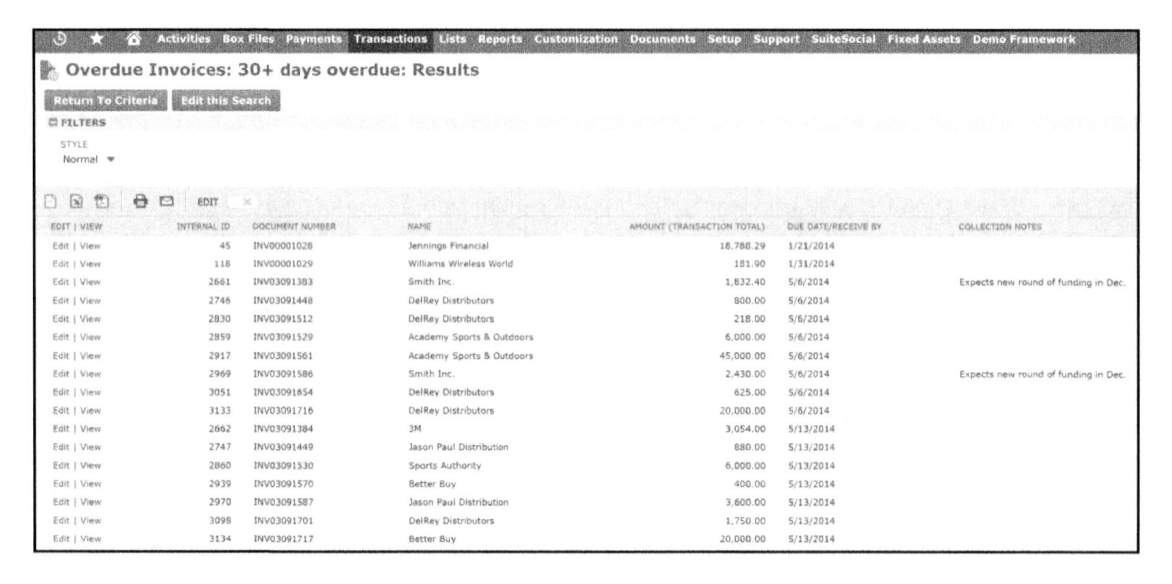

Saved search results

This portlet fixes the list portlet's greatest weakness: the number of records that will be displayed on the dashboard. With this portlet, you can limit the results by using the saved search criteria. A sales rep can display opportunities closing in a particular month, instead of all of the opportunities that are available in the list portlet.

It is still a judgment call, at the end of the day, to determine just the right amount of data to display on the dashboard. Too little, and the users may not have all the data they need to perform their tasks. Too much, and the dashboard is no longer operating as a summary.

Trend graphs

A **Trend Graph** shows the trend for a particular metric over time, and has its own section under the personalized dashboard. Once enabled, the user chooses specific trend graph(s) to display:

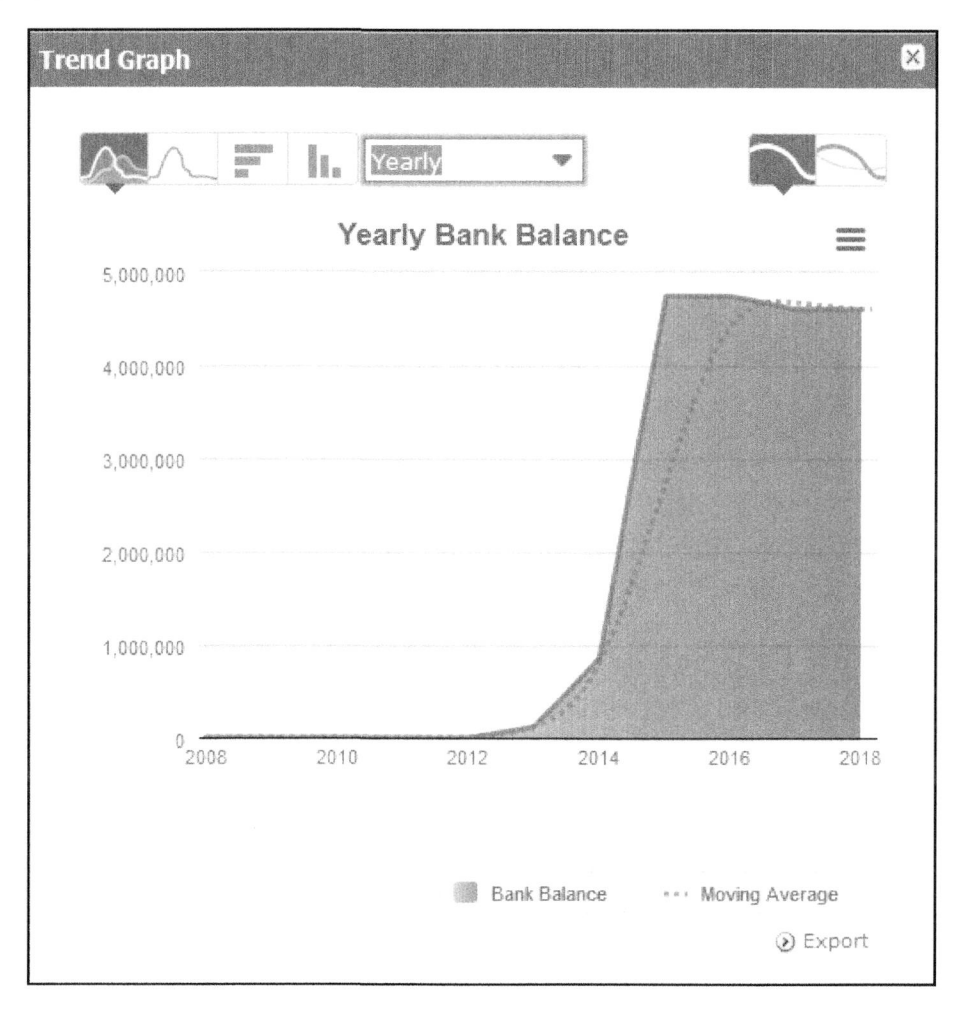

Trend Graph

Exploring NetSuite Tools

Report snapshots

The following are mini reports, as we do not have the space to show the full report on the dashboard. They are merely a summary of the report; for instance, the *top 5 items by sales* would be displayed on the dashboard, instead of a comprehensive *sales by item* report:

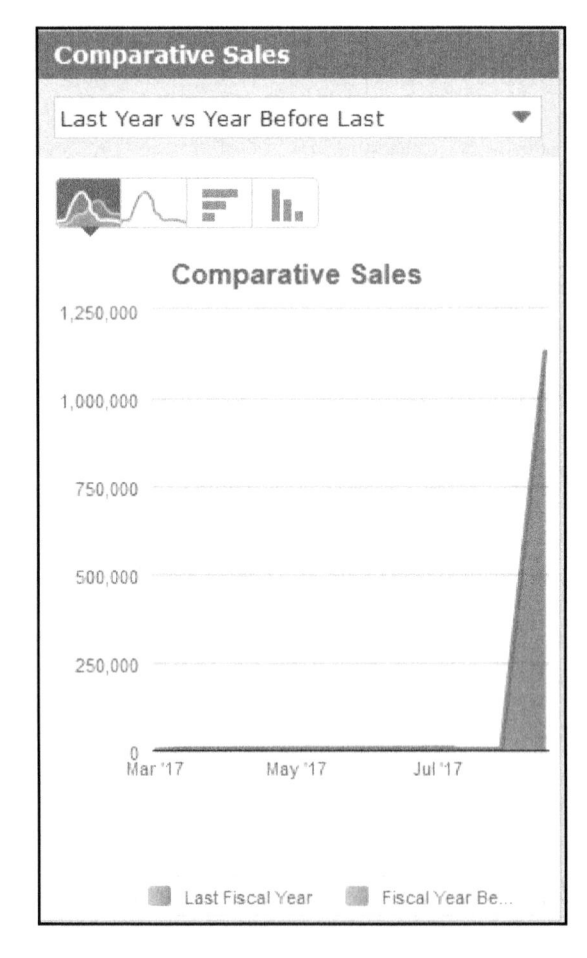

Report snapshot

They are set up in the normal way, using **Personalize Dashboard**, and have their own section for you to choose from.

Pivoting data on the dashboard

Accountants familiar with Excel usually like to pivot the dashboard to see information from different perspectives. Does that mean that he or she needs to reset the dashboard each time he or she wants to pivot the data? No.

NetSuite has two tools to help you accomplish this. The first is **Portlet date settings**, which appears in the top right-hand corner of the dashboard. It can be used to change the date range of the dashboard to specific date ranges, such as **Today vs Yesterday** or **This month vs Last Month**. The KPIs will then respect those date ranges until the user resets the portlet date settings or logs out of the system. The date range will then return to the individual date ranges set up in those portlets:

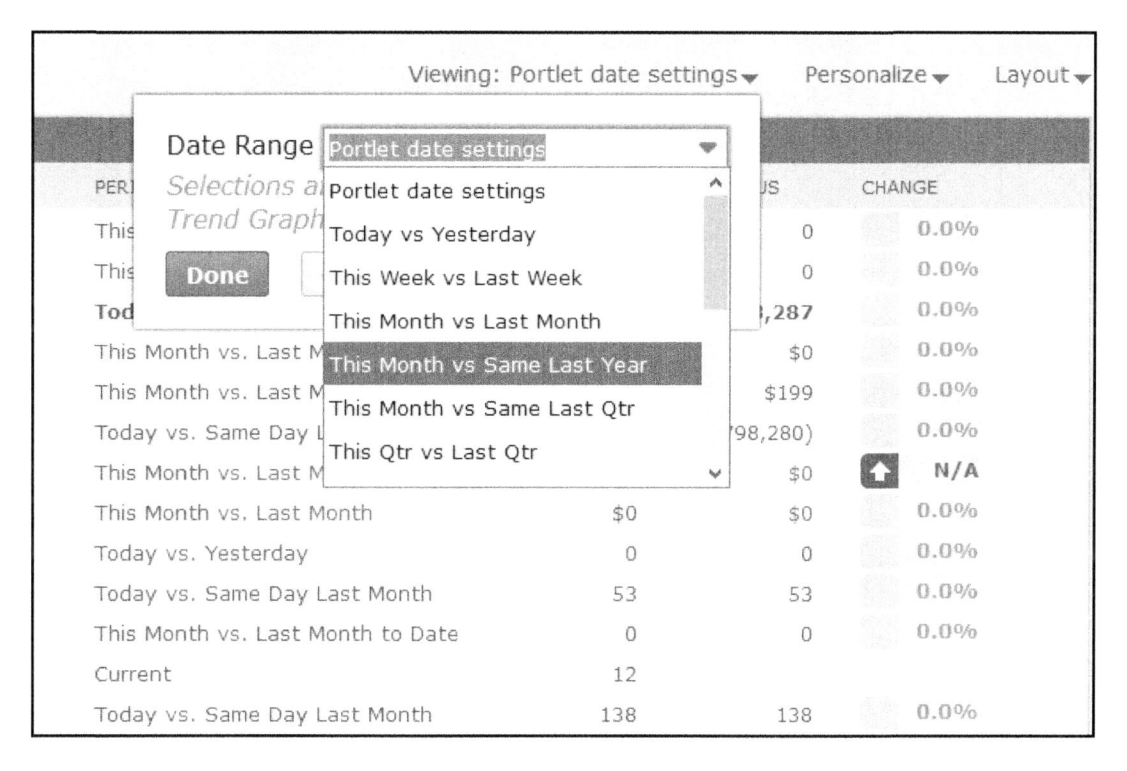

Changing the dashboard date settings

[47]

Exploring NetSuite Tools

It is often useful to view information from the perspective of a certain location or line of business. You can pivot the dashboard to accomplish this by going to **Home | Set Preferences** and selecting the **Restrict View** tab. The user can restrict the view by class, location, and departments (as well as the subsidiary for a `OneWorld` account). The data will refresh once the setting is saved, and it will appear as if you are in a database for that class, location, or department. In fact, you will not be able to see outside that restriction:

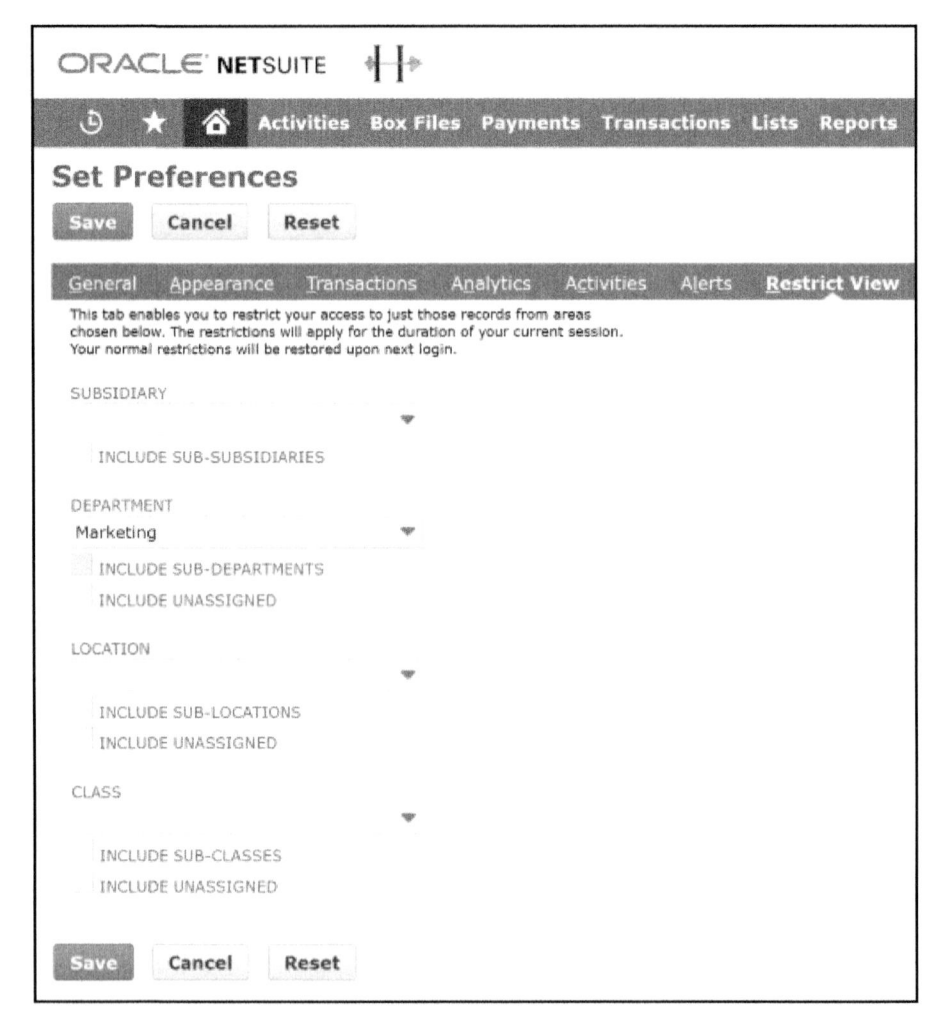

Personal preferences

Once again, the restriction can be removed manually, by reversing the steps or logging out.

Global search

Global search is a powerful search tool to quickly search for a specific record, such as an individual customer or transaction. It operates like a Google search throughout your NetSuite database, and returns any record that contains a given search term:

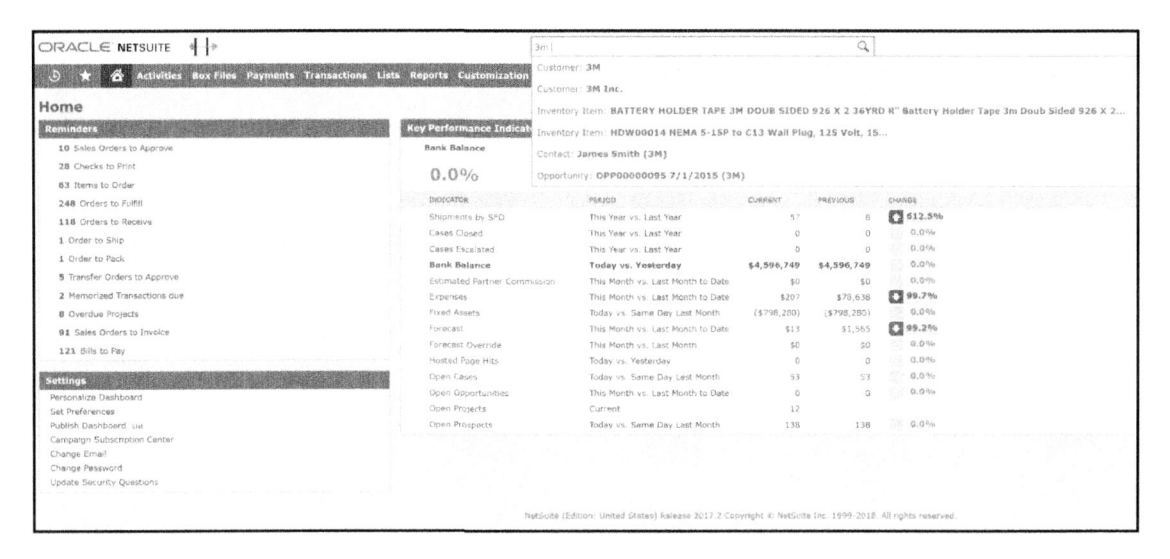

Autosuggest on global search

As you can see in the preceding screenshot, a global search doesn't differentiate whether it's a customer, vendor, item, or opportunity; it returns all records containing the search term. Therefore, depending on the search, the results can be substantial, and it can be very difficult to go through all of them to find the one record you are looking for. To solve this, NetSuite provides a way to limit search results to specific records, by using global search prefixes. Using the search prefix `cu:` before the search term will limit the results to customers. The prefix `sa:` will only return sales orders:

Exploring NetSuite Tools

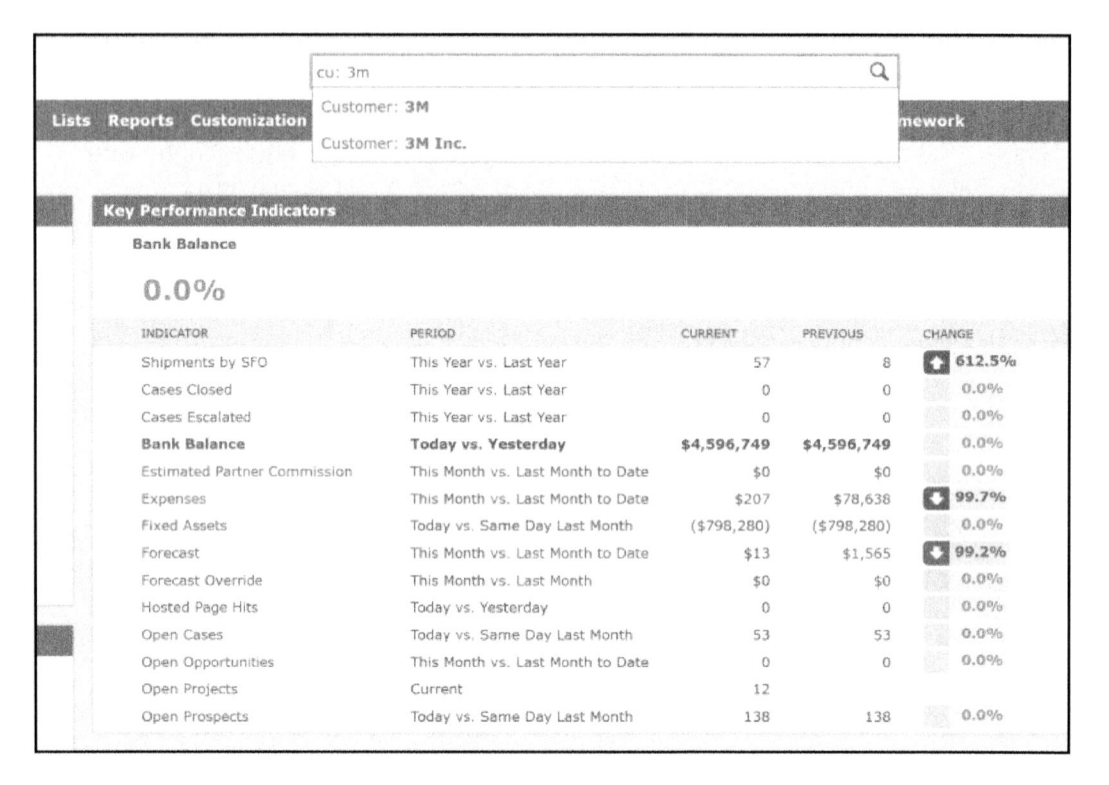

Global search with customer prefix

On the other hand, you can expand a search result by using wildcards. Let's suppose that I'm searching for a contact named Micky Mouse. He could be recorded in the database as Mickey, Michael, Mike, Mick, and so on. So, I would use a search term to encompass all of the possible variations. I would use the search term `cu: mi% mouse`. The `%` is the wildcard that will return all possible letters to represent the `%`.

Memorized transactions

Some transactions repeat throughout the year. Rent is one example; it is paid in the same amount on the same day of each month. NetSuite provides an automation feature to help the user in this case. The user memorizes the transaction after creating it. The memorized transaction occurs on a specific, set schedule, and the transaction can be automatically created; however, I recommend using the **REMIND ME** option instead. This places a reminder on the user's dashboard, to prompt a review of the transaction. The transaction is created for you, but is not posted until the user elects to enter it:

Setting up memorized transactions

Summary

In this chapter, we demonstrated many of the standard functionalities that are available to solve the challenges faced by your business. We divided this up into three sections, based on the audience experiencing the challenge. You can use the *Features that support businesses* section to guide your management on strategic business decisions. You can use the *Features that support users* section to help end users perform their day-to-day tasks easily and efficiently. You can use *Features that support administrators* to save yourself time and hassle, with more of an impact on the company's use of the ERP.

Many of you will be administering NetSuite's multi-company consolidation module, so we will look at NetSuite `OneWorld` in the next chapter. We will provide a framework for understanding `OneWorld`, in order to simplify this complex module.

3
OneWorld

OneWorld is NetSuite's name for its multi-subsidiary consolidation module, and if you are not using a OneWorld account, feel free to skip this chapter. Consolidation is the accounting treatment for multiple independent business units that are owned by the same holding company. The business units are referred to as subsidiaries. These subsidiaries can operate in the same country as the holding company or in different countries, which adds the complication of operating in multiple currencies.

Big deal, you might say. Can't we just treat the subsidiaries as independent and create the financial statement for each subsidiary? We could then simply add up the results of all the subsidiaries to arrive at the consolidated income statement. The problem is that a significant number of transactions may be between different subsidiaries, where one subsidiary purchases goods from another. This has the effect of overstating sales if we were simply adding all the individual results together. It also would allow an unscrupulous accountant to overstate income by selling millions of dollars' worth of inventory from one subsidiary to another.

Accounting principles have stringent rules on consolidation to prevent this kind of abuse. It removes double counting by setting off intercompany transactions against an elimination subsidiary. To translate that into a NetSuite configuration, we would need to set up a holding company as well as each business unit as independent subsidiaries. We would also need to set up elimination subsidiaries in order to remove double counting.

Another implication of what we have said so far is that intercompany transactions are dealt with differently from regular transactions, which is the case in NetSuite. These are the only transactions that can be posted for more than one subsidiary. Every other transaction is posted against one subsidiary only.

OneWorld

NetSuite makes it even easier for us by removing the user's ability to choose a subsidiary of a transaction. It does so by sourcing the subsidiary based on the customer, vendor, partner, and employer that you are transacting with. In other words, we will select the subsidiary on that entity and all transactions from there on for that entity will be recorded against that subsidiary. Now, let's drill-down a little deeper into the details of setting up OneWorld.

Subsidiary hierarchy

The first step is to set up the subsidiaries and subsidiary hierarchy; in other words, to determine which subsidiaries report to parent subsidiaries. This may be very simple, where all subsidiaries report to the same parent:

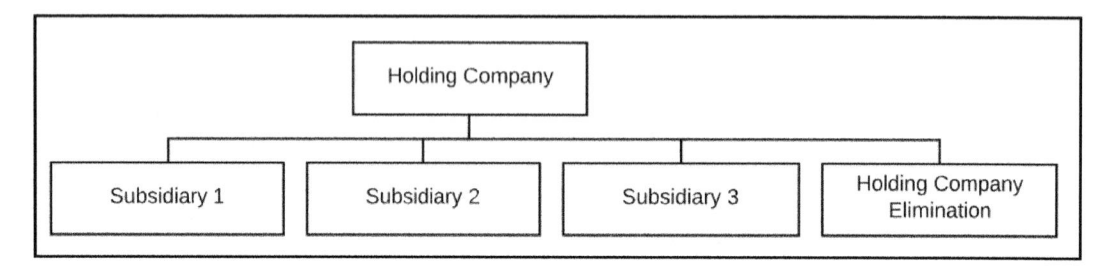

Subsidiary hierarchy example

Alternatively, it can be more complex, as follows:

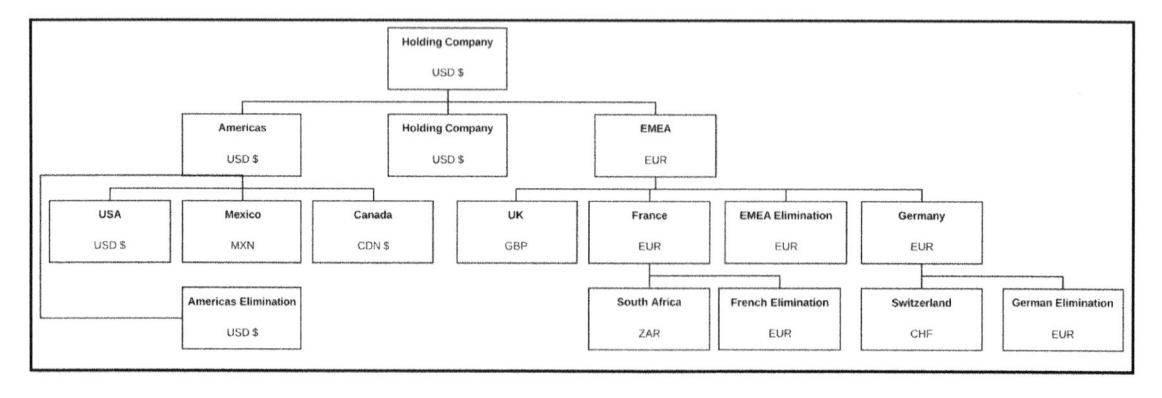

Complex subsidiary hierarchy example

Once set up, NetSuite has the ability to report by each subsidiary individually (such as the UK or South Africa) or for a group of subsidiaries. A financial report for Americas, for instance, would incorporate all the transactions for all of the children of Americas, namely USA, Mexico, and Canada, and a report for the entire consolidated company would return the results for the subsidiaries.

The report would be displayed in the currency of the node or level that is being reported on, so EMEA financials are reported in € irrespective of whether all the children use €. Transactions in the UK, Switzerland, and South Africa would all be converted from their base currencies into € for the purposes of the report. In addition, the financial statements for the entire company would be reported in USD $ even though only one of the subsidiaries reports in USD $.

The currency and order of the hierarchy are therefore crucial. This group of companies should be set up differently if you need to report on the German and Swiss subsidiaries in Swiss Francs, or if South Africa reports to Americas and not EMEA. One needs to be very sure of the hierarchy before setting this up, because it is very difficult to unscramble this egg after the fact.

This demonstrates the true value of NetSuite OneWorld, in that the CFO can analyze the performance of a subsidiary or a group of subsidiaries by simply selecting that subsidiary or node in the subsidiary context field of virtually all reports. Furthermore, a transaction in South Africa in ZAR will update the Group CEO's dashboard reflected in USD $, one second after the transaction is entered into the system.

The subsidiary record is also used in streamlining operations, because it has its own logo, shipping, and return addresses, which can be placed on transaction forms; as well as subsidiary-specific preferences, such as time zone, to ensure that transactions are recorded at the correct time for auditing purposes. It also has its own tax setup to ensure that the correct local taxes are charged by the subsidiary and remitted to the appropriate tax authorities:

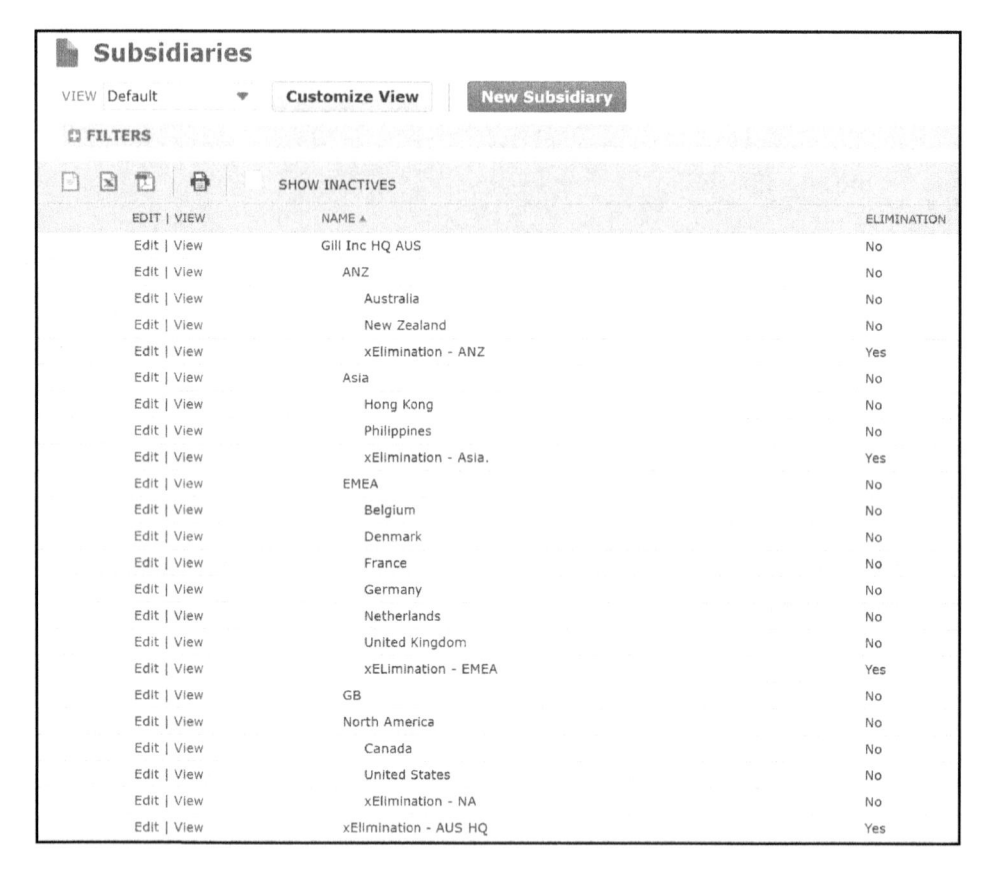

EDIT | VIEW	NAME ▲	ELIMINATION
Edit | View	Gill Inc HQ AUS	No
Edit | View	ANZ	No
Edit | View	Australia	No
Edit | View	New Zealand	No
Edit | View	xElimination - ANZ	Yes
Edit | View	Asia	No
Edit | View	Hong Kong	No
Edit | View	Philippines	No
Edit | View	xElimination - Asia.	Yes
Edit | View	EMEA	No
Edit | View	Belgium	No
Edit | View	Denmark	No
Edit | View	France	No
Edit | View	Germany	No
Edit | View	Netherlands	No
Edit | View	United Kingdom	No
Edit | View	xELimination - EMEA	Yes
Edit | View	GB	No
Edit | View	North America	No
Edit | View	Canada	No
Edit | View	United States	No
Edit | View	xElimination - NA	No
Edit | View	xElimination - AUS HQ	Yes

Subsidiary hierarchy setup in NetSuite

List records

The subsidiary is set on the list record, and is sourced into transactions using that list record.

Customers

A customer is, by default, associated with a specific subsidiary when it is created, and all the transactions with this customer will inherit the customer's subsidiary. A customer can only be associated with one subsidiary. In the event that the same customer does business with multiple subsidiaries, duplicate customer records will be set up, one for each subsidiary.

Chapter 3

The 2018.1 release introduced the *multi-subsidiary customer* feature, which enables us to share customers (and sub-customers, for that matter) between subsidiaries. A primary subsidiary is set up on the customer record, as well as any additional subsidiaries that are deemed necessary. The primary subsidiary that is selected on the customer record is selected as the default subsidiary on transactions; however, this can be changed when the transaction is created:

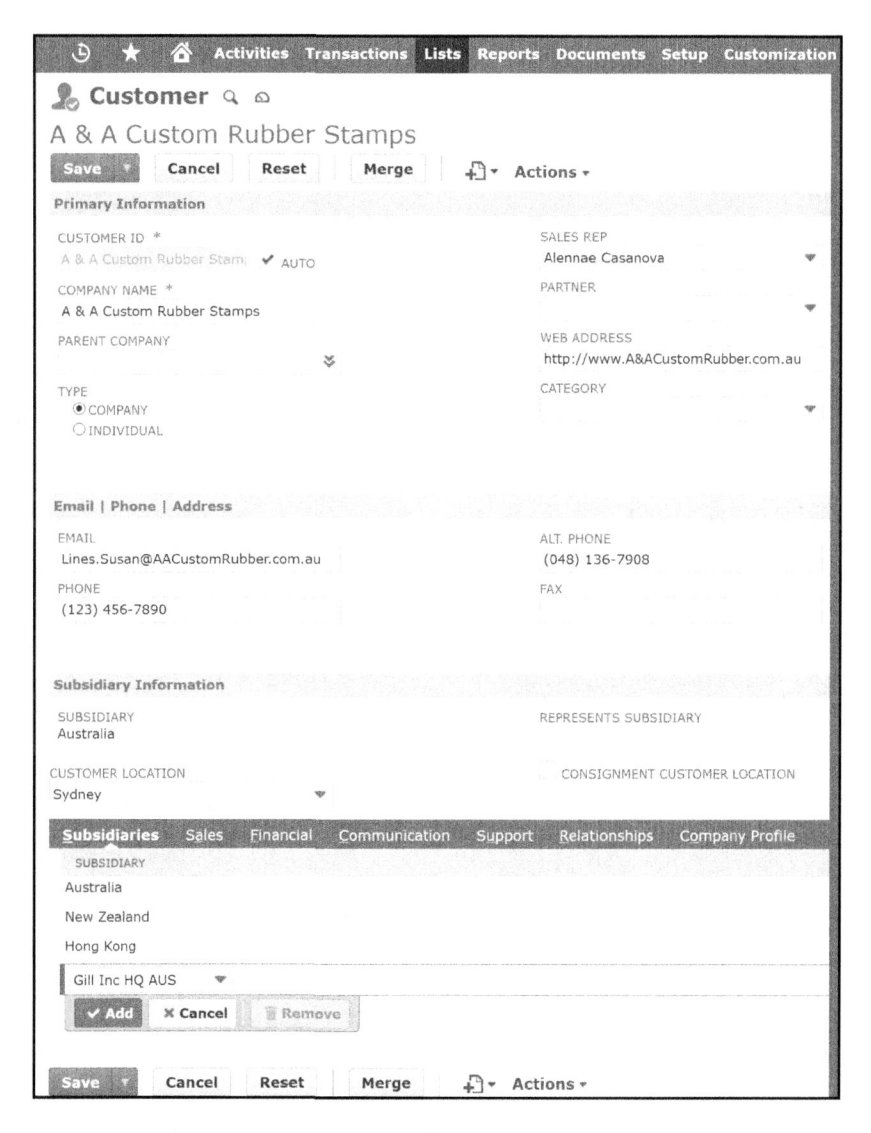

Multi-subsidiary customer

[57]

Vendors

Vendor records are typically related to one subsidiary only; however, they can be shared between subsidiaries, if a specific feature is purchased and enabled. In that case, the vendor will always have a primary subsidiary and could have additional subsidiaries attached to it. The user will be able to choose a subsidiary when entering the transaction. A transaction can only be entered with one subsidiary at a time:

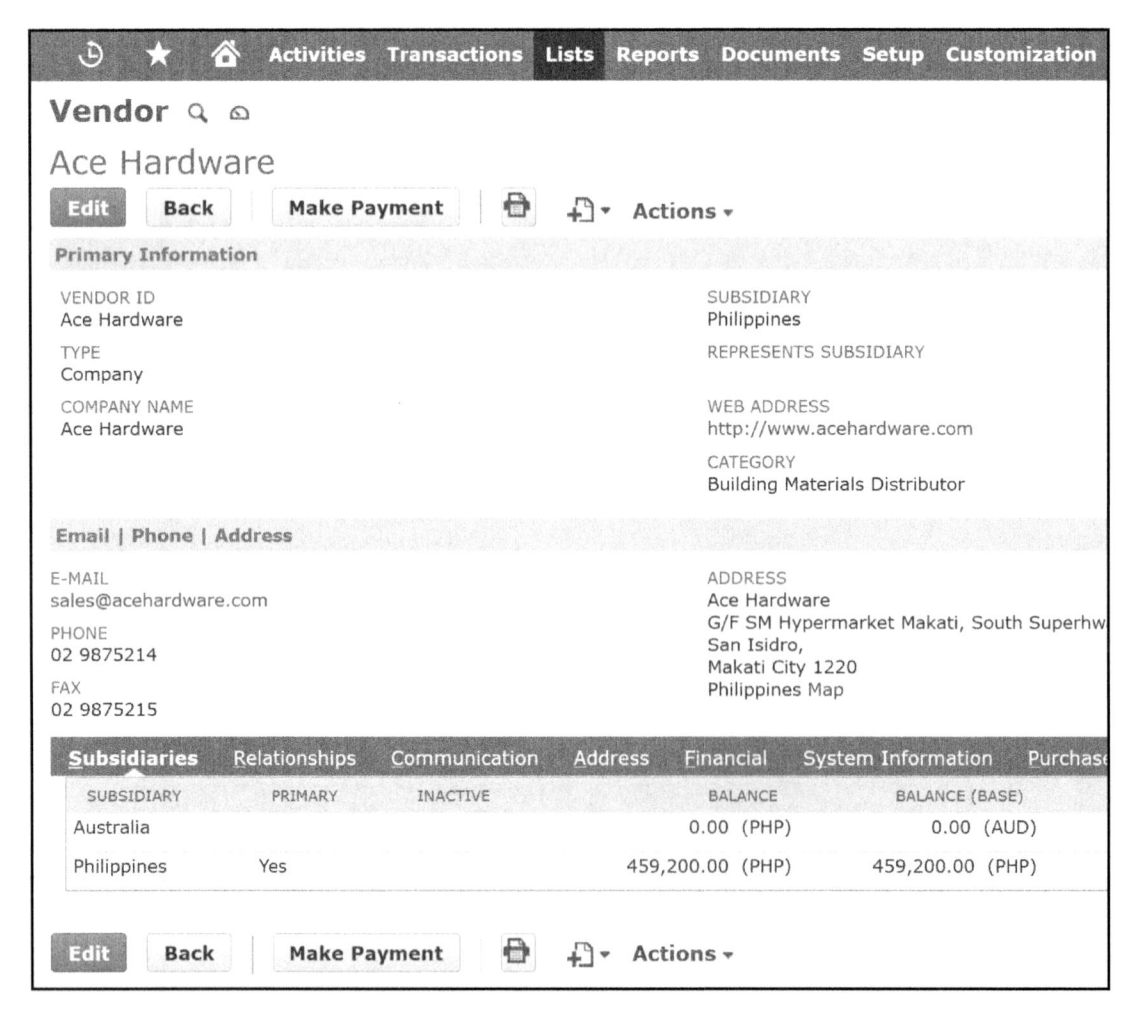

Vendor

Ace Hardware

[Edit] [Back] [Make Payment] [Actions ▼]

Primary Information

VENDOR ID
Ace Hardware

TYPE
Company

COMPANY NAME
Ace Hardware

SUBSIDIARY
Philippines

REPRESENTS SUBSIDIARY

WEB ADDRESS
http://www.acehardware.com

CATEGORY
Building Materials Distributor

Email | Phone | Address

E-MAIL
sales@acehardware.com

PHONE
02 9875214

FAX
02 9875215

ADDRESS
Ace Hardware
G/F SM Hypermarket Makati, South Superhw
San Isidro,
Makati City 1220
Philippines Map

SUBSIDIARY	PRIMARY	INACTIVE	BALANCE	BALANCE (BASE)
Australia			0.00 (PHP)	0.00 (AUD)
Philippines	Yes		459,200.00 (PHP)	459,200.00 (PHP)

[Edit] [Back] [Make Payment] [Actions ▼]

Multi-subsidiary vendor

Items

Items can be shared by multiple subsidiaries, so there is no need to create duplicate items when selling or buying items and inventory. The item will need to be attached to the subsidiary in order to be available on transactions with vendors and customers of that subsidiary:

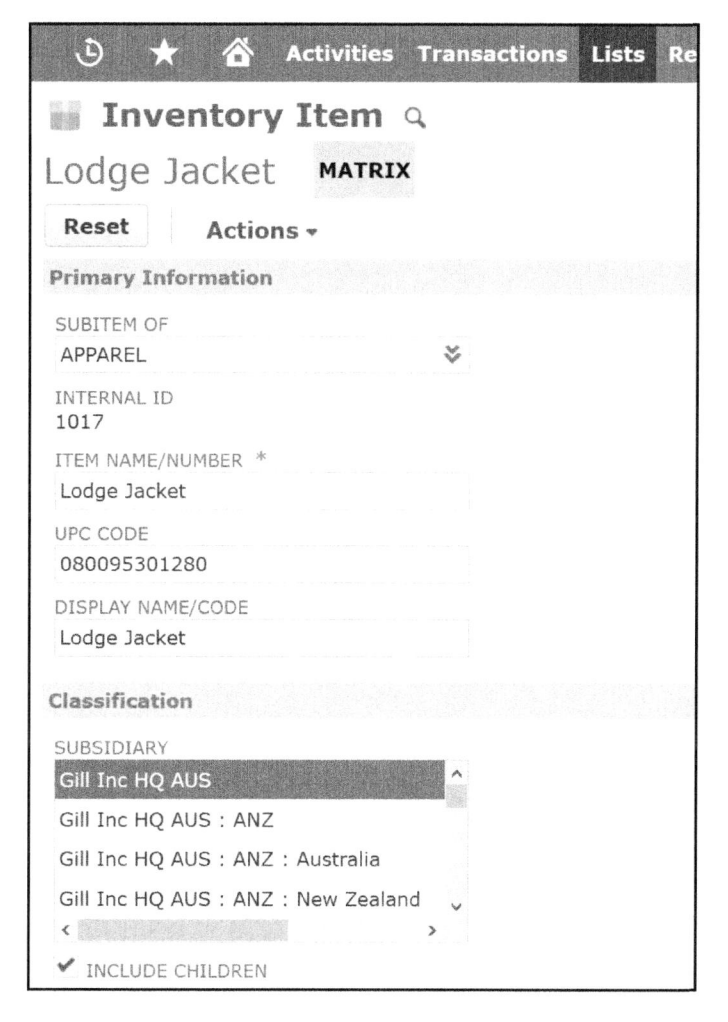

Subsidiaries sharing items

Employees

Employees can only be associated with one subsidiary. This has implications for role setup, because the employee will be restricted to data within his/her subsidiary when he/she is given access to a standard NetSuite role. This is one reason why I recommend that you always use custom roles, which can be customized to include multiple subsidiaries. This allows employees with that role to view the data in all the subsidiaries referenced in that role:

Providing a role with access to multiple subsidiaries

Chart of accounts

Accounts can be associated with multiple subsidiaries. The fact that subsidiaries can share accounts simplifies the list of accounts. Any transaction with that account will be recorded against the subsidiary referred to in the transaction:

Sharing accounts between subsidiaries

Transactions

OneWorld has limited implications for most transactions, as the subsidiary is automatically set based on the people or companies who are entering into the transaction:

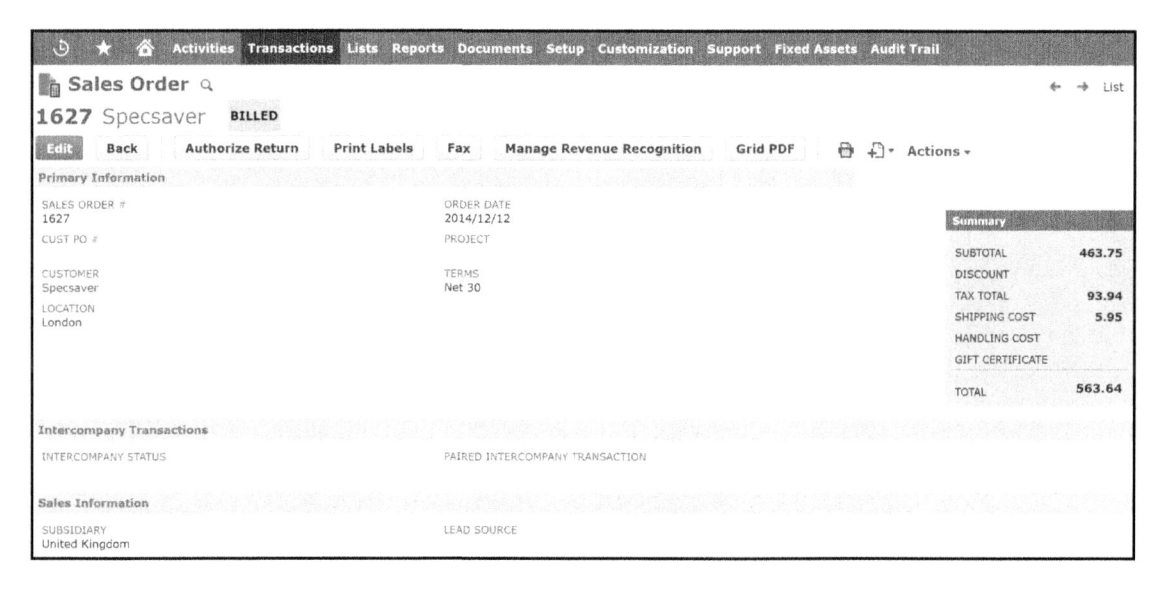

Standard transaction limited to one subsidiary

There are, however, exceptions called intercompany transactions.

[61]

Intercompany journal entries and advanced intercompany journals

Intercompany journals span different subsidiaries, by definition, and enable accountants to create journals to remove any double counting that may occur as a result of transactions between members of the group of companies. They usually involve a subsidiary called an elimination subsidiary, which is set up for the purpose of removing intercompany transactions. The elimination subsidiary is set up in the same way as a normal subsidiary, but with the elimination checkbox checked on the subsidiary record. Speak to your accountant about how he/she wants the elimination subsidiaries set up and at what position in the subsidiary hierarchy:

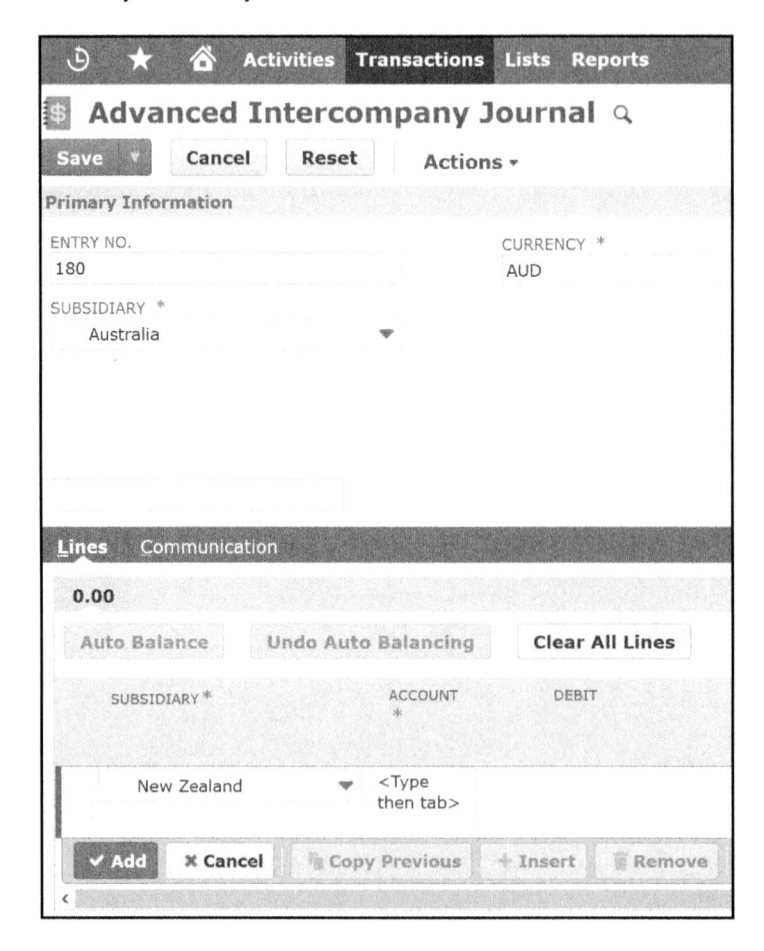

Intercompany journal entry between different subsidiaries

Summary

In this chapter, we looked at setting up a subsidiary hierarchy:

- OneWorld
- Customer
- Vendor
- Item
- Employee
- Roles
- Chart of accounts

The selection of the correct subsidiary/subsidiaries on those records will flow into the majority of transactions. Once you have done that, your accountant will take care of the rest!

In the next chapter, we will focus on the standard processes and built-in workflow that enable us to run the entire company on one system.

4
Implementing

You may be thinking "Oh my gosh, this interface looks confusing. There are so many different options; how am I going to learn how to set up and implement in this complex ERP?" Well, that's the focus of this chapter. We want to distill the concept in NetSuite into easy-to-use steps that we can leverage to implement new features that will also give us the opportunity to learn about some of the standard processes that NetSuite uses for common transactions.

In this chapter, I will introduce my methodology for implementing features and we will set up and configure new features.

In this chapter, we will cover the following:

- Enabling the feature
- Configuring the defaults and preferences
- Setting up the building blocks of the transaction
- Creating transactions on the transaction menu

In this chapter, we will focus on NetSuite's main processes of procure-to-pay and order-to-cash as our use cases in order to configure them for use.

Procure-to-pay process

We will start by looking at a simple process to purchase items that we intend to sell. The process starts with an employee entering a purchase request. The purchase request specifies the vendor and the items, as well as the quantity of those items to be purchased. Being a purchase request, it requires the approval of a manager in order to be transformed into a valid purchase order. The purchase order is then sent to the vendor, which the vendor fulfills by sending the items to our warehouse. The warehouse manager receives the order and places the items in stock.

Implementing

It is up to the accountant to enter the bill into NetSuite, however, the bill has the same details as the purchase order, so the accountant will simply transform the purchase order into a bill at the click of a button. The **Accounts Payable (AP)** Clerk will now recognize which bill is required to be paid in accordance with the terms with that vendor. The AP Clerk will then wait until the bill is due and pay the bill by issuing a check.

Enabling the feature

Go to **Setup** | **Company** | **Enable Features** and check the **A/P**, **ACCOUNTING**, and **ACCOUNTING PERIODS** checkboxes on the **Accounting** tab and the **PURCHASE ORDERS** checkbox on the **Transactions** tab:

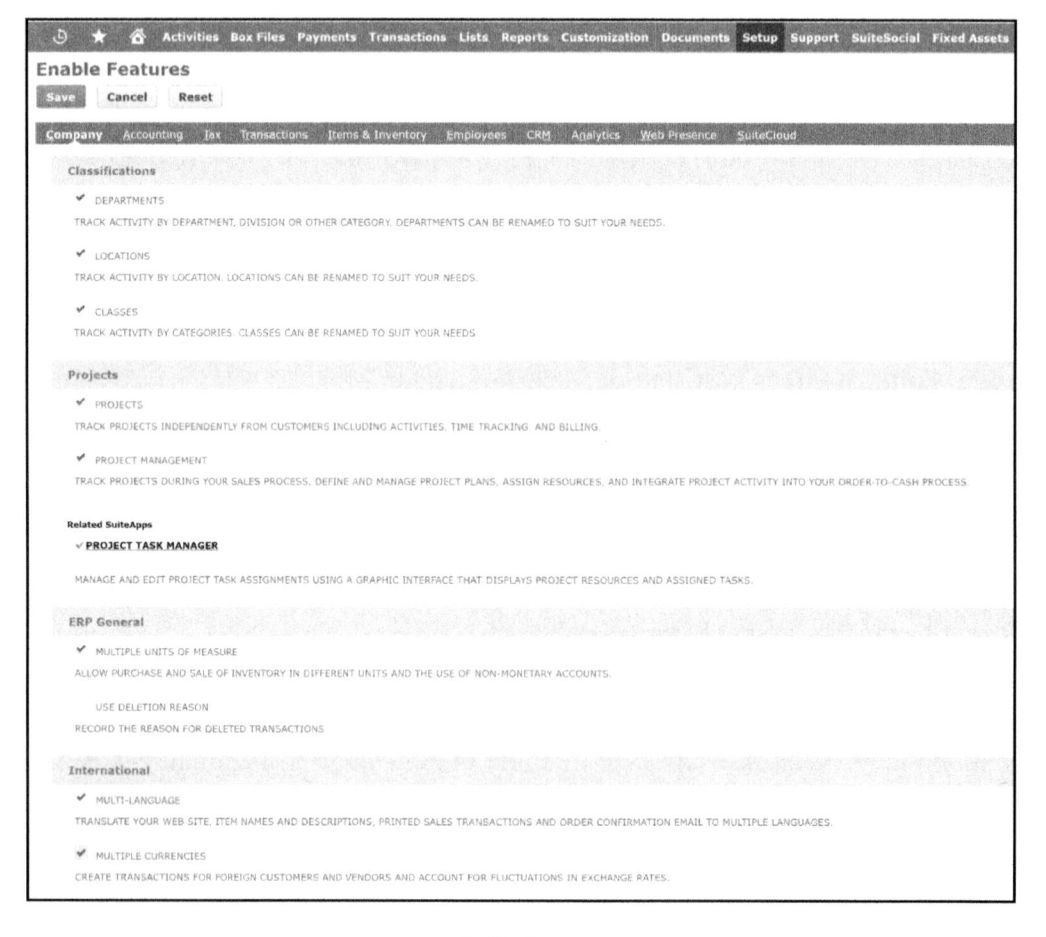

Enabling features

Chapter 4

Configuring the defaults and preferences

The next step is to configure the preferences for this process. The preferences for any process are found on the drop-down menu of the associated transaction, for instance, as in the following:

- Sales preferences are set up at **Setup** | **Sales** | **Sales Preferences**
- Support is set up at **Setup** | **Support** | **Support Preferences**
- Accounting preferences are configured at **Setup** | **Accounting** | **Accounting Preferences**

Accounting Preferences Page

[67]

Implementing

This is the heart of the ERP. If there are any tweaks to be made to a process, this is the place to look. It covers virtually all options for the ERP, from purchasing and selling to advanced processes such as revenue recognition and billing schedules. Let's review the important preferences regarding the process we are configuring.

General tab – Accounts Payable

This section contains the triggers we can use to adjust the **Accounts Payable** process; for instance, in NetSuite, the **DEFAULT VENDOR PAYMENTS TO BE PRINTED** option puts the payments in a check queue waiting for the check run instead of printing each payment one by one. The **VENDOR CREDIT LIMIT WARNINGS** enables the accountant to set the credit limit on each vendor record. The user is prompted with a warning in the event that this order will exceed our credit limit with the vendor:

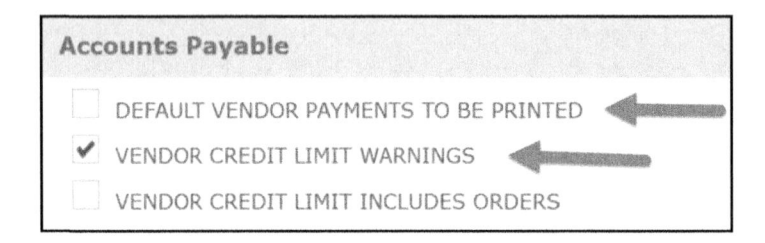

Accounts Payable

☐ DEFAULT VENDOR PAYMENTS TO BE PRINTED ⬅
☑ VENDOR CREDIT LIMIT WARNINGS ⬅
☐ VENDOR CREDIT LIMIT INCLUDES ORDERS

Accounts Payable Section in Accounting Preferences

Items/Transactions tab

Ask your accountant to review the account selections on this tab, as this will determine the default accounts that will be used for all these transactions. The **DEFAULT EXPENSE ACCOUNT** and **DEFAULT PAYMENT ACCOUNT** are the selections that are most applicable to this process. The **DEFAULT PAYABLE ACCOUNT** selection will appear by default when the accountant is paying bills. The default **COSTING METHOD** is a crucial selection that will affect all your processes. The options are **FIFO**, **LIFO**, and **Average**. There is also a *standard costing feature* that can be enabled if necessary and, if you purchase this feature, you will find it under **Setup | Company | Enable Features**:

Chapter 4

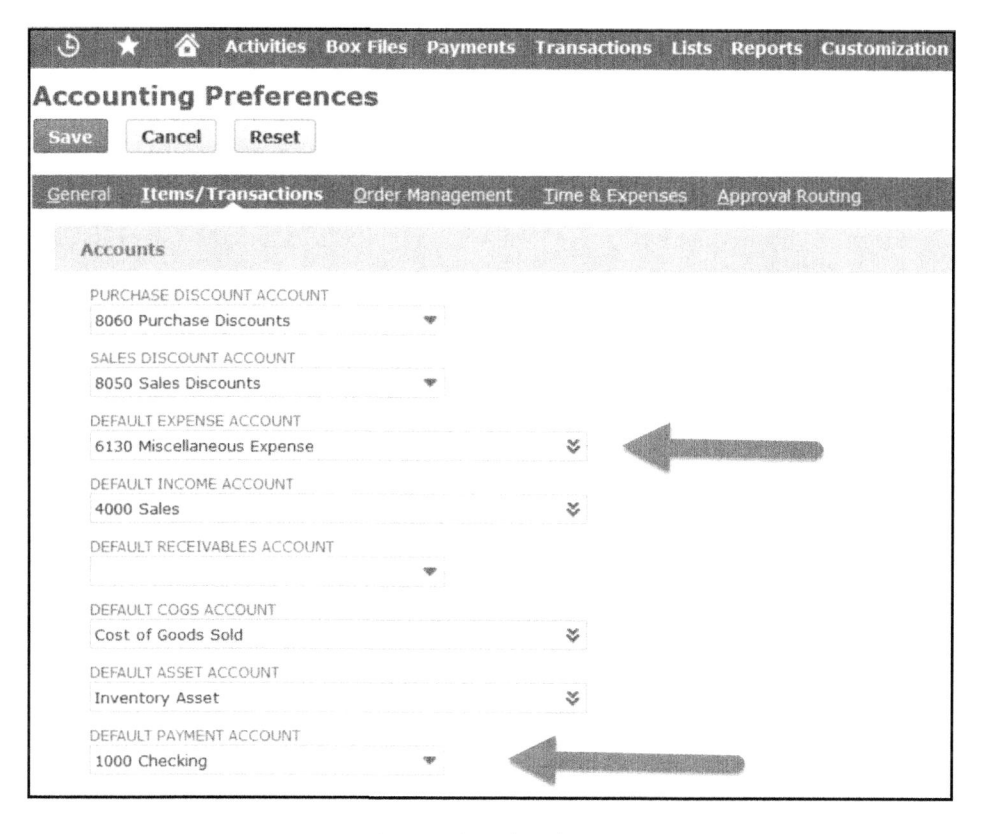

Accounts on Accounting Preferences

Order Management – Purchasing

Go to the **Purchasing** section of the **Order Management** tab:

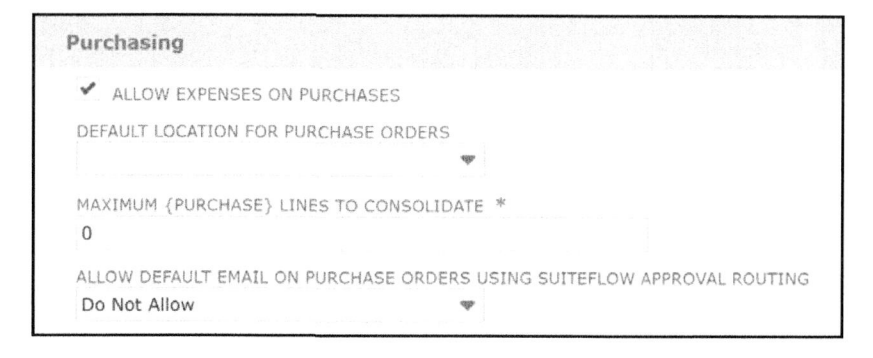

Purchasing section on Accounting Preferences

[69]

Implementing

We can choose to allow expenses on purchases, which places an **Expenses** tab on the **Purchase Order** screen. This can be used to create a **Purchase Order** and post the transaction directly to the expense account without needing to set up an item record first:

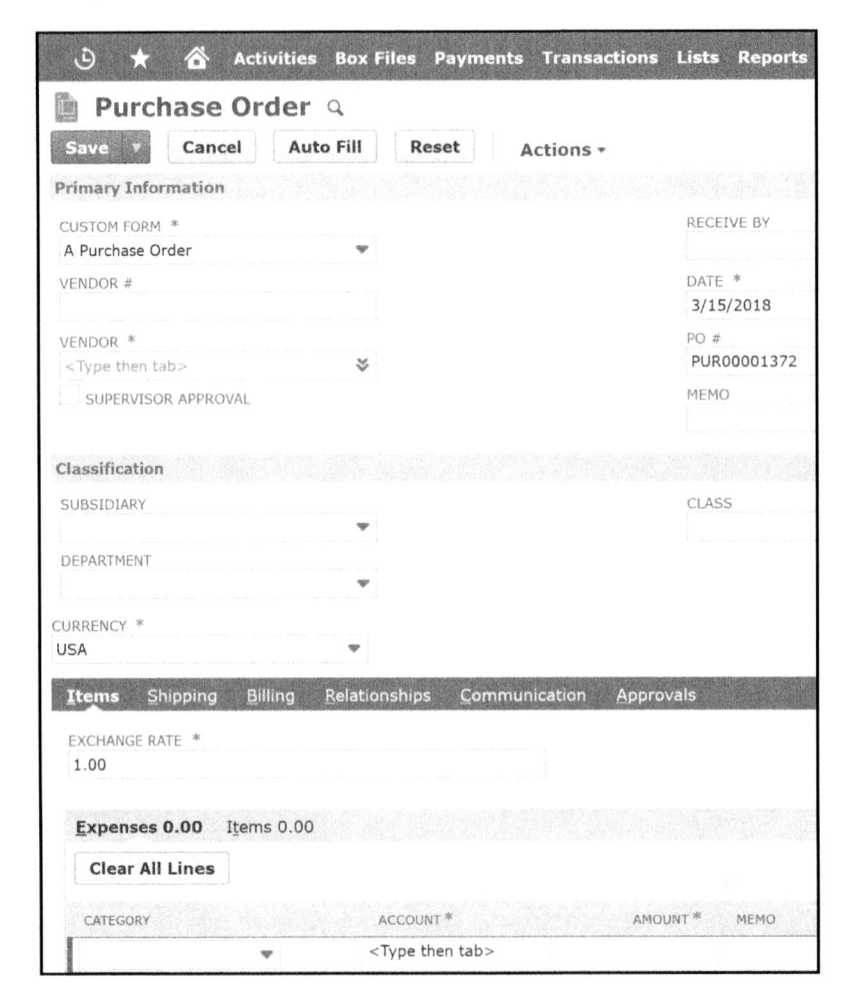

Purchase Order page showing Expenses subtab

In our example, we are purchasing inventory, so we need to know the quantity of inventory purchased, in addition to the amount paid. For this, we can use the item tab and add the inventory items to our purchase order. The option to **Allow Expenses** is, however, open to you, if required.

[70]

We can also choose a **Default Location for Purchase Orders** to automate the selection of location when creating purchase orders. The default can be changed on the purchase order itself. There is an option to enter the **Maximum lines to consolidate on a Purchase Order**, where, for instance, we use the system to prompt reordering when inventory falls below the reorder point of particular items. NetSuite will create the purchase order for us, placing all the items requiring replenishment onto a single purchase order, by vendor. This selection determines the maximum number of lines on such a purchase order.

Order Management – Receiving

The **BILL IN ADVANCE OF RECEIPT** checkbox enables us to tweak the purchase-to-pay process. The standard procure-to-pay process requires a receipt to precede the billing of the purchase order. In fact, the **BILL** button will not appear on a purchase order until the purchase order has been received. By enabling this checkbox, NetSuite gives us the option of billing before receiving a purchase order.

Will we allow the warehouse manager to receive more items than were ordered on the purchase order? This option is determined by checking or unchecking the **ALLOW OVERAGE ON ITEM RECEIPTS** checkbox.

LANDED COST is a feature that is enabled separately. It allows us to allocate the costs of shipping the items to us to the cost of the items themselves. We may buy Widget A from our vendor in China at $10 per item. It may, however, cost us thousands of dollars to ship the items to our warehouse in San Diego and even more in customs duties. In that event, is the cost of the item really $10 or should we apportion the freight and duty to each of those items? The **LANDED COST ALLOCATION PER LINE** feature will allow you to do so. Here, we are presented with the option to apportion the costs per order or per line on that order:

Receiving

✔ BILL IN ADVANCE OF RECEIPT
✔ ALLOW OVERAGE ON ITEM RECEIPTS
DEFAULT RECEIVING EXCHANGE RATE
Use Order Exchange Rate

  USE PURCHASE ORDER RATE ON BILLS
  LANDED COST ALLOCATION PER LINE

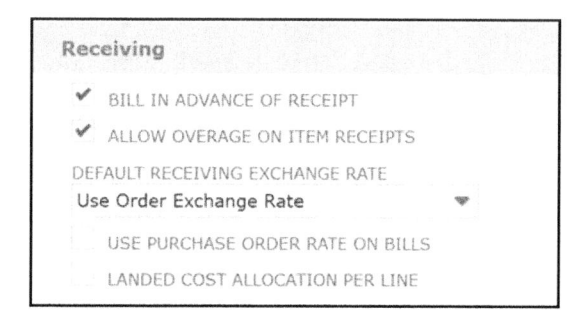

Receiving section on Accounting Preferences

Implementing

Order Management – Vendor bills

We can choose to enable an approvals process for vendor bills using this selection by setting this field to **PENDING APPROVAL**, which will require a supervisor to approve a bill before a payment can be made on that bill:

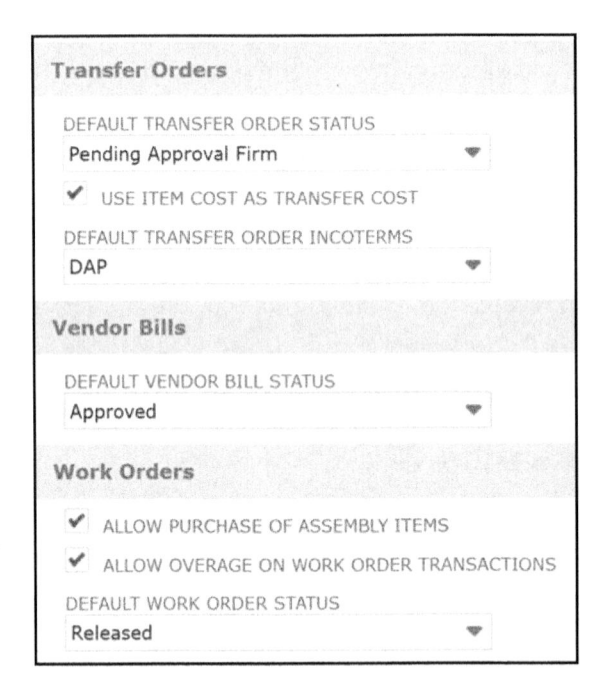

Vendor Bills section Accounting Preferences

Approval routing

Check the **Purchase Order** checkbox and the system will automatically email a notification to the appropriate purchase approver when a purchase request has been entered.

Building blocks

Now that we have set up the configuration, return to set up the building blocks, representing the components of the transaction. The building blocks are usually found on the **Lists** drop-down menu. In the case of a purchase order, those components are employees, vendors, and items.

Employees

Let's start with the employee record. Go to **Lists** | **Employees** | **Employees** | **New**. We are concerned with the approval hierarchy when reviewing the employee records. The **Employee** hierarchy is on the **Human Resources** tab. We can choose the employee's **PURCHASE APPROVER**, **PURCHASE LIMIT**, and **PURCHASE APPROVAL LIMIT**. The **PURCHASE APPROVER** is the manager who is responsible for approving this employee's purchase request. If this field is left blank, the approval will be routed to this employee's supervisor, instead, for approval. The **PURCHASE LIMIT** enables the employee to self-approve any purchase orders below that amount, whereas the **PURCHASE APPROVAL LIMIT** sets a limit on this employee's authority to approve their subordinate's purchase requests.

Naturally, we will also need to assign this user with a role that includes the permissions to enter and/or approve purchase orders, among others.

On the subject of roles, purchase requests are entered using the employee center role, so it will be necessary to grant that role to the employees who will be entering the purchase requests:

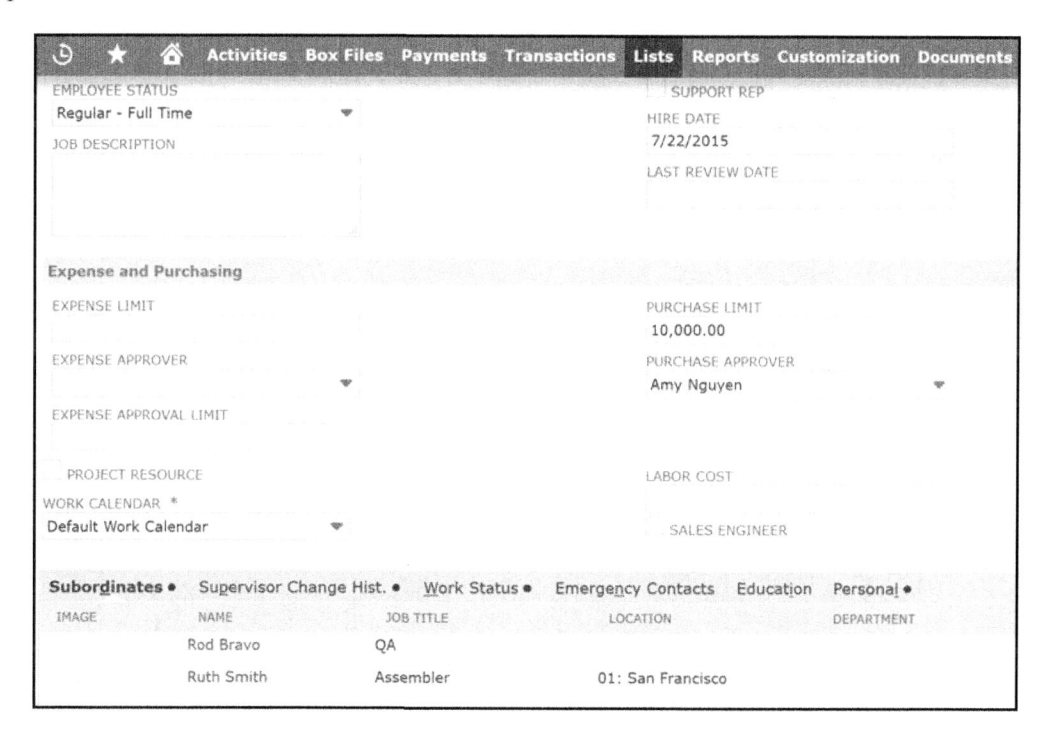

Setting Purchase Approver and Purchase Limit on the Employee record

Implementing

Vendors

The information on the vendor record will be sourced into any transaction with that vendor. We can save time that would be spent editing each individual purchase order by setting up the defaults on the vendor record, for instance, the email address is necessary if we want NetSuite to email purchase orders to each vendor.

The necessary options are available on the **Financial** tab of the vendor record. We can also set a specific **Expense Account** and **Payables Account** for this vendor if they are different from the default accounts specified under **Setup | Accounting | Accounting Preferences**. Set up the **TERMS** and **CREDIT LIMIT** that we have with that vendor. The **CREDIT LIMIT** prompts the user when it is about to be exceeded, whereas the **TERMS** will prompt the AP Clerk to pay the bill before it is due. If you're using the multi-currency feature, you can select the **Currencies** that you transact with this vendor in. We can also set up **Pricing Schedules** to automate pricing where we have preferential pricing with this vendor. So, for instance, if we get a 7% discount if we purchase more than 100 items from this vendor, NetSuite can automatically apply the discount based on the quantity pricing schedule selected on the vendor record:

The Financial tab of the Vendor record

Item record

The item record allows us to specify a **Vendor Name/Code** where the vendor has a different name for the item than we do. In that case, the item will appear internally using our SKU but will automatically default to the vendor's SKU number when processing Purchase transactions.

We can specify the **COSTING METHOD** for each individual item. This overrides the default costing method for all items, it is set up in the heart of the ERP... Yes, you guessed it! **Setup | Accounting | Accounting Preferences**!

The item record also allows us to specify the **PURCHASE PRICE** of the item, as well as whether we will be tracking landed cost on this item and even the vendor or vendors that we purchase this item from. In addition, we can specify whether this item is a drop-ship or special-order item. NetSuite can automatically create a purchase order when a **DROP SHIP ITEM** or **SPECIAL ORDER ITEM** is sold. The difference is to be found on the ship to address of the purchase order. The Drop Ship purchase order instructs the vendor to ship the item to the customer directly, whereas the **SPECIAL ORDER ITEM** specifies our warehouse address on the purchase order. We will send it on to the customer as soon as we receive it:

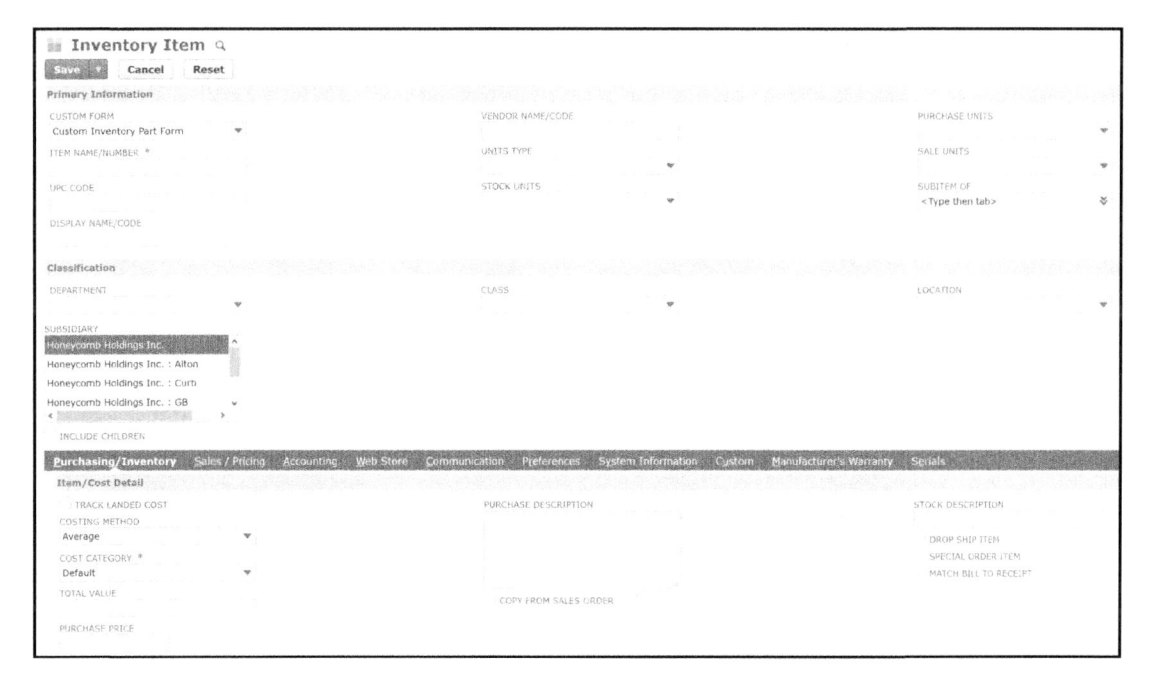

Cost details of Item record showing DROP SHIP ITEM and SPECIAL ORDER ITEM fields

Implementing

Transactions

The purpose of accounting is to record transactions and, as a result, these are the objectives of the entire configuration and need to be tested with end users to confirm that the transaction complies with the company's requirements.

The first transaction in this process is the purchase request, which can be accessed by users with a limited set of permissions. Permissions are determined by the user's role:

1. Click the **Change Role** button on the top-right corner of the screen and select **Employee Center**:

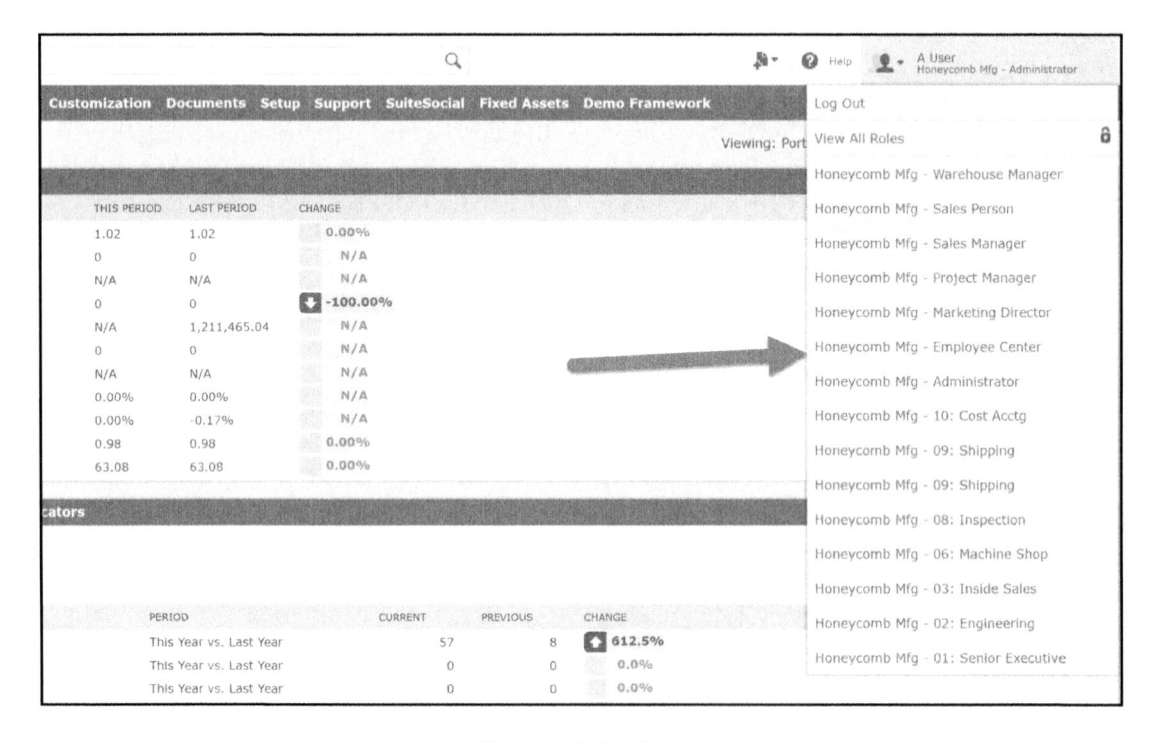

Change role to Employee Center

2. Select the **Purchase Request** button on the dashboard, which will open the purchase request form:

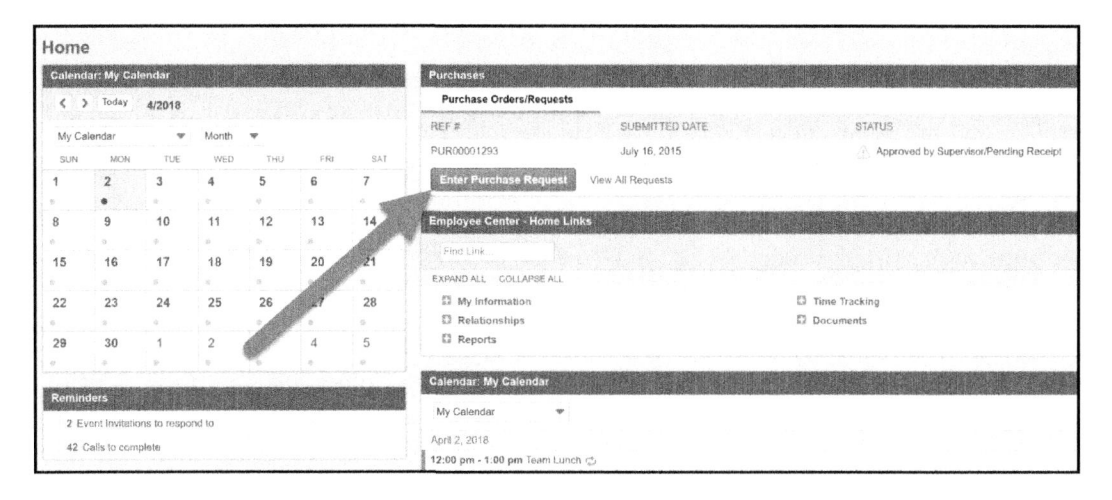

Employee Center role dashboard

3. Select the vendor and the items you wish to purchase. The purchase price will auto-populate from the item record as will all the necessary information from the vendor record. Enter the number of items that you need to purchase.
4. Click **Save**:

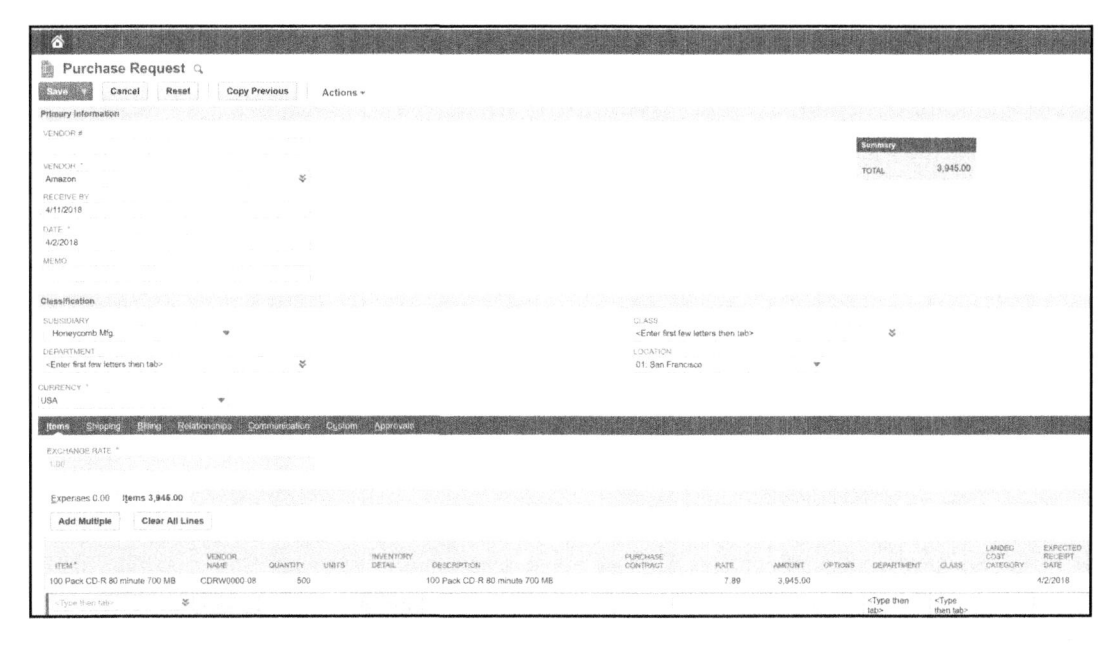

Entering a Purchase Request

Implementing

The **Purchase Request** has now successfully been entered and an automated email has been sent to the appropriate approver to alert that person to approve the purchase request. The notification is, of course, on the preceding accounting preferences screen.

The supervisor would go to the **Reminders Portlet** on receiving the email notification.

The **Purchase Requests to Approve** reminder will have increased by one and the supervisor would click on the **Purchase Request** link to be taken to a list of purchase requests that needs to be approved.

The approval can be made en masse to a number of purchase requests at one time; alternatively, the supervisor can click on the specific purchase request and approve it individually.

Once approved, the purchase request becomes a valid purchase order and can be sent to the vendor.

The warehouse manager would access the **Reminders Portlet** when the package arrives at the warehouse. The relevant reminder is the **Items to Receive** reminder; by clicking on it, the warehouse manager will be taken to the list of orders to be received.

Click **Receive**, next to the appropriate order. The information in the order has been pre-populated directly from the purchase request including the items and their quantities. The warehouse manager only needs to click the save button if the items have been received in the correct quantities. The warehouse manager can edit the quantities to ensure they record the correct number of items actually received:

Chapter 4

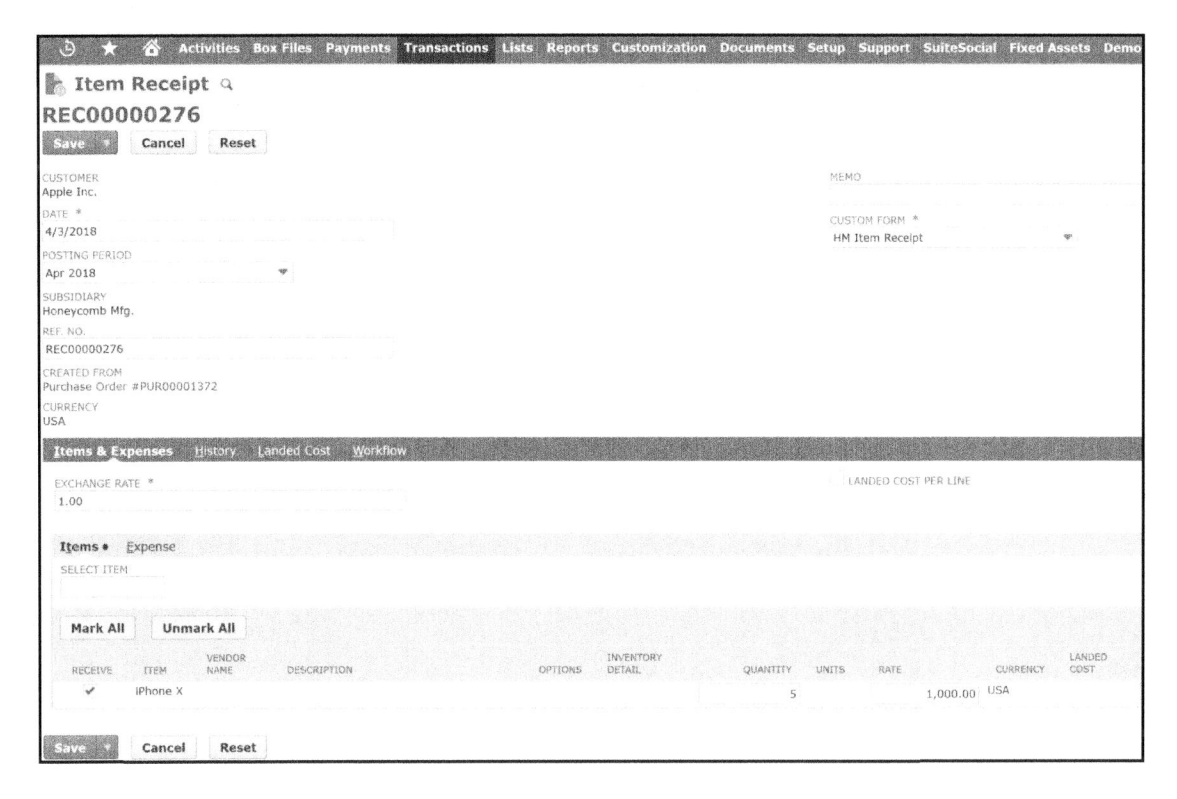

The Item Receipt

There is a preference on the **Accounting Preferences** screen to allow the warehouse manager to receive items on orders if appropriate. Once the warehouse manager saves the receipt, the order goes into a received-pending billing status.

[79]

Implementing

This, in turn, sets off a reminder on the **Accounts Payable** clerk's dashboard to **BILL TO** the purchase order. The **Accounts Payable** clerk simply clicks that reminder on the dashboard to be taken to the list of purchase orders to **BILL**. The AP clerk can bill multiple purchase orders simultaneously, provided that all those selected are for the same vendor. We can use the vendor filter at the top of the screen to limit all the purchase orders in the list to those belonging to that vendor:

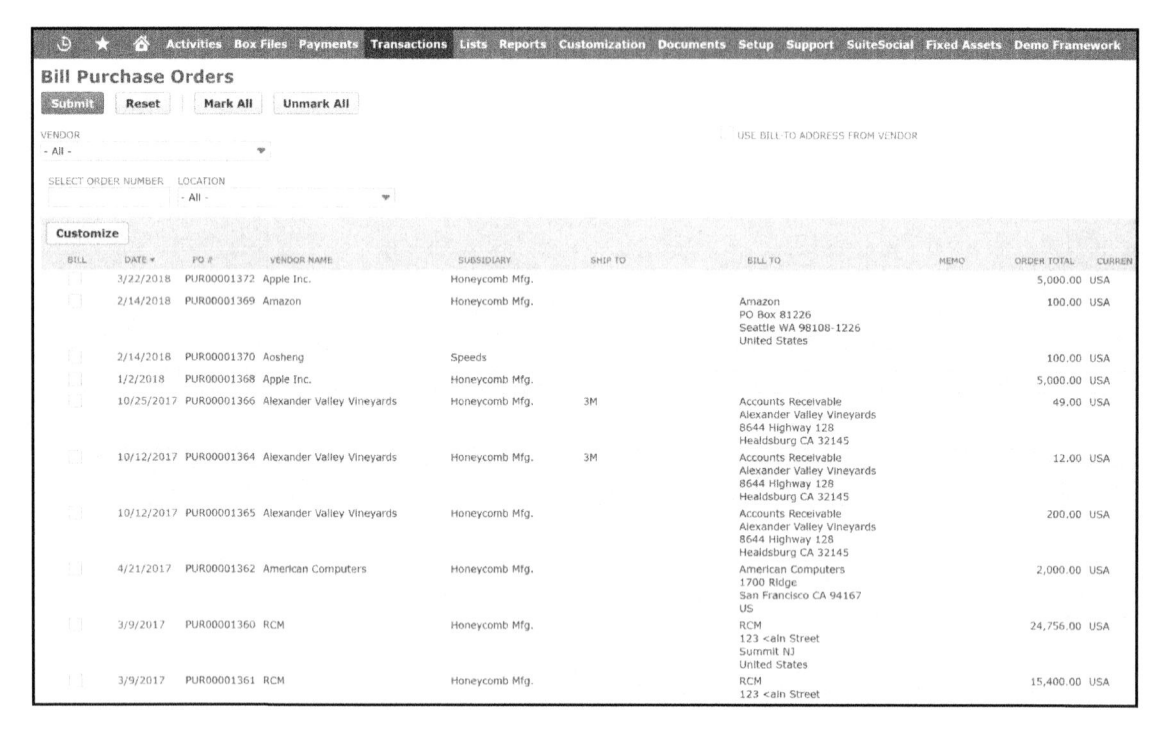

Bill Purchase Order in Bulk Screen

Chapter 4

Alternatively, the AP Clerk can focus on one purchase order at a time by selecting a purchase order from the list. All of the necessary information has been pre-populated from the vendor, item, and purchase orders, and all the AP clerk needs to do is click the **Save** button:

Bill Purchase Order

Implementing

The system monitors all outstanding purchase orders and will alert the **Accounts Payable** clerk when the purchase orders need to be paid in accordance with the terms. This also will be reflected in the reminders posted on the home dashboard as **Bills to Pay**.

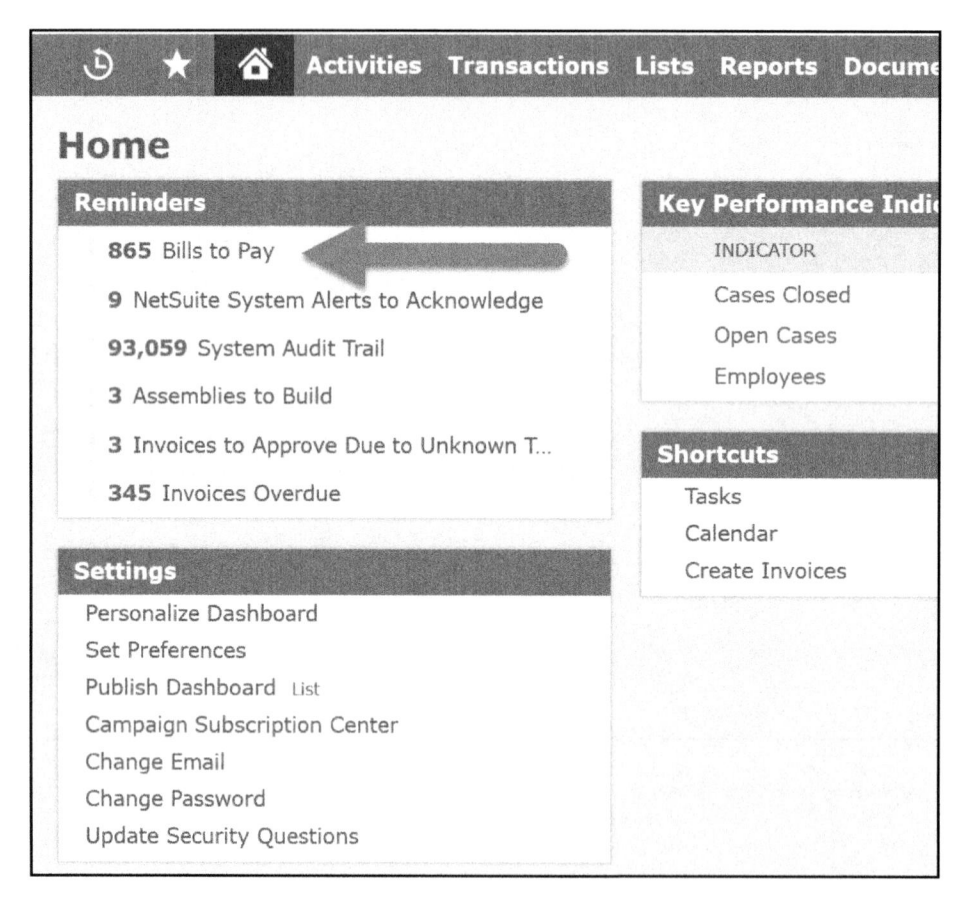

Bill to Pay reminder

The AP clerk simply needs to click the **Bills to Pay** button to be taken to that screen to pay those bills. It is a list of multiple bills enabling the clerk to pay more than one bill at a time:

	DATE DUE	TYPE	VENDOR	REF NO.	CURRENCY	EXCHANGE RATE	ORIGINAL AMOUNT	AMOUNT DUE	DISC. DATE	DISC. AVAIL.
		Bill	Office Depot		USA	1.00	999.00	999.00		
		Expense Report	Jill Muscat	2012	USA	1.00	75.00	75.00		
		Bill	The Office Shop Inc		USA	1.00	9.99	9.99		
		Bill Credit	American Express		USA	1.00	-5.00	-5.00		
		Bill Credit	Coopers Office Furniture		USA	1.00	-189.99	-189.99		
		Bill Credit	Coopers Office Furniture		USA	1.00	-385.96	-385.96		
		Bill Credit	Koka Office Supplies		USA	1.00	-2,593.40	-2,593.40		

Bill Payment in bulk screen

Implementing

Alternatively, the AP clerk can go to a specific vendor by clicking on the link to that transaction. All the outstanding bills for that vendor appear in the following tabs and the AP clerk can select to pay some or all of the outstanding bills by simply clicking on the checkbox beside it. If paying by check, it may be best to click the **TO BE PRINTED** checkbox, which places this bill payment in a check queue on saving:

Bill Payment screen

The checks to print will, of course, be available as a link on the **Reminders** portlet:

Chapter 4

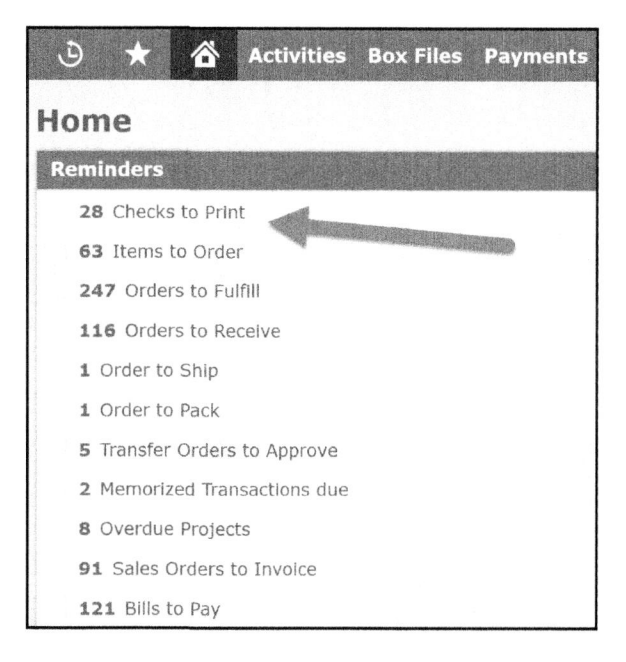

Checks to Print reminder

The AP clerk can select that link in order to do the check run at the end of the day:

Print Check queue

Implementing

That concludes a simple demonstration of the procure-to-pay process and, as you can see, the efficiency is determined by the selections on the accounting preferences screen as well as the building blocks.

Order-to-Cash

The order-to-cash process starts with a sales order combined with a possible sales order approval step. The order is then sent to the warehouse for fulfillment, followed by the invoicing step completed by the accountant. The AP clerk then monitors outstanding invoices to ensure the cash flow of the company.

Enabling features

Go to **Setup** | **Company** | **Enable Features**. ACCOUNTING, ACCOUNTING PERIODS, and **A/R** on the **Accounting** tab need to be enabled for the order-to-cash process.

We can also enable specific item types, allowing us to sell different types of products. We find the options on the **Items & Inventory** tab:

Chapter 4

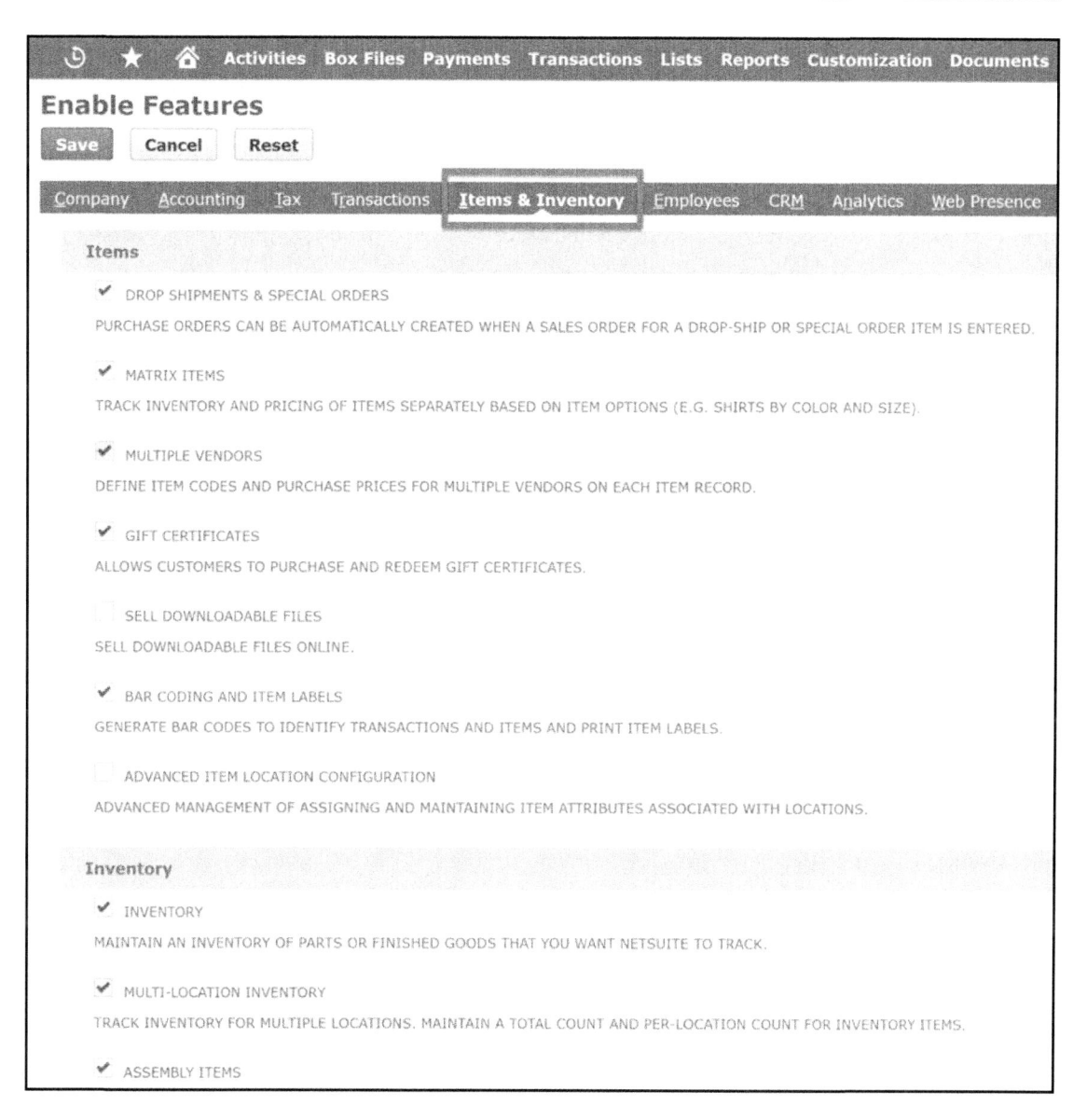

```
                  Activities  Box Files  Payments  Transactions  Lists  Reports  Customization  Documents
Enable Features
 Save    Cancel    Reset

 Company   Accounting   Tax   Transactions   Items & Inventory   Employees   CRM   Analytics   Web Presence

 Items

    ✔ DROP SHIPMENTS & SPECIAL ORDERS
    PURCHASE ORDERS CAN BE AUTOMATICALLY CREATED WHEN A SALES ORDER FOR A DROP-SHIP OR SPECIAL ORDER ITEM IS ENTERED.

    ✔ MATRIX ITEMS
    TRACK INVENTORY AND PRICING OF ITEMS SEPARATELY BASED ON ITEM OPTIONS (E.G. SHIRTS BY COLOR AND SIZE).

    ✔ MULTIPLE VENDORS
    DEFINE ITEM CODES AND PURCHASE PRICES FOR MULTIPLE VENDORS ON EACH ITEM RECORD.

    ✔ GIFT CERTIFICATES
    ALLOWS CUSTOMERS TO PURCHASE AND REDEEM GIFT CERTIFICATES.

    ☐ SELL DOWNLOADABLE FILES
    SELL DOWNLOADABLE FILES ONLINE.

    ✔ BAR CODING AND ITEM LABELS
    GENERATE BAR CODES TO IDENTIFY TRANSACTIONS AND ITEMS AND PRINT ITEM LABELS.

    ☐ ADVANCED ITEM LOCATION CONFIGURATION
    ADVANCED MANAGEMENT OF ASSIGNING AND MAINTAINING ITEM ATTRIBUTES ASSOCIATED WITH LOCATIONS.

 Inventory

    ✔ INVENTORY
    MAINTAIN AN INVENTORY OF PARTS OR FINISHED GOODS THAT YOU WANT NETSUITE TO TRACK.

    ✔ MULTI-LOCATION INVENTORY
    TRACK INVENTORY FOR MULTIPLE LOCATIONS. MAINTAIN A TOTAL COUNT AND PER-LOCATION COUNT FOR INVENTORY ITEMS.

    ✔ ASSEMBLY ITEMS
```

Items and Inventory page

INVENTORY is just one of the options. It is used to purchase physical goods from a vendor and resell them to a customer while tracking the location of the inventory throughout that process.

Implementing

ASSEMBLY ITEMS are items that we manufacture from components. The components are therefore set up as inventory items and the manufacturing process results in an assembly item.

MATRIX ITEMS are used to manage situations where the item can be ordered in multiple configurations. A shirt, for instance, may be sold in different sizes (small, medium, large, and extra-large), different colors (red, green, blue, and white), and with different logos (Manchester United, Chelsea, Manchester City, and Liverpool). That is a lot of permutations to manage, but the NetSuite matrix item feature helps you to do so by creating a parent item that can be used to update the various combinations very easily.

We can also create **Serialized Inventory** items providing the ability to track the movement of a specific piece of inventory based on its serial number. This feature necessitates entering the serial number on any transaction containing this item. Any item receipt, fulfillment, or transfer requires us to specify the specific item that was received or sent, identified by its serial number. There is also the ability to sell **Gift Certificates** and **Downloadable Items**, as well as **DROP SHIPMENTS & SPECIAL ORDERS** item.

The **Transactions** tab contains some important options, including **SALES ORDERS**, which recognize the customer's commitment to purchase from you and can create the instruction to the warehouse to ship the item and the accountant to invoice the sale. We can also enable **RETURN AUTHORIZATIONS** to record any customer returns.

The **Transactions** tab also contains important options regarding the fulfillment itself. **ADVANCED SHIPPING** splits the shipping function from the billing function, whereas **PICK, PACK AND SHIP** splits the fulfillment into three separate steps. This allows us to easily split those tasks among different people while the system manages the process to ensure that no fulfillments get missed.

SHIPPING LABEL INTEGRATION enables us to print FedEx, UPS, and USPS shipping labels directly in NetSuite. It automatically creates the shipping label and updates the NetSuite tracking number field with the correct tracking number supplied by those shippers.

MULTIPLE PRICES gives us the ability to charge two different customers different prices for the same items. **QUANTITY PRICING**, on the other hand, helps us to specify bulk discounts provided to customers if they purchase in large quantities. In the case of **MULTIPLE PRICES**, a wholesale customer will be charged the wholesale price even if they're purchasing only one item. **QUANTITY PRICING**, on the other hand, lets us charge a different price per item, if the customer purchases more than 10 items on the same order, as an example:

Chapter 4

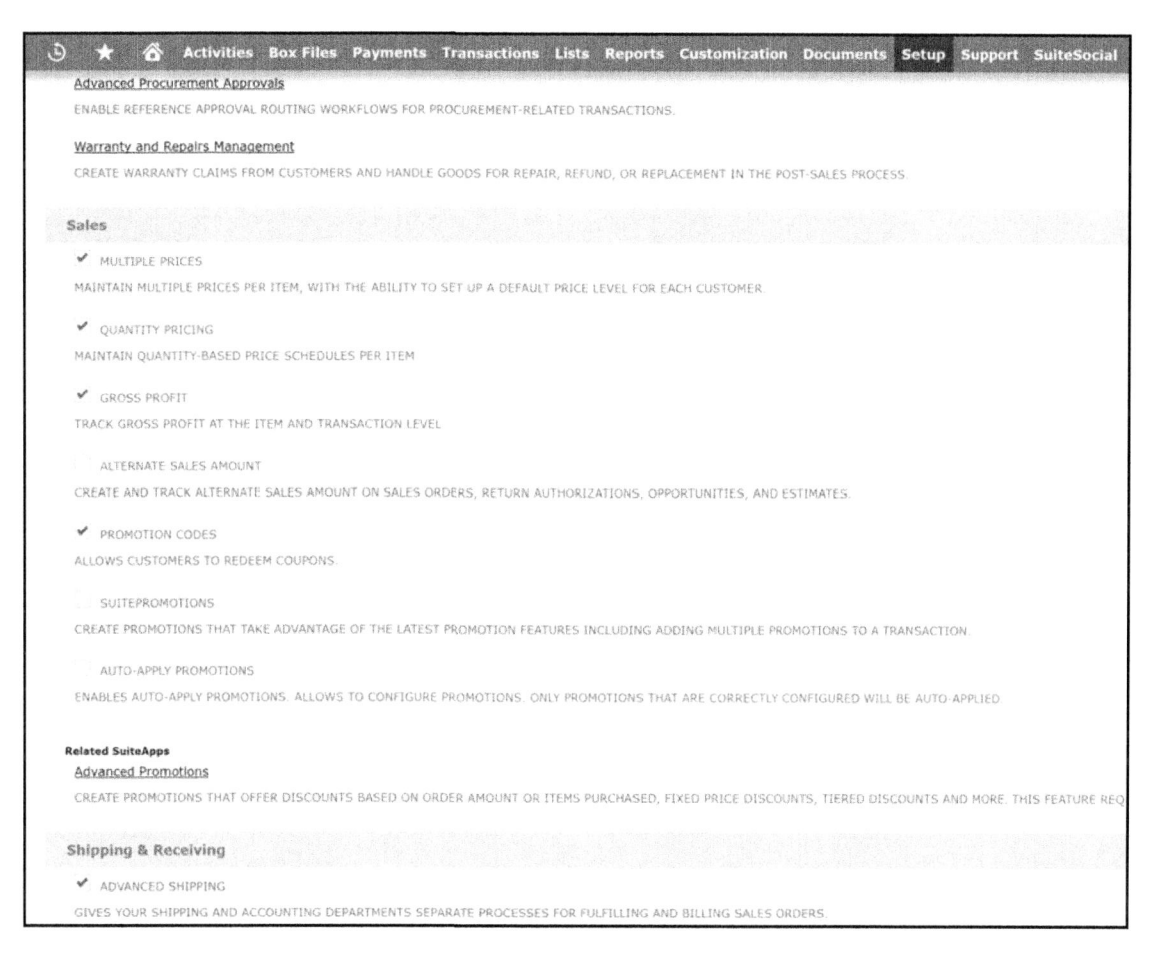

Sales section of the Transactions tab

Configuring the defaults and preferences

The key to configuring the ERP is the **Accounting Preferences** screen; however, in this section, we will also briefly touch on shipping and tax, which are also necessary for transacting with customers.

Implementing

Shipping and tax

We'll begin the configuration by going to **Setup** | **Accounting** | **Shipping** and in **FedEx/USPS/More**, inserting our USPS account details to be used in the integration. We can also go to **Setup** | **Accounting**:

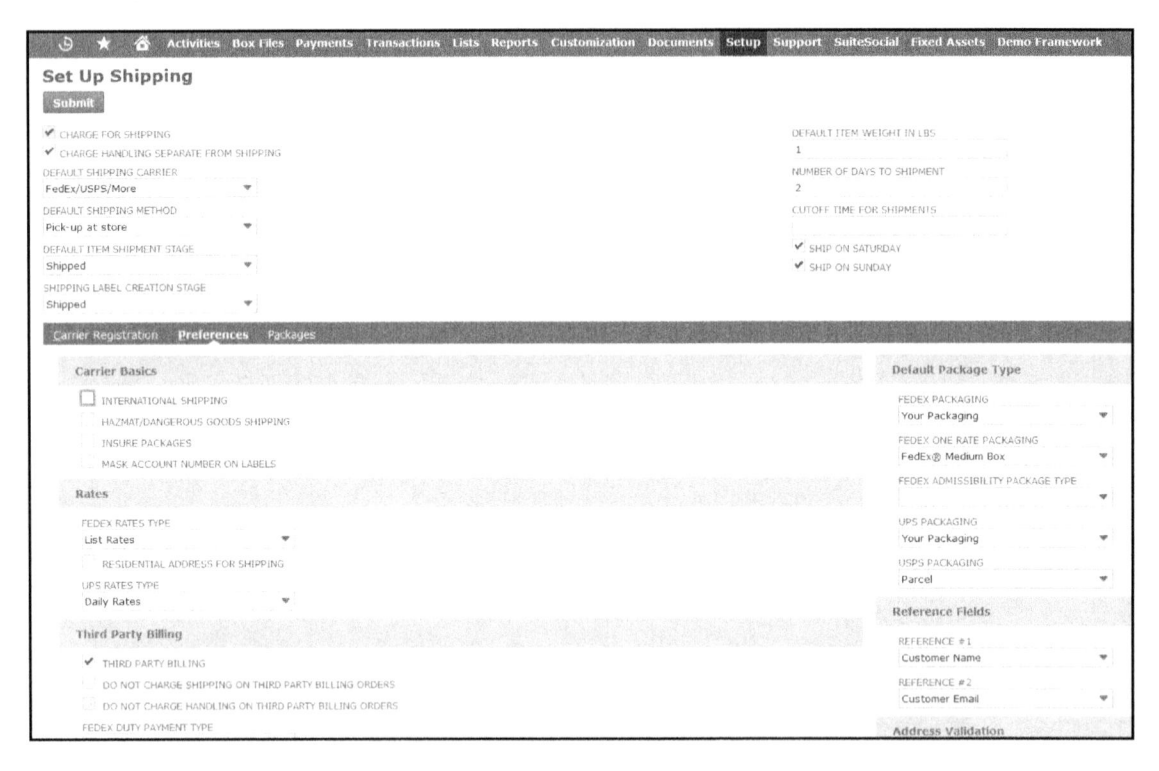

Setup Shipping screen in Accounting

Payment Processing sets up the integration with the preferred credit card processor. The tax setup is also on the **Setup** | **Accounting** menu and will need to be entered for the correct tax to be charged to the customer.

Accounting Preferences – Order Management

Like any other ERP process, the crux of the order-to-cash process is set up on **Setup** | **Accounting** | **Accounting Preferences**.

The **Order Management** tab has a section on sales orders. The **DEFAULT SALES ORDER STATUS** is used to determine whether an approvals process will be used for sales orders. It has two options, **Pending Approval** and **Pending Fulfillment**. We can set the location for orders to a specific location by default using the **DEFAULT LOCATION FOR SALES ORDER** field, as well as choosing whether NetSuite will commit items to orders in the following fields. **Commitment** sets specific items aside for specific orders based on various criteria, such as the date of the order or the importance of the customer:

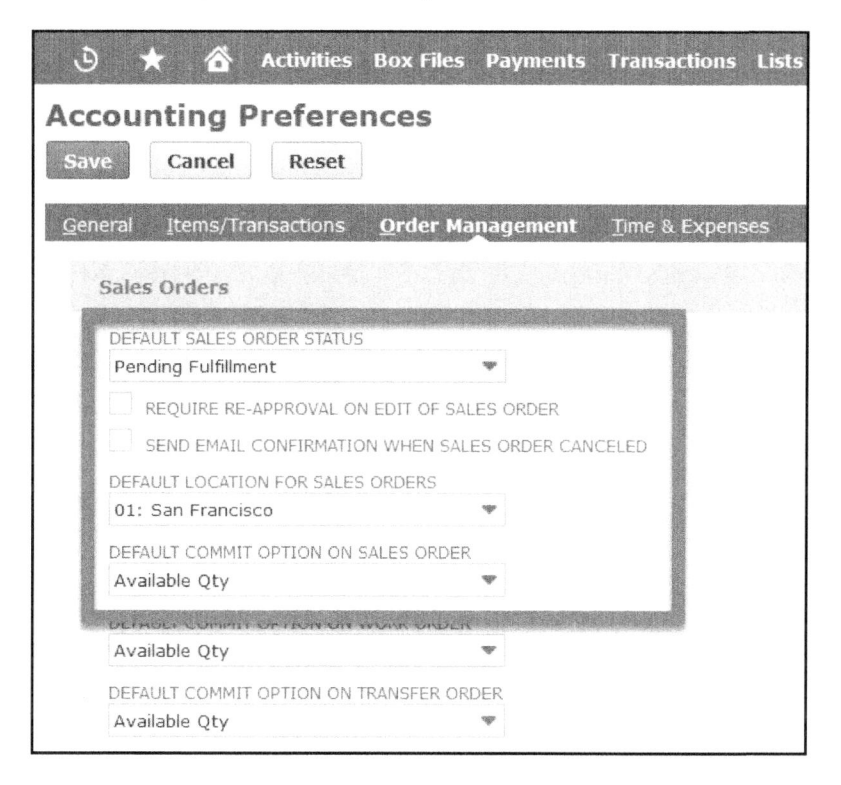

Sales Orders section in Order Management tab in Accounting Preferences under Accounting in Setup

The **Pick/Packing** and **Fulfillment** sections contain options for the default values that will appear on the screens during the fulfillment, as well as automation options, such as generating an automated email to the customer when the order has been fulfilled. The **Invoicing** section contains the **INVOICE IN ADVANCE OF FULFILLMENT** option. The fulfillment is required prior to invoicing when the checkbox is left unchecked. On the other hand, we can enable the accountant to invoice prior to fulfillment by merely checking the **INVOICE IN ADVANCE OF FULFILLMENT** checkbox:

Implementing

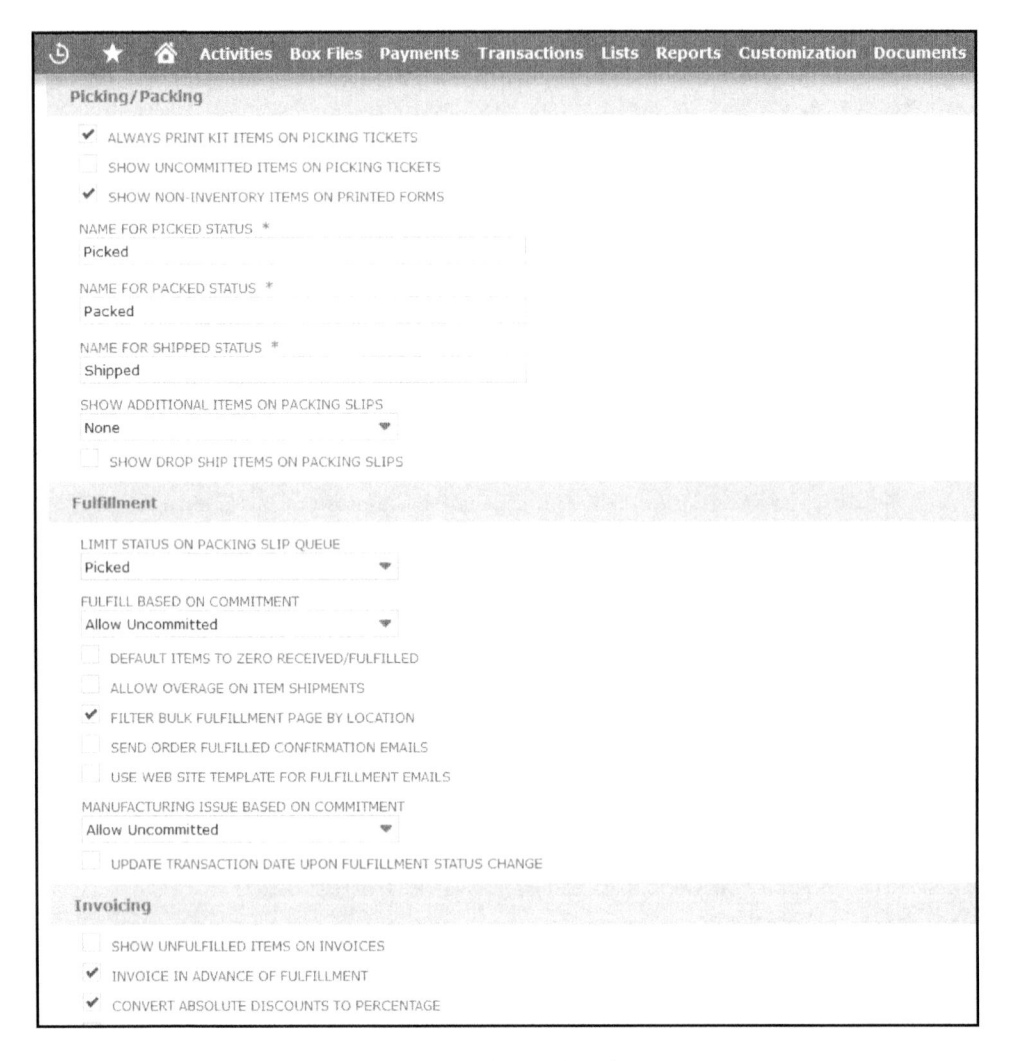

Order Management tab in Accounting Preferences

The **DEFAULT RETURN AUTH. STATUS** status field in the **Returns** section determines whether we will be using an approvals process when processing returns. The **Pending Approval** selection requires the approval step as opposed to the **Pending Receipt** selection, which sends a reminder to the warehouse manager to expect delivery of the return. There is also a **REFUND IN ADVANCE OF RETURN** checkbox, as well as the option to restock returned items by default, as opposed to writing them off.

Accounting Preferences – Items/ Transactions and Accounts

Work with your accountant to choose the correct **DEFAULT INCOME ACCOUNT**, **DEFAULT RECEIVABLES ACCOUNT**, and **DEFAULT PAYMENT ACCOUNT**. Best practice is to leave the **DEFAULT PAYMENT ACCOUNT** field blank. This places payments into an **Undeposited Funds** holding account which are then transferred to the actual bank account. We will be making the bank reconciliation process easier by inserting this intermediate step:

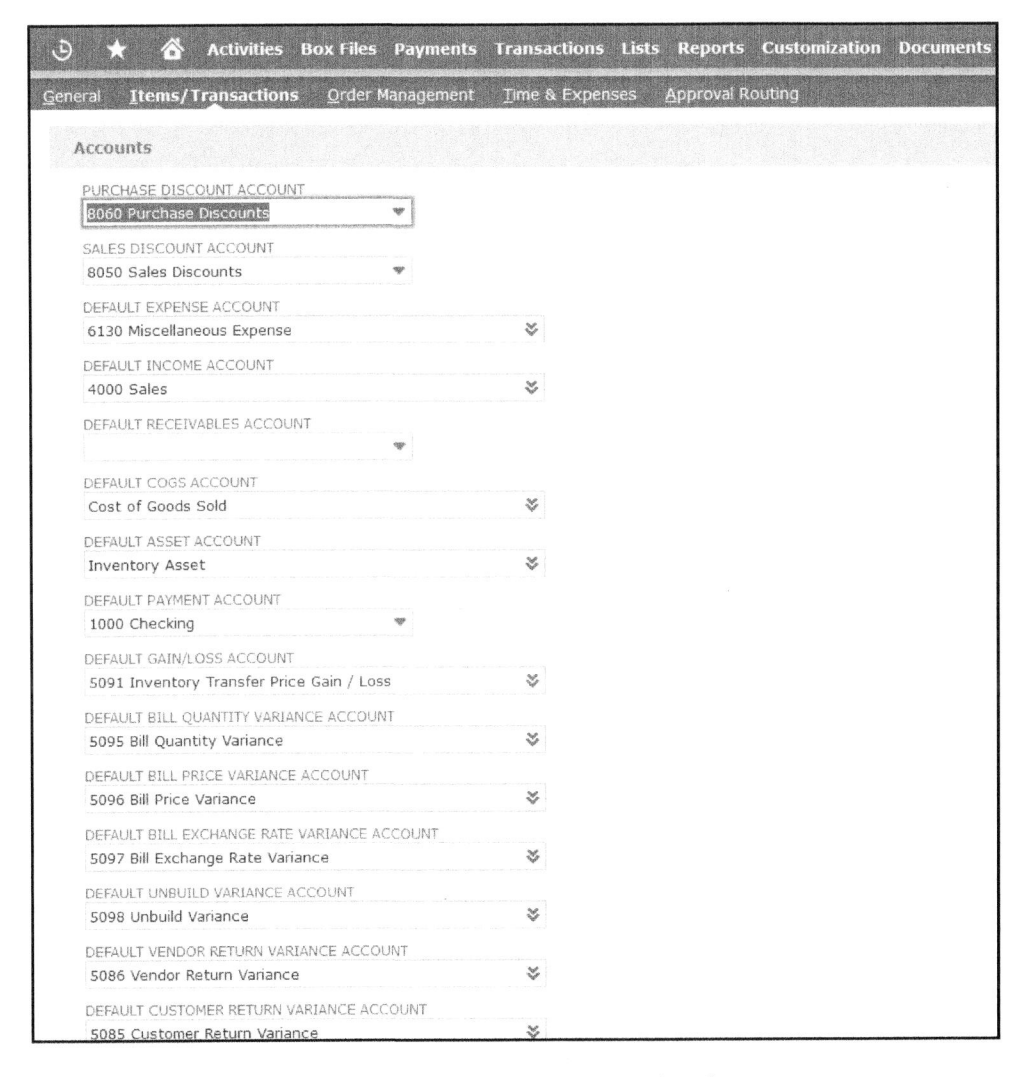

Accounts section in Items and Transactions tab under Accounting Preferences

Implementing

Sales & Pricing section in Accounting Preferences

The **Maximum # of Quantity – Based Price Levels** determines the number of quantity buckets available when applying a discount. The following screenshot has 5 levels set, enabling us to set up discounts at levels of 0-10, 11-20, 21-50, 51-100, and 100 and above.

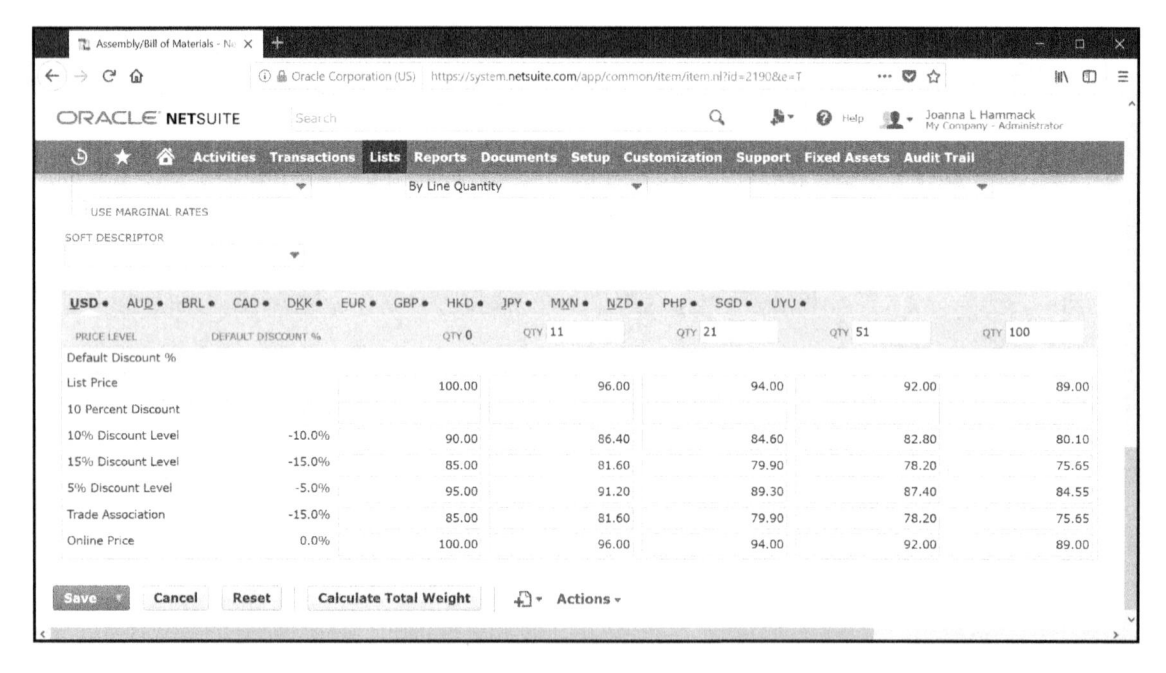

Quantity Based Pricing Setup

Accounts Receivable in Accounting Preferences

NetSuite can record a relationship between customers where one customer is owned by another company. The **APPLY PAYMENTS THROUGH TOP LEVEL CUSTOMER** checkbox enables us to enter an order on behalf of the child customer, for instance, Pepsi Canada, and accept payment from the Parent, such as Pepsi USA, on behalf of the child.

There is a **SHOW ONLY OPEN TRANSACTIONS ON STATEMENTS** checkbox to determine whether statements will be limited to transactions that have been completely fulfilled.

The **CUSTOMER CREDIT LIMIT HANDLING** selection determines what happens when a Sales Rep tries to enter an order that will exceed the customer's credit limit. The options are to **Warn Only**, **Ignore**, or **Enforce The Hold**.

The **DAYS OVERDUE FOR WARNING/HOLD** enables us to grant a grace period to customers who have overdue invoices. The customer will be prevented from entering any orders after the grace period has started and without paying the overdue invoice:

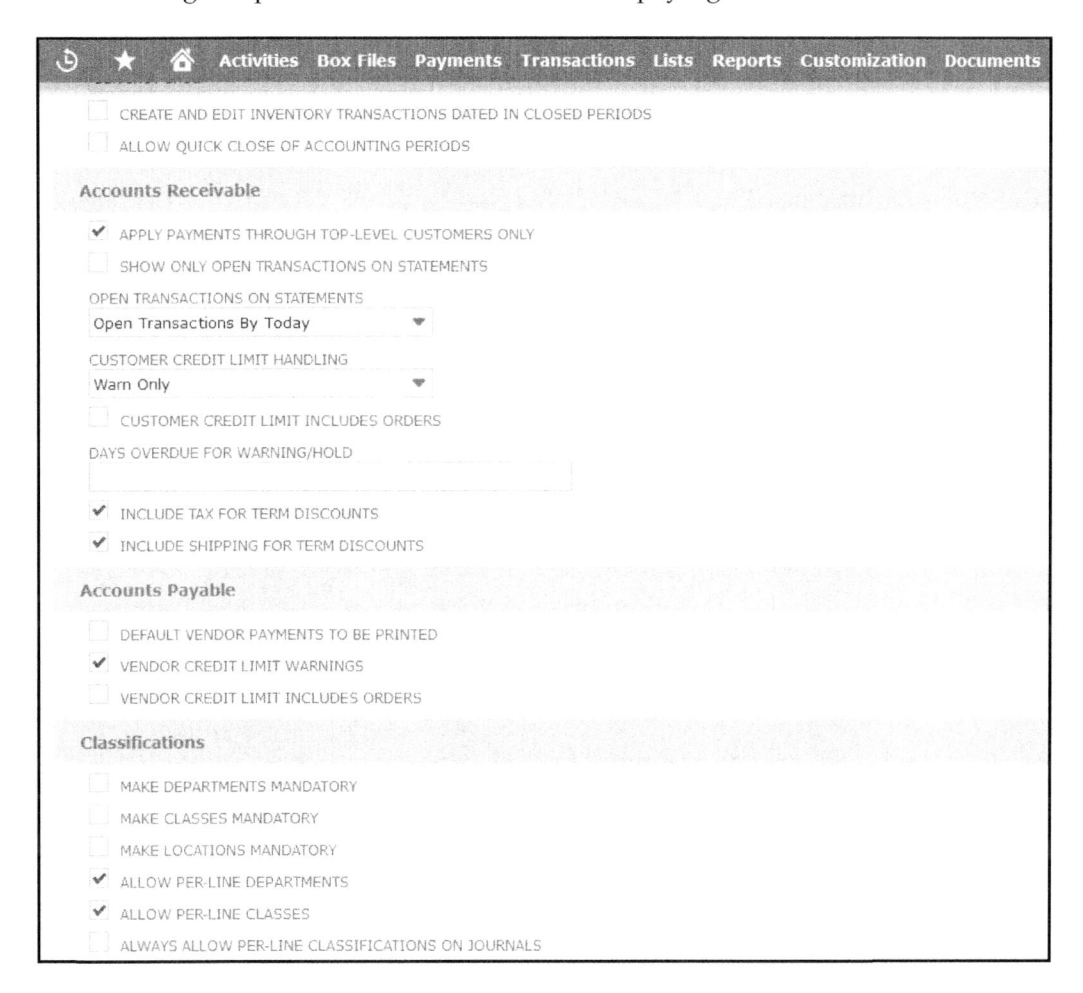

Setup | Accounting | Accounting Preferences | General

Building blocks

Now let's shift focus to the list menu to set up the settings that will be sourced in the sales transactions. We will focus on the customer and item records in setting up the lists to be used in the order-to-cash process.

Customer

The customer record has a number of important fields that need to be entered accurately to enable the order-to-cash process to proceed efficiently. The email address field is used to email customers copies of the sales order, the invoice, as well as updates when the order is fulfilled. Naturally, this setting is enabled at **Setup | Accounting | Accounting Preferences**.

The subsidiary field is crucial if you are working in the OneWorld account because it determines which legal entity will receive the revenue generated by sales to this customer.

The **Address** tab contains a list of addresses for this customer. There may be only one address or there could be multiple addresses. It is important to specify the default billing and default shipping address in order to automate those selections in the sales order and invoice.

The **Financial** tab contains very important information. The **Default Receivables Account** can be set to a different account for this customer if it conflicts with the system preference set up on the accounting preferences screen.

We can also select the terms that will default into any transaction with this customer. These terms are used to notify the accountant in the event that an invoice becomes overdue. It can also be used to automatically calculate a discount if the customer's terms include a discount for early payment.

There's also the enter the customer's credit limit field. The system can enforce the credit, and disallow any transactions where the customer has exceeded this credit limit, as discussed previously in the set up accounting preferences screen.

There is a field to specify the **PRIMARY CURRENCY** that we transact with this customer in. That field is only available if you're using the multicurrency feature. The price level is very useful because it enables us to enable customer-specific pricing. The price level is enabled on **Enable Features** and the various price levels will be setup on the setup menu under **Setup | Accounting | Accounting Lists**. The selection in this field will provide this customer with its associated price on a per item basis. For instance, most customers may receive their retail price by default, however, this customer may be entitled to the wholesale price. If the wholesale price is set as the price level on this customer's customer record, then the item that this customer purchased will automatically be priced at the wholesale level:

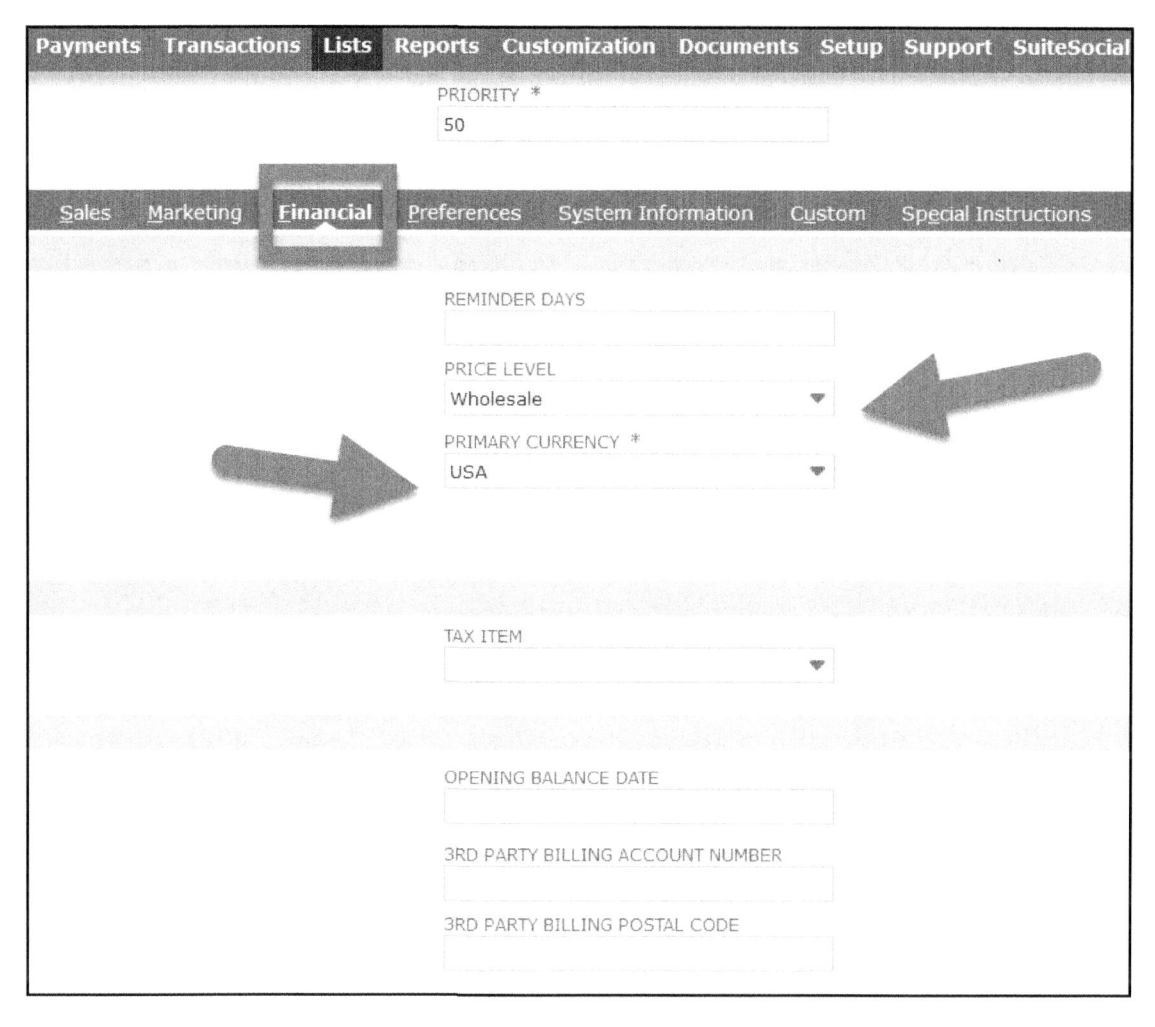

Financial tab on the Customer Record

Item record

The specific settings of each item are obviously dependent on the type of item. A non-inventory item, for instance, does not need to be fulfilled. In this example, I am focusing on inventory items; however, the concepts we will be discussing may also be applicable to different item types.

Implementing

The sales related options on mainly found on the **Sales/Pricing** tab of the item record. The different currencies are listed as subtabs at the bottom of the screen and the different price levels are listed going down the screen, enabling you to set different prices for the same item. The quantity breaks provided for bulk purposes are listed as columns going across the screen and of course, the number of these Maximum Number of Quantity Based Pricing levels is set up under **Setup** | **Accounting** | **Accounting Preferences**:

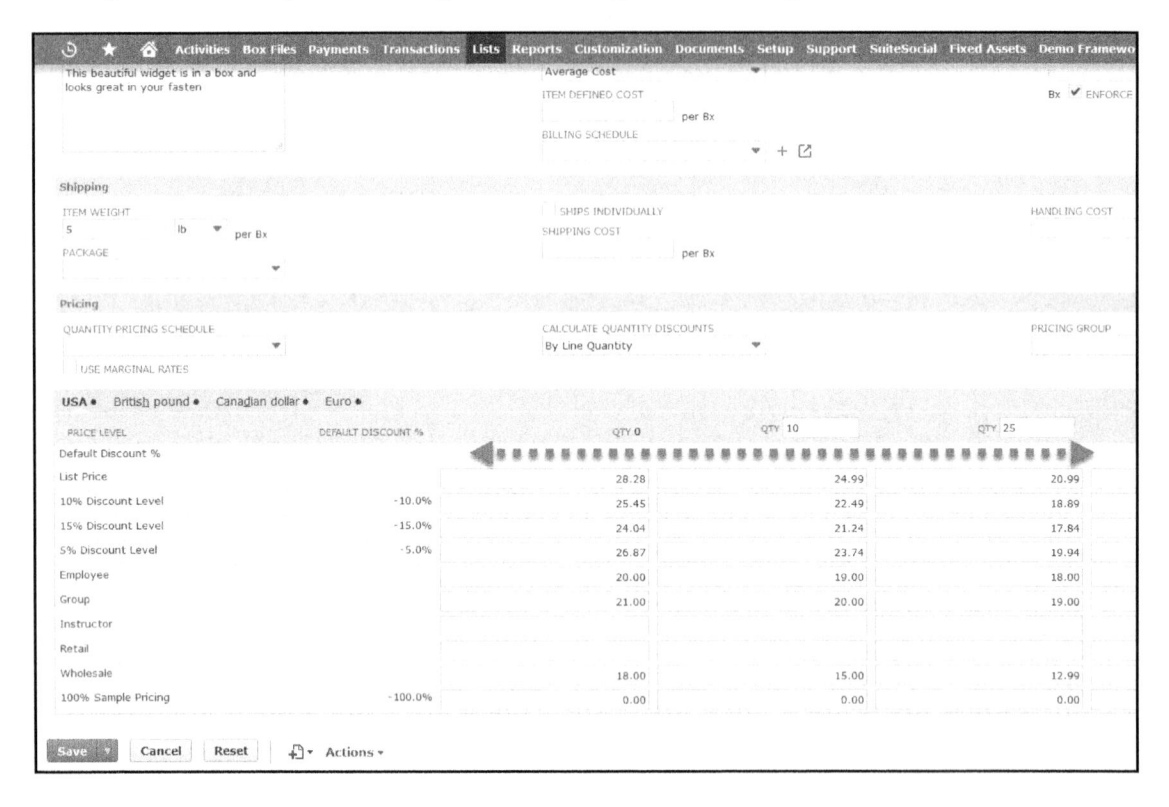

Sales and Pricing tab on the Item record

Shipping Items

We also need to set up the options that can be selected to ship the order to the customer. Go to **Lists** | **Accounting** | **Shipping Items** to create new shipping items.

[98]

Chapter 4

Name the new shipping item and select the account that will be used to record the revenue generated by shipping. We can then specify the rate, whether a flat rate, percentage of total, or by creating your own custom rates using your own shipping table. The most common option is to use the real-time rates generated by UPS, Fedex, and USPS. We will need to create different shipping items for each shipping method and will specify the integrated shipping label to use on the **Shipping Labels** tab:

Shipping method setup at Lists | Accounting | Set up Shipping page

[99]

Implementing

The remaining tabs on the **Shipping Item** give us options to provide free shipping for specific items or to charge customers reduced pricing for shipping.

Transactions

The order-to-cash process starts with the sales order. The sales order is made up from the appropriate building blocks, namely, the customer, the item, the shipping item, and potentially the tax.

The sales rep goes to the **Create New Toolbar** and selects **Sales Order**. The sales rep then selects the customer and the items that will be purchased in the appropriate quantities. The system will integrate the information on the item and customer records to calculate a price per item for the order. So, for instance, if the customer is set to the price level of wholesale price, the wholesale price will default in each of the items that I ordered:

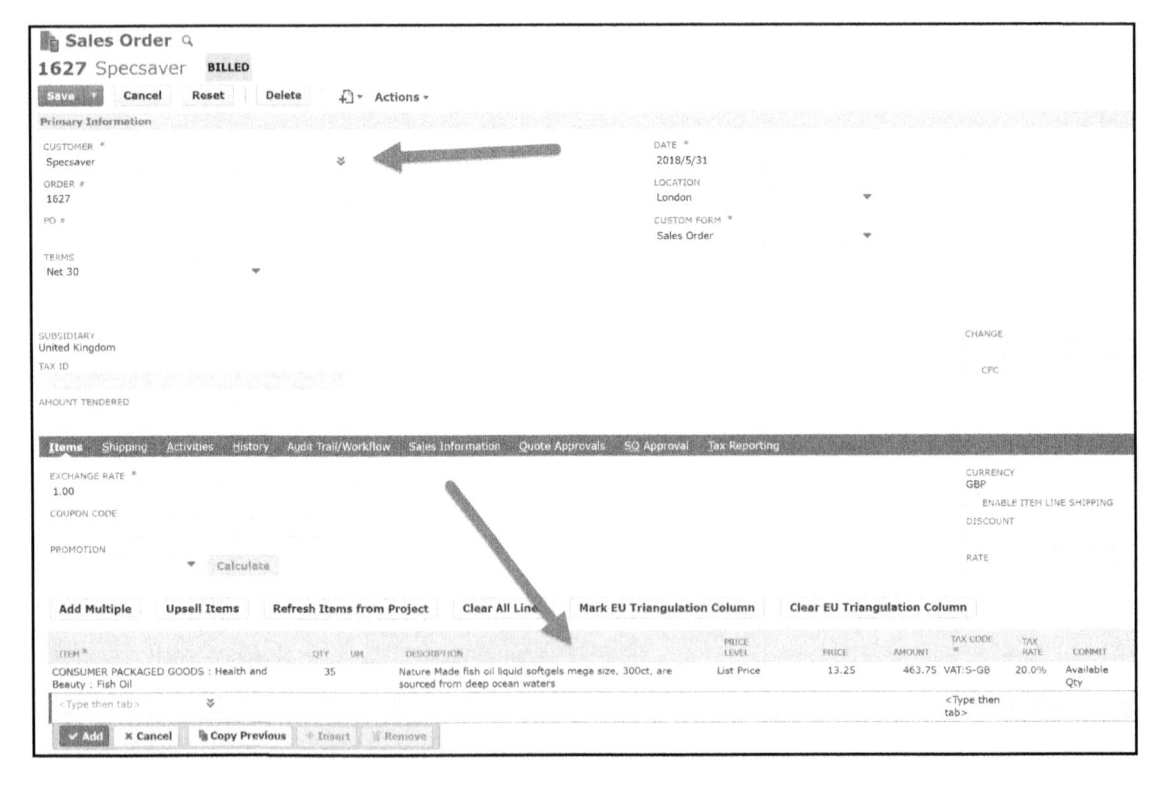

Entering a new Sales Order

The user will then go to the **Shipping** tab and select the preferred shipping method, which should default in from the selection on the customer record. Alternatively, a different shipping method can be selected. In the event that an integrated shipping method is selected, the user needs only click the calculate button for the system to enter the correct shipping cost for this order. The text information should prepopulate based on the ship-to address, provided that the customer record is set to charge sales tax to this customer. Once all this information is entered, the sales rep clicks save:

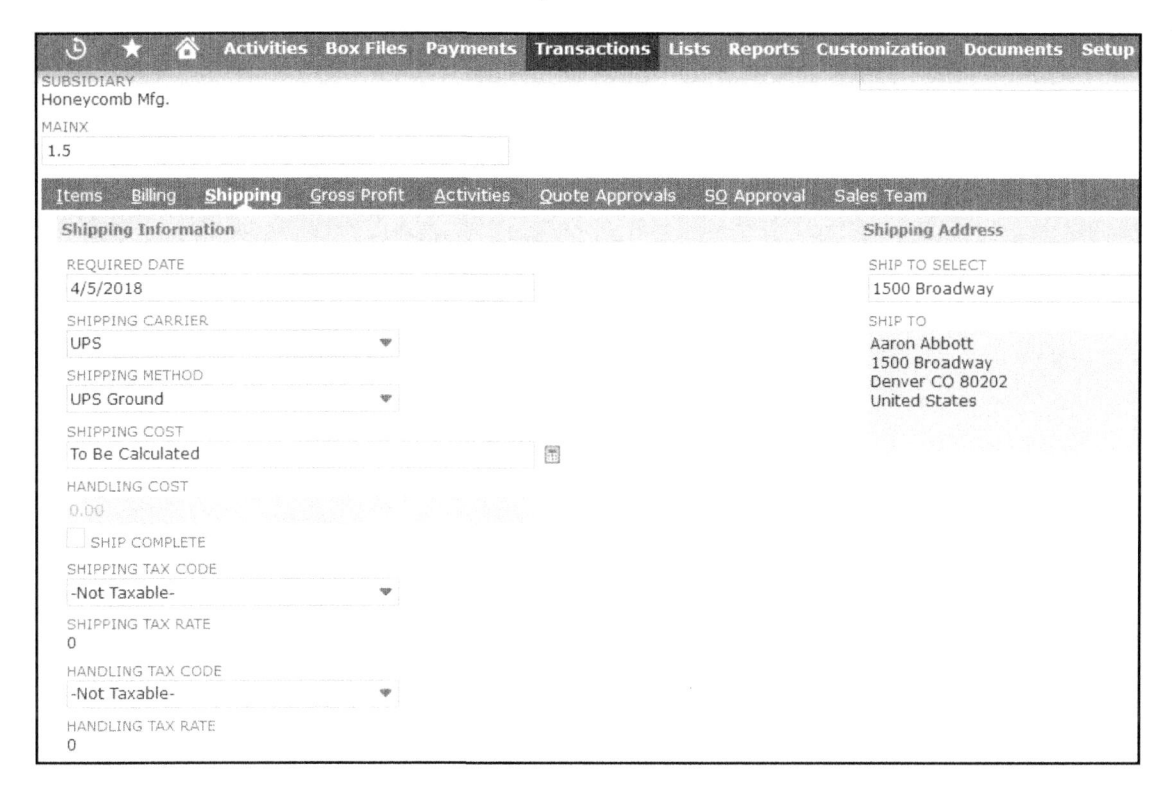

Select shipping method on new Sales Order

An email is then generated for the supervisor or sales manager to approve the sales order. The sales manager goes to the home dashboard, select sales orders to approve, and is taken to the list of all sales orders pending approval. The sales manager then approves orders on the screen or drills down to the specific sales order in order to approve them by clicking the approve button.

Implementing

Once approved, the order is placed in the **Fulfillment** queue. The warehouse manager can access the Fulfillment queue from the home dashboard by clicking the **Orders to Fulfill** Reminder. This takes the warehouse manager to the fulfillment screen, where multiple orders can be fulfilled at once, or the user can select a specific order to fulfill.

The user may prefer to print out the **Pick Picking Tickets** prior to fulfilling the orders; that can be done at the **Print Checks and Forms** screen found at **Transactions | Management | Print Checks and Forms | Picking Tickets**. The user takes the pick tickets and walks around the warehouse, selecting the items that need to be fulfilled. The user then returns to the computer and records that the items have been picked on the item-fulfillment screen:

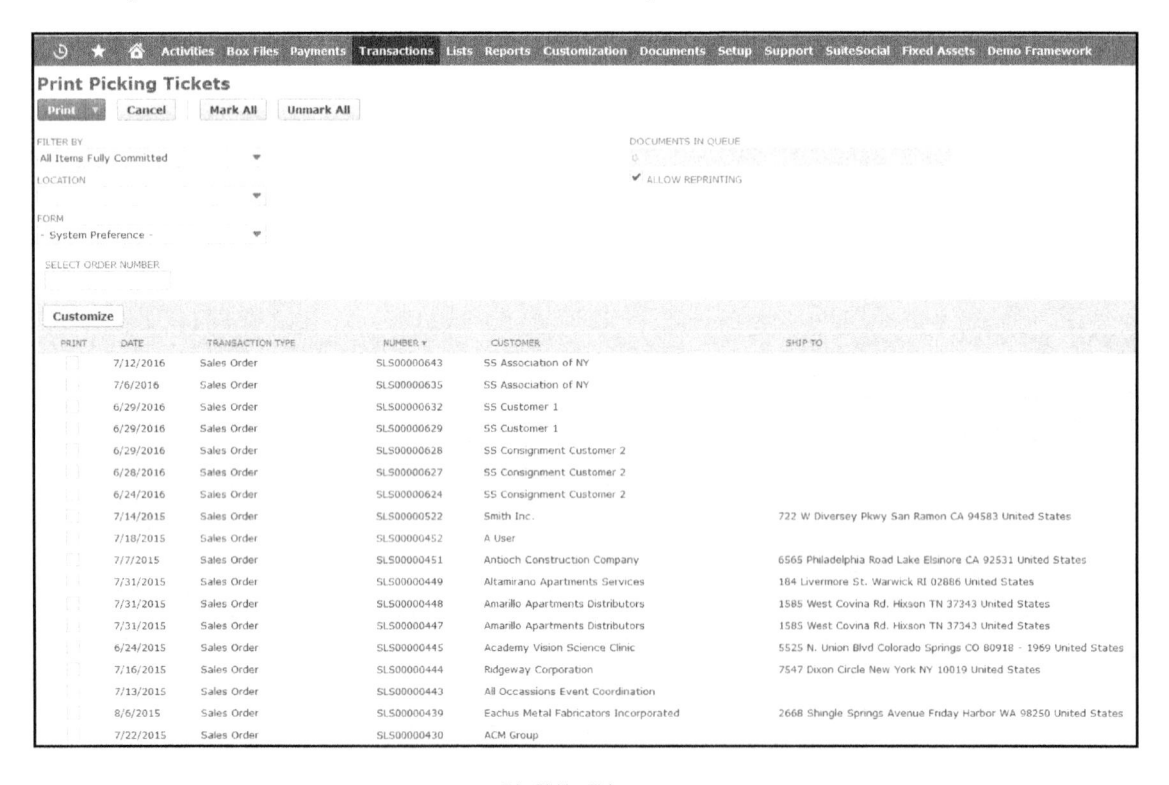

Print Picking Tickets page

[102]

These orders will be set to the next status and will appear as a Reminder entitled **Orders to Pack**.

Order to Pack Reminder

The user clicks on the link to be taken to the list of items that need to be packed. The order is selected and set to the Packing status by clicking save. The user can also print out the packing slip at this time by checking the print icon.

Implementing

The next step is obviously shipping and, once again, it is reflected on the Home dashboard. The user clicks into the **Items to Ship** link on the Reminders portlet on Home dashboard and is taken to the list of orders that need to be shipped. The user goes into the specific order that will be shipped and clicks the save button to record that it has been shipped. The user can then click the print icon in order to print the integrated shipping label, which will print out on the thermal printer ready to be affixed to the package:

Order Fulfillment page

This places the order in a fulfilled-pending billing status and sets of the reminder on the **Accounts Receivable** clerk's dashboard to bill this order. The user clicks on the link from the dashboard to be taken to the list of orders to bill. The user can either bill a number of orders simultaneously on that screen or drill down into a specific order to Bill it individually. The user can then click the print button to print out the invoice that has been created by billing the order.

The system begins to monitor outstanding invoices and will alert the **Accounts Receivable** clerk when this invoice is due and still unpaid. The user can click on the link to be taken to the **Outstanding Invoices Report** and can then follow up with the customer if necessary.

When the payment is received, the AR clerk will go to the accept payment screen and select the appropriate customer. This will default in all of the outstanding invoices for this customer and the clerk can select those that are being paid at this point. The clerk can also choose which account the payment will go into. The account that is defaulted in here is set up on the account preferences screen and the AR clerk can merely click save to pay it into that particular account:

Chapter 4

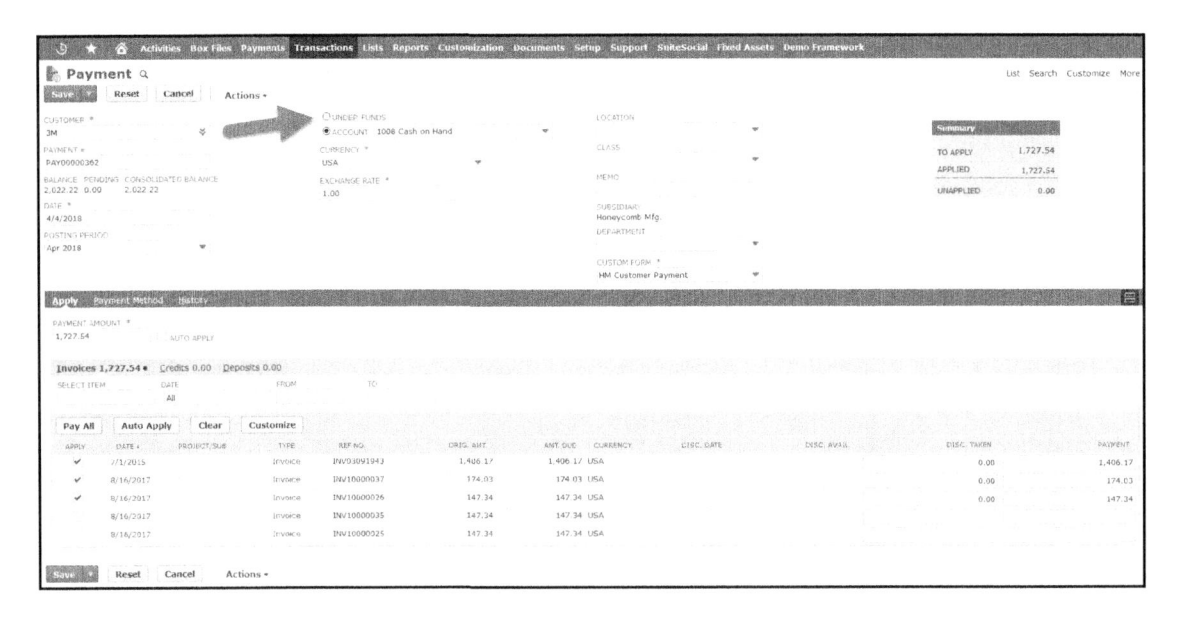

Accept Customer Payment page

I advise using the **UNDEP. FUNDS** account as it works best when reconciling the bank statement at the end of the month. This requires an additional step after accepting the payment; the AR clerk will need to deposit these funds into the actual bank account when doing the banking. That screen is found under **Transactions | Bank | Deposit Funds**.

Summary

In this chapter, we demonstrated how an administrator can configure the procedure-to-pay and order-to-cash processes. It gives us a feel for the end user process and it identifies the levers that the administrator can use to tweak the process if necessary. It also provides us with a methodology to implement new features in our account by enabling the feature, configuring the settings on the **Accounting Preferences** screen, and then setting the defaults on the **Building Block/List** records that will flow into the **Transactions**.

In the preceding chapters, I've given you a context on the way in which NetSuite works while identifying the functions you can use to enable end users to perform their daily jobs. In the next section, we will shift gears to specific administrative tasks that you will need to perform, secure, update, and customize the application, starting with the next chapter on roles and permissions.

Security and Permissions

There is always a trade-off in application security. On the one hand, we are interested in permitting access, and on the other hand, we want to restrict access. While we typically think of permitting and restricting access to data, this could also be applied to forms, custom reports, or custom saved searches, as well as documents stored in the file cabinet. In addition, the methods we will use need to be simple to manage, otherwise we risk having something fall through the cracks, creating a vulnerability.

We'll begin by focusing on the tools available to authenticate users when they log in to NetSuite. We will then shift our focus to their permissions on records and forms once logged in, which is encapsulated in the user's role. Next, we will review tools to record changes the user has made to the database. We will then look at controls on specific functions, namely searches, reports, and documents in the file cabinet.

This chapter will cover the following:

- Authentication
- Roles and permissions
- Audit trail
- Custom reports

Authentication

Let's look at the options we have to manage access to the NetSuite database.

Username and password

NetSuite grants access based on a username and password. The username is in the form of an email address, which is set up on the appropriate user record. The standard user's email address is set up on the employee record, whereas a customer's access to the **Customer Center** is set up on the customer record, the vendor's access to the vendor center on the vendor record, and the partner's access on the partner record.

The administrator determines the company's password policy at **Setup | Company | General Preferences**. The options are **Weak**, **Medium**, and **Strong**. We can exceed the password policy's minimum password length by overriding it in the **MINIMUM PASSWORD LENGTH** field if required. We can also set the days before the password expires and how long it will take before the system automatically logs a user out due to inactivity:

Password settings

Security questions

NetSuite also provides a second layer of authentication in the form of *security questions* and *answers*, which the user can set up for authentication purposes. The questions and answers are accessed in the setting portlet of the user's home dashboard. The security question performs two functions, enabling the user to reset their password without the assistance of an administrator and to authenticate the user when logging in from a new computer, such as a home PC when working from home or spending the holidays with their in-laws.

IP address rules

An administrator may want to restrict the users' ability to log in from any computer, and NetSuite provides a feature to accomplish this. The **IP Address Rules** feature is found on the **Access Section** of the **General** tab on **Setup** | **Company** | **Enable Features**. It allows us to restrict rules based on specific IP addresses. Be very careful when using this feature, however, as you risk locking yourself out of the application if set up incorrectly.

Login URL

The user typically logs in from the login page at http://www.netsuite.com.

Security and Permissions

There is an exception for the **Customer Center**. Each NetSuite account has its own private **Customer Center** login page. We can find the URL for the **Customer Center** in our database by going to **Setup | Company | Company Information**:

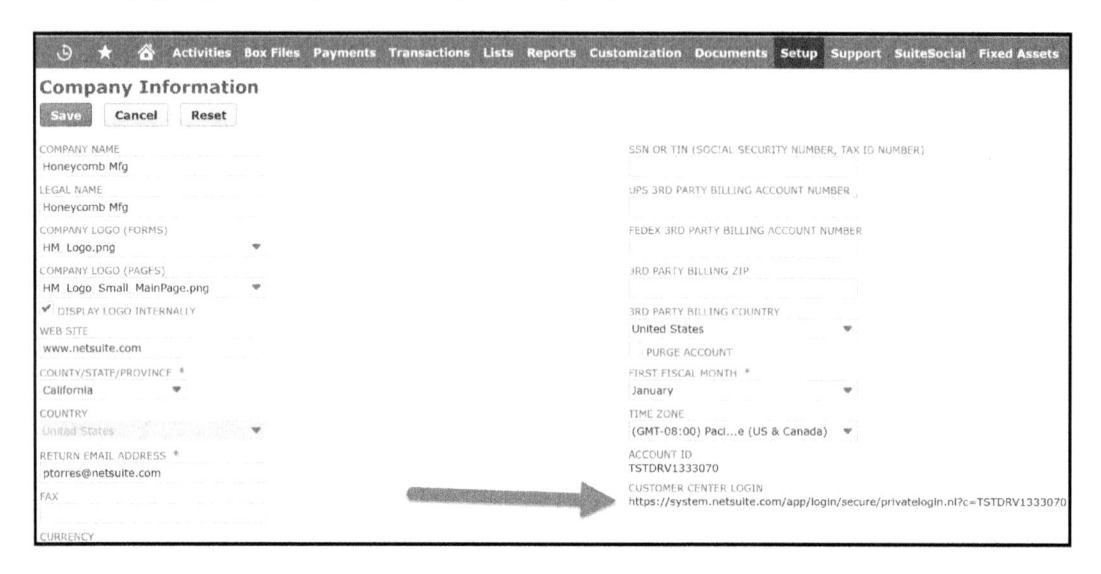

Customer Center URL

There are also tools we can use to manage login authentication, found in the **Managed Authentication** section of the **Setup | Company | Enable Features | SuiteCloud** tab. We can use a Google ID to authenticate users, as well as any SAML-compliant provider, by enabling these options:

Authentication options

Roles and permissions

Whenever you give a person access to NetSuite, you need to select a role or a number of roles that can be used. This applies to employees as well as customers, vendors, and partners, who would be assigned to the customer center, vendor center, or partner center to access those portals.

The administrator can permit or restrict access to any screen in NetSuite, so there are many options to choose from. The good news is NetSuite provides standard templates, so we don't need to set these roles up from scratch. You'll find the role templates under **Setup** | **User & Roles** | **Manage Roles**. There are standard roles for most, if not all, users in the company, from an AP clerk to the controller to the warehouse manager to the CEO:

Roles

Best practice is to always set up your own copy of a template before assigning it to users. This applies even if you want to use the substance of the standard role. Just click **Customize**, change the name of the role to include your company name, and then click **Save**. Remember, you can never overwrite a standard role, so there is no concern about messing up the standard template.

Center

NetSuite tries to make the interface as intuitive as possible for each user. The **Lists** menu makes no sense to an AR clerk, so it provides a menu called **Customers** instead. A group of menus is called a *center* and you should consider which center should be chosen for each role you will set up. Each role has a corresponding center and we can see examples of different centers in the following screenshot comparing the administrator role with a sales role and a warehouse manager role:

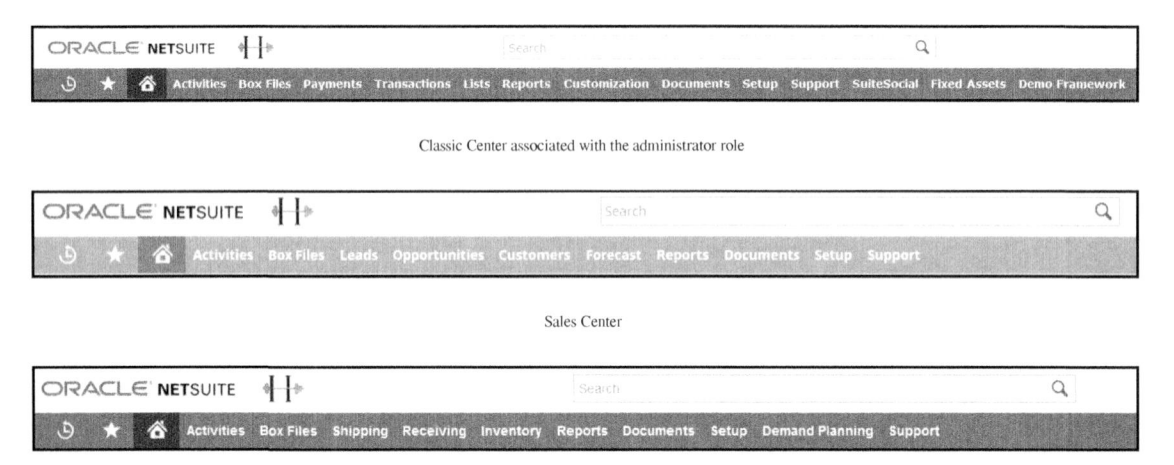

Classic Center associated with the administrator role

Sales Center

Warehouse Center

Permissions, restrictions, and forms

Roles, permissions, restrictions: what do these all mean and how do we combine them to get the result we want? Let's illustrate by way of an example:

Record	Assigned Sales Rep	Field	Role
Sales Order #10	Brian	Customer Credit Check Rating	AB sales manager
Sales Order #11	Jason	Customer Credit Check Rating	AB sales rep
Sales Order #12	Kathy	Customer Credit Check Rating	AB sales rep
Sales Order #13		Customer Credit Check Rating	AB sales rep

Let's configure Brian's sales manager role while assuming that Jason reports directly to Brian, and Kathy reports to a different sales manager.

Permissions

Permissions apply to the record. It answers the question, Do we want Brian to be able to see any sales order data at all?

Permissions are naturally found on the **Permissions** tab and segmented by type of record, namely, by **Transactions**, **Reports**, **List**, and **Setup**.

If the record does not appear in the list of the saved roles, the user with that role will not be able to see those records at all. If we were to remove **Sales Orders** from the **Transactions Permissions** for the AB sales manager role, sales orders would be invisible to Brian when he logs in with that role. Sales orders would not appear in his menus, and searches for existing sales orders will not return results.

That would be an odd choice for a sales manager role, so we will add access to sales orders in the AB sales manager role. We must then decide what level of access he will get to sales order records:

- **View access**: Read-only access. He cannot enter new sales orders or change existing orders in the system. A sales order menu selection will now appear and a search for sales order will return results.
- **Create permissions**: Enables the role to enter new sales orders and includes the view permission. The **New Sales Order** button is now available for Brian to use. If, however, Brian makes a mistake in entering a new sales order, he will not be able to amend the record once it is saved.
- **Edit permissions**: Includes create and view, as well as enabling the user to change existing sales orders. Brian can view sales orders, enter new orders, and make changes to existing sales orders if need be. He cannot, however, delete a sales order that was created in error.

- **Full access**: Includes all the other permissions in addition to being able to delete records. Brian can view orders, create new ones, edit existing orders, and delete existing sales orders.

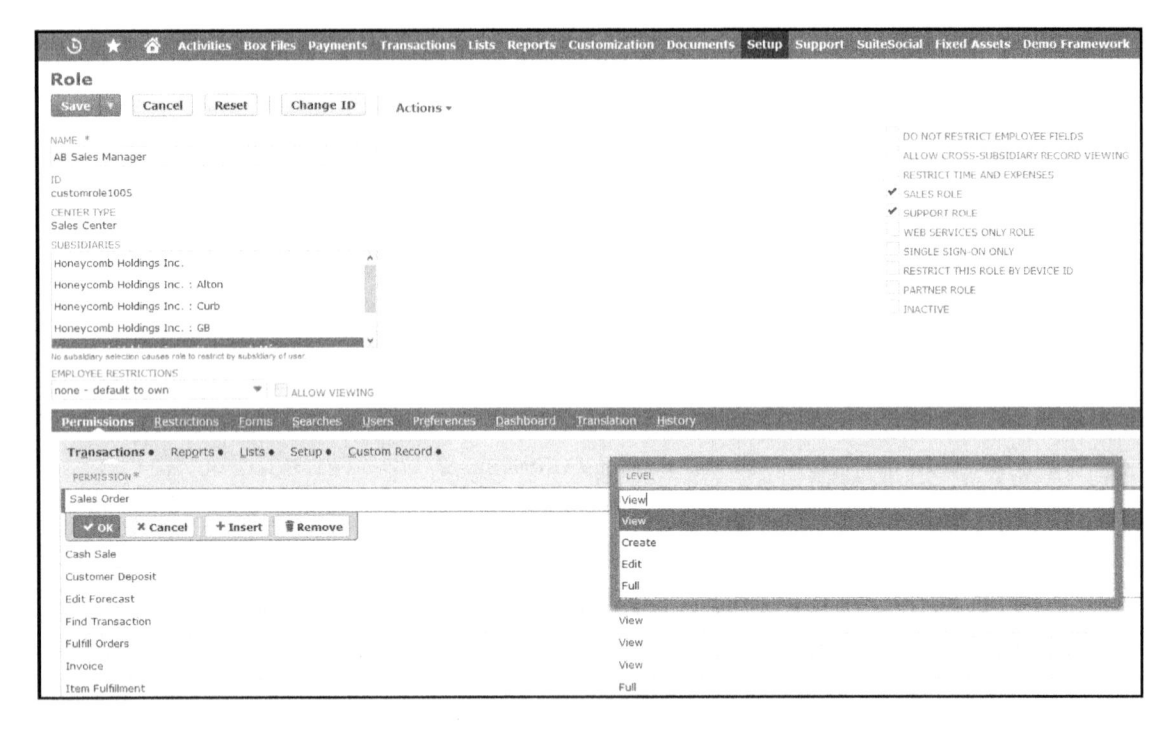

Role permission options

Restrictions

Now that we have given Brian permission to see sales orders, we need to determine which sales orders he should be able to see. He presumably needs to see sales order #10, as he is the assigned sales rep, but what about order #11 and #12? Should he be able to review order #11, which is assigned to his direct report, Jason, and sales order #12, which is assigned to Kathy, who is a member of another team?

Chapter 5

While permissions provide access to the **Sales Order** record, restrictions determine the specific sales orders the role can access:

- **None–No Default**: The first selection in the **Employee Restriction** is **None–No Default**. In this case, Brian would be able to view, edit, and delete Sales Orders #10, #11, and #12.
- **None–Default to Own**: The second selection, **None–Default to Own**, enforces no restriction but merely a default.
- **Own, subordinate & unassigned**: Brian can see, edit, and delete his own order, Jason's order, and as well as the unassigned order. Sales Order #12, belonging to Kathy, is invisible to him.
- **Own–subordinate only**: This will limit Brian's ability to see sales orders. While he can view, edit, and delete the order belonging to Jason, as well as his own, the remaining two orders will be invisible to him:

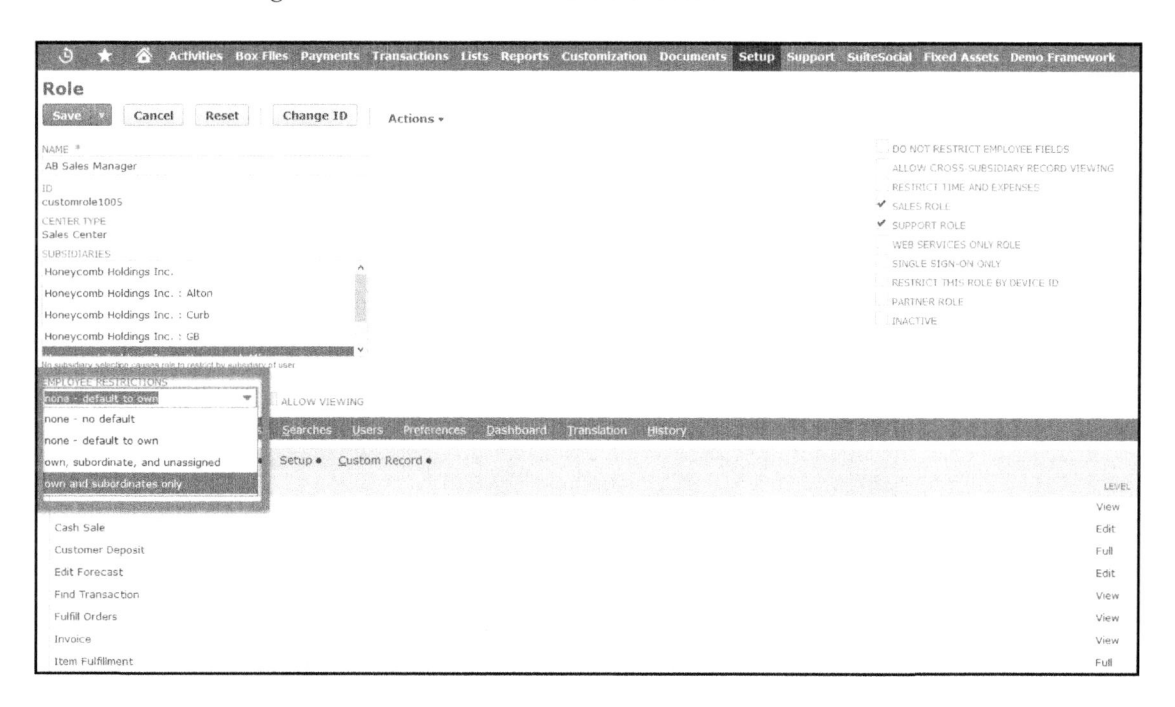

Employee restrictions

Security and Permissions

View access to specific records

In many cases, we want to restrict access to edit and delete records belonging to other users, records but to give view access to those records. Access to the custom record is a great example of this. We don't want sales reps to be able to edit customer records belonging to other reps because an unethical sales rep would simply reassign another's customer to themselves. On the other hand, we want reps to be able to search the entire database prior to creating a new customer, in order to determine whether it is a duplicate. NetSuite, therefore, provides an override to the restriction in the form of a view only checkbox. The restriction would apply to the editing and deleting of records belonging to others; however, these records would still be viewable:

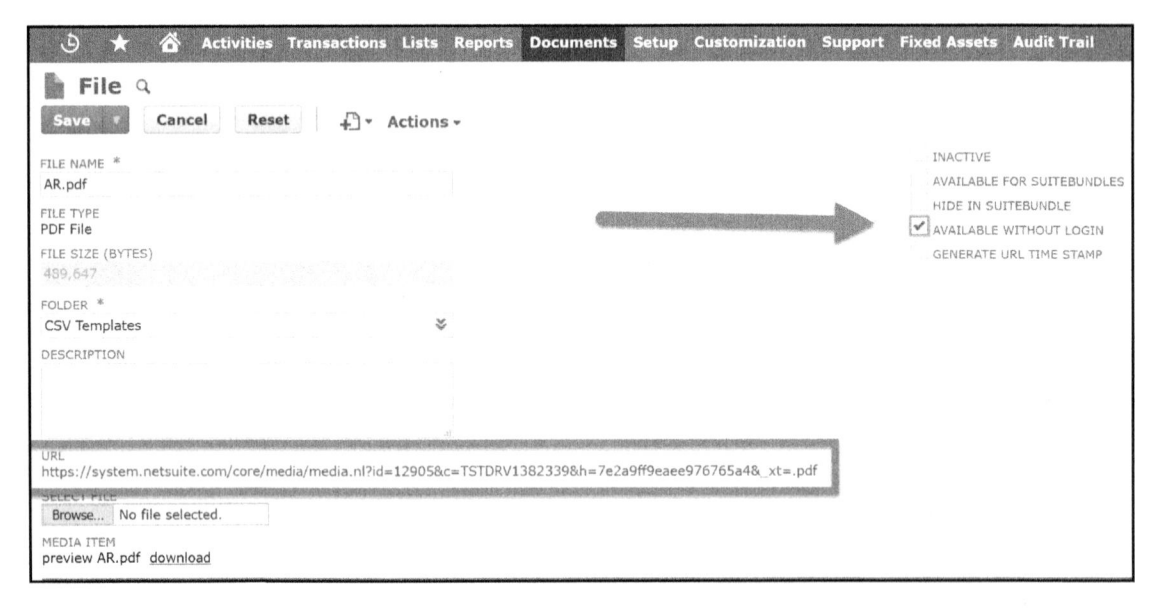

Allow Viewing selection

Restrictions by segment

Restrictions can also be applied using different criteria. The **Restriction** tab enables us to apply this concept based on segments such as department, class, and location. We can, therefore, restrict certain user's access to only records within their respective departments, classes, or locations. The selection of department, class, and/or location on the transaction would, therefore, need to match the department, class, and/or location on the user's employee record to have access. There is also an **ALLOW VIEWING** option that can be used in the same way as the option on **EMPLOYEE RESTRICTIONS**:

Restrictions by segment

These restriction selections of the **none - default to own** options can also be used as an automation tool, where 99% of a user's transactions are with class A, yet the user is forced to select this value on each and every transaction. You can help automate the selection of class B on this user's transactions by choosing **none - default to own** on the class restriction, which will automatically place the class on the employee's record into the transaction but still allow them to edit it in the remaining 1% of cases.

There are additional options for OneWorld administrators. The **SUBSIDIARIES** field restricts the role's access to records within one or more subsidiaries selected on the role. While this removes any and all access to records outside of that subsidiary window; there is also an **ALLOW CROSS-SUBSIDIARY RECORD VIEWING** checkbox on the role.

Security and Permissions

Forms

We have shown ways to limit or allow access to types of records and specific records. Sometimes, we need to apply similar limitations to specific fields on a record. Let's take the **Customer Credit Check Rating** field on the **Sales Order** as an example. We may not want to allow sales reps to see the value in this field. How can we hide it from them?

We can do so by creating a new form for the sales order record and removing the field from that form. We demonstrate how to do this in `Chapter 6`, *Customization*, however, once the form is created, we can determine which forms will be available for this role to be able to view. This is done on the **Forms** tab of the role, where we can select whether a form will be viewable to users with this role, as well as selecting a preferred form that will load by default:

Forms selection for role

To continue with the example, we may need the sales manager to view the values in this field, yet prohibit Brian from changing the value. We can once again use a form to do so by changing the form to include the field but set it as read-only (which NetSuite calls inline text) and then make it available to the `AB Sales Manager` role.

It is important, in both cases, to remove the forms that allow editing of this field from the AB sales manager and AB sales rep roles by unchecking the checkbox on the row next to that form, as listed on the **Forms** tab.

User Roles

Now that we know how to configure roles, the next question is which users are assigned which roles. We can see the list of roles assigned to a user by going to that user's employee record. We can only see one employee record at a time, which makes this rather inefficient. Luckily, NetSuite has included a general view to display all users and their associated roles. We will find this at **Setup** | **Users/Roles** | **Manage Users**:

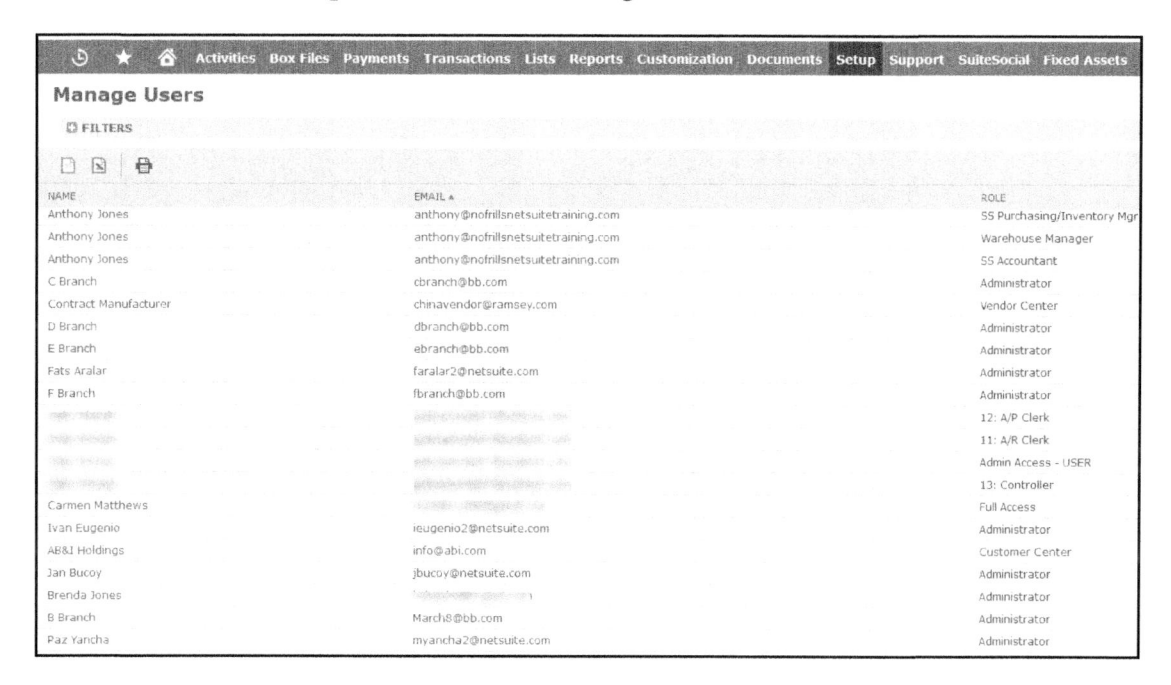

NAME	EMAIL	ROLE
Anthony Jones	anthony@nofrillsnetsuitetraining.com	SS Purchasing/Inventory Mgr
Anthony Jones	anthony@nofrillsnetsuitetraining.com	Warehouse Manager
Anthony Jones	anthony@nofrillsnetsuitetraining.com	SS Accountant
C Branch	cbranch@bb.com	Administrator
Contract Manufacturer	chinavendor@ramsey.com	Vendor Center
D Branch	dbranch@bb.com	Administrator
E Branch	ebranch@bb.com	Administrator
Fats Aralar	faralar2@netsuite.com	Administrator
F Branch	fbranch@bb.com	Administrator
		12: A/P Clerk
		11: A/R Clerk
		Admin Access - USER
		13: Controller
Carmen Matthews		Full Access
Ivan Eugenio	ieugenio2@netsuite.com	Administrator
AB&J Holdings	info@abi.com	Customer Center
Jan Bucoy	jbucoy@netsuite.com	Administrator
Brenda Jones		Administrator
B Branch	March8@bb.com	Administrator
Paz Yancha	myancha2@netsuite.com	Administrator

Manage Users page

We can sort the columns by **Name** or **Roles** and even export the results to Excel, using the Excel icon at the top of the page, for further analysis.

[119]

Security and Permissions

Identifying differences between roles

There are a lot of roles and even more permissions available. How can we easily identify the differences between roles? NetSuite provides us with this functionality at **Setup** | **Users/Roles** | **Show Role Differences**:

Show permission differences between roles

We can choose a base role and compare it to other roles. Clicking the **Show** button runs a report to display the specific differences between the roles, which, once again, can be exported for further analysis:

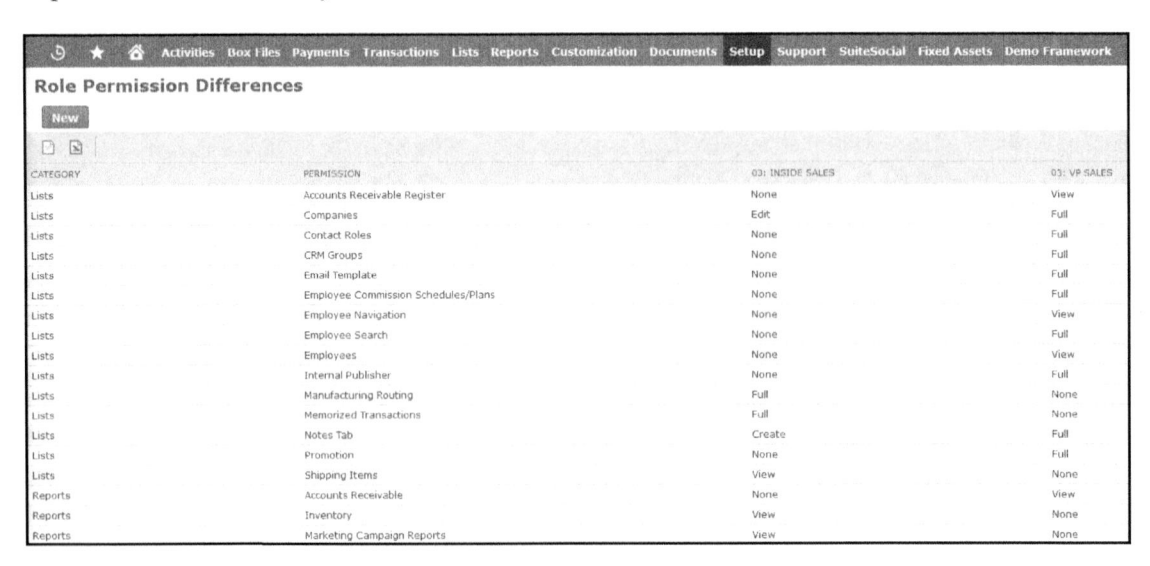

Role Permission Differences page comparing Inside Sales and VP Sales

Global permissions

It invariably happens that management identifies a superuser who needs more permissions than were granted to their role. The sales manager, for instance, may ask for one of their reports to be given additional permissions for searches and exports because that person is required to perform extra analysis for the company. The standard sales rep role that was assigned to all sales reps, including this user, is insufficient for this task.

What do we do? Creating a new role and assigning it to this user seems like overkill and increasing the number of roles complicates the setup even more. NetSuite has therefore introduced a feature to address this. It is called **Global Permissions** and is found in the **Permissions** section at **Setup** | **Company** | **Enable Features** | **Employees**.

Once enabled, a new subtab appears on the employee record. The tab contains a list of permissions that can be selected. Each permission will provide this specific employee with that permission, irrespective of whether the permission is included on this user's role:

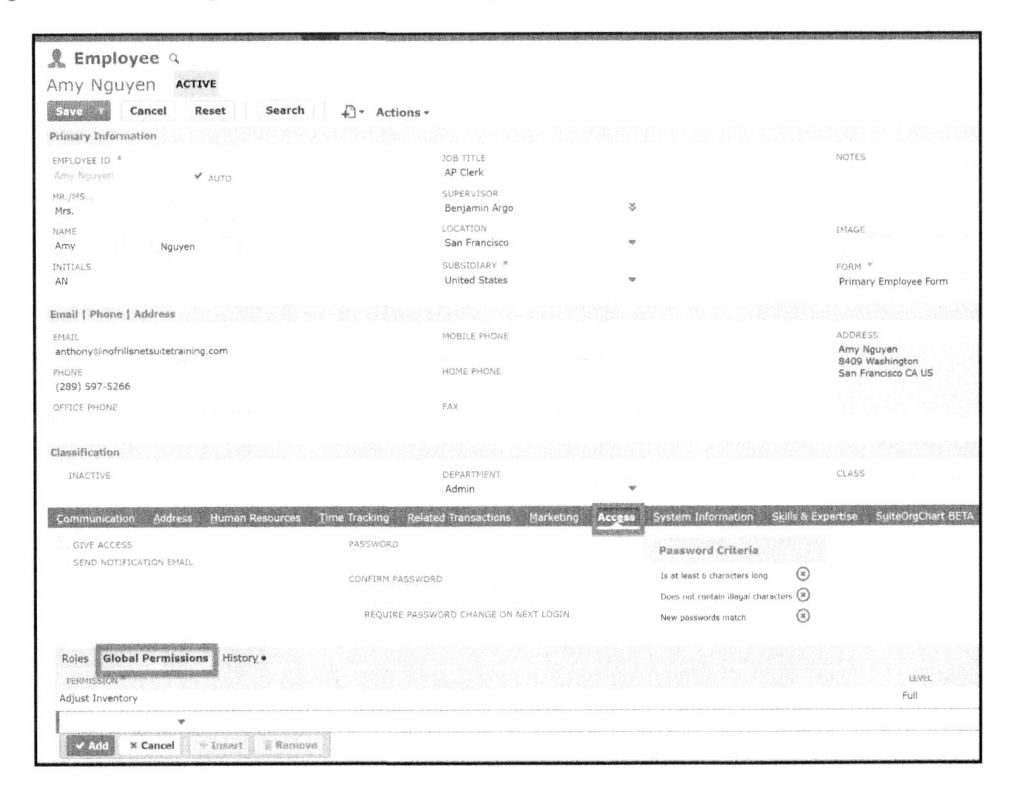

Global Permissions selection on the Employee Record

Security and Permissions

Audit Trail

Now that we've seen how to control a user's access to information, let's look at recording what the user does with that information.

View login Audit Trail

There is a prebuilt search to review the login **Audit Trail**, which can be found at **Setup** | **Users/Roles** | **View Login Audit Trail**. We can filter the results by user, role, or a specific date range, and can even add additional filters to it by clicking **Personalize Search**:

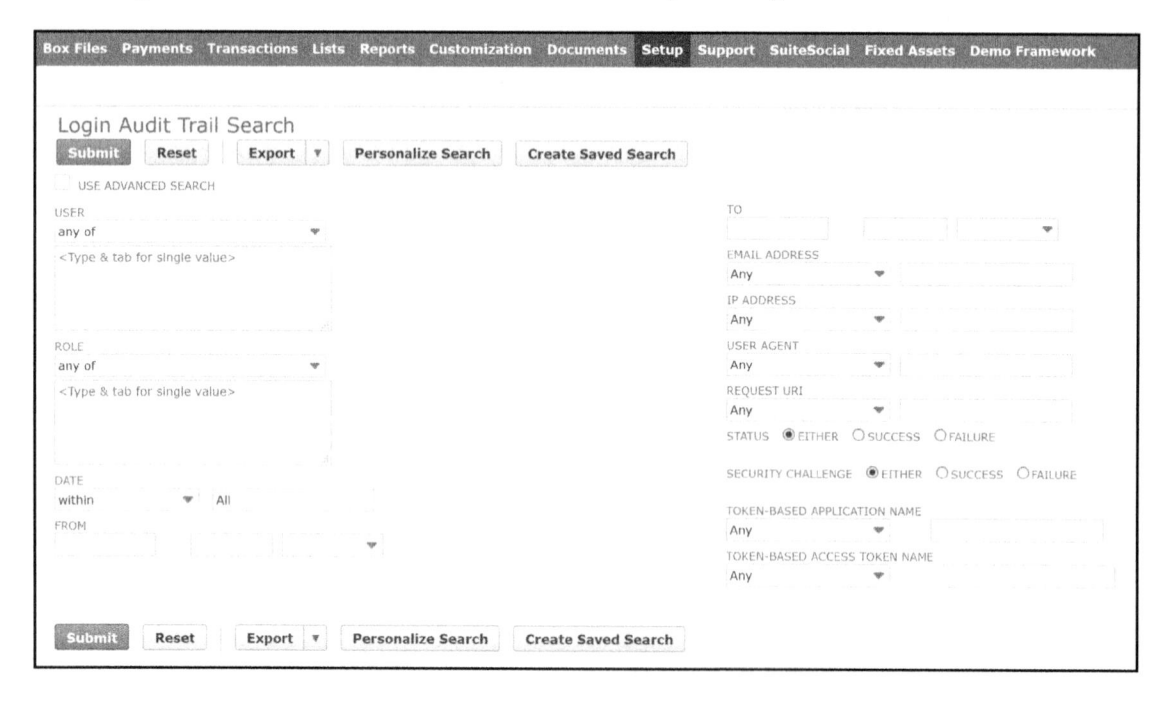

Login Audit Trail Search filters

The results of the search return the date and time, user, user's email address, role, and IP address:

Chapter 5

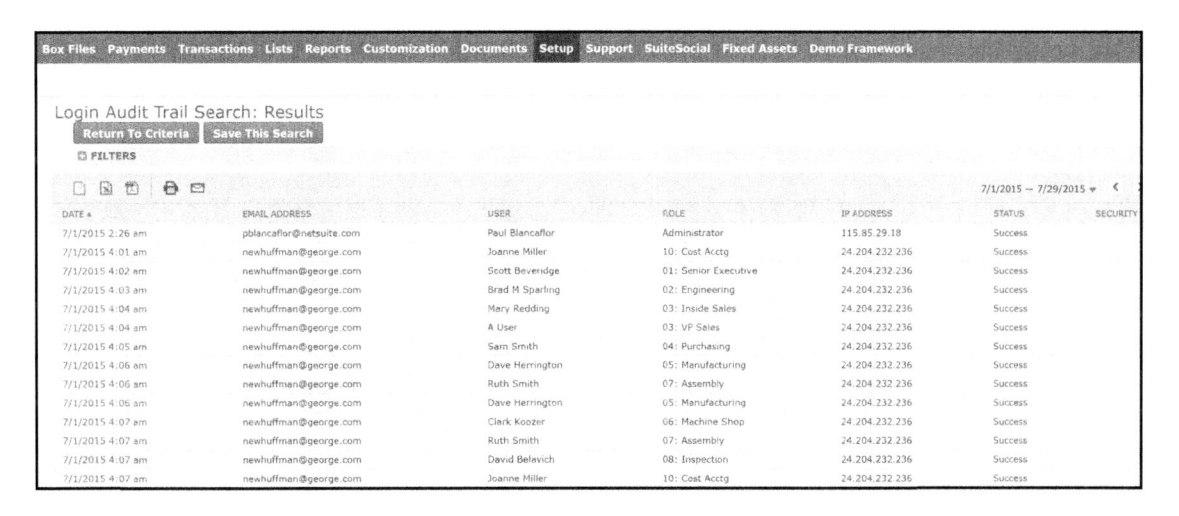

Login Audit Trail Search Results

In addition, each user can review their own login audit trail using a portlet that can be set up on the **Home** dashboard. Click **Personalize** dashboard and select the portlet for it to appear:

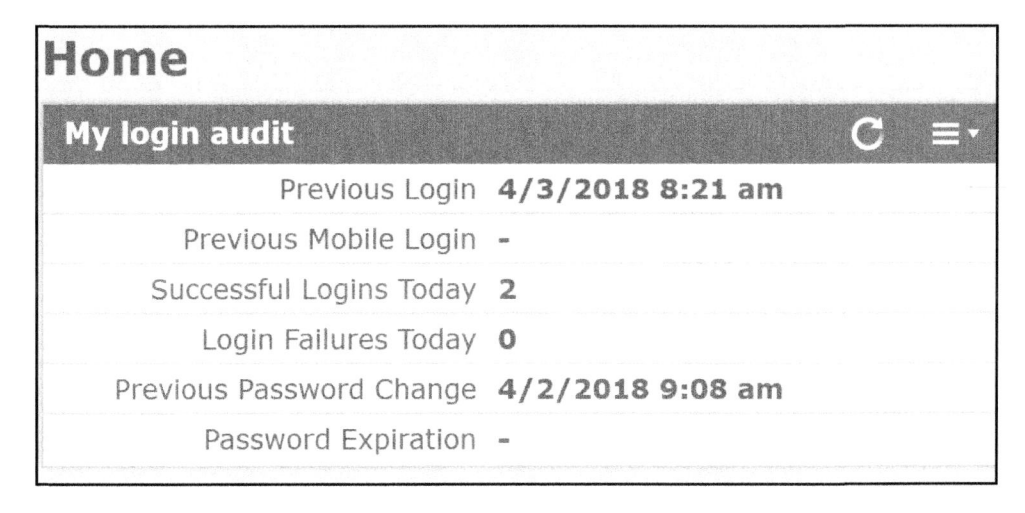

My login audit portlet on the Home dashboard

[123]

Security and Permissions

System notes

NetSuite records changes on every record and displays them in a subtab on the record, called **System Notes**:

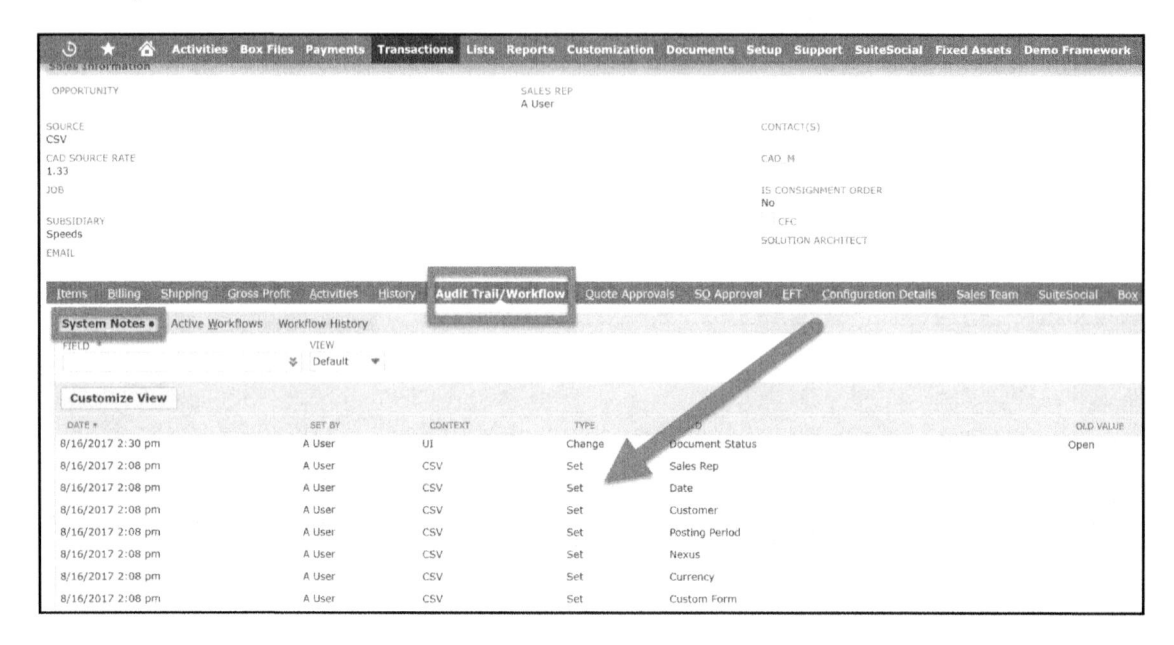

System Notes tab on Transaction

The **System Notes** tab specifies the following:

- **DATE** of the change
- **USER** who made the change
- **CONTEXT** or, rather, the way in which the change was made
- **TYPE** of change, such as **Set** or **Created** versus **Change**
- The **FIELD** that was changed
- The **OLD VALUE**
- The **NEW VALUE**

This tab is used when reviewing transactions on a one-by-one basis but is of limited help when we need to analyze multiple records to assess changes, for instance, where an integration has gone awry and updated a number of records that it shouldn't have. How do we identify the transactions that need to be set back to their original value?

NetSuite can restore from a backup for you in such a circumstance. It requires you to contact NetSuite Support and can be rather costly, or so I am told. So this is another opportunity for the administrator to shine and save the company some money.

The **System Notes** are available in saved searches, which we discuss in `Chapter 9`, *Workflows*. You'll be able to build the saved search using the tools we discuss there and update the appropriate records with the knowledge you'll gain in `Chapter 7`, *Imports*, where we demonstrate how to make updates to records using CSV imports.

Suffice to say for the moment, there are two types of system notes available in saved searches. The **System Notes** table records changes to the header level of transactions and to customers, items, and so on. The column or item level of transactions are accessed in the **System Line Notes** table. If you need to see whether someone changed the date or department of the transaction, use **System Notes** in your search, whereas, when enquiring on changes to the quantity of a widget ordered in the transaction, use the **System Line Notes**.

Security and Permissions

Audit Trail

The **Audit Trail Transaction** is found at **Transactions | Management | View Audit Trail**. It is a prebuilt search and shows changes to all transactions in NetSuite. It is will show whether the record was created, changed, or deleted. Simply running the audit trail will likely result in thousands of results, so NetSuite has included a number of filters to help us specify parameters, such as **USERS, ACTION, TRANSACTION DATE, AMOUNT**, and **TRANSACTION TYPE**:

View Audit Trail filters

Analyzing the audit trail is always tricky, especially when working out why a particular transaction was deleted. The **Use Deletion Reason** feature requires a user to enter a reason for deleting a transaction prior to executing the deletion. The feature is found in the **ERP General** section at **Setup | Company | Enable Features | General Tab** and will likely get you some brownie points with the accountant.

[126]

Saved Search Execution Log

Wondering whether the CEO exported the full customer list before giving their notice to leave the company? Look no further than the **Saved Search Execution** log. This tab is found on the edit screen of any saved search and specifies when the search was executed and by whom, as well as whether the data was exported from NetSuite:

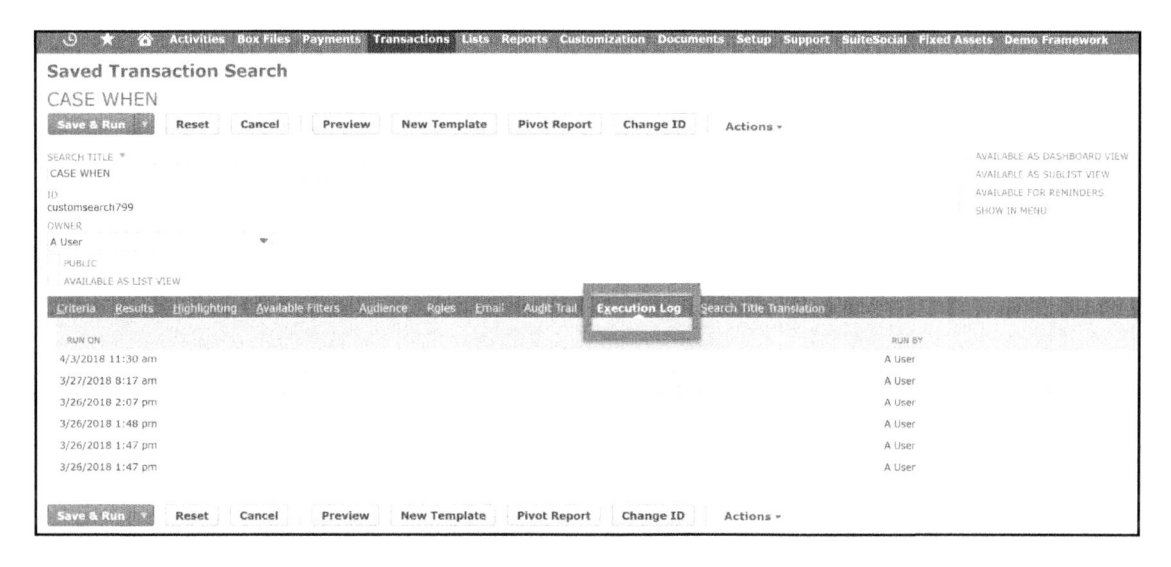

Execution Log Tab on a Saved Search

Security and Permissions

Custom reports

Access to standard reports is handled by the role's set of permissions, however, it does not provide access to a custom report that I just created. Access to custom reports is provided on the **More Options** tab on the **Report Builder**, for instance, go to **Reports** | **Sales** | **Sales by Customer Summary** | **Customize**, and open the **More Options** tab:

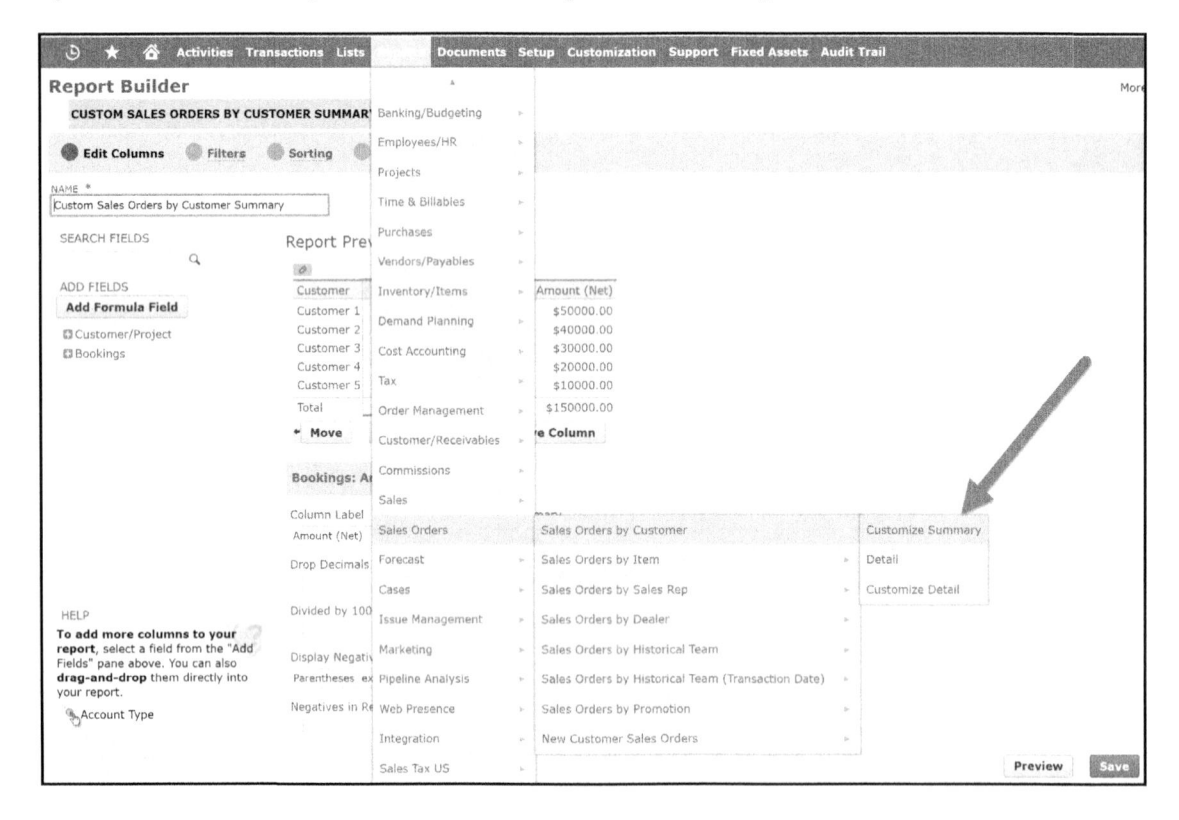

Customize a report

[128]

The Audience subtab

We can specify the ability to view this report by an individual employee, role, subsidiary, or department, or by setting up dynamically-generated groups of users, for instance, `All Sales Reps who report to Jim`:

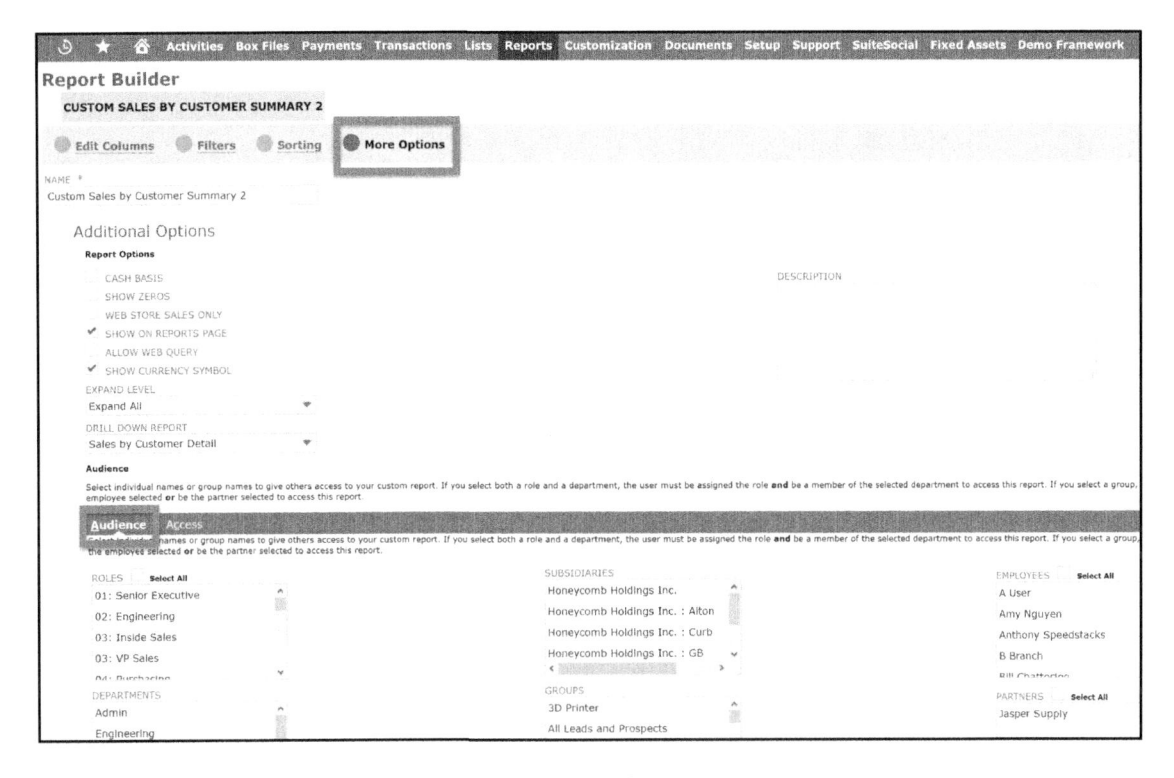

Audience Tab on Report Customization

The selections on this tab respect the permissions in the role. In other words, if an employee is specified as a member of the audience of this custom report, but does not have the permission to see this category of the report in their role, they will not be able to view this report.

The Access subtab

There are occasions when we would like a user who is not able to see this category of report because the role does lacks permissions to see this data. The **Access** subtab can be used to facilitate this as it overrides the permissions of the role. A user who is added to the **Access** tab will be able to view the report, irrespective of whether the user is assigned to a role with those permissions:

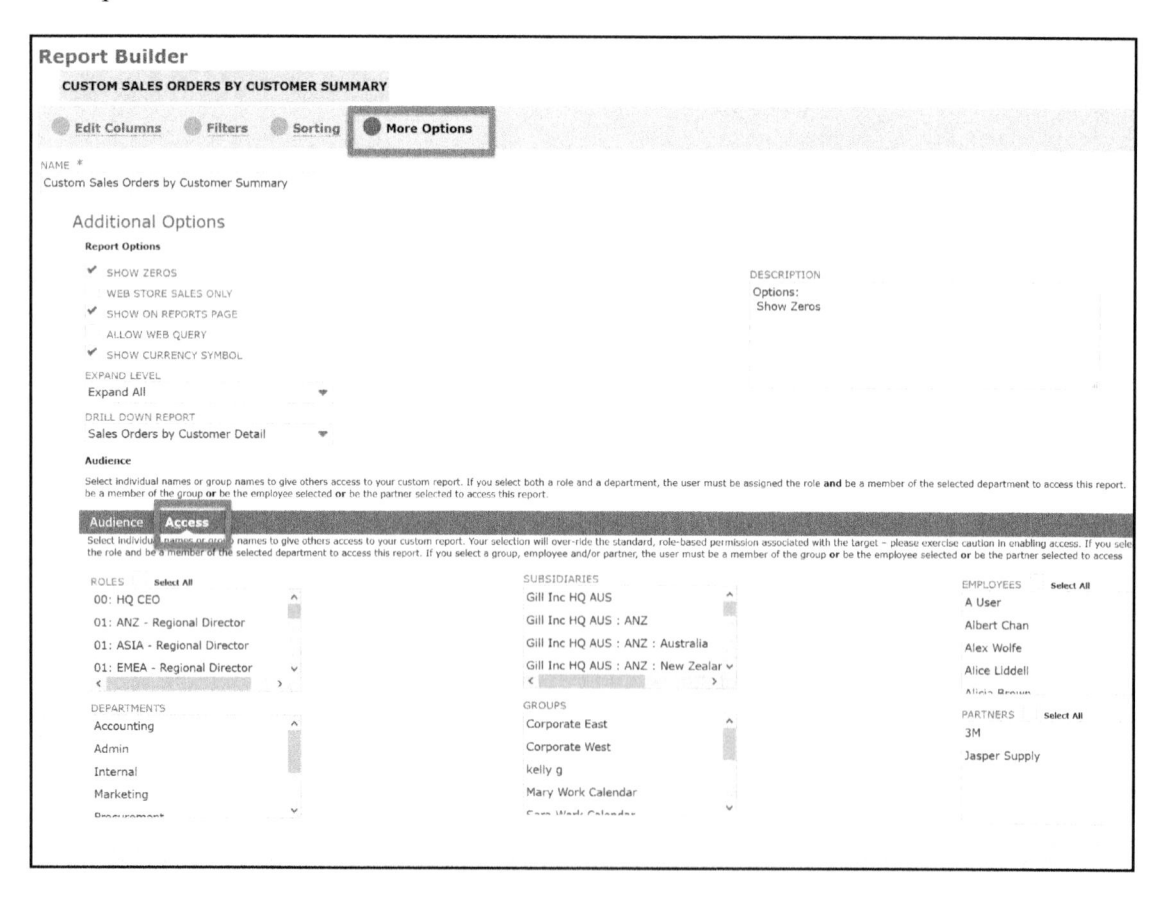

File Cabinet

The NetSuite **File Cabinet** is a file-management system enabling us to store and back up important files, such as images, logos, sales collateral, and Microsoft Word and PowerPoint files that have been presented to customers. These files can either be added from within the cabinet itself or using the **Files** tab on an associated record or transaction. While the file is physically stored in the **File Cabinet**, a link to the file is displayed on the record or transaction if the document is uploaded from the respective customer or transaction.

The **File Cabinet** is organized into folders, and we can add or edit folders by going to **Documents** | **Files** | **File Cabinet**:

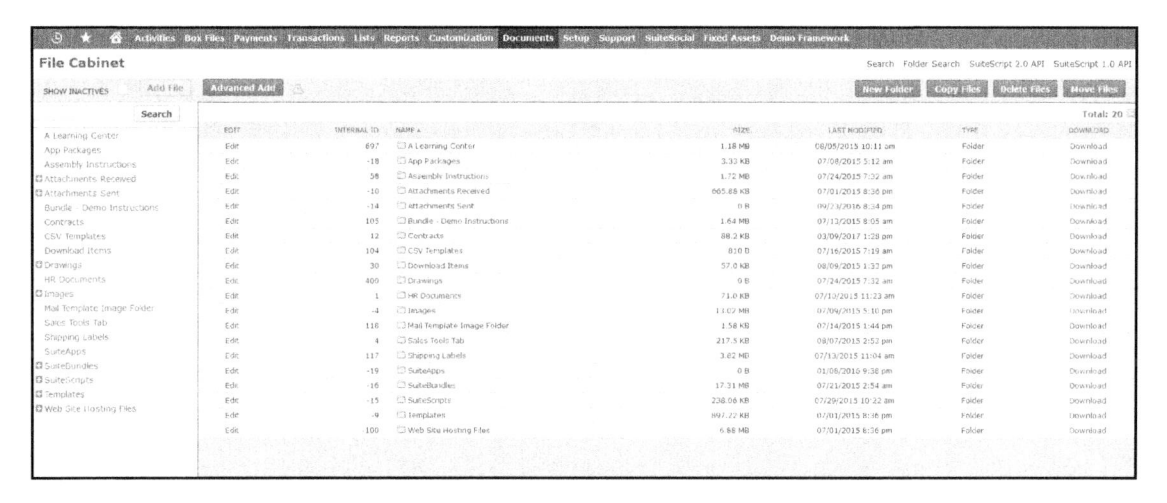

NetSuite File Cabinet

Security and Permissions

Folders can be added on the root level or by migrating through the folder structure to the appropriate section. This gives us the ability to implement security on the folders in the **File Cabinet**. A folder has a name and its place in the folder structure is set up in the **Sub-Folder of** field. The security aspects are set up using the restrictions on the right of the screen. Access to the folder can be restricted to a specific class, department, or location, as well as **SUBSIDIARY** for OneWorld users. The folder can also be set to private, which restricts access to the folder to the user who created it and any administrator. There is also the ability to **RESTRICT BY GROUP**, which gives us the flexibility to secure the folder providing access to specific members comprising that group. Please review the section on creating groups in `Chapter 8`, *Analytics – Searches, Reports, and the Dashboard*:

Editing a folder in the File Cabinet

Chapter 5

A user's access to a file is determined by the user's access to the folder with one exception. A file can be set to available without login, in which case the file will be viewable by anyone on the file's unique URL, which is generated when the file is first updated. This gives the user the option of sharing files with external parties, such as customers, by simply providing the URL:

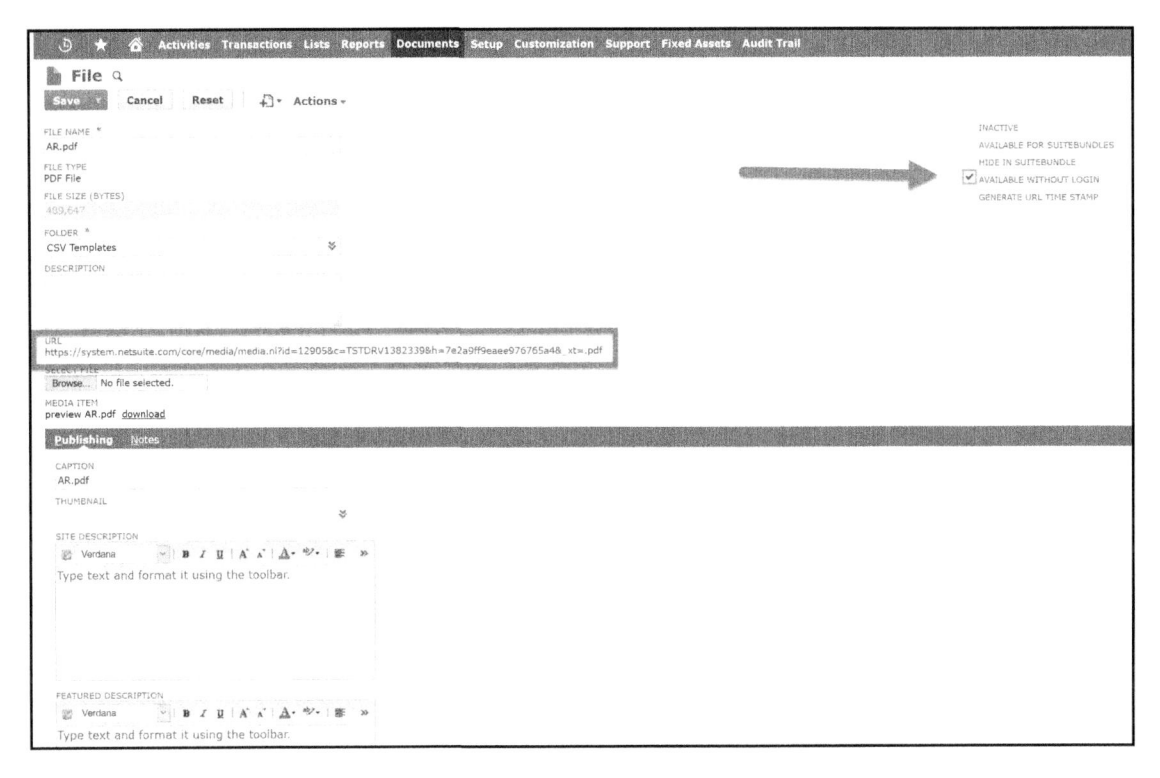

Make File Available without Login

Summary

NetSuite has given us a myriad of options to secure the data in our accounts. We can determine the complexity of a user's password and ensure a second level of authentication through the use of security questions. We can also determine the locations where the users are permitted to login via IP address rules, as well as other authentication options, such as single sign-on.

We can easily track which user logs in, when, and from which IP address, and we can track the changes that the user makes while logged into the database. We can even tell how often the user runs searches and more importantly if they proceed to export the results of the search.

We can also determine the type of data that the user can access by using permissions, and which specific transactions the user can access by using restrictions. We control what the user can do with the record if access is provided, such as edit or delete permissions.

We can also restrict the user to specific forms containing specific fields. That begs the question, *How do we customize forms?* That question and more will be answered in the next chapter, where we focus on creating custom fields, editing forms, and other customization options.

6
Customization

Usually, when we think of customization, we think of adding fields to a database. Customization, however, can take different forms. It includes the ability to edit forms to hide specific fields, or even to make those fields read-only. We can also edit forms in order to move the field to a different section of the form, for instance, if we need to place a field from one of the tabs into the main area of the screen. Forms are not just for internal use so that your users can access the information easily. The information also needs to to be printed or emailed to the people we transact with. They will likely need to see different information from what your users need to access so we need to specify the data they need to see on those documents. NetSuite gives us the ability to edit the external forms as well as internal forms to ensure that everyone sees the information that they are entitled to. In this chapter, we will examine the tools that NetSuite provides for this type of customization.

This chapter will cover the following:

- Understanding the different customization options available
- The difference between entity, item, CRM, and transaction custom fields
- Adding custom fields
- Editing forms and creating new forms
- Editing external forms and placing fields on external forms
- Creating and using custom records

Customization options

NetSuite offers a comprehensive toolkit of customization options in order to build and implement complex processes and integrations. They are all found on the customization drop-down menu and are subject to the specific features that have been enabled.

The first option we will look at is the ability to add custom fields to store data that is specific to your company and your industry. This includes the ability to determine where the outfield will appear on forms, provide field level help for your users, and optimize the import of data, for instance, by using picked lists.

Form customization is usually used when we have different processes requiring data to be placed in different forms will stop the classifications of department. Class and location provide an excellent example of this forestall in most situations. We may find that the class field applies to an entire transaction, and therefore needs to be placed on the main area of the transaction form to stop particular transactions; it may require multiple values for class, so class would need to be placed on a line level instead. That would require two forms, with an ability for the user to change from one form to the other. It also allows us to set specific forms as default forms, as well as setting up different default forms for different roles.

NetSuite provides two options to create the PDF and HTML layouts that will form the templates for external documents sent to the people we transact with. The older tool is called transaction form layouts. The new tool, called advanced PDF HTML templates, will only appear once the feature has been being enabled on **Setup** | **Company** | **Enable features** | **SuiteCloud** tab.

Customer records is another feature that needs to be enabled before it's available to be used in NetSuite. It is also enabled on the **Setup** | **Company** | **Enable features** | **SuiteCloud** tab. The Custom records feature give us the ability to add a new table to the NetSuite database. It may be a freestanding table or could be joined to existing records, for instance, a customer satisfaction survey that needs to be related to the specific customer who has filled out that survey.

Features such as sweet flow, client SuiteScript, and server SuiteScript are used to automate processes. Suitescript requires scripting, as you would expect. Suiteflow, on the other hand, is a GUI-based tool that is used to automate data entry that would otherwise be done manually. It can be used to set field values, create records, send emails, or even to create new records. That's not even the full list of the actions you can take using Suiteflow. It enables us to create this automation without needing any coding, but it has its limitations, particularly when we need to alternate actions at the sub-list level, such as on an item that is added to an order. We will need to look to Suitescript to solve complex problems like that.

Tips and tricks

New Custom fields are found at the **Customization** | **Lists** | **Records and Fields** menu path. **Entity fields** | **Transaction body** fields, item, and CRM fields all sound very complicated. Let's keep it really simple. Just go to the record you need to add the file to and click **Edit**. **Customer**, **Vendor**, **Sales Order**, **Item**, whatever. Now, select the **Customize** button in the top-right corner of the page and click **New Field**:

Select New Field from the record

Customization

We are now taken to the new custom field for that specific record. We selected new field from the customer record in our example and are therefore taken to the new **Custom Entity Field** page; the **Applies to Customer** checkbox is automatically checked:

Custom Entity Field setup

We can now proceed to configure our new field, as well as applying it to other records, for instance, contacts, and printing the custom field on statements or price lists:

Placing the custom field on different records

Chapter 6

Forms can also be accessed from a specific record. Go to a sales order in the edit mode, for instance, click the customize button on the top-right corner of the screen, and click **Customize Form**:

Customize form from the record

This selection takes us to the page used to customize this specific form where:

1. We can select which tabs will appear on the form
2. We can select the field that will appear on the form and determine the label of the field, as well as whether it will be editable (**normal**) or read-only (**inline text**)
3. The buttons that will appear on the form enable the user to take specific actions from the form
4. Whether it will be the default form (**preferred form**) for all users or just for users with a specific role/ series of permissions
5. We can select whether to use a basic or advanced layout when printing the external, customer-facing form

Customization

6. We can select which specific customer external form layout to use when printing or emailing this form

Customer Form Setup

[140]

Common characteristics

Most features when creating a new custom field are available for all records. A generic name, such as `customentity12`, will be auto-generated if we leave the field blank. It's best to give the new field a descriptive ID, or the developer may be ticked with you if and when a script needs to be written referencing this custom form. Best do it now, or you might have to treat the developer to an apology lunch. We usually use an underscore prefix to identify the ID, followed by the name of the company to distinguish the field from one created by your NetSuite partner. The ID looks something like this: `_abccospouse`.

The description is useful to elaborate on the need for this field if ambiguous in the future.

The type of field is obviously crucial:

- Text is for the value to be typed by the user.
- Text area is for a note.
- Rich text is a notes field that gives users formatting tools for the note.
- Lists are picklists providing the user with a number of selections to choose from.
- The **List/ Record** field becomes available when we choose **List/ Record** or **Multiple Select** as the field **Type** field. We use it to reference the specific values that will be displayed for the user to choose from. We can either select the list to be used or click the plus sign to create a new list.

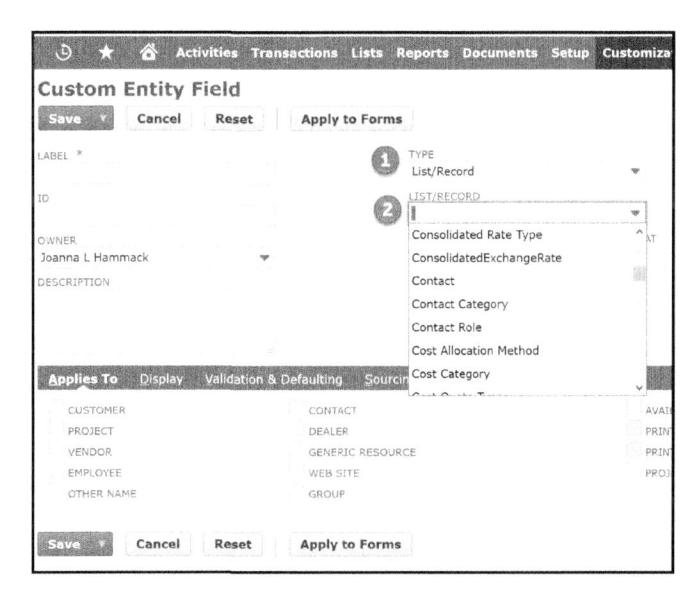

List/ Record Type opens the List/ Record field

Customization

- Date displays a calendar to the user, so they can select a date value for the field.
- Phone is for phone numbers.
- Currency is for currency.

Store value seems to be an odd option because it seems that we would only create fields with an ability to save the data placed therein.

There are, however, circumstances where we do not want to store the data, such as when we source in data from another record using the sourcing and filtering tab. We will look at an example of this later in the chapter.

The **Applies To** tab is used to determine which records and/or forms this new field will apply to.

The **View** tab determines where this custom field will appear in forms by default. Failure to make a selection here will result in a **Custom** tab being added to the record and this field will appear on that tab.

Select the area of the screen this needs to appear in. Is it a crucial field that needs to be available in the main area of the screen, or can it be hidden in one of the tabs?

The **Help** field sets the field-level help for this field. The instructions for this field will appear when a user clicks the label of the custom field.

Mandatory make this field mandatory on all forms, meaning that the system will prevent a user from saving the record until or unless the user has made a selection from this field. This should be used with caution. Placing too many mandatory fields on a form will result in user frustration. This increases the likelihood that the user will make any selection in the field just to be able to save the record and move on. Selecting a random value instead of the correct value in the field defeats the purpose of creating the field in the first place.

Custom entity field

Let's focus on a custom entity field in our first exercise. We will add a new field on the contact record to save a contact's spouse's name.

Go to a contact record using **Lists** | **Relationships** | **Contacts** | **New**. Then, click on the **Customize** button on the top-right corner and choose **New Field**.

Add Spouse Name to the **Label** field:

1. Add an **ID** such as `_hmspouse`.
2. Choose **Free-Form Text** from the **TYPE** field.
3. Ensure that **STORE VALUE** is checked.
4. Review the **Applies to** tab and ensure that the contact is selected:

Configure Custom Entity Field

Customization

5. Go to the **Display** tab and choose the **Main** subtab.
6. Enter any applicable field-level help in the **Help** field:

Determine the Display options for a custom field

7. Click **Save**.
8. Go to a contact record and verify that the new field is available. (This may require you to edit the form, which we will be discussing later in this chapter.)
9. Test the new field by entering data into that field on a contact record:

Custom field on customer record

Employee and transaction fields use case

In this use case, we will add a new field to sales orders to display the name of the solution architect who helped close this deal.

Go to a sales order and click the **Customize** button. We are faced with a few choices for transaction fields. We will select transaction body field, as the solution architect worked on the entire deal (unlike transaction column field, which would be used if different architects worked on different items sold in the same transaction):

1. Name the new field by entering `Solution Architect` into the **Label** field.
2. Enter `_hmsolarc` into the **ID** field.
3. There is no need for the name of the solution architect be typed onto each transaction. We will set the **Type** to list in order to select from a list of values instead.

Customization

4. The **List/ Record** becomes available once the type is changed to list. We can add a list of solution architects by clicking the plus sign next to the list/record field, however, this would require us to maintain this separate list. The list will need to be changed when a solution architect joins or leaves that team. Alternatively, we already have a list of employees in the system so we can simply reuse that list by selecting employees in that drop-down menu.
5. Select **Show in List** in order for us to see the field in the list of transactions.
6. Review the **Applies to** tab and ensure that **Sale** is selected:

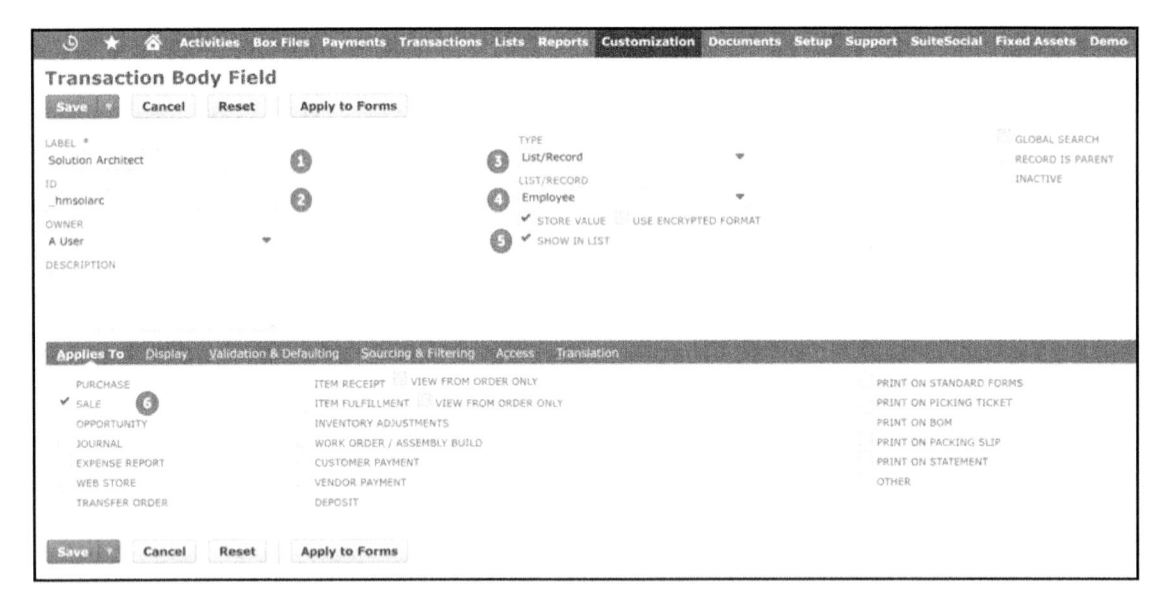

Custom Transaction Body Field

7. Go to the **Display** Tab and choose the **Main** subtab.
8. Enter any applicable field-level help in the **Help** field:

[146]

Chapter 6

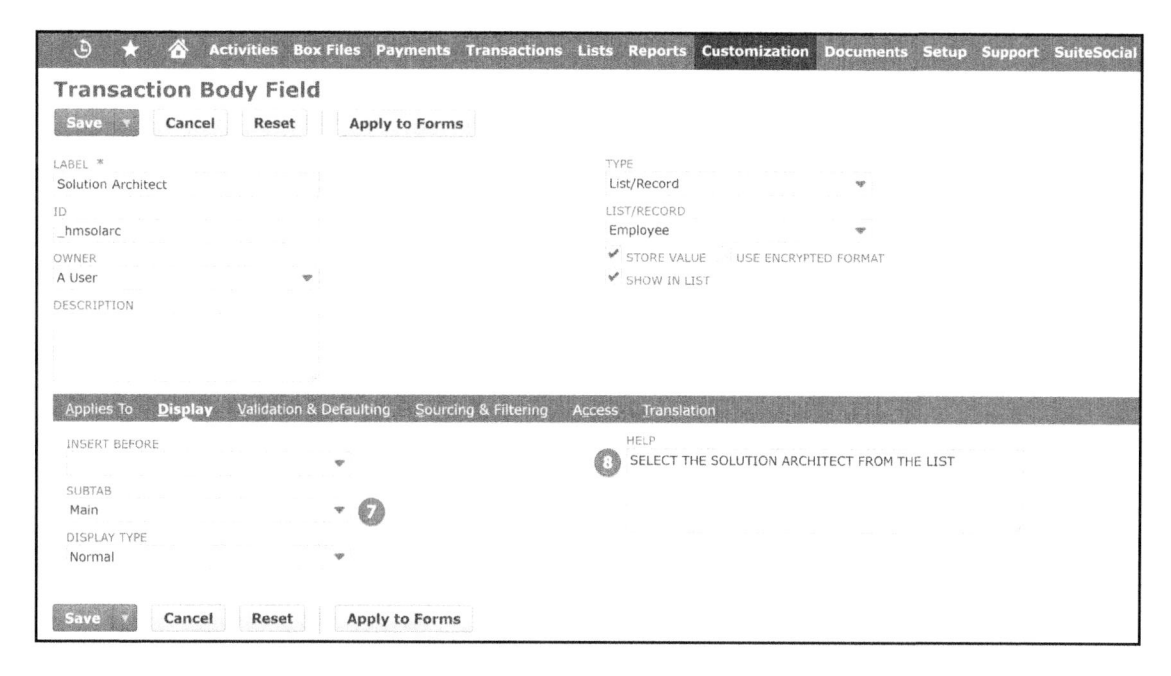

![Screenshot of Transaction Body Field customization screen showing Display tab with fields for Insert Before, Subtab (Main), Display Type (Normal), and Help text "Select the solution architect from the list". Numbered callouts 7 and 8 point to the Subtab and Help fields respectively.]

Custom Transaction Body field Display Options

9. Click **Save**.
10. Go to a sales order and verify that the new field is available. (This may require you to edit the form, which we will be discussing later in this chapter.)

The elephant in the room is that the list of employees is much larger than the list of solution architects, yet a user would need to go through the entire list to select the one solution architect. Wouldn't it be preferable to limit the names in the list to solution architects only?

Yes, it would, however that requires further customization. We need to add a field to the employee record to identify specific employees as solution architects. We can then use that field to filter the list of employees on the transaction record:

1. Go to **Lists** | **Employees** | **Employees** | **New**.
2. Click the **Customize** button on the top-right corner of the screen and select **New field**.
3. Name the field `Solution Architect`.
4. Enter the **ID** as `_emplsa`.

[147]

Customization

5. Select checkbox from the **Type** dropdown.
6. Check **Show in List** to make this field available in a list (and therefore inline editable as we learned in `Chapter 2`, *Exploring NetSuite Tools*).
7. Go to the **Display** tab and select **Human Resources** from the **SUBTAB** field:

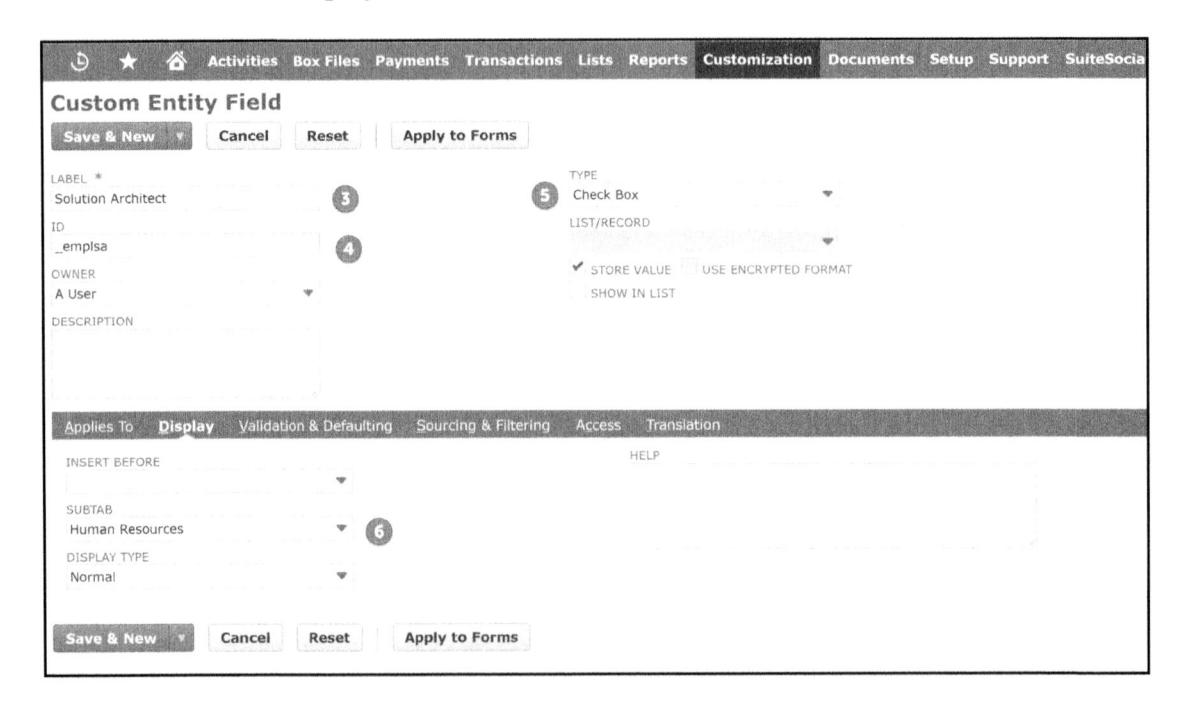

Chapter 6

8. Click **Save**.
9. Go to the **Human Resources** tab on the employee record.
10. Test the new field:

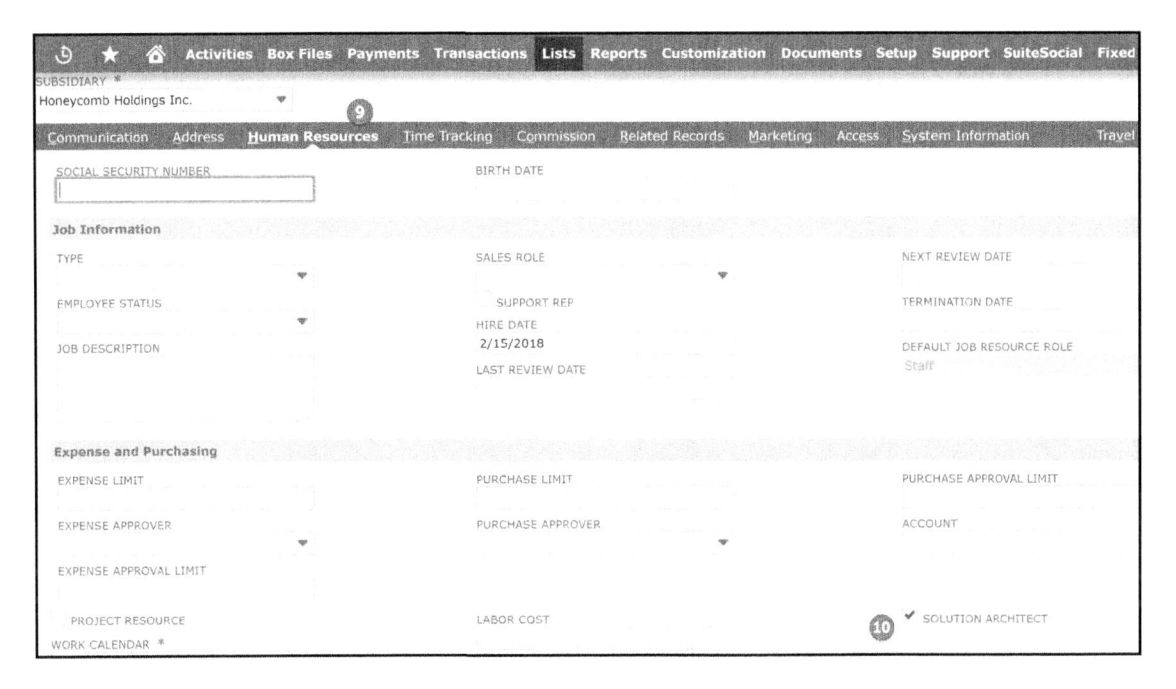

Custom Field on Employee Record

Customization

The next step is to apply that field to the transaction body field:

1. Go to **Customization** | **Lists Records & Fields** | **Transaction Body Fields**.
2. Select **Solution Architect** from the list.
3. Go to the **Sourcing & Filtering** subtab.
4. Choose **Solution Architect** from the **Filter Using** drop-down menu.
5. Ensure that the **Is Checked** field is checked:

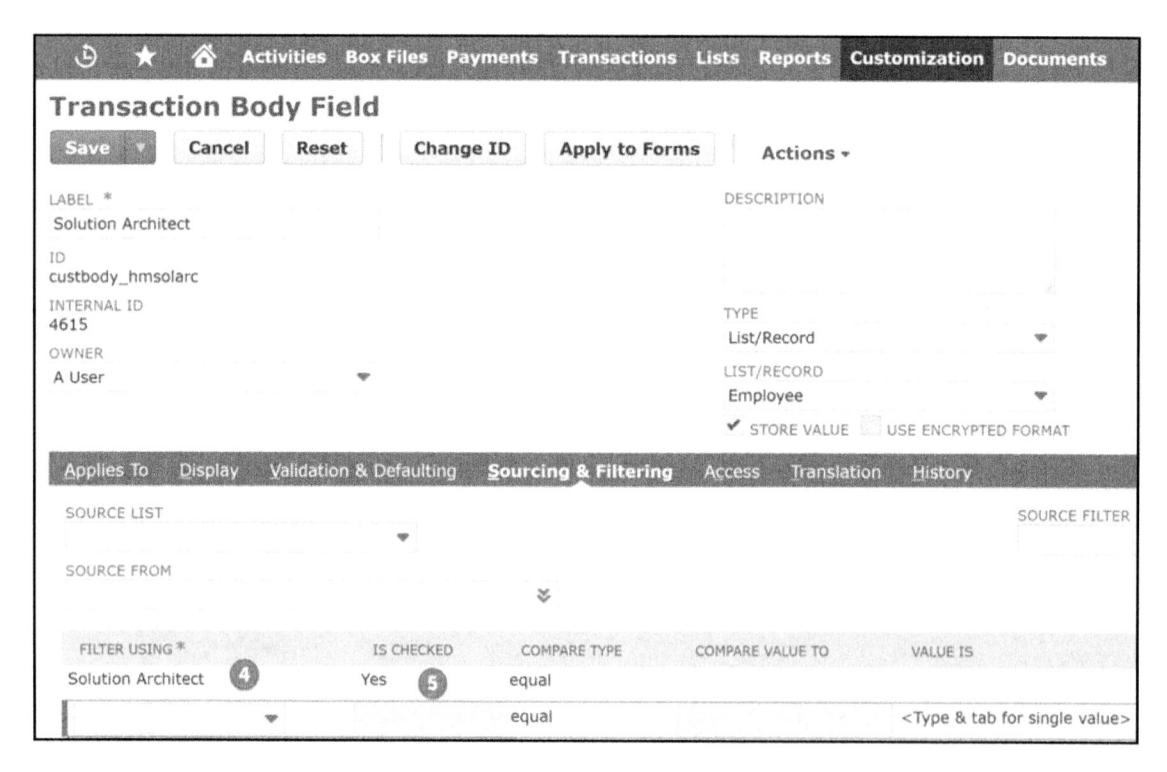

Sourcing & Filtering custom field options

6. Click **Save**.
7. Go to the sales order and click the **Solution Architect** drop-down menu. Confirm that the list of employees is limited to the employees that have the **Solution Architect** checked on their employee record:

Chapter 6

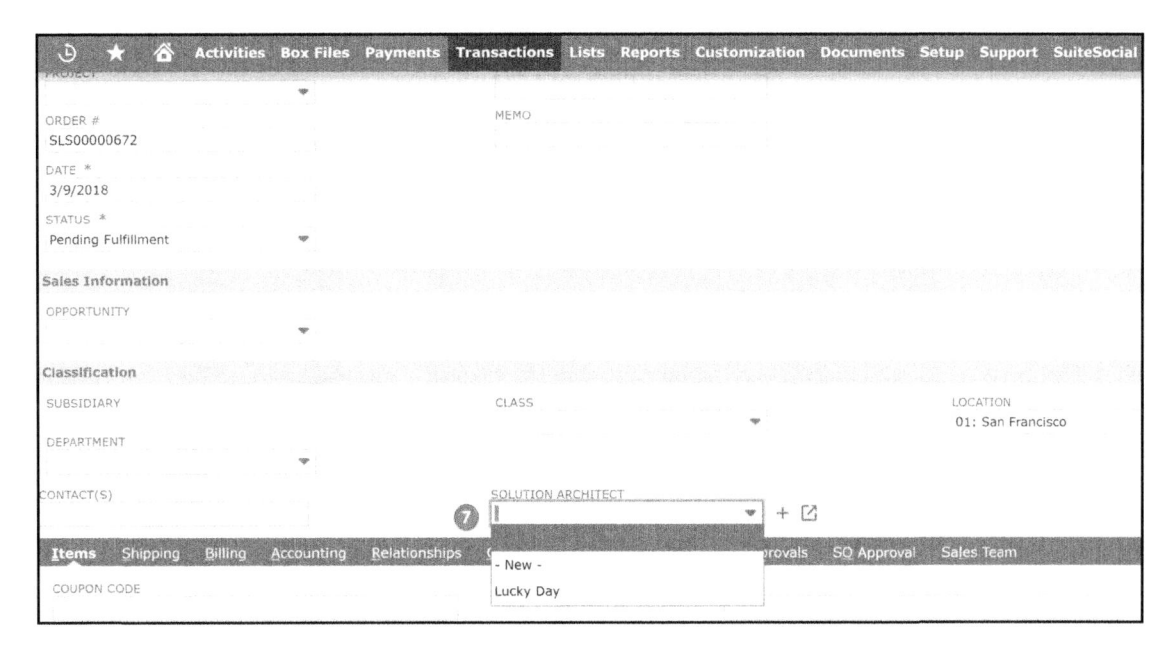

Custom Field drop-down contains filtered list

Custom records

Now that we've seen custom fields, what are custom records? The easiest way to understand customer records is to expand on our previous example, recording the name of a contact's spouse on the contact record. Let's assume we also need to record the names of the contact's children.

While children can be added as custom fields, just as a spouse can, the fundamental difference is that a contact can only have one spouse but can have multiple children. So, how many children fields do we need to create? Two? Three? What if Octomom becomes a customer? Will we need eight fields, one for each of her eight children? Yet, those fields will be empty for most (if not all) of the other contacts.

Customization

This is where a custom record comes into play. It is a new table that can be associated with an existing table, for instance, the contact table, and it can have one or more records related to the parent record, which is the contact record in our example.

To put it differently, custom fields are based on a one-to-one relationship, whereas custom records are based on a one-to-many relationship.

Online forms

Another advantage of custom records is that they have built-in online forms. The online form can be easily created from within the NetSuite UI. This creates a unique URL that can be used to populate the data in the custom form. It is accessed on the web and does not require additional NetSuite licenses to go to that URL, meaning that external customers and contacts can enter their own information directly into your NetSuite, making it a perfect option for a customer satisfaction survey.

Custom record example

Let's assume we've been tasked with creating a customer satisfaction survey, which will be periodically sent out to customers. The survey follows the **Net Promoter Score** (**NPS**) methodology, which is based on asking customers one question, namely, "How likely are you to recommend our business to a friend or colleague?" According to NPS, that's the only question that matters. All other questions are superfluous to customer loyalty.

We could build a custom field on the customer record, of the type-list record, with an associated list containing values from 1-10, but it would be incorrect. The primary reason we need a custom record is not that the survey has multiple questions, which in this case it does not. The reason is that customers will be sent the survey many times over their life cycle with the company. If we were to use one custom field on the customer record, the results of previous surveys will be overwritten each time a new survey is completed.

The custom record also gives us the ability to enable the customer to fill it out on their own, without any manual entry on our side:

1. Go to **Customization** | **Lists, Records & Fields** | **Records Types** | **New**:

Add new Custom Record

2. Name the custom record NPS Survey.
3. Provide an **ID**: _hmnpssurvey.
4. Uncheck **Include Name** field.
5. Click **Save**:

Customization

6. Go to the fields subtab and click the **New Field** button.
7. Enter the name as Customer.
8. Enter the ID: _npscustomer.
9. Select field type of list.
10. Select the **List/Record** of **customer** to link to the existing list of customers.
11. Check the checkbox that was previously greyed out but is now available—**Record is Parent:**

Link Custom Record to Parent record

12. Click **Save**.
13. Go to a customer record to review the changes. The **NPS Survey** subtab appears on the **Custom** tab:

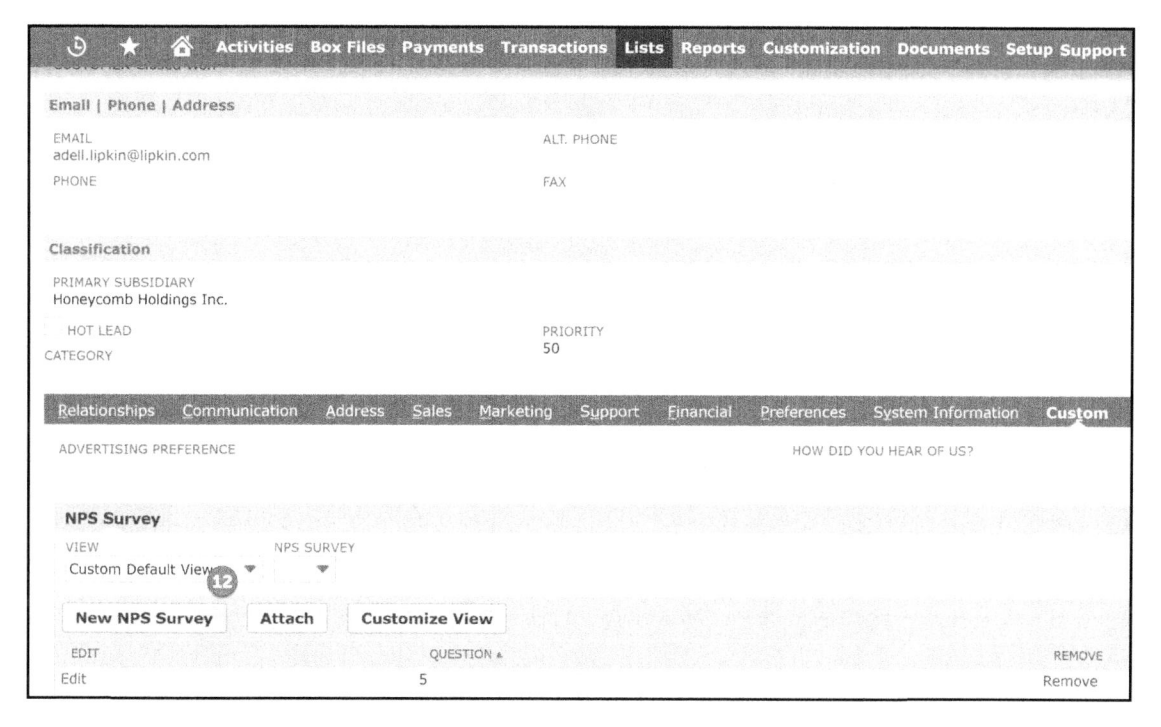

Add New record in the NPS Custom Record

14. Return to the custom record and click **New Field**.
15. Name the field `Question`.
16. Name the **ID** `_hmquestion`.
17. Select the type field as list.
18. Go to the **List/Record** field and click the **+** sign on the right of that field.
19. Name the list `Answers`.
20. Enter the values of 1-10 in the list.
21. Click **Save**.

[155]

Customization

22. Go back to the **NPS Survey** subtab on a customer record.
23. Click **New Survey**.
24. Select the dropdown next to **QUESTION** and select the answer **5**:

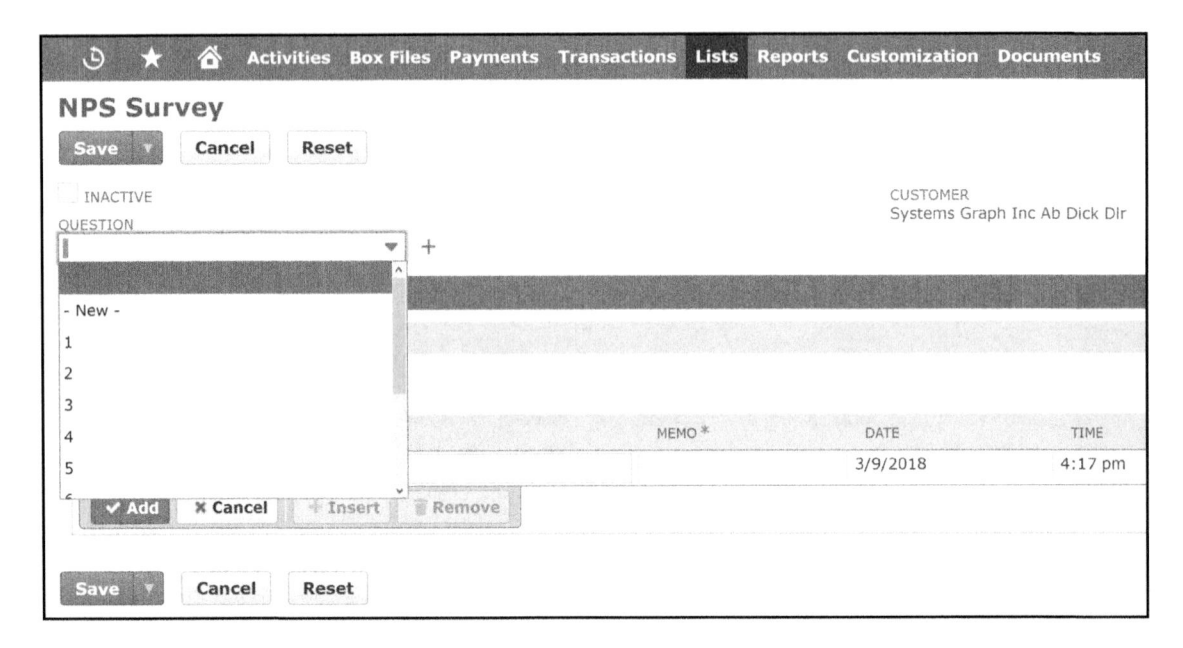

Update field value on Custom Record

25. Click **Save**.

26. The new survey appears on the customer record, however the answer to the question does not appear; we need to customize the view to show it on the subtab:

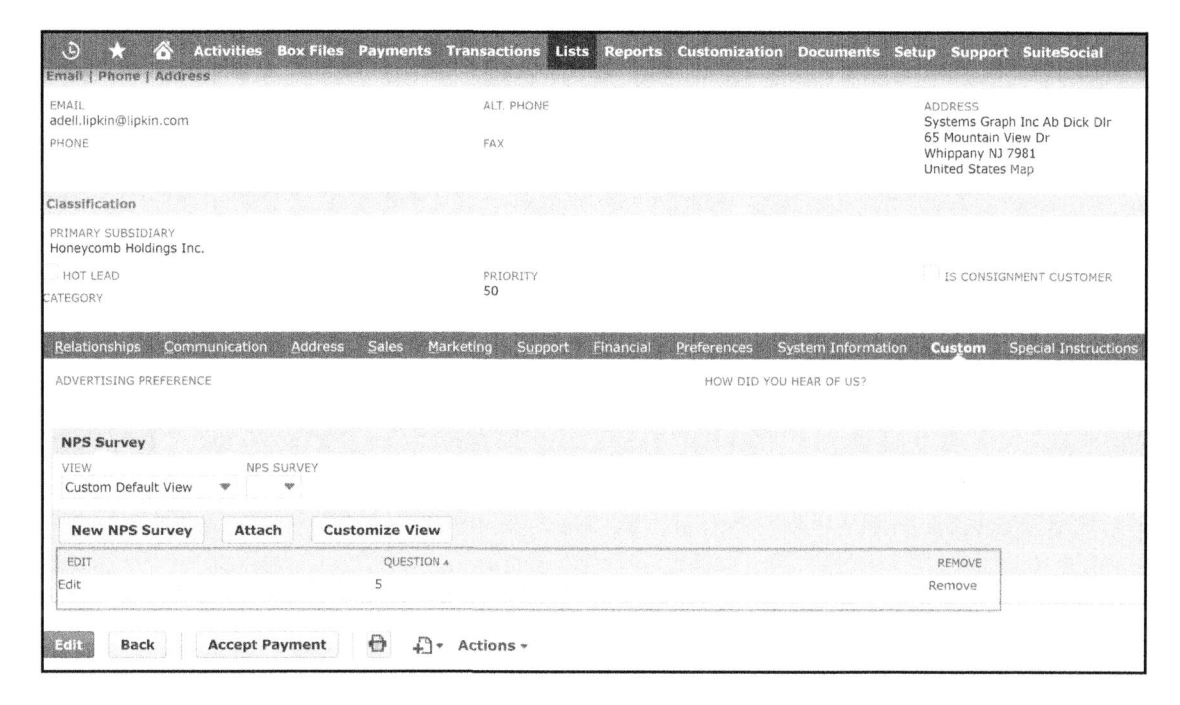

Custom Record Sublist View

27. Click the **Customize View** button to change the sublist view.

Customization

28. Add the **Question** field to the **Results**:

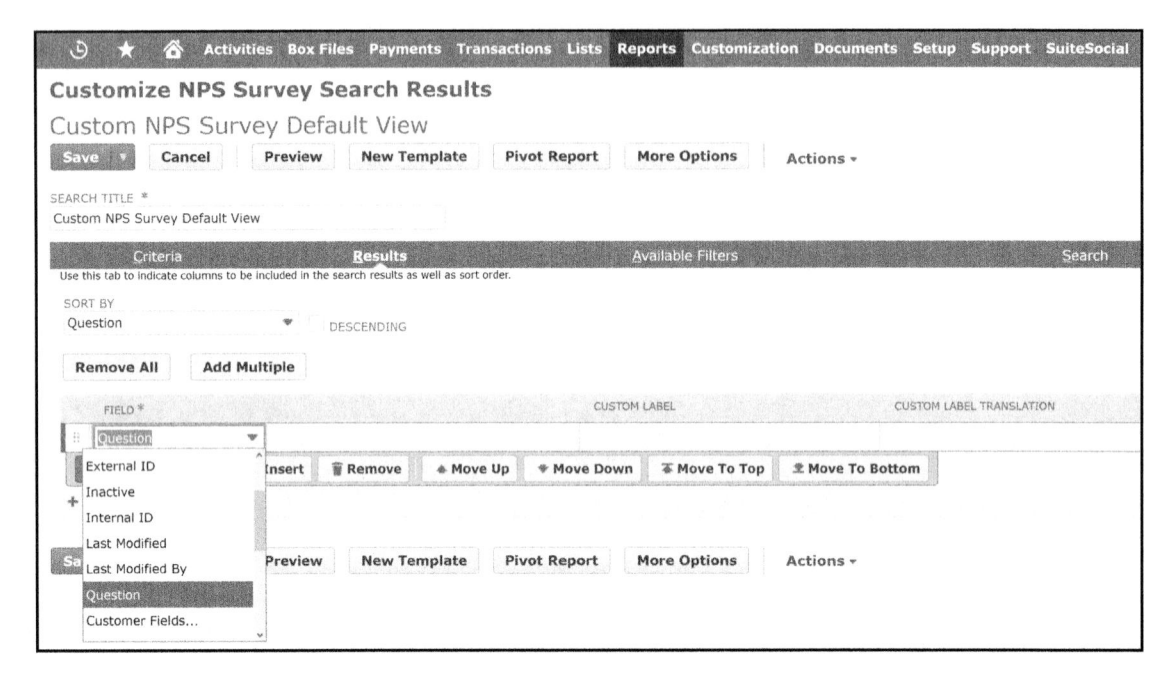

Edit custom record sublist view

29. Click **Save**—the results of the survey now appear in the sublist view on the customer record:

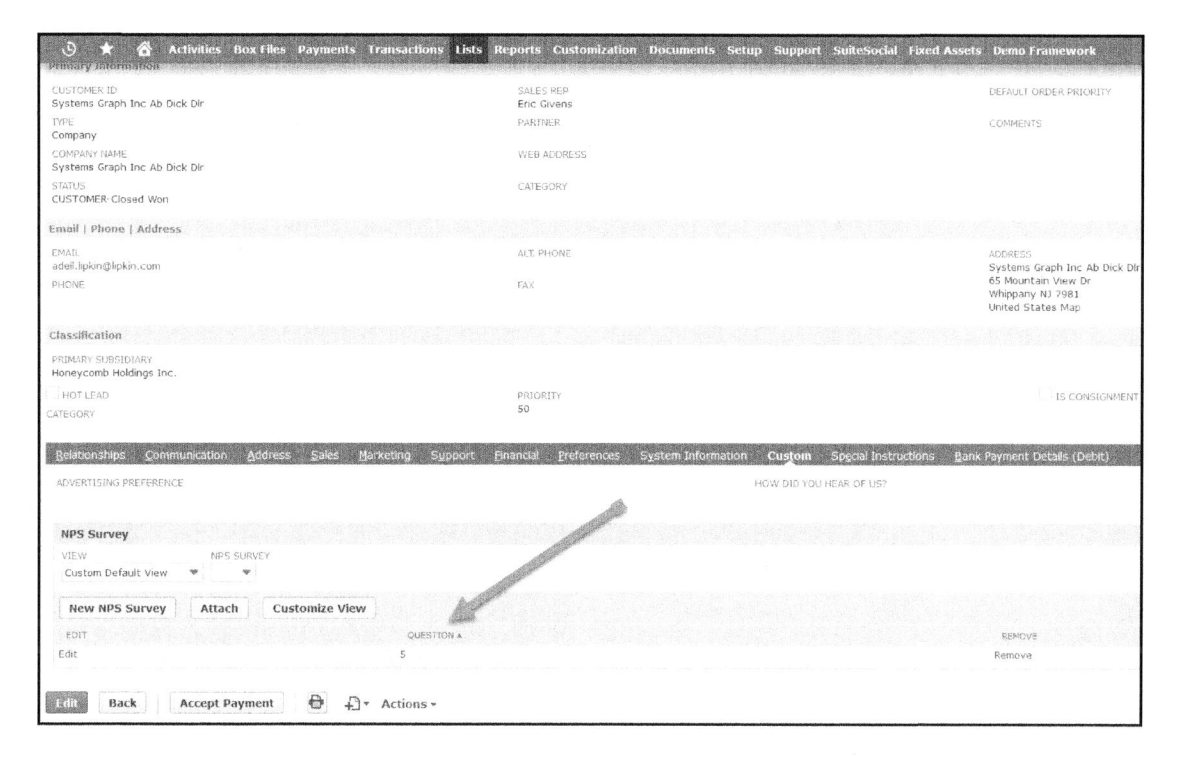

Columns appearing on custom sublist view

Customization

Reporting on custom records

The custom record is now available in saved searches, allowing us to report on the results of the survey, such as the average score. We can see the **NPS Survey** appear under **Lists | Search | Saved Searches | New**:

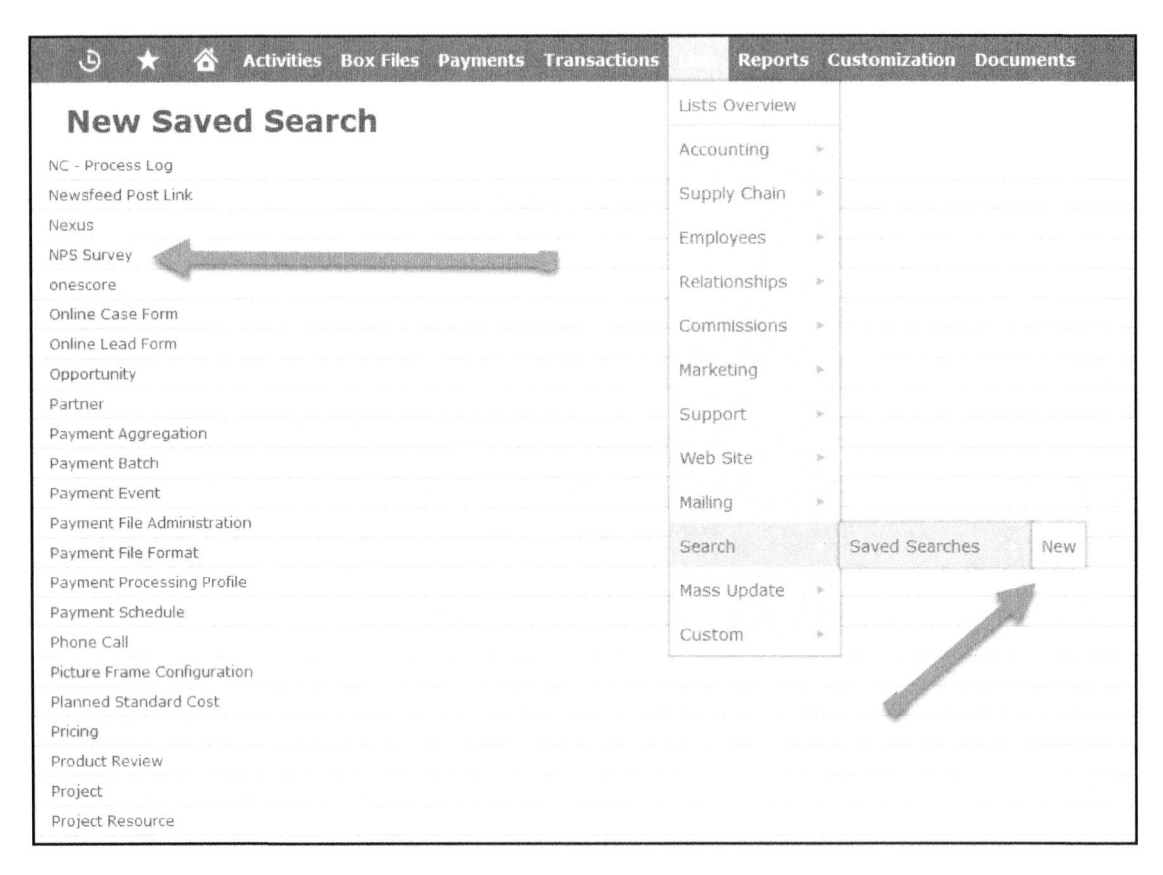

Create Saved Search based on Custom Record

Custom Record online form example

The objective here is to create an online form that customers use to fill out the customer satisfaction survey, which will be attached to each customer's customer record:

1. Return to the custom record by going to **Customization | Lists, Records & Fields | Records Types**, then select the NPS survey custom record.

[160]

2. Go to the **Online Form** tab:

Custom Record Type

NPS Survey

[Edit] [Back] Actions ▼

NAME
NPS Survey
ID
customrecord_hmnpssurvey
INTERNAL ID
485
OWNER
A User
DESCRIPTION

☐ INCLUDE NAME FIELD
☐ SHOW ID
SHOW CREATION DATE ☐ ON RECORD ☐ ON LIST
SHOW LAST MODIFIED ☐ ON RECORD ☐ ON LIST

SHOW OWNER ☐ ON RECORD ☐ ON LIST ☐ ALLOW
ACCESS TYPE
Require Custom Record Entries Permission
✔ ALLOW UI ACCESS
☐ ALLOW MOBILE ACCESS
✔ ALLOW ATTACHMENTS
✔ SHOW NOTES
☐ ENABLE MAIL MERGE
☐ RECORDS ARE ORDERED
✔ SHOW REMOVE LINK ☐ ALLOW CHILD RECORD EDIT
☐ ALLOW QUICK SEARCH

Fields • Subtabs Sublists Icon • Numbering • Forms • **Online Forms** Permissions Links Managers Translation

[New Online Form] [New Online HTML Form]

NAME ▲   ENABLE ONLINE
No records to show.

[Edit] [Back] Actions ▼

Custom Record Online form options

There are two options, **New Online Form** and **New Online HTML Form**. The online form is a cookie-cutter form with limited opportunity for customization. The online HTML form, however, gives you complete control to create an online form that looks and feels like your website. You build the page and simply include tags to represent the NetSuite fields on the custom record.

3. We will demonstrate how to create a simple online form that does not require any HTML. Click the **New Online Form** button.
4. Enter the title of the online form: Customer Satisfaction Survey.
5. Enter the instructions in the **Message** field.

Customization

6. Add the **Question** field to the form.
7. Add the **Customer** field to the form; after all, it will be important to attach the response to the correct customer. We cannot, however, allow the customer to choose their name from the complete list of our customers because this would expose the names of all our customers. This violates their privacy and risks a data breach. While we need to have the field on the form, it does not have to be viewable by the customer, so check the hidden checkbox:

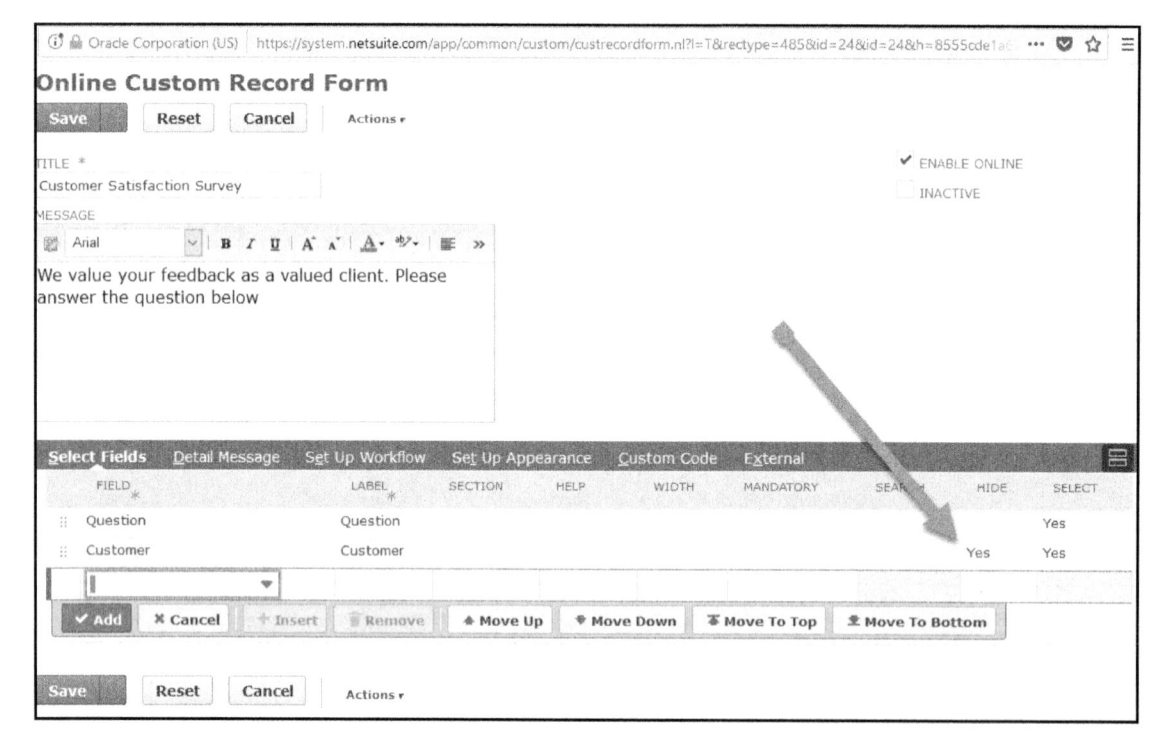

Hide field on Online Form

8. Go to the **Set up Workflow** tab.
9. Enter your email address into the **NOTIFY BY EMAIL** field, which will send you an email whenever the form is submitted.

[162]

10. Enter the company URL into the **REDIRECT TO URL** field. This will redirect anyone submitting the form to that specific page:

Setup Workflow on submission of Online Form

11. Click **Save**.

Customization

12. Reselect the online form you've just created. A new tab has been named `External`. This tab contains the publishable form URL, which is the live form that the customer will use to fill out their customer satisfaction survey:

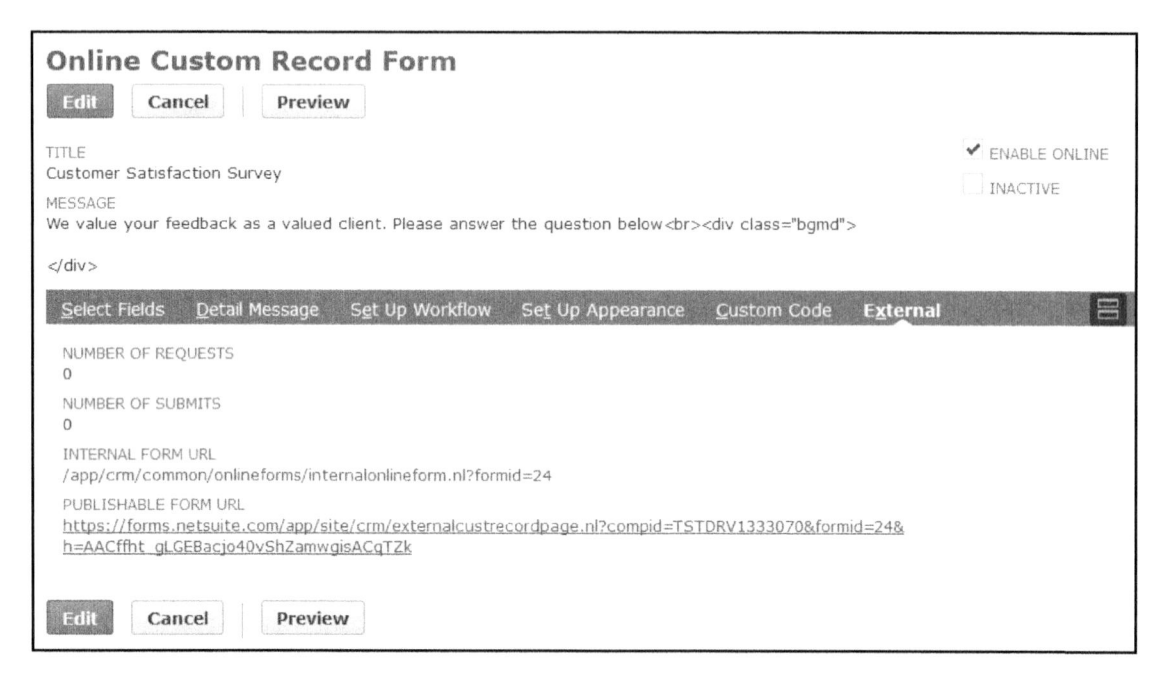

<div style="border:1px solid #000; padding:10px;">

Online Custom Record Form

[Edit] [Cancel] [Preview]

TITLE
Customer Satisfaction Survey

✔ ENABLE ONLINE
☐ INACTIVE

MESSAGE
We value your feedback as a valued client. Please answer the question below\
\<div class="bgmd">
\</div>

Select Fields | Detail Message | Set Up Workflow | Set Up Appearance | Custom Code | **External**

NUMBER OF REQUESTS
0

NUMBER OF SUBMITS
0

INTERNAL FORM URL
/app/crm/common/onlineforms/internalonlineform.nl?formid=24

PUBLISHABLE FORM URL
https://forms.netsuite.com/app/site/crm/externalcustrecordpage.nl?compid=TSTDRV1333070&formid=24&h=AACffht_gLGEBacjo40vShZamwgisACqTZk

[Edit] [Cancel] [Preview]

</div>

Online Form URL link

We're almost done. We've created a survey and an online survey form, but are not done yet. The online form, in its present state, is virtually useless as it is not associated with a customer record. Our next step is to ensure that the customer name is populated when someone accesses the form.

We can append `custrecord_npscustomer='CUSTOMERNAME'` to the URL to automatically enter the customer's name into the form: Let's unhide the customer field on the publishable form and test the new URL:

```
https://forms.netsuite.com/app/site/crm/externalcustrecordpage.nl/compid.
TSTDRV1333070/.f?formid=24h=AACffht_gLGEBacjo40vShZamwgisACqTZkcustrecord_
npscustomer=3M
```

[164]

Chapter 6

![Browser screenshot showing Customer Satisfaction Survey online form with Question dropdown and Customer 3M field, with Submit button]

Online form as it appears to the user

Now that we can automatically set the customer name on the **Customer Satisfaction Survey** online form, we can create individual links for all customers and send each customer their individual URL via mail merge.

Customizing forms

Now we will focus on customizing forms. Go to **Customize** | **Forms** | **Transaction** forms to see the list of transaction forms in your system.

There are a number of different records available, but it can also include multiple forms for the same record.

There is also a column showing the preferred form, which is the default form that will appear when anyone accesses the record.

Yet, as usual, the place to start is with the form that you wish to customize in the UI itself. So, start from the sales order, for instance, by going to **Transactions** | **Sales** | **Enter Sales Order** and click the **Customize** button on the top-right corner of the screen, click **Customize**, and then **Form**.

The first step is to name the new form. Once named, we should save this form before doing any further customization. Click the **Save** button or preferably the **Save As** button, if it appears (save appears when initially customizing a standard form, whereas save as appears when editing a form that had already been customized).

[165]

Customization

Main screen

The main screen contains the name of the form, as well as the selection of the category of the external form used in conjunction with this transaction form. This is where we select whether this form will be linked to the basic (legacy) external form or the advanced PDF/HTML layouts. The external forms determine the format of the printed version that will be given to the customer. The specific layout chosen appears just below this field and is dependent upon the selection of either the basic or advanced forms.

We can also enter a disclaimer for this transaction and a specific logo for this form, if different from the standard logo. We can also designate this form as the preferred form:

Custom Transaction form

We determine the tabs and fields that will appear on the form by checking and unchecking the options on the **Tabs** and **Screen Fields** subtabs. Turn a tab on or off by toggling the **Show** checkbox on the **Tabs** subtab.

We can even change the order in which the **Tabs** appear by selecting the line and dragging into a different order, or by using the **Move To Top** and **Move To Bottom** buttons:

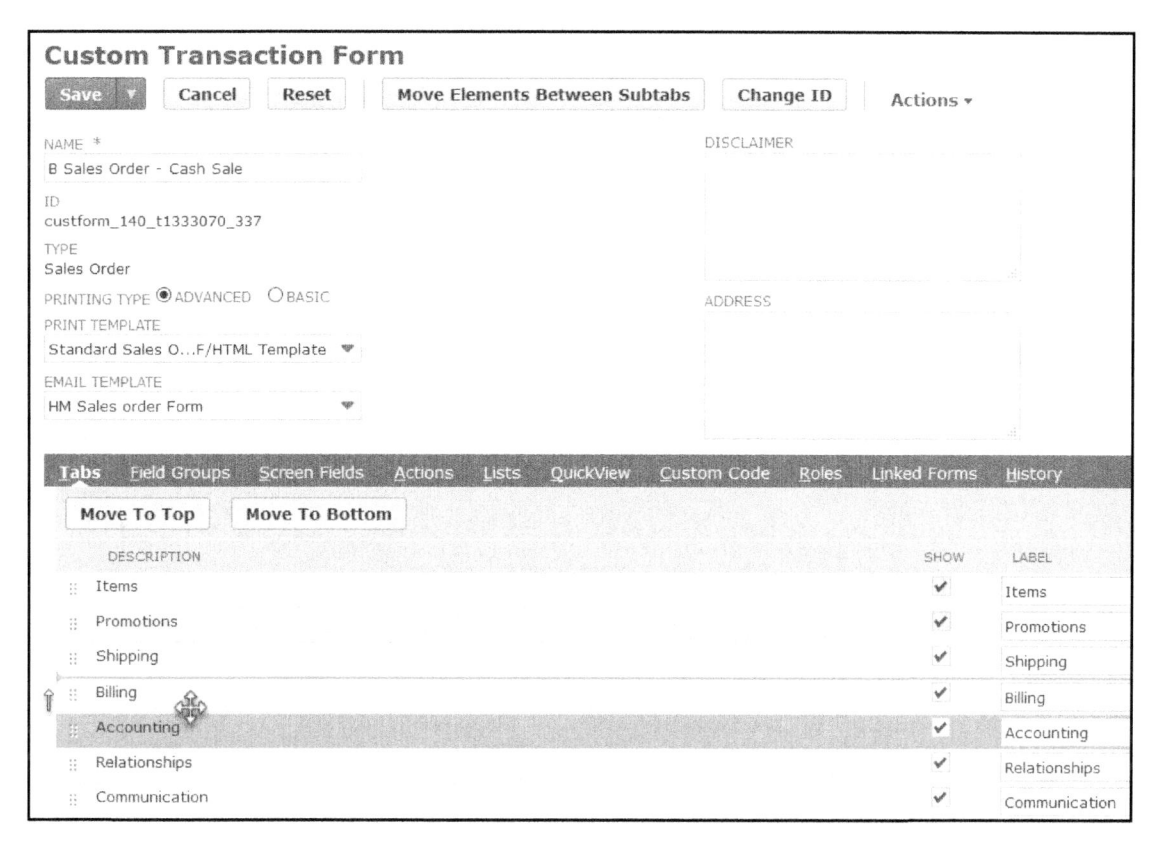

Edit Order of Tabs on Custom Transaction Form

The **Screen Fields** subtab displays the fields that can appear on the form. We can change the order of the fields by dragging and dropping in the same way as we do for the **Tabs**, and decide whether to show the field by toggling that checkbox. There is also a **Mandatory** checkbox to ensure that this field will be entered when filling out this form. Beware of making too many fields mandatory, otherwise, you risk frustrating the user to the point where they make any selection just to be able to save the record and move on, thereby affecting the integrity of the data.

Customization

The **DISPLAY TYPE** field provides three options: **Normal**, **Inline text**, and **Disabled**. Normal is used to enter and edit data in that field, while inline text displays the data in that field as read-only for anyone accessing this form. It is not possible to edit a disabled field–it is used for making calculations on this form.

We can set defaults for checkboxes on this form by selecting the field row in the **CHECK BOX DEFAULT** column. We can also change the label that will appear next to that field on the form, and we can change the section that this field will appear in on the form using the **FIELD GROUP** column:

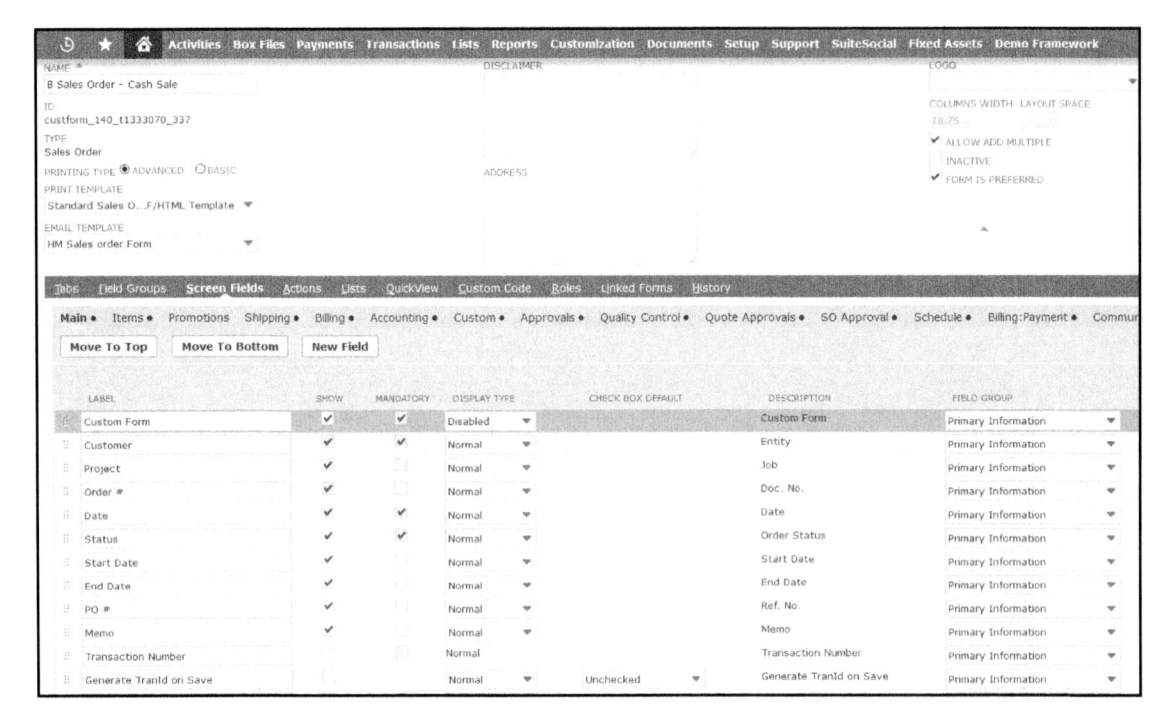

Edit the field that can appear on Custom Transaction Form

[168]

Chapter 6

In many cases, multiple forms are used to show and hide data to and from different roles. The **Roles** subtab enables you to set this form as preferred by role, as opposed to the preferred form for the entire company. The standard form may be preferred for all roles whereas the **Sales Rep SO Form** will be the preferred form for the **Inside Sales** role only:

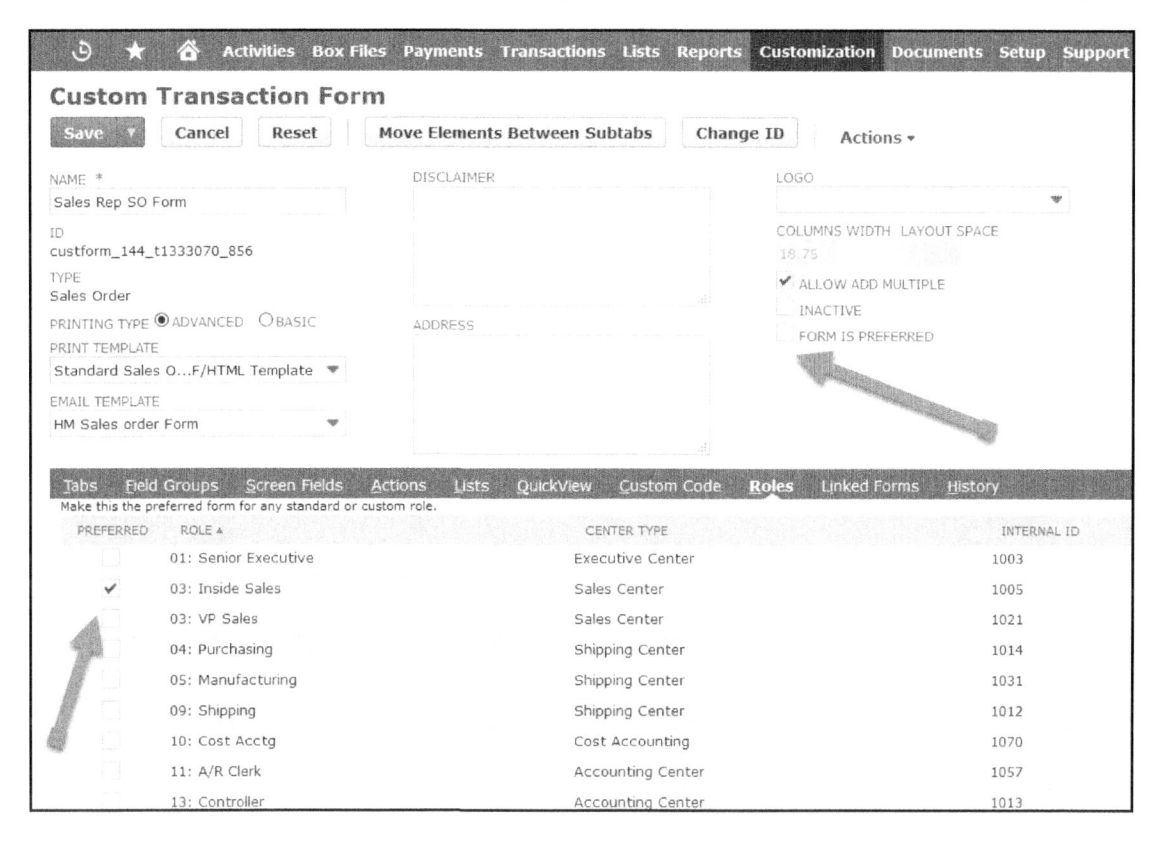

Set Custom Form as Preferred for all users or by Role

Advanced PDF/HTML layouts

Advanced PDF/HTML layouts are located at **Customization** | **Forms** | **Advanced PDF/HTML Templates**. It lists the prebuilt templates, as well as any custom templates that we have created by customizing a standard template. The **TYPE** field shows the record that each template is associated with, and the preferred column, the template that is assigned by default to any new transaction forms of that type. The key word is `new` because the selection is not retroactive. If you wish to change the print template of the existing transaction forms, you'll need to return to the transaction form after finalizing the custom PDF/HTML layout and select your new version as the new print template:

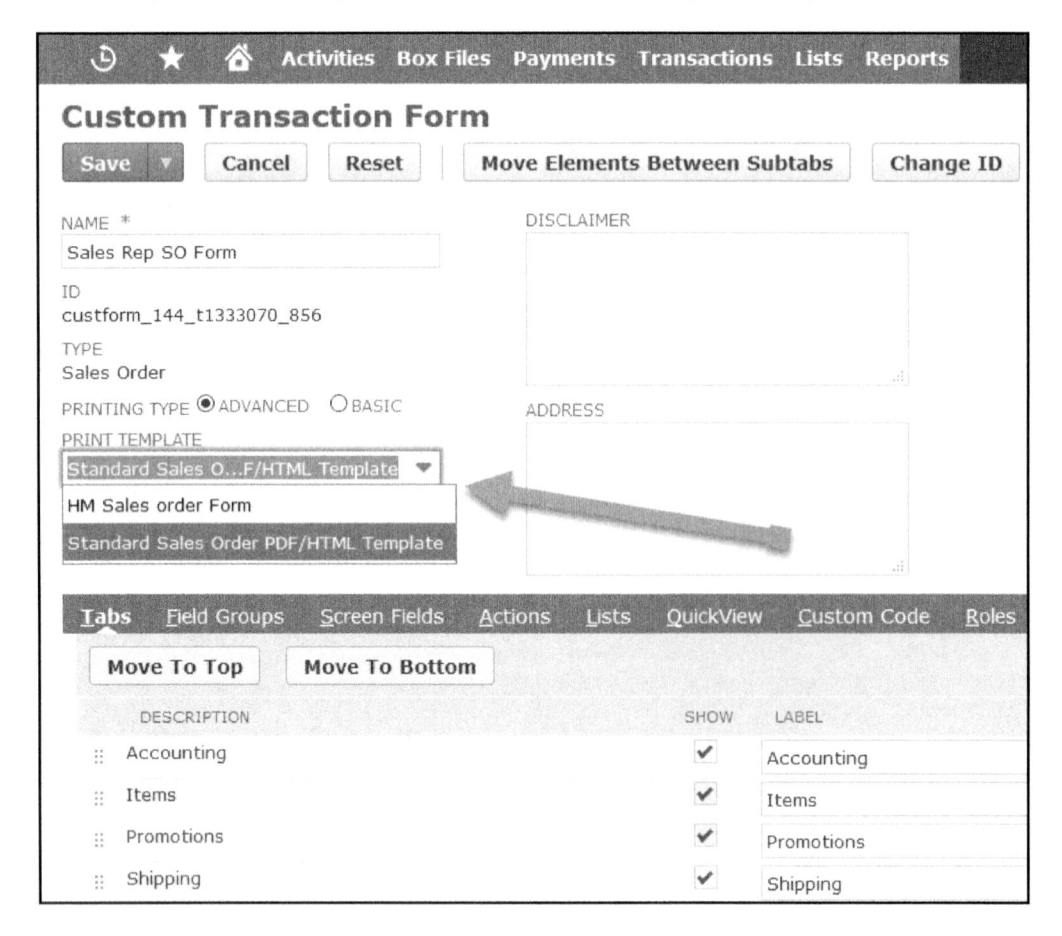

Select form to Print on Custom Transaction Form

Standard PDF/HTML templates have a **Customize** button next to them, whereas a custom template has an **Edit** button. NetSuite does not allow us to overwrite a standard template, so we can always refer back to the original, if necessary. It does, however, make the process of customizing a little more cumbersome.

Start by clicking **Customization** and click the **Template Setup** option. We can then rename the template and click **Save**:

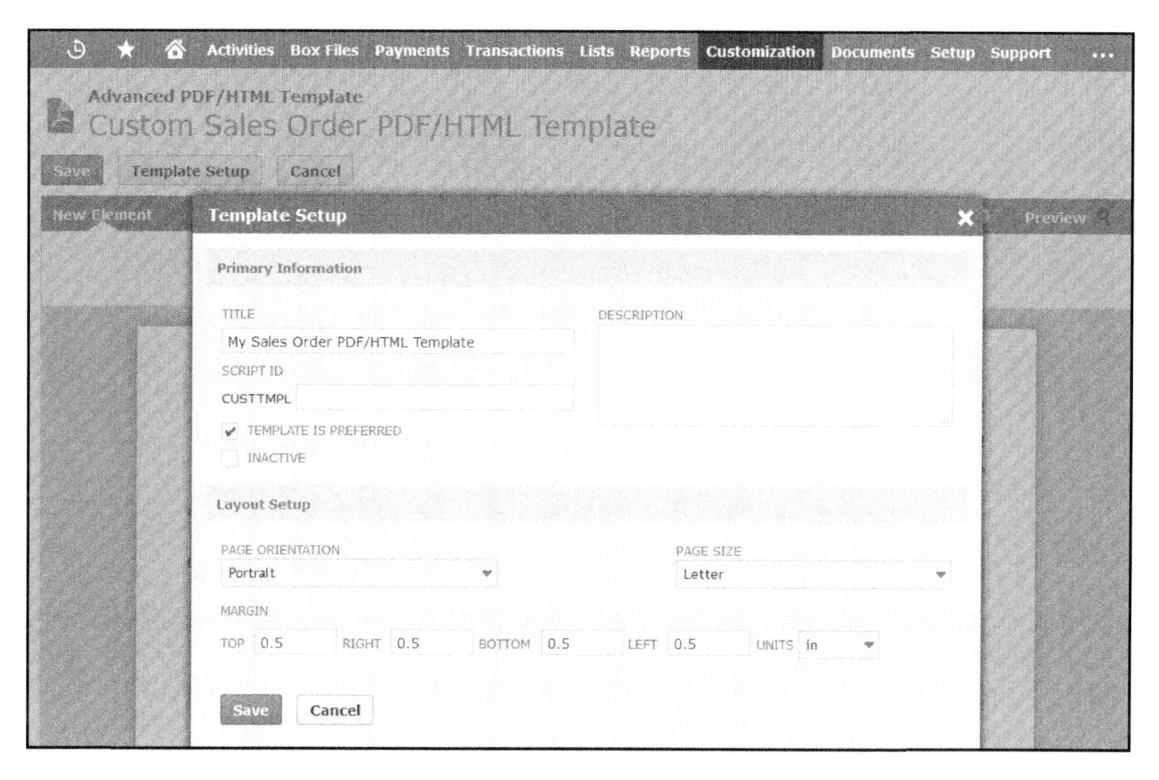

Rename Custom PDF/ HTML Form

Customization

The form itself is made up of tables that work similarly to the tables in Microsoft Word. Right-click in a cell and receive a menu to edit the cell, column, and row. Additional menus within those options allow you to insert and delete cells, rows, and columns, as well as merge cells. You can also delete the table or insert one if necessary:

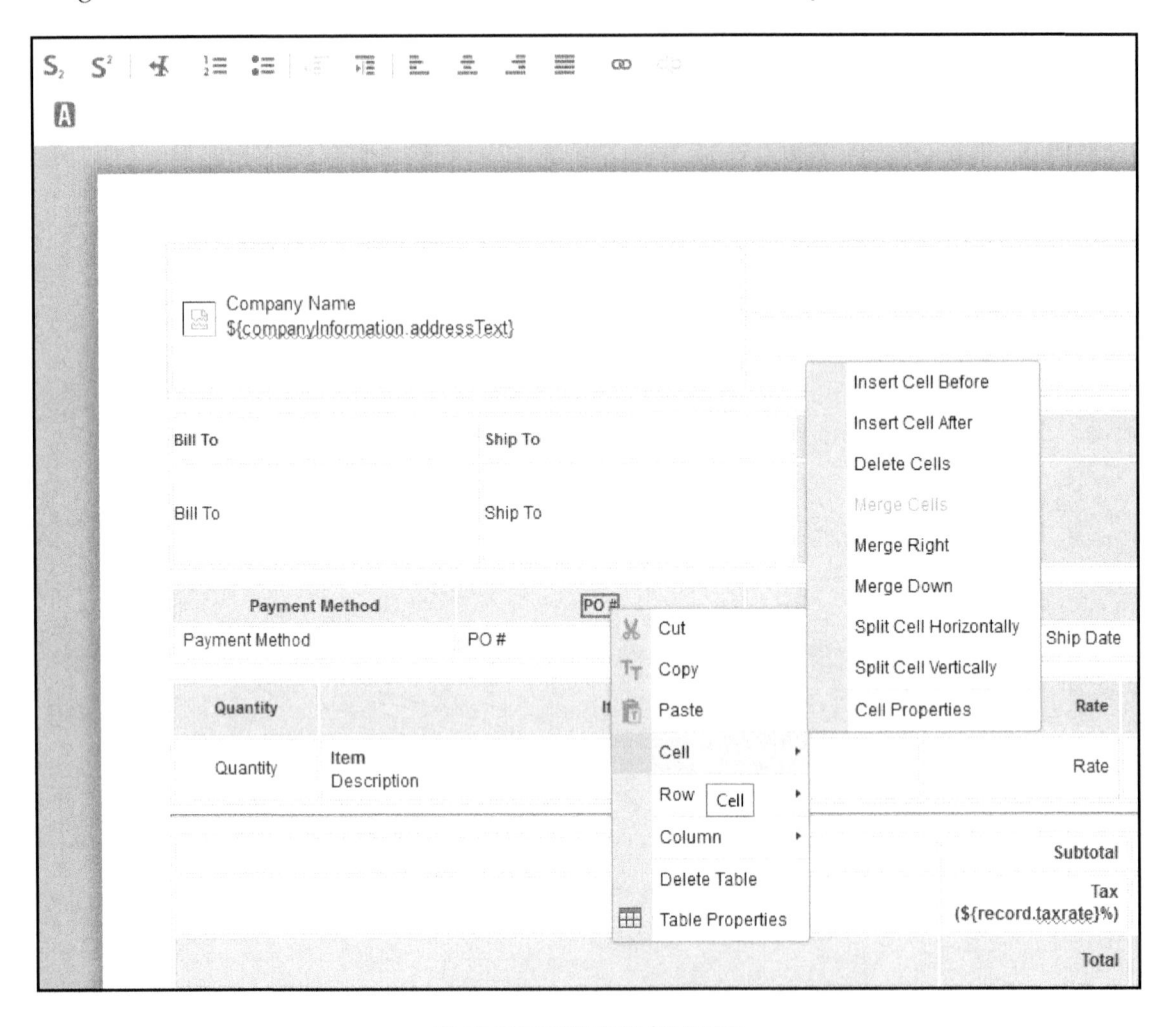

Edit cells on Custom PDF/ HTML form Template

We can control the design of the cell itself by selecting the **Cell Properties** option, such as alignment, colors, borders, and the number of rows and columns within that cell:

Chapter 6

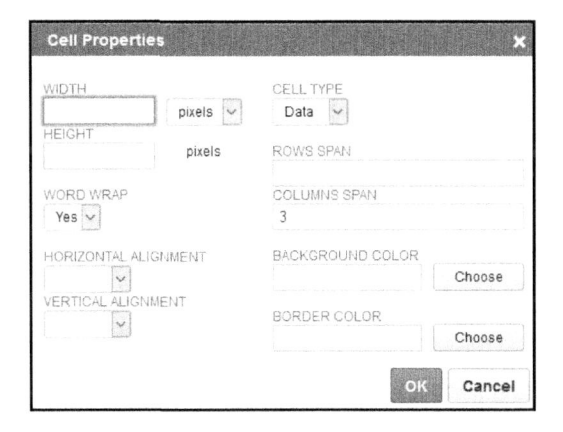

Edit cell properties

The template contains a number of fields sourcing the data directly from the transaction. We can delete fields that are not necessary on our form and insert fields by clicking on the giant + icon on the toolbar. Note that custom fields will also appear in the list so can be placed on your printed forms:

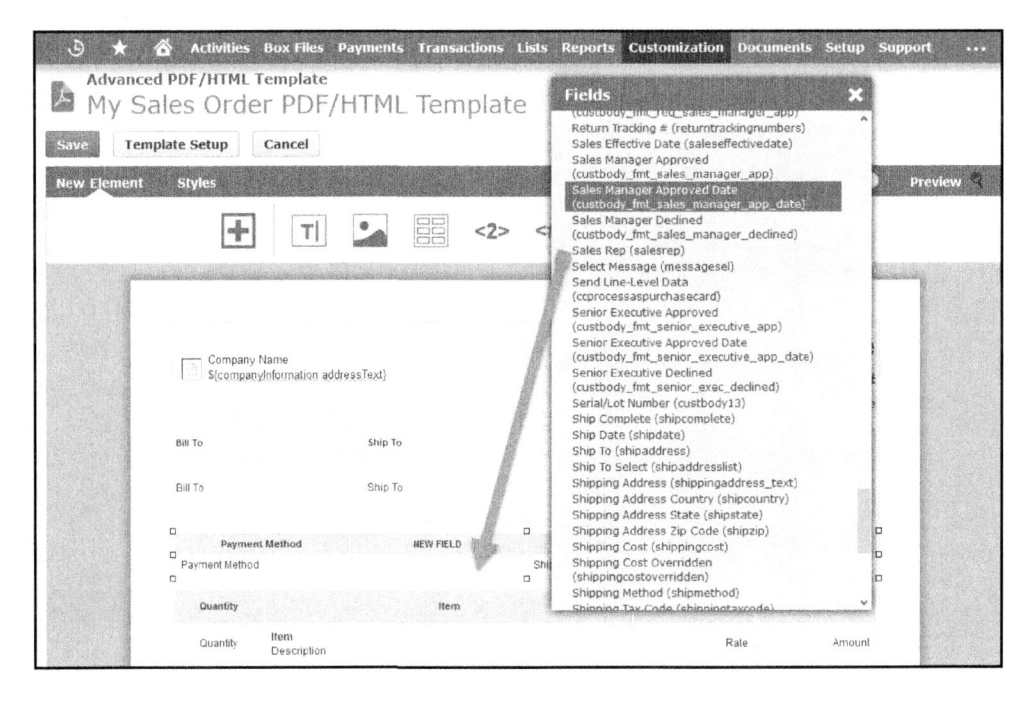

Add Field to appear on printed form

[173]

Customization

The toolbar is made up of additional icons to add text, images, and tables. The image option allows you to reference image URLs that will be sourced into the form. We use the options on the **Styles** tab to change the font, size, color, and so on of the printed form:

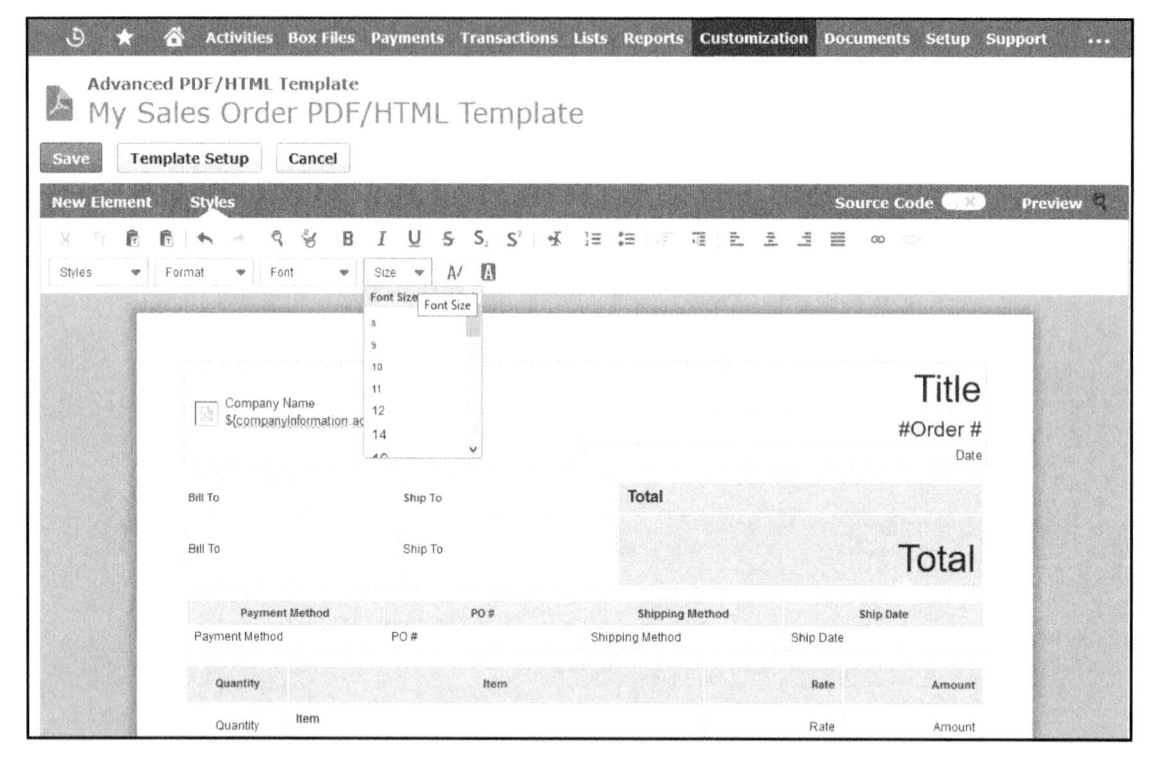

Change font size on printed form

There is also a button that will switch to the source code of the form and you can simply amend the HTML, if you're more comfortable doing so:

View HTML of custom printed form

Customizing the advanced PDF/HMTL layouts can be tedious, so it's best to make small incremental changes and click the preview button, in order to see whether your change has the results you expected. If it has, save the form and come back in to edit it to take the next step. Sometimes the edit results in a catastrophic error and the preview cannot even load. There is no need to start again. All you need do is to cancel out of the form without saving and re-edit the previously-saved version in order to continue. Believe me, it will save you a lot of time and frustration in the long run.

Summary

In this chapter, we focused on personalizing the NetSuite database to be able to record all the data that is relevant to your industry. We looked at adding fields to records and displaying them on the right forms for users to enter information. We also showed the different options that are available to make the users' job easier when entering that information, such as picklists, multi-select picklists, and checkboxes. We also looked at how to reuse information, such as existing picklists of employees, and filter that list so that it doesn't contain the values that don't apply to this record.

We created a custom record and placed it on the web for customers to fill it out on their own; we also as explored how to customize internal and external forms to display the data that needs to be entered and reviewed.

Now that we have the fields available for all our data, we'll shift focus to entering data into those fields. While this can be done manually, it is more efficient to automate the input using data imports, which we'll cover in the next chapter.

7
Imports

CSV imports are a valuable tool in the administrator's toolbox. They can be used to import new data into the database during the initial deployment or on an ongoing basis, such as when importing new leads into the system gathered from trade show. You can also use the import wizard to update existing data, such as updating the prices of your products or changing the item sold in specific transactions. They can even be used to execute workflows on existing records.

We'll start the chapter by focusing on the theory behind CSV imports and then illustrate it by importing three kinds of records.

This chapter will cover the following:

- A Review of the NetSuite Import Wizard
- Setting up the prerequisites for successful importing
- Understanding how to prepare the source data to comply with NetSuite's data requirements
- Formatting the source data
- Understanding how to map information based on the ID and name value
- Knowing how to import new data into the database and updating existing data in the database
- Understanding the mapping tools available
- Saving import templates for reuse in the future
- Troubleshooting errors

Imports

The CSV Import Assistant

The Import Assistant is, of course, a wizard, so the system will try to guide you as you start to import information into NetSuite.

NetSuite allows you to import most records, and we see the list of records by going to **Setup | Import Export | Import CSV**. We begin by choosing the type of records we need to import, for example, when importing sales orders, we will need to use **Transactions**, or if importing customers, we will need to choose **Relationships**. For items, select the item's type and then choose the subtype of that original type. In the case of items, for instance, one could choose **Inventory** item, a kit, or package, among others:

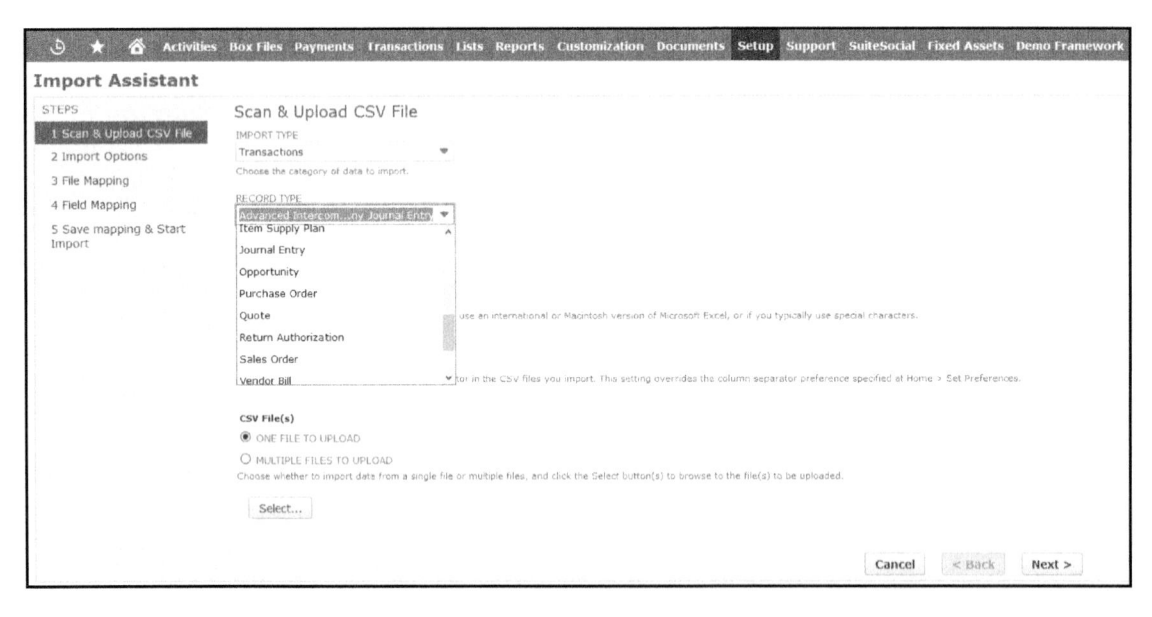

Record type selection on the Import Assistant

Select the source file, which will be a file saved as the CSV type; after all, we are using the import CSV wizard!

NetSuite performs a preliminary test for errors, so if there is a column in the source data with a blank header, it will return an error. We will not be able to proceed with that source file until we edit and amend the source file by giving that column a heading:

Chapter 7

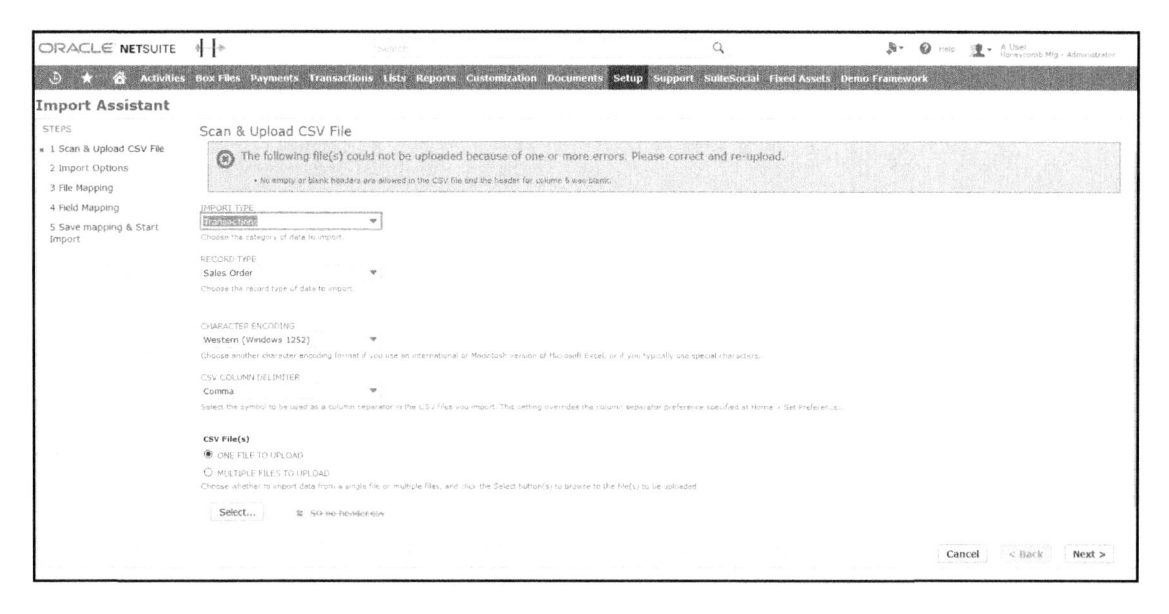

Preliminary error checking of source file

The wizard then provides options to either **ADD**, **UPDATE**, or **ADD OR UPDATE**. The first option will add these records in a new record in NetSuite, whereas the second option updates the appropriate record with new information contained in the source file.
ADD OR UPDATE really should be called update or add because NetSuite will first look to see whether it finds that particular record in the system, in which case it will update it with new information. If it does not find it, NetSuite will add it as a new record in the system:

Data-Handling option in the Import Wizard

[179]

Imports

The next step in the wizard is the mapping screen. NetSuite will try to automatically map fields for you based on the name of the column headers. It's not always correct, so I would recommend that you do a check to make sure that it is mapping to all the right fields:

Automapping on the mapping page of the Import Wizard

Automapping can be very useful, especially where you're going to be using this to update existing information. Let's assume I need to post an update to existing information, such as change the sales rep assigned to a sales territory or reclassify a set of customers. There are a few ways to accomplish this. One option is to use the inline editing as described in `Chapter 2`, *Exploring NetSuite Tools*. The second option is a mass update, which was also described in `Chapter 2`, *Exploring NetSuite Tools* (in fact, NetSuite has a specific mass update dedicated to sales-territory realignments).

Both inline editing and the mass update options are really powerful, however, they suffer from the same inherent weakness: that not all fields are exposed for inline editing and mass updating, as you can see from the following graphic showing the **Mass Update** field screen for a sales order mass update. Fields that are not on that list cannot be updated using inline editing or mass update and require a CSV import:

Chapter 7

![Mass Update screen]

Mass Update screen

The implication of auto-mapping is to build the source data using the field names already contained in NetSuite. In the case of an import to update records, create a saved search containing the records you wish to update, including the field you need to change. Export those search results to CSV and replace the old field value with the new one. Then, simply use the import wizard to import the change you made in Excel. The field mapping will be done for you automatically because the source file was initially exported from NetSuite, so it contains the same field names.

Imports

The last step in the wizard contains the option to name and save your import map prior to executing the import. This is important as it allows you to create map templates that can be reused to import data with the same structure. That saves time on future imports, as well as helping you troubleshoot errors you may encounter during an import:

Name import template and execute import

Best practices

Let's begin by reviewing some best practices that will save you a lot of time and frustration when performing your imports.

Internal IDs

My first recommendation may sound inane and irrelevant; however, I suggest the first thing you do is go to Home icon | **Set Preferences** and check the **SHOW INTERNAL IDS** checkbox:

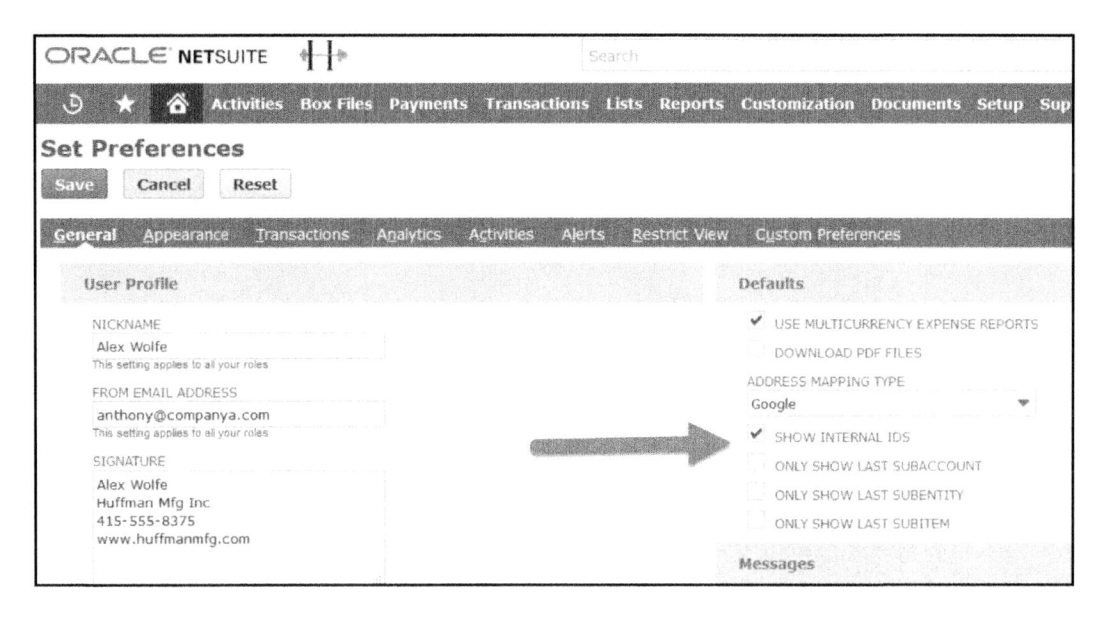

Set Preferences

The easiest way to add or update data is to use the internal ID for a record. Incidentally, you can see the internal ID of each record by looking at the URL of that record. It is easier to reference the ID than it is to reference the name of the record because you can't make spelling mistakes when referencing an ID. A name, on the other hand, can be misspelled or contain slight changes that will result in an import error, such as an extra space in the field:

Transaction internal ID

Imports

Don't worry, you don't need to identify internal IDs manually using their URLs as long as you turn on the **SHOW INTERNAL IDS** checkbox. Now each record's internal ID will appear in a list of that record. This applies equally to customers as well as picklist values, such as terms. We can, therefore, update the sales rep assigned to customer X using the internal ID of 2615, or add a new customer who has terms of **NET 30 DAYS** by referencing terms internal ID 4 instead of the words **NET 30 DAYS**.

Source data

Imports usually take a lot longer than you initially expect, and I find myself spending more time manipulating the source data than working inside the import wizard. The key to successful importing is to focus on your source data. NetSuite is very unforgiving of failure to conform with its data standards for each field. If the phone number field in 1 record out of 24,022 customer records to import contains the value **AP555-555-8896** instead of just the phone number, the entire import will be prevented from running. The same is true if it finds alphanumeric characters in an internal ID field or the lack of an @ symbol in an email field, so we need to be very precise when preparing our source data. Make sure your data is clean, precise, and consistent.

It is good practice to include a unique identifier in the source data, which is then imported into the external ID field of each record. The external ID is usually the ID of the legacy system you are importing from, however, if you don't have a unique identifier for each record being imported, then I suggest creating one. That is how important an external ID is because it identifies the record for the purposes of updates.

Importing tips

Following are some importing tips:

- There's a limit of 25,000 rows per import file so, obviously, if you have more than 25,000 in your import source file, it will result in an error. Instead, we will need to break the master file up into multiple files. This can be done manually but, in the event of an import comprising hundreds of thousands (or even millions) of lines, you can use tools, such as Kutools, to automate the breakup of the files.
- Imports are limited to executing one at a time, so they are queued and run consecutively, one after the other. There is, however, a NetSuite add-on that can be purchased, which gives us five different streams going at the same time.
- Make sure that the fields containing dollar values are formatted as numbers, and not as currency, in the source file.

- Break up your various types of items into their individual categories in order to import them correctly. **INVENTORY** items records are different from **Kit** records and different from **ASSEMBLY ITEM** records. Each record has its own specific properties and default values, so it does need to be stored in a separate source file. We can use the **Subtype** drop-down menu to view the different types of imports.

Customer import

It is important to identify whether an entity being imported is an individual or a company. Individual customers have **Firstname** and **Lastname** fields, which are missing from a company customer. That information is recorded on the contact record for a company customer. I recommend splitting entity imports into an individual file and a company file because they require different import maps.

Example 1 – Customer import use case

Let's analyze this table for import as an example:

Company	Firstname	Lastname	Email	Street address	City	State	Country	Terms
Disney	Donald	Duck	dd@disney.com	123 Main Street	Orlando	Florida	United States	Net 30
Universal	Harry	Potter	h@potter.com	905 Young Street	Orlando	FL	US	Net 30
Mi6	James	Bond	007@mi5.co.uk	100 Church Street	London		UK	Net 60
N/A	Katy	Perry	kphotmail.com	102 7th Ave	New York	NY	USA	Net 15

The values in the country field need to be changed:

- United States is named three different ways and these need to be changed to the value in NetSuite, which is United States.
- UK has been set up in NetSuite as United Kingdom, so the source data needs to be changed to mirror that value.
- The Katy Perry email address lacks the @ sign, which needs to be corrected.

- The values in the terms must already exist in NetSuite. Terms are found under **Setup | Accounting | Accounting Lists** and select terms from the drop-down menu. It's best to replace the terms with the internal ID. Export the values to Excel and then perform a VLOOKUP to replace the terms with the appropriate internal ID:

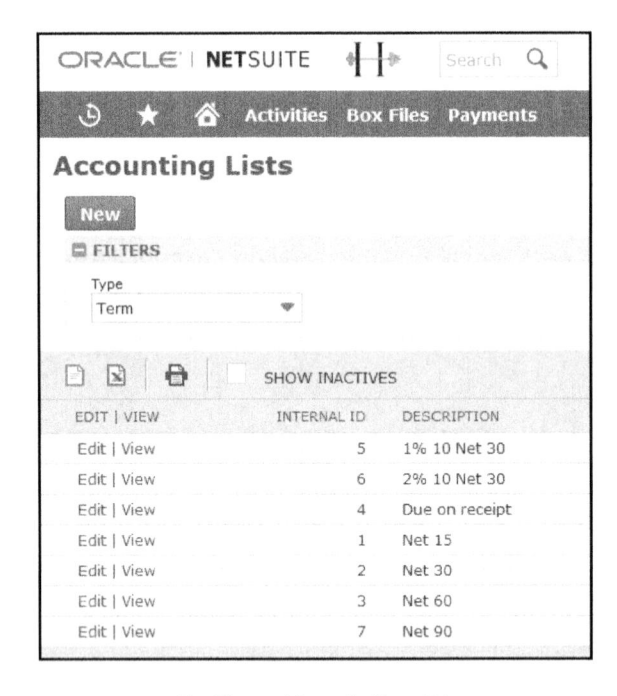

List of Terms and the associated internal ids

- The file is made up of companies and individual customers. Donald, Harry, and James work for companies, so in NetSuite terms, the company is the customer (because it is ultimately responsible for paying the bill) and the people are contacts at that company. Katy, on the other hand, is an individual so should be placed in a separate file.

The resulting files look as follows after the data has been manipulated:

File 1: Companies and Contacts

Company	Firstname	Lastname	Email	Street address	City	State	Country	Terms
Disney	Donald	Duck	dd@disney.com	123 Main Street	Orlando	FL	United States	2
Universal	Harry	Potter	h@potter.com	905 Young Street	Orlando	FL	United States	2

| Mi6 | James | Bond | 007@mi6.co.uk | 100 Church Street | London | | United Kingdom | 3 |

File 2: Individuals

Firstname	Lastname	email	Street address	City	State	Country	Terms
Katy	Perry	kp@hotmail.com	102 7th Ave	New York	NY	United States	1

Perform the following steps to import companies and contacts:

1. Go to **Setup** | **Imports & Exports** | **Import CSV records**.
2. Select **Relationships** from the **IMPORT TYPE** field.
3. Select **Customers And Contacts Together** from the subtype.
4. Browse to and select the company file:

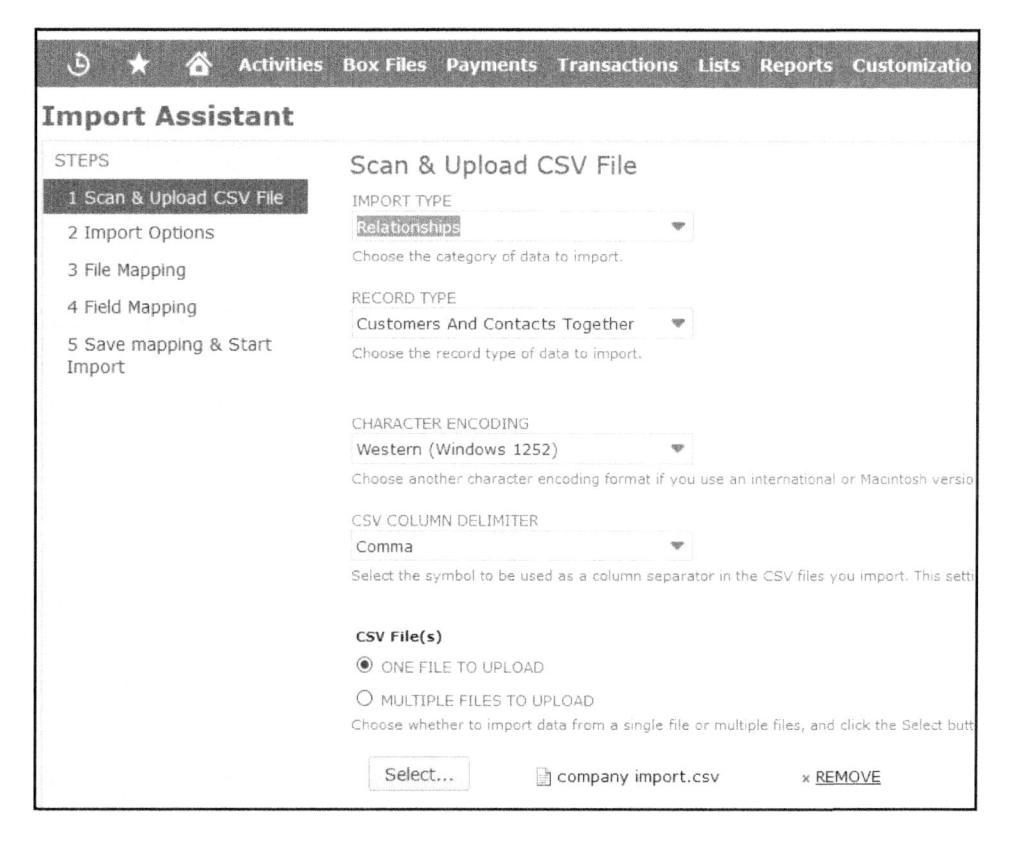

Select the source file to be imported

[187]

Imports

5. Click **Next**.
6. We are looking to add records to the database, so select the add radio button and click **Next**.
7. We perform the mapping in the fourth step of the wizard:
   1. Review the mandatory fields, which are signified by a suffix (req) and ensure they are filled out. We can map a field from our source data by dragging and dropping it into the middle of the screen. Alternatively, we can set a default value by clicking the pencil icon on the left of the source field and typing in the value that will apply for all records imported using this map:

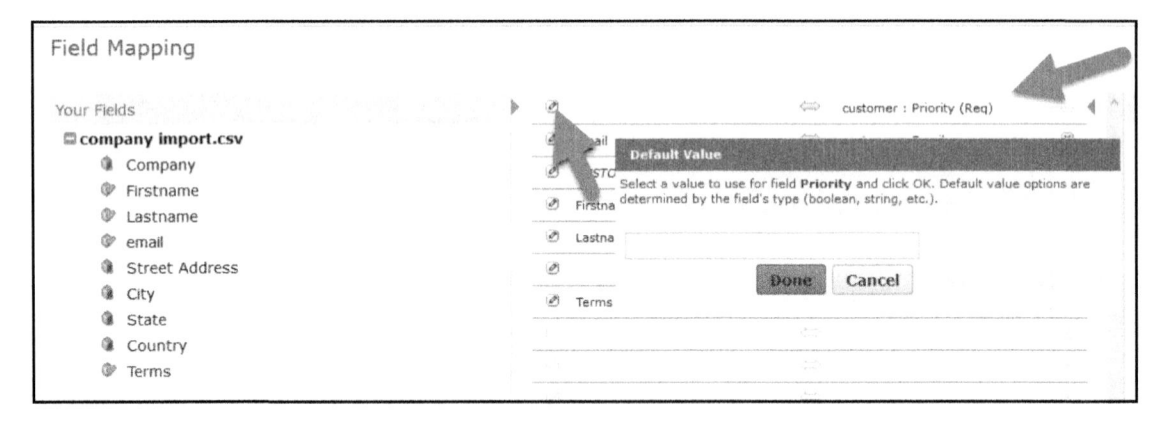

Set a Default Value on a field in the import

   2. Map the remaining fields from the source list to the NetSuite list by dragging and dropping the selections into a new line.

[188]

3. The **Firstname** and **Lastname** are incorrectly mapped by default, as NetSuite has mapped these fields to the customer first and last name. This is a company import, however, so the customer is the company and the first and last names belong to the contacts or people that work at the company. We find the contacts in the contact folder that is listed under the customer folder. Minimize the customer folder, scroll down to the contact folder on the right, and map the first and last name to the values of the source data:

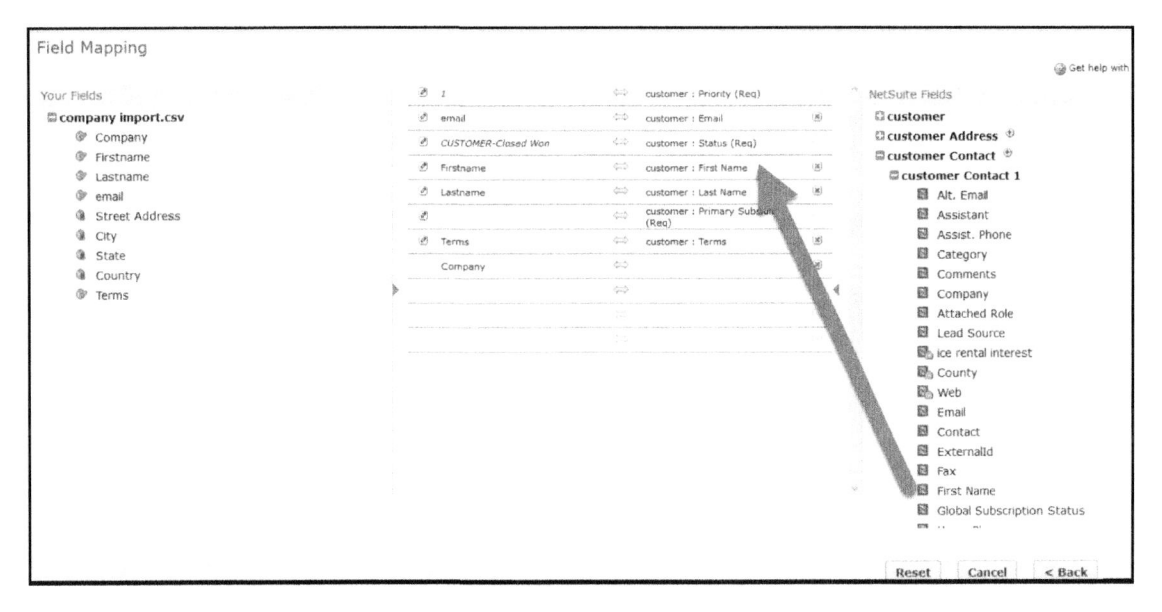

Mapping from the source file to NetSuite fields

4. Drag and drop the **Company** field from the source file on to a new line and map it to the **Company** field on the NetSuite customer folder.
5. The address fields are found in the address folder in NetSuite. Open the folder and map the address fields from the source to NetSuite.

Imports

5. The reason for the folder structure is that customers may have more than one address, for instance, a shipping address that is different from the billing address. In that case, the addresses would be set in additional columns in the source data. We can map the first address to the customer **Address 1** folder and select the **Default Shipping** field and set the default to **Yes**. Add the billing address by clicking the + sign to add an additional customer address folder (customer **Address 2**). The billing address from the source would be mapped to the fields in customer **Address 2** and default billing would be set to the default of **Yes**:

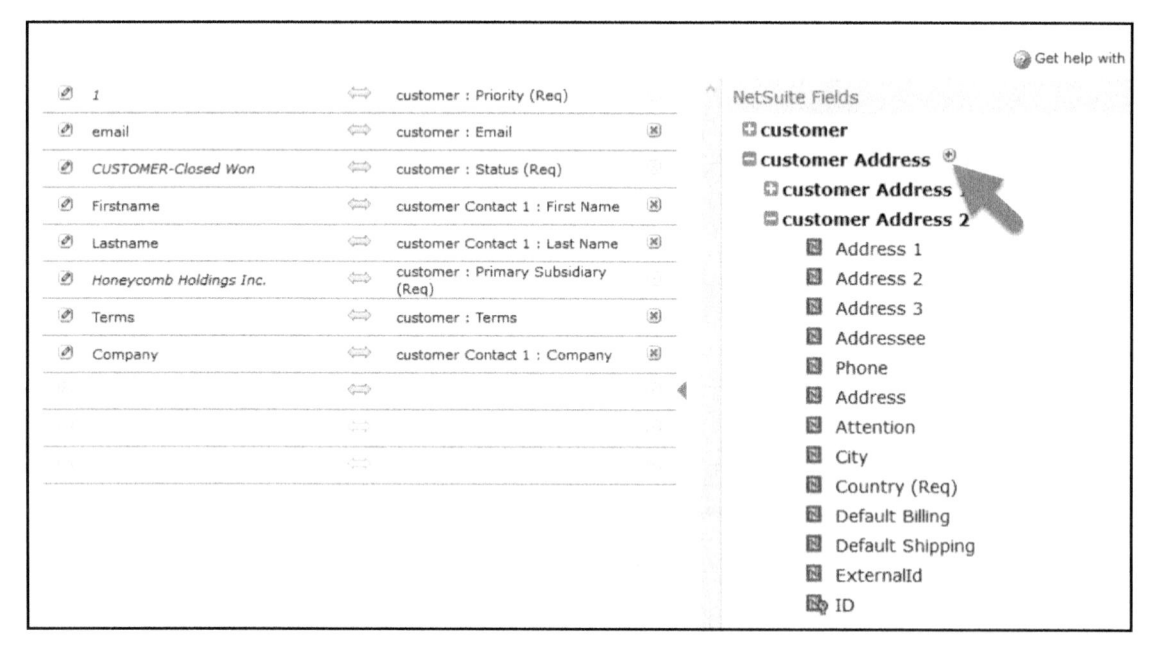

1	⇔	customer : Priority (Req)	
email	⇔	customer : Email	✕
CUSTOMER-Closed Won	⇔	customer : Status (Req)	
Firstname	⇔	customer Contact 1 : First Name	✕
Lastname	⇔	customer Contact 1 : Last Name	✕
Honeycomb Holdings Inc.	⇔	customer : Primary Subsidiary (Req)	
Terms	⇔	customer : Terms	✕
Company	⇔	customer Contact 1 : Company	✕

NetSuite Fields
- customer
- customer Address ⊕
  - customer Address 1
  - customer Address 2
    - Address 1
    - Address 2
    - Address 3
    - Addressee
    - Phone
    - Address
    - Attention
    - City
    - Country (Req)
    - Default Billing
    - Default Shipping
    - ExternalId
    - ID

Mapping multiple address records

7. The terms field has been mapped, however, we used the **Terms** internal ID in our source data, instead of the name. This must be reflected in the map in order for NetSuite to be matched on internal ID instead of name. We do so by clicking the pencil icon next to terms and choosing internal ID from the drop-down menu:

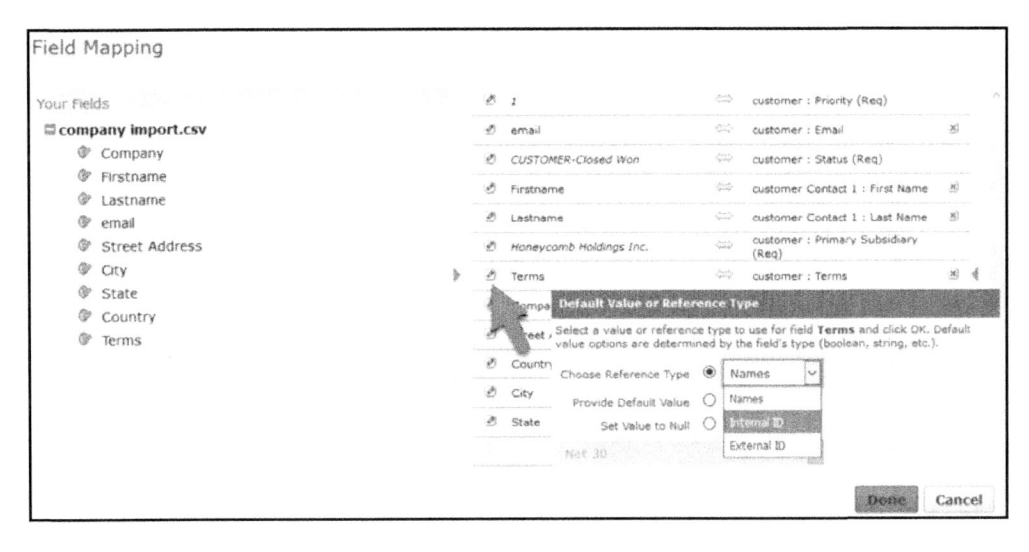

Change reference from Name to Internal ID

8. The mapping will look like this now that we are finished. Click **Next**.

Import Mapping screen

Imports

9. We can now choose to name our import map template, click **Save and Run** to save the template and run the import.

In some imports, it is preferable to break up the data into multiple source files, such as assemblies and kits. Both assemblies and kits are made up of components. The first file will store the assembly or kit information, whereas the second file will store the component information. The two files are linked together using a primary key contained in both files:

Import using multiple source files

Test the import map with a small subset of records. Troubleshoot the errors until you get the import just right, then reuse the import template you've been tweaking through the testing, and apply it to the full import.

If your import includes references to other records, ensure that those records exist prior to your import. As simple as this sounds, we sometimes forget this in the midst of an import; for instance, a customer import that references the parent company (for example, Walmart in Kalamazoo is the child of Walmart Corporate in Bentonville, AK) requires the parent to be already in the system. If both records are in the same source file, ensure that the parent appears in the list before the child.

Item import

Now, we'll look at an item import. Let's review the following file to be imported:

	A	B	C	D	E	F
1	SKU	Name	Description	Wholesale Price	Retail Price	
2	C1	Computer Desktop		750	800	
3	P1	Printer		100	150	
4	M1	Monitor		200	220	
5	B1	Bluetooth Keyboard		50	75	
6	C2	Computer Bundle	Made up of C1, P1, M1 & B1	999	1050	

Item import source file

This is essentially a kit import because the **Computer Bundle** is a Kit, made up of a **Computer Desktop, Printer, Monitor,** and **Bluetooth Keyboard**. Our first step is to check whether the components already exist in the database. Assuming they do not, we will need to execute two imports containing three files in order to accomplish this.

Inventory import

We will import the components of the Kit as inventory items and the inventory source file will look like this:

A	B	C	D	E
SKU	Name	Description	Wholesale Price	Retail Price
C1	Computer Desktop		750	800
P1	Printer		100	150
M1	Monitor		200	220
B1	Bluetooth Keyboard		50	75

Manipulated source file containing inventory components of the Kit

This file needs to be saved and imported as inventory items:

1. Save as the file type as CSV.
2. Go to **Setup | Company | Import /Export | Import CSV records**.
3. Select **Type Item**, **Subtype of Inventory**.
4. Select the file and click **Next**.
5. Choose **Add** and click **Next**.
6. Map the required fields, such as tax schedule, or select a default value.
7. Map the remaining fields.
8. Use the pricing folder to enter pricing information by adding the pricing fields. Select the appropriate default for the **Price Level** field:

Chapter 7

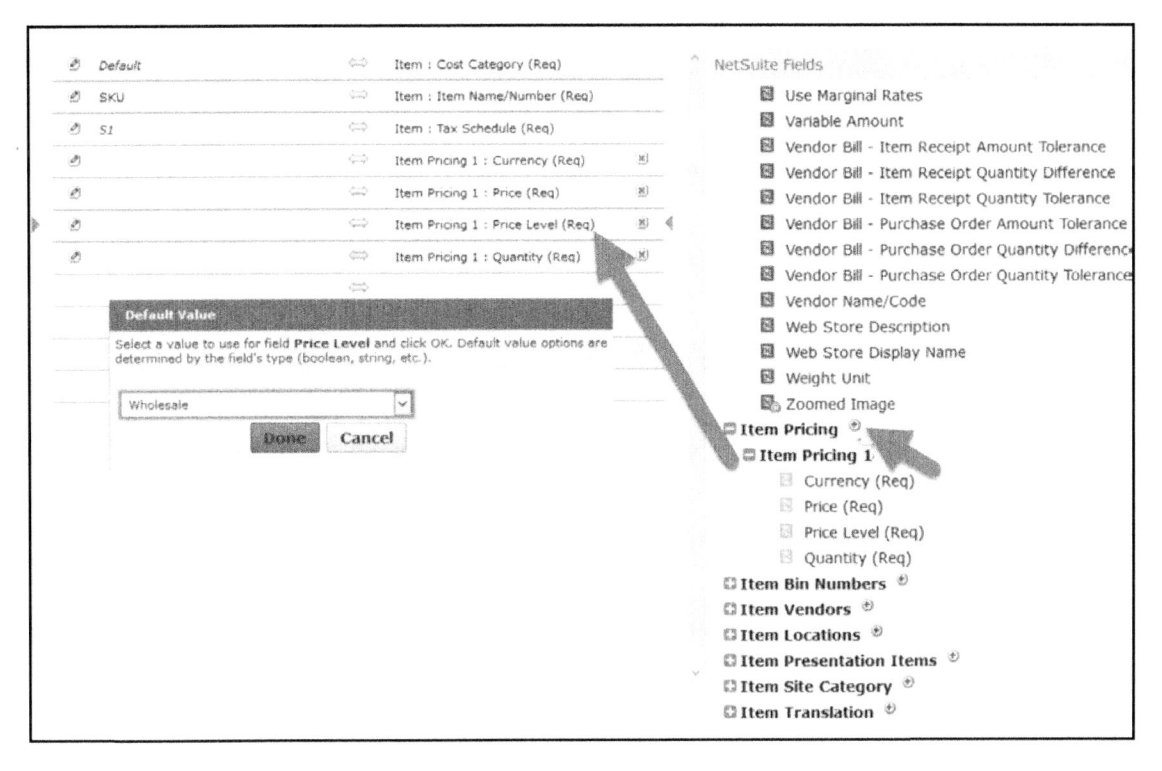

Importing multiple price levels

9. Add additional item prices for all the pricing columns in the source data.
10. Click **Next**.
11. Name the import template and click **Save and Run**.

Imports

Kit import

We can focus on importing the Kit now that the components are in the system. The Kit should be separated into two files, one for the Kit and another for the components. Each file needs to have one field that links the components to the kit. The files look like this:

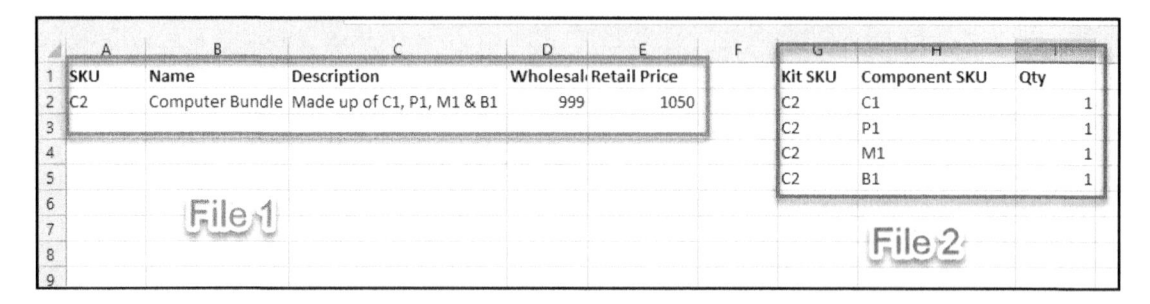

SKU	Name	Description	Wholesale	Retail Price		Kit SKU	Component SKU	Qty
C2	Computer Bundle	Made up of C1, P1, M1 & B1	999	1050		C2	C1	1
						C2	P1	1
						C2	M1	1
						C2	B1	1
	File 1						File 2	

Kit items (File 1) linked to the Kit components (File 2)

Both files need to be added to the import. **File 1** creates the kit item whereas **File 2** links the kit to its component inventory items:

1. Save both files as the type CSV.
2. Go to **Setup | Company | Import /Export | Import CSV records**.
3. Select type **Item** and subtype of **Kit/ Packaged Item**.
4. Choose multiple files to upload. Select the `kit file` as the main file and select the `components` file as **Item Members**. Click **Next**:

Scan & Upload CSV File

IMPORT TYPE
Items
Choose the category of data to import.

RECORD TYPE
Kit/Package Item
Choose the record type of data to import.

CHARACTER ENCODING
Western (Windows 1252)
Choose another character encoding format if you use an international or Macintosh version of Microsoft Excel, or if you typically use special characters.

CSV COLUMN DELIMITER
Comma
Select the symbol to be used as a column separator in the CSV files you import. This setting overrides the column separator preference specified at Home > Set

CSV File(s)
○ ONE FILE TO UPLOAD
⦿ MULTIPLE FILES TO UPLOAD
Choose whether to import data from a single file or multiple files, and click the Select button(s) to browse to the file(s) to be uploaded.

Primary File - Item	Select...	kit file.csv	× REMOVE
Linked File (Optional) - Item Pricing	Select...		
Linked File (Optional) - Item Members	Select...	components.csv	× REMOVE
Linked File (Optional) - Item Presentation Items	Select...		
Linked File (Optional) - Item Site Category	Select...		

Selection of multiple source files for import

5. Choose **Add** and click **Next**.

6. Choose the primary key from each file to link the multiple files together:

Link values in source file via a primary key

7. Map the required fields, such as **Tax Schedule**, or select a default value.
8. Map the remaining fields while ensuring that the fields are being mapped from the correct folder. The item name/number field is in the header information so it is in `File 1` of the source files, and in the `Item` folder in NetSuite. The members, however, are contained in `File 2` of the source files, so be sure it has been added to the map. The remaining components fields are added from the `Item Members` folder on the right, such as quantity, which maps to **Qty** in `File 2`.
9. Map the pricing fields in the same way as the previous example import, using the item pricing folder from the list of NetSuite fields. `Folder 1` will use the `Pricing Folder 1`.

10. Add a second pricing folder to map the retail price information:

Import Mapping screen in Import Wizard

11. Click **Next**.
12. Name and click **Save and Run**.

Transaction import

I'm going to focus on an update as the transaction import. Let's assume we need to change a specific item that appears on sales orders, such as `Product A rev. 1` needs to replaced by `Product 1 rev. 2` on all open sales orders.

Updates are best done by starting with the data that is already in the system. Create a saved search to identify the data you are looking to update with the plan to export the data, manipulate it in Excel, and then re-upload the changes. The internal ID of the transaction will be used to ensure that the correct record is being updated.

Imports

There are two options to update the line level of a transaction. The first option is to overwrite the entire line level with the information in the source file. This works especially well when there is only one line on each sales order and it is the line item that we want to replace. The key is to use the **OVERWRITE SUBLISTS** option in step 2 of the import wizard, which will overwrite the entire sublist of line items with the information in the source file:

Overwrite sublists option

The second option is to replace the individual line item only. This is done by identifying the line of the specific line item that needs to be replaced. The hard work is done by identifying the line ID when creating the saved search. We will be covering saved searches in depth in Chapter 8, *Analytics – Searches, Reports, and the Dashboard*. Suffice to say, the key is to include a criteria filter of **Main Line** = "**No**" and add the **Line ID** field in the **Results** of the saved search:

Chapter 7

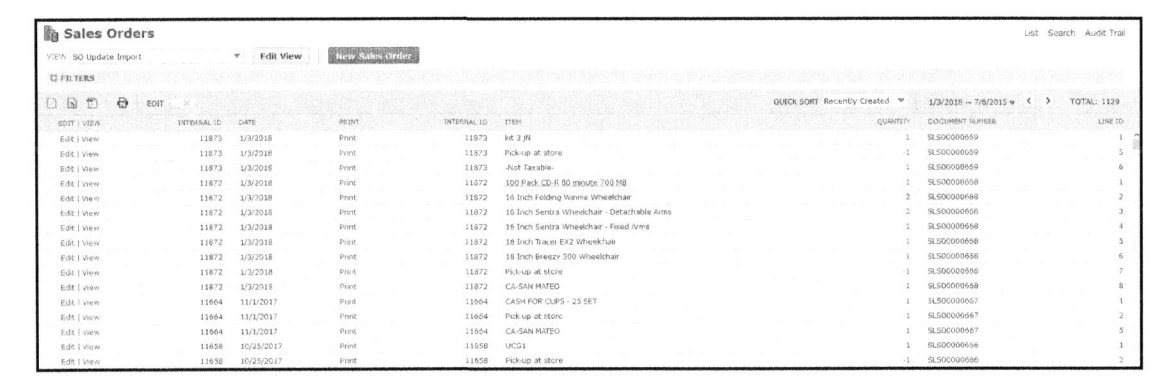

Saved Search results

The result is to show us the ID of the line, which we will use to update that line item:

Add the Line ID to the saved search to produce the export file

[201]

Imports

We can then export the search to CSV and remove all lines that do not need to be updated. Then, identify the internal ID for the new item that will replace the old item on the sales order. Create a new column and give it a heading of **New Item Internal ID** and copy that internal ID to all the rows in the file. Then simply re-import the same file.

The CSV file that will be imported will look like this:

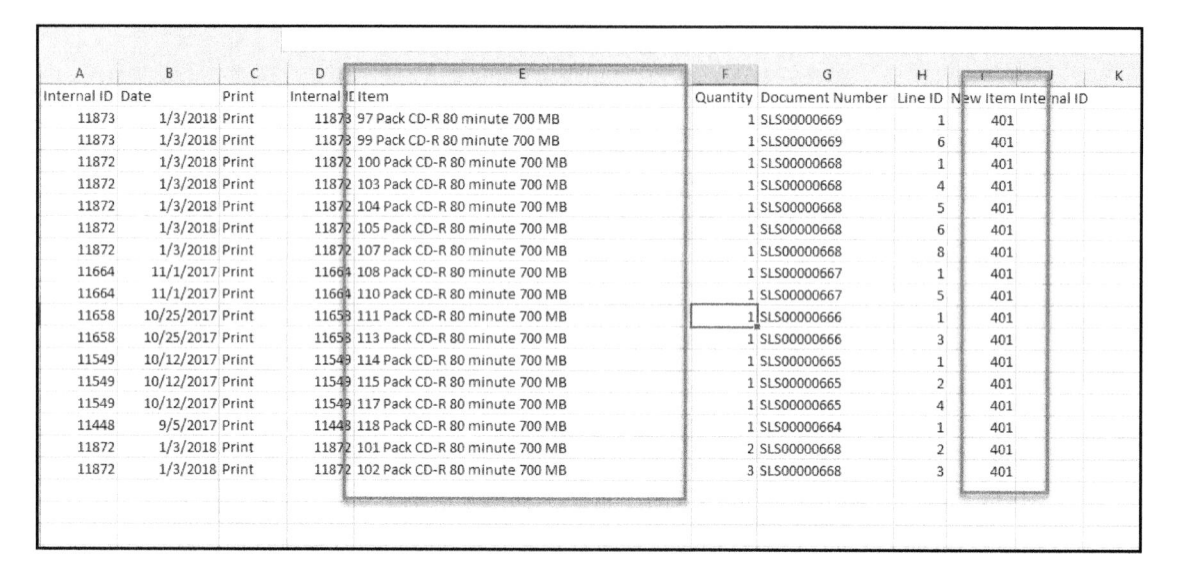

Internal ID	Date	Print	Internal ID	Item	Quantity	Document Number	Line ID	New Item Internal ID
11873	1/3/2018	Print	11873	97 Pack CD-R 80 minute 700 MB	1	SLS00000669	1	401
11873	1/3/2018	Print	11873	99 Pack CD-R 80 minute 700 MB	1	SLS00000669	6	401
11872	1/3/2018	Print	11872	100 Pack CD-R 80 minute 700 MB	1	SLS00000668	1	401
11872	1/3/2018	Print	11872	103 Pack CD-R 80 minute 700 MB	1	SLS00000668	4	401
11872	1/3/2018	Print	11872	104 Pack CD-R 80 minute 700 MB	1	SLS00000668	5	401
11872	1/3/2018	Print	11872	105 Pack CD-R 80 minute 700 MB	1	SLS00000668	6	401
11872	1/3/2018	Print	11872	107 Pack CD-R 80 minute 700 MB	1	SLS00000668	8	401
11664	11/1/2017	Print	11664	108 Pack CD-R 80 minute 700 MB	1	SLS00000667	1	401
11664	11/1/2017	Print	11664	110 Pack CD-R 80 minute 700 MB	1	SLS00000667	5	401
11658	10/25/2017	Print	11658	111 Pack CD-R 80 minute 700 MB	1	SLS00000666	1	401
11658	10/25/2017	Print	11658	113 Pack CD-R 80 minute 700 MB	1	SLS00000666	3	401
11549	10/12/2017	Print	11549	114 Pack CD-R 80 minute 700 MB	1	SLS00000665	1	401
11549	10/12/2017	Print	11549	115 Pack CD-R 80 minute 700 MB	1	SLS00000665	2	401
11549	10/12/2017	Print	11549	117 Pack CD-R 80 minute 700 MB	1	SLS00000665	4	401
11448	9/5/2017	Print	11448	118 Pack CD-R 80 minute 700 MB	1	SLS00000664	1	401
11872	1/3/2018	Print	11872	101 Pack CD-R 80 minute 700 MB	2	SLS00000668	2	401
11872	1/3/2018	Print	11872	102 Pack CD-R 80 minute 700 MB	3	SLS00000668	3	401

Export file referencing the Line ID of the item on the transaction

We will now import the file to update the specific line items on the transaction:

1. Go to **Setup** | **Import/Export** | **Import CSV records**.
2. Select type: **Transaction** and subtype: **Sales Order**.
3. Select the source file by browsing to it on your computer and click **Next**.

4. Select **UPDATE**. Ensure that **OVERWRITE SUBLISTS** has not been checked because doing so will overwrite the entire transaction with the new item, as opposed to merely updating one line item on the transaction:

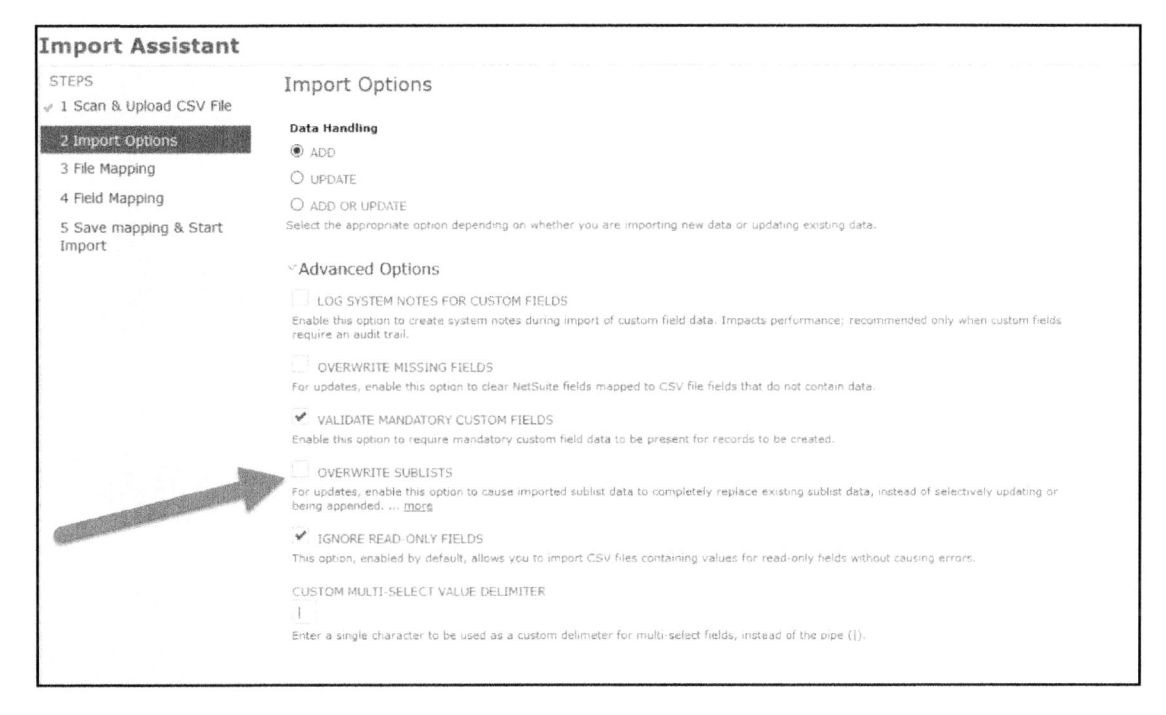

Update a line instead of all line items by unchecking 'Overwrite Sublists'

Imports

5. Map the **Sales Order** item from NetSuite to the **New Item Internal ID** in the source data and click the pencil icon to change the matching criteria from **Names** to **Internal ID**:

Match on Internal ID

6. Ensure that the (**Transaction**) **Internal ID** is mapped to the **Sales Order: Internal ID**, the **Quantity** is mapped to **Sales Order Items: Quantity**, and **Line ID** is mapped to **Sales Order Items: Line Id**:

Chapter 7

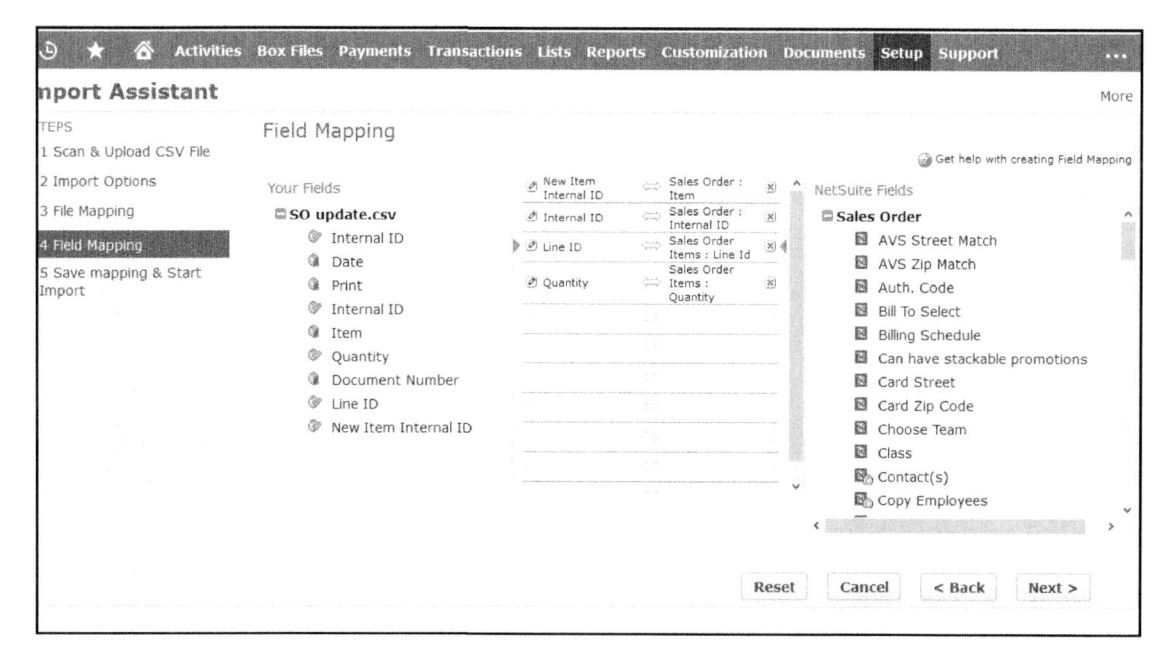

Final Mapping

7. Click **Next**.
8. Name the import template.
9. Click **Save and Run**.

Edge cases

Imports are so powerful, they can often help us automate processes in many different situations.

[205]

Imports

Change a transaction form via import

Transaction forms are typically saved with the transaction itself. The form is selected from the **CUSTOM FORM** field on entering the transaction. If no selection is made, the preferred form is used and is saved with the transaction record:

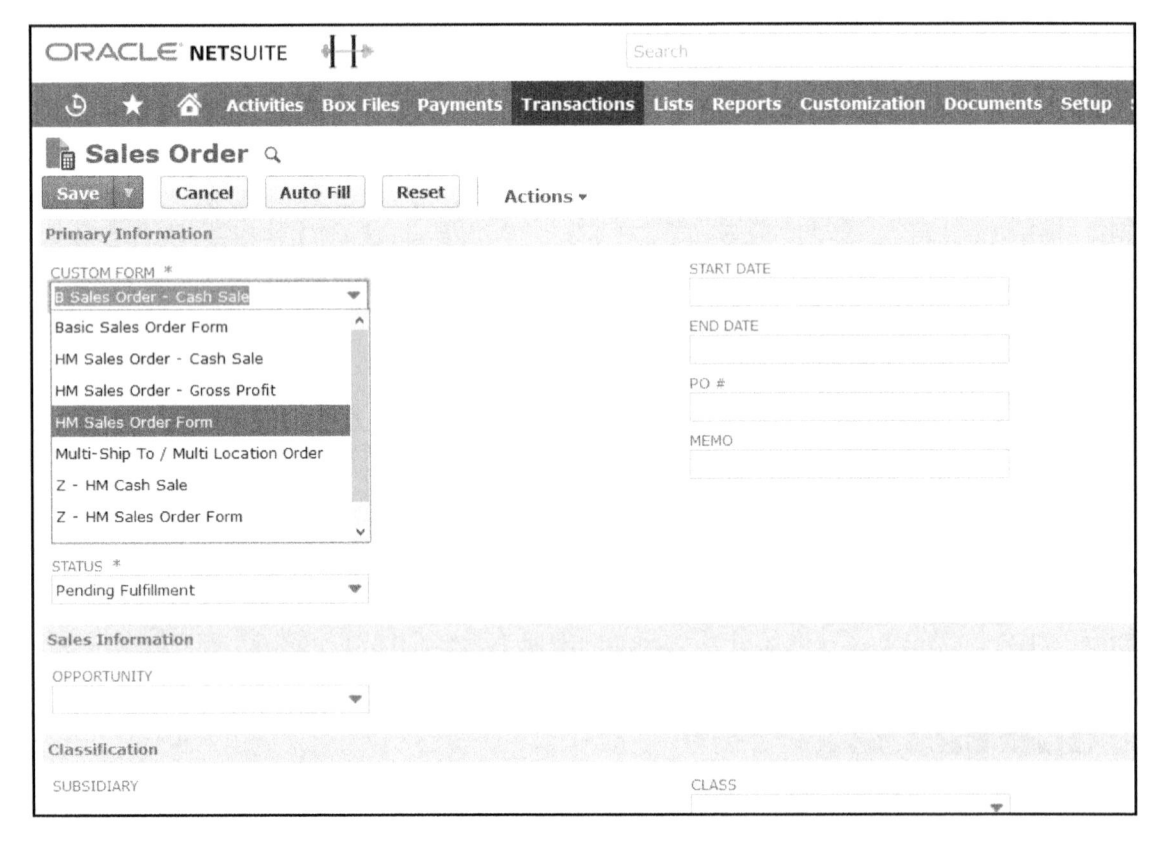

Custom form selection on a transaction

There are occasions where we may need to change the form that was originally selected in order to display or hide specific fields from our users. Our first option would be to edit each individual transaction and select the new form that needs to be used but, if you prefer spending your weekends on more exciting activities, we can use the CSV import wizard to mass update all of those transactions:

1. Export a list of the transactions that need to be changed to a CSV file.
2. Go to **Setup** | **Import/Export** | **Import CSV**.

3. Select **Transaction** from the import type and select the subtype of the transaction, for instance, **Sales Order.**
4. Select the file that was just exported and click **Next**.
5. Select **Update** from **Data Handling**.
6. Open **Advanced Options** and select the correct form from the **CUSTOM FORM** dropdown:

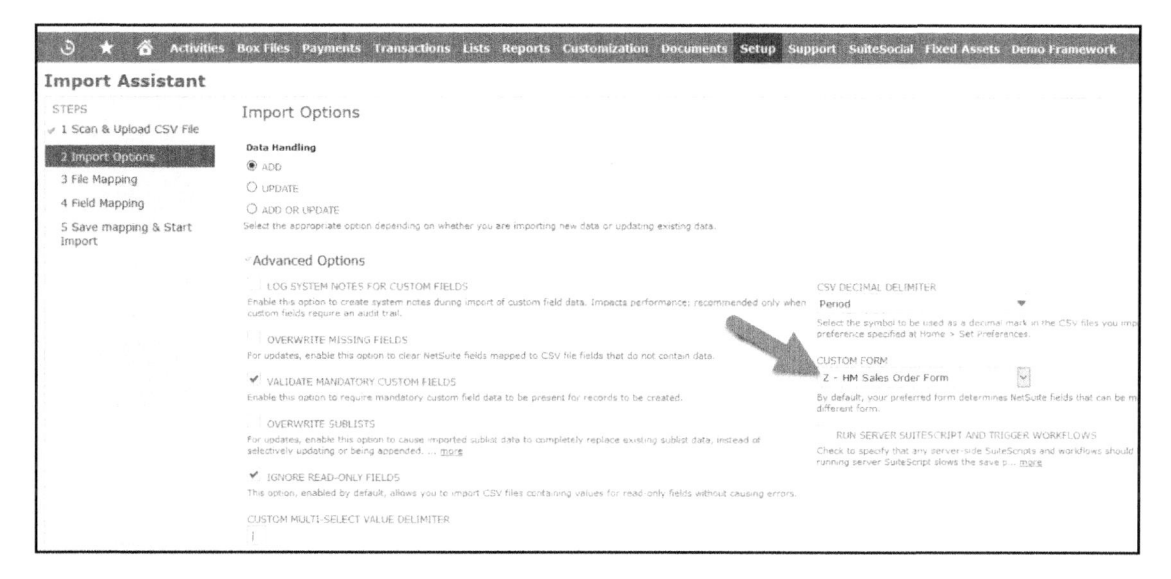

Advanced Import Options in the Import Wizard

7. Click **Next**.
8. Map only one field, namely internal ID, in the source data to the NetSuite internal ID. There is no need to map any other fields as we only want to change the form and nothing else. Click **Next**.
9. Give the import template a meaningful name
10. Click **Save and Run**.

Imports

Extending CSV imports

The import wizard gives us access to change almost every field in the database. Almost. So what do you do if you can't find the field you need to change? We can use this workaround.

NetSuite has a lot of built-in functionality but the developers can't think of every possible automation. After all, if they did, there would be no need for upgrades! So, NetSuite provides us with a tool to automate processes and transform records, named the workflow manager. The workflow manager can be used in conjunction with CSV imports to accomplish things that either one could not do on its own.

An approval process for purchase orders is one example. An approval process may be very complex when combined with approval limits, meaning that a purchase of $1 million will require approvals from the direct supervisor, the VP of purchasing, the executive VP, CFO, and CEO. What happens when there is a reorganization of the company, requiring the supervisor approval hierarchy to be changed for existing purchase orders that have already been entered into the system? We would not be able to change the hierarchy for the existing orders using the import wizard, as all those fields are not available for upload. We may be able to build a workflow that could automate this process, however, it would only be triggered for new purchase orders. It is like having a gun without a trigger, leaving us between the proverbial rock and hard place.

The answer is to combine both tools. Build the workflow and then export the appropriate transactions to CSV:

1. Go to **Setup** | **Import/Export** | **Import CSV**.
2. Select **Transaction** from the import type and select the subtype of the transaction, for instance, **Purchase Order.**
3. Select the file that was just exported and click **Next**.
4. Select **UPDATE** from **Data Handling**.
5. Open **Advanced Options** and check the **Run Server Script and Trigger Workflows** checkbox:

Chapter 7

Import Options page of the Import Wizard

6. Click **Next**.
7. Map only one field, namely internal ID, in the source data to NetSuite internal ID. There is no need to map any other fields as we only want to change the form and nothing else. Click **Next**.
8. Give the import template a meaningful name
9. Click **Save and Run**.

Troubleshooting

The import status page displays the results of an import. It is found at **Setup** | **Import/Export** | **View CSV Import Status**:

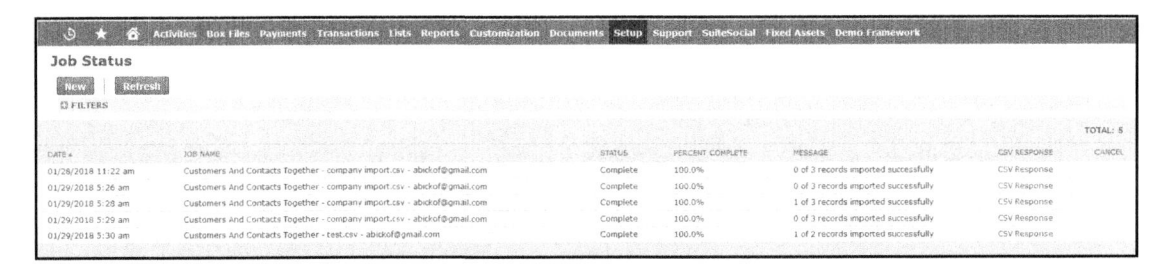

Import Job Status page

[209]

Imports

The import may take a few minutes to a couple of hours to complete, depending on the size and complexity of the data in the file. Click the **Refresh** button on the status page to update the progress. The **Refresh** button works like the traffic-light WALK button pedestrians press to change the light at an intersection–it doesn't make the process go any faster but it certainly makes me feel better while waiting!

Each import creates a CSV response file, which is opened by clicking on the link in the **CSV RESPONSE** row on the import **Job Status** page. The file replicates the data that was not imported and provides an error message for each line:

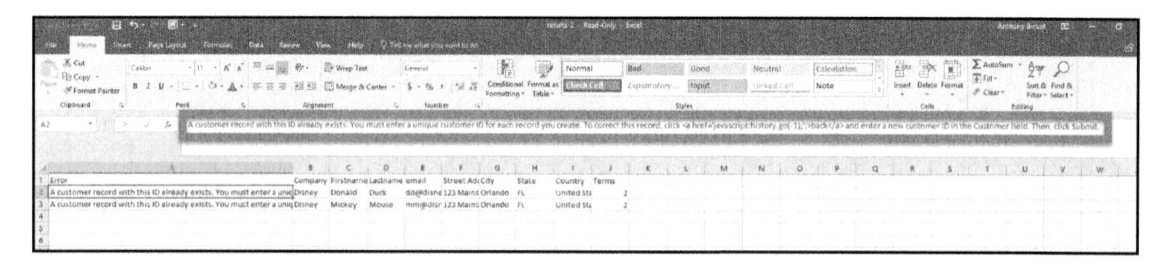

Example of import error message

We now need to address the error in our source data or import map and re-execute the import using the saved template.

Common errors include the following:

- **Missing a value for a mandatory field,** requiring us to include a value in our source data.
- **That record does not exist,** meaning that the source data refers to a record that does not exist in the database.
- **Invalid item reference key,** meaning that the source data refers to an item that does not exist, for instance, on a transaction import referencing the item that was sold.
- **Invalid Parent Reference Key,** which occurs when we import records in the wrong order, such as importing a child that references the parent before importing the parent. Reorder the source data to ensure that the parent is imported before the child records.

The list of possible errors messages is extensive, however, an error is displayed for each failure, so sort the results file by the error column so that the errors are shown in groups. We can then address each error, save as CSV, and reimport.

Summary

The import wizard can be used to add additional records to the database or to update existing records. Focus on manipulating your source data to ensure it meets the criteria NetSuite requires for each field. Convert the data in fields referencing picklist values to the internal ID corresponding with the appropriate picklist value.

We can only import one subtype of a record at a time, for instance, importing the inventory and assembly items will need to be done in two separate imports. We can import one file only or multiple files simultaneously, where the data is stored in different tables in NetSuite, such as customers and contacts.

NetSuite provides us with advanced mapping tools in addition to simply mapping a field from the source data to the corresponding NetSuite field. The mapping screen enables us to set default values and match picklist values based on internal ID. The NetSuite fields on the mapping screen are displayed in different folders. The first folder represents the header information on the NetSuite record that we are importing, and the folders represent the sublists or tabs associated with that record.

The import wizard allows us to save import maps for further use, enabling us to set up and reuse our own import templates. This makes future imports much easier, as we can simply focus on manipulating the source data to conform to the template data structure.

Imports enable us to increase the numbers of leads, customer, vendors, and transactions in our NetSuite database, but a larger dataset poses its own set of challenges, namely, summarizing the data into actionable business intelligence. That is the focus of our next chapter.

8
Analytics – Searches, Reports, and the Dashboard

How do we provide our users with the real-time, actionable business intelligence that they need to run their business? NetSuite has three features to accomplish this: searches, reports, and dashboards.

As a rule of thumb, I believe I can gauge a company's use of NetSuite by looking at three screens: the CEO's dashboard, the CFO's dashboard, and the dashboard of a random user. If the dashboard is set up, my assumption is that the system is being used properly. Failure to setup these dashboards is a reflection on the use of NetSuite; I suspect the company won't be renewing their NetSuite contract when they need to.

That's how crucial the dashboard is. A strong dashboard enables the user to operate tactically and strategically. Tactically, it displays the day's priorities and highlights any issues that need to be immediately addressed. The dashboard also shows longer-term goals and trends that the user needs to be keeping track of.

On the other hand, searches and reports are two different functions that serve very similar ends, namely the ability to turn more data into business intelligence. They have very similar functionalities and the question is always whether to summarize data using a search or the report.

These three concepts are inextricably linked because the dashboard is comprised of underlying searches and reports. This allows the user to drill down from a dashboard summary right into the details. It also provides us with the ability to extend the dashboard by customizing searches and reports and linking them to the dashboard.

In a sense, the dashboard is the beginning and the end of the discussion on business intelligence in NetSuite. We will start by exploring the built-in features of the dashboard because we need to learn what is available before we look at creating other searches and reports. We will then look take an in-depth look at searches and then reports. Finally, we will link all the concepts by showing how you can place your custom searches and reports onto the dashboard.

In this chapter, we will do the following:

- Define the dashboard.
- Explain the different mechanisms that are provided on the dashboard in order to display data in the best way in which it will be understood.
- Discuss the types of data to present on the dashboard segmented by the user, such as a manager versus an individual contributor.
- Compare searches and reports, showing the advantages and disadvantages of each.
- Look at searches and start by comparing specific tools to their Excel equivalent to apply the administrator's existing skills to NetSuite.
- Look at all the various options that are available in searches and show use cases where these can be used.
- Build commonly used searches and reports demonstrating the filtering and formatting options available.
- Learn how to centralize the creation of searches and reports. We will cross-reference this with `Chapter 5`, *Security and Permissions*, by showing you how to make the searches and reports available to specific users.
- Leverage searches and reports to set them up on the dashboard.

Dashboard overview

Dashboards operate in the same way as a dashboard in a car because they are designed to summarize data for the user. But the driver does not need to open up the gas tank prior to a long drive in order to check whether there is enough gas to make it to the destination. Instead, the driver just needs to focus on the dashboard, which will summarize information such as speed and the level of gas. The car dashboard also has the ability to highlight certain information that requires immediate attention, for instance, the blinking light as we are running out of gas and need to fill up.

The NetSuite dashboard does a similar thing. It summarizes data for the user to be able to manage the business from from one screen. It is dynamic and can highlight metrics that require immediate attention. It is very powerful and should be used by all NetSuite users in order for them to keep up to date with their job responsibilities.

We're going to start with the dashboard because it not only has many built-in features that we can use without the need to start from scratch, but is also the likely destination for many of the searches and reports that we will be building. The dashboard is organized by portlets, which are different ways to display information.

Each portlet must be enabled to appear on the dashboard. Click the **Personalize** button in the top right-hand corner of the dashboard to select the portlets you wish to see on the dashboard:

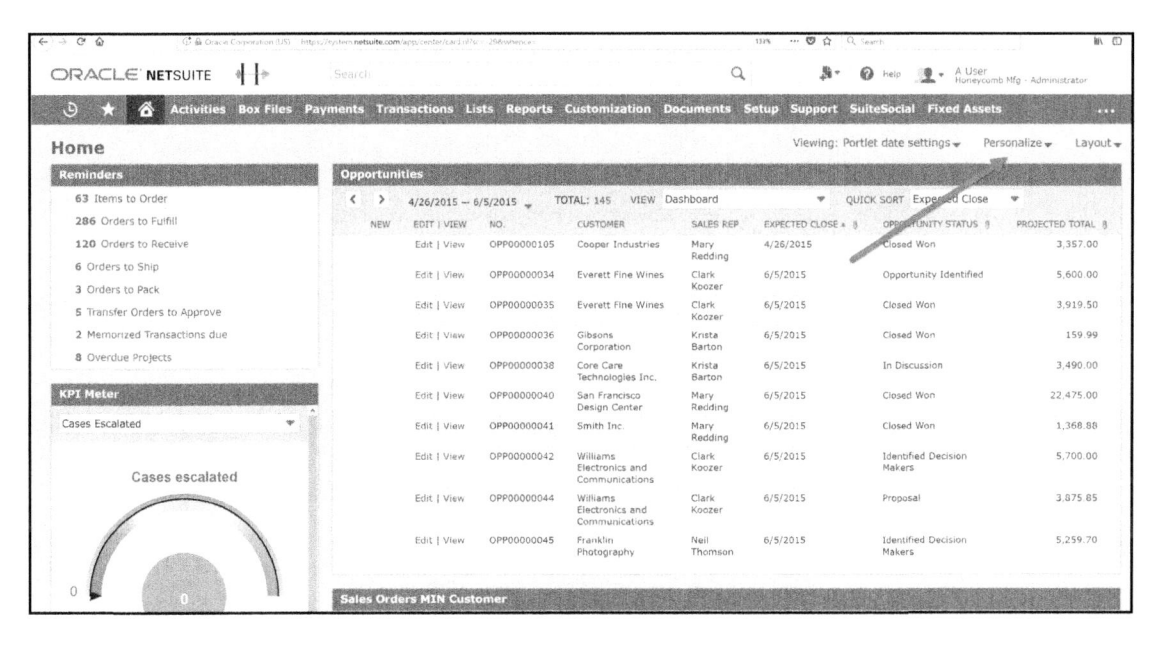

Personalize dashboard

Analytics – Searches, Reports, and the Dashboard

The options are divided up into sections including **Standard Content**, **Report Snapshots**, and **Trend Graphs**, and we will explain all of those options in the pages ahead. The portlets are merely mechanisms to display content. We still need to choose the content we wish to display on each portlet individually. Each portlet has its own setup options which we access by clicking on the ellipses button in the top right-hand corner of the portlet. The ellipses button becomes visible as soon as we hover the mouse over the top-right corner:

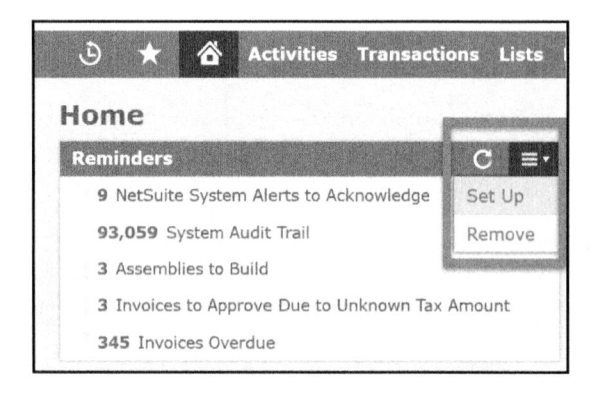

The Set Up button on each portlet

Click the **Set Up** button to setup the content to be displayed on each portlet.

Here is a list of the most important portlets and how they can be used:

- The reminders are in the form of a punch list summarizing work that needs to be done with a built-in hyperlink to the details of that task. It is closely integrated with the default processes in NetSuite and contains standard reminders for all the steps in a process. It can be augmented with custom reminders, which we will learn how to build in this chapter:

The reminders portlet

[216]

- The list portlet is mainly used by individual contributors, giving them a list of the specific records they work with. It is not a summary but details of the actual records, with links to the records:

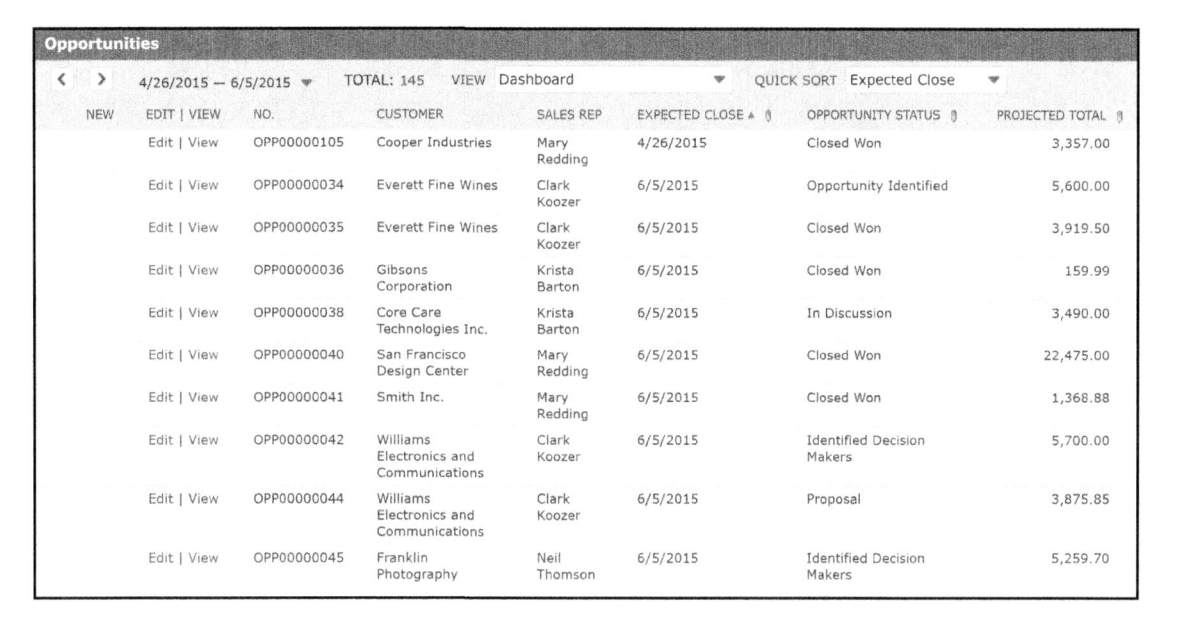

	EDIT | VIEW	NO.	CUSTOMER	SALES REP	EXPECTED CLOSE ▲	OPPORTUNITY STATUS	PROJECTED TOTAL
NEW	Edit | View	OPP00000105	Cooper Industries	Mary Redding	4/26/2015	Closed Won	3,357.00
	Edit | View	OPP00000034	Everett Fine Wines	Clark Koozer	6/5/2015	Opportunity Identified	5,600.00
	Edit | View	OPP00000035	Everett Fine Wines	Clark Koozer	6/5/2015	Closed Won	3,919.50
	Edit | View	OPP00000036	Gibsons Corporation	Krista Barton	6/5/2015	Closed Won	159.99
	Edit | View	OPP00000038	Core Care Technologies Inc.	Krista Barton	6/5/2015	In Discussion	3,490.00
	Edit | View	OPP00000040	San Francisco Design Center	Mary Redding	6/5/2015	Closed Won	22,475.00
	Edit | View	OPP00000041	Smith Inc.	Mary Redding	6/5/2015	Closed Won	1,368.88
	Edit | View	OPP00000042	Williams Electronics and Communications	Clark Koozer	6/5/2015	Identified Decision Makers	5,700.00
	Edit | View	OPP00000044	Williams Electronics and Communications	Clark Koozer	6/5/2015	Proposal	3,875.85
	Edit | View	OPP00000045	Franklin Photography	Neil Thomson	6/5/2015	Identified Decision Makers	5,259.70

The list portlet

- The Custom Search portlet is similar to the list portlet and is also mainly used by individual contributors. It serves the same purpose but the results are usually based on a filter, such as the opportunities expected to close this month:

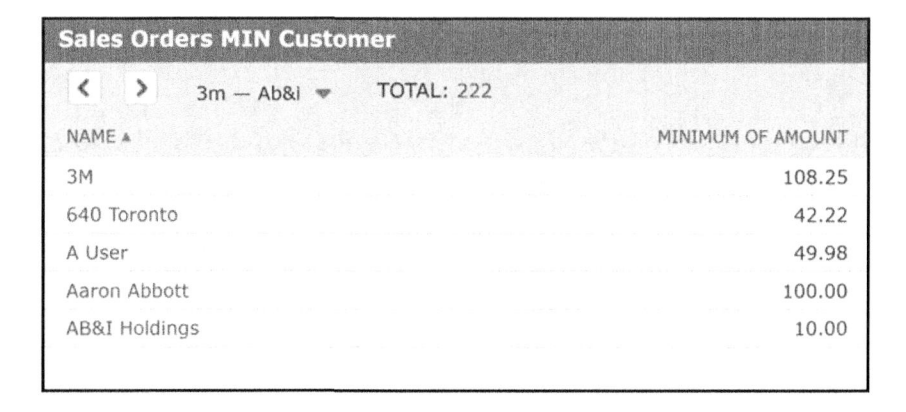

Sales Orders MIN Customer

3m — Ab&I ▼   TOTAL: 222

NAME ▲	MINIMUM OF AMOUNT
3M	108.25
640 Toronto	42.22
A User	49.98
Aaron Abbott	100.00
AB&I Holdings	10.00

The Custom Search portlet

- **Key Performance Indicators** are text-based reports used by both executives and individual contributors. The Corporate Executive's KPIs will likely be more extensive because they have more information to keep track of, whereas the AR clerk may have two KPIs visible, for instance, **Payables** and **Bank Balance**. They are summaries with hyperlinks to the actual report and can appear in bold if a certain threshold has been met, such as the bank balance falling below a certain minimum balance. KPIs also provide a comparative date range to compare against so that you are not looking at a metric by a certain period but are able to compare it to a previous date range. They can be customized, and we will learn how to do that a little later:

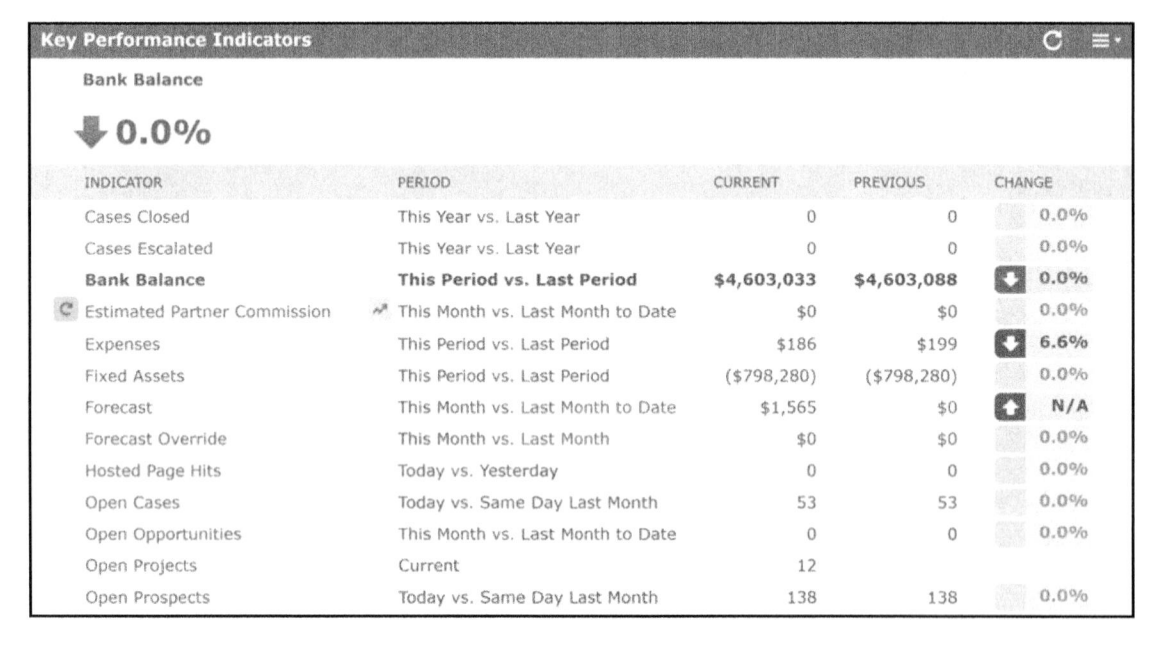

Key Performance Indicators

Bank Balance

⬇ 0.0%

INDICATOR	PERIOD	CURRENT	PREVIOUS	CHANGE
Cases Closed	This Year vs. Last Year	0	0	0.0%
Cases Escalated	This Year vs. Last Year	0	0	0.0%
Bank Balance	**This Period vs. Last Period**	**$4,603,033**	**$4,603,088**	0.0%
Estimated Partner Commission	This Month vs. Last Month to Date	$0	$0	0.0%
Expenses	This Period vs. Last Period	$186	$199	6.6%
Fixed Assets	This Period vs. Last Period	($798,280)	($798,280)	0.0%
Forecast	This Month vs. Last Month to Date	$1,565	$0	N/A
Forecast Override	This Month vs. Last Month	$0	$0	0.0%
Hosted Page Hits	Today vs. Yesterday	0	0	0.0%
Open Cases	Today vs. Same Day Last Month	53	53	0.0%
Open Opportunities	This Month vs. Last Month to Date	0	0	0.0%
Open Projects	Current	12		
Open Prospects	Today vs. Same Day Last Month	138	138	0.0%

The Key Performance Indicator portlet

- **KPI scorecards** take KPIs to the next level with two additional matrices. Scorecards let you add more than two possible date ranges, as well as providing the ability to execute calculations such as KPI 1 minus KPI 2 or KPI 3 as a percentage of KPI 4. As a result, it is a wonderful way to provide executives with real analytics:

Customer Statistics					
INDICATOR	Q1 2011	Q2 2011	Q3 2011	Q4 2011
New Customers	0	0	0	0
Lost Customers	0	0	0	0
Net Customers	243	243	243	243
Total Revenue	$0	$0	$0	$0
Revenue Per Customer	$0	$0	$0	$0

The KPI scorecard portlet

- Trend graphs provide a visual representation of the metric over time:

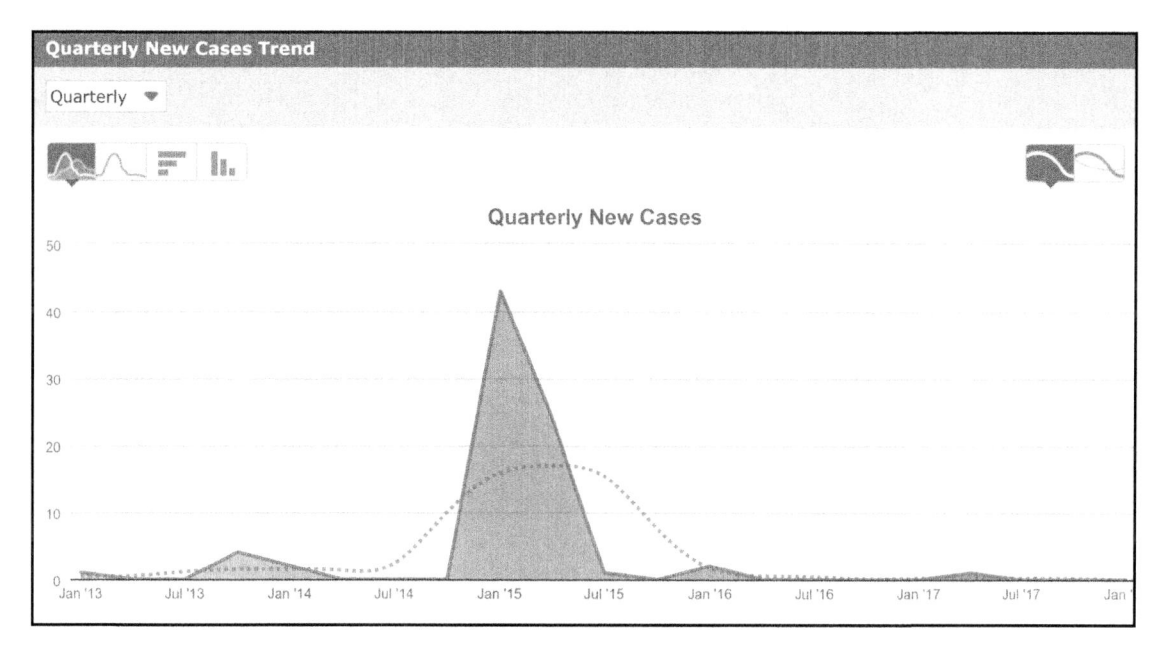

The trend graph portlet

Analytics – Searches, Reports, and the Dashboard

- Report snapshots are mini reports that appear on the dashboard. The dashboard doesn't have space for large reports because it contains so much other information. The report snapshot is a summary of the report, such as the top five customers based on sales this month to date:

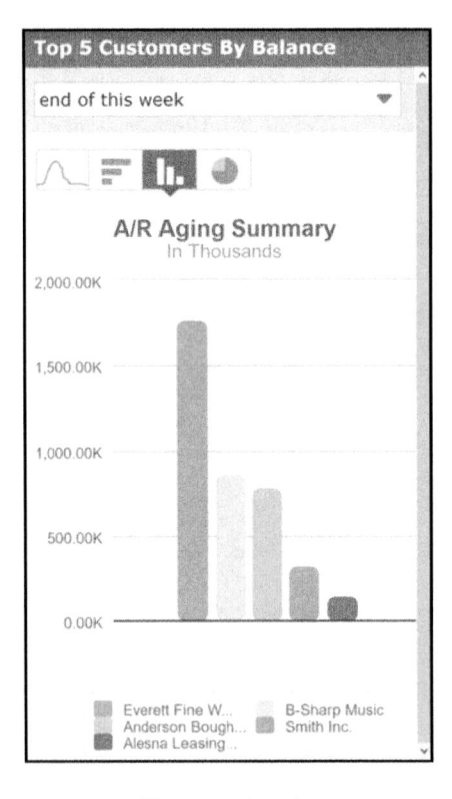

The report snapshot portlet

- KPI meters are visual representations of KPIs and are in the form of a traffic light, showing whether we are in the green, the yellow, or the red with respect to a goal we have set for that metric:

Chapter 8

The KPI meter portlet

When people use the term dashboard, they are usually referring to the home dashboard, accessed by clicking on the home icon on the toolbar, however, this is not strictly correct. There are multiple dashboards available; in fact, each tab on the toolbar links to its own dashboard, providing us the real estate to add additional content, using the same portlets on each of those screens:

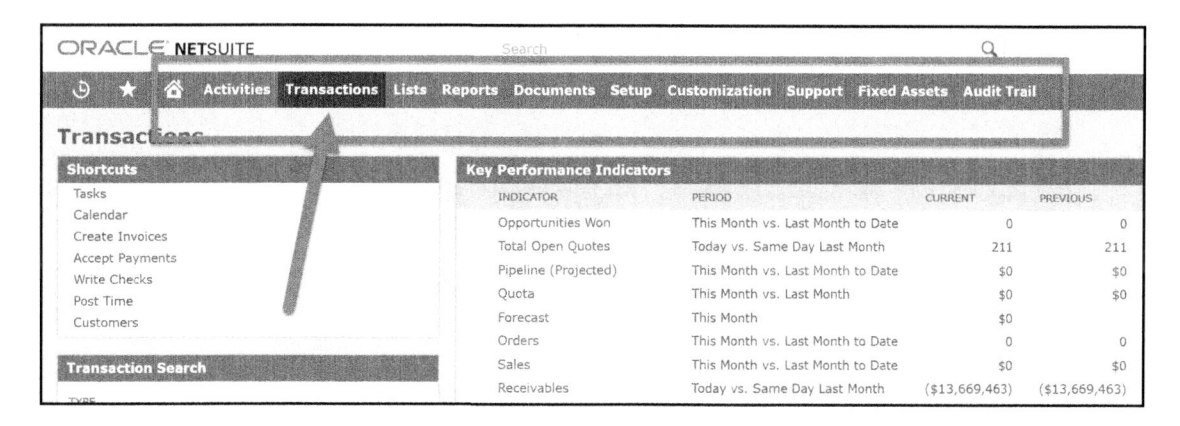

The Transactions dashboard

[221]

Analytics – Searches, Reports, and the Dashboard

There are also **Customer** and **Vendor** dashboards available. These dashboards summarize the relationship between individual customers and vendors, providing us with a snapshot of our interactions with each. Click the dashboard icon on a specific customer or vendor record to access their dashboard:

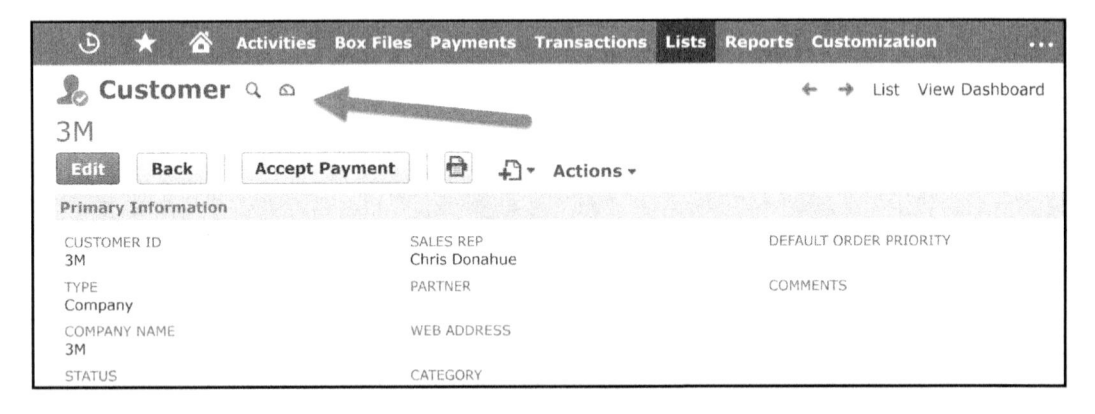

Link to Customer dashboard

The **Customer** and **Vendor** dashboards use the same portlets to summarize information, and the tools we will be learning in this chapter can also be used to customize the dashboards to provide your users with the information they need to make strategic decisions about individual customers and vendors:

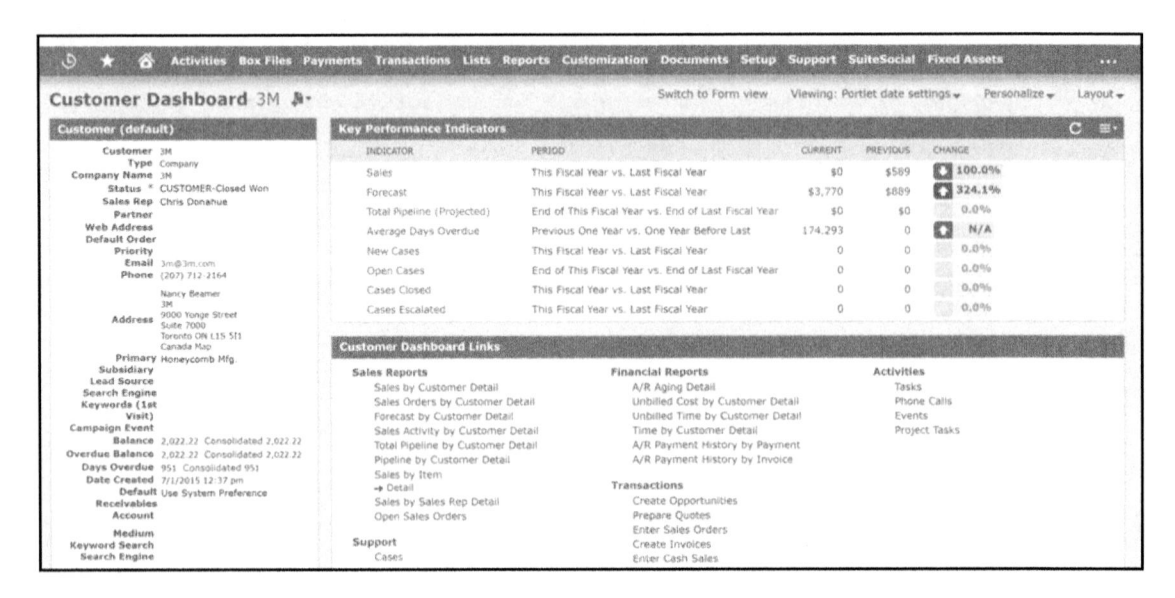

The Customer Dashboard

[222]

Searches versus reports

If you are wondering what the difference is between searches and reports, the answer is: not very much. They both perform similar tasks and are to some extent duplicates, yet NetSuite contains both options. Let's outline the advantages of each to help you decide when to use searches or reports.

Advantages

Let's review the advantages of searches and reports.

Advantages of Saved Searches

Saved Searches have the following advantages over Reports:

- Saved Searches are better at providing lists of data, for instance, a list of customers in California.
- The results of a saved search can be leveraged elsewhere in the system, for instance, mail merges, marketing campaigns, mass updates, and, of course, the dashboard. All the custom BI tools on the dashboard, with the exception of report snapshots, are built on custom saved searches.
- As a general rule, when you're looking to report on entities (customers, vendors, employees, and partners) saved searches are usually the way to go.
- Searches have a function to initiate event-based alerts to send an email if a particular event (outlined in the search criteria) occurs, for instance to email the CFO in the event that a check is created for $1 million or more.
- Searches are also used in conjunction with workflows to limit automation tasks to specific records.

Advantages of Reports

Reports have the following advantages over Saved Searches:

- Reports contain better formatting options and can provide a better mechanism for analyzing data with built-in charting, as well as better integration with classifications.
- Reports also provide better pivoting options if you're looking to pivot data by subsidiary, department, class, or location.

- NetSuite ships with a number of existing reports which can also operate as templates. You can build a report by customizing the existing report, so you don't have to start from scratch, unlike saved searches.

Saved Searches

I'm going to explain searches in NetSuite by contrasting them with a tool that you likely know very well, Microsoft Excel. Start by going to **Lists** | **Search** | **Saved Search** | **New** and select **Customer**.

Criteria tab

Let's start at the bottom of the screen with the tabs. The NetSuite **Criteria** tab is used to build the query, which is analogous to the advanced filter option in Excel:

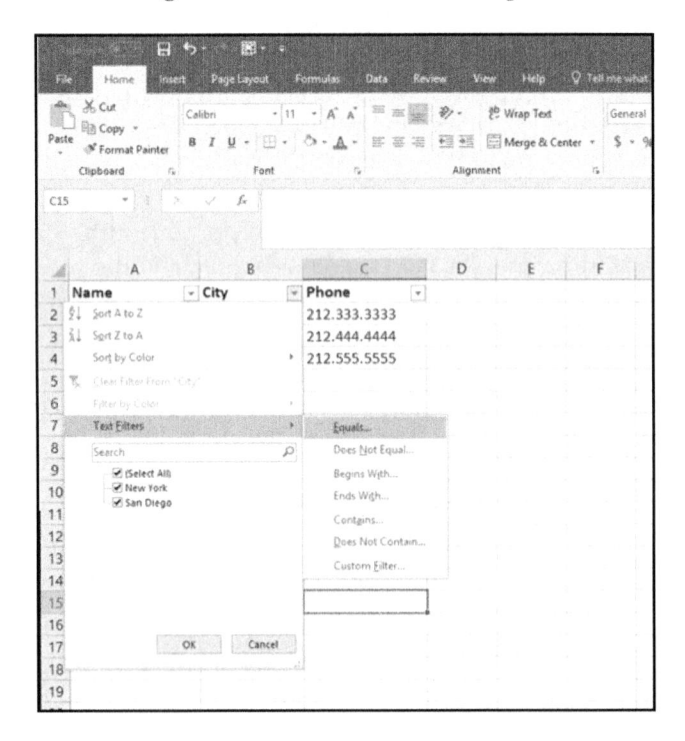

Excel filter

The Excel filter of `City = 'New York'` is represented as criteria in NetSuite:

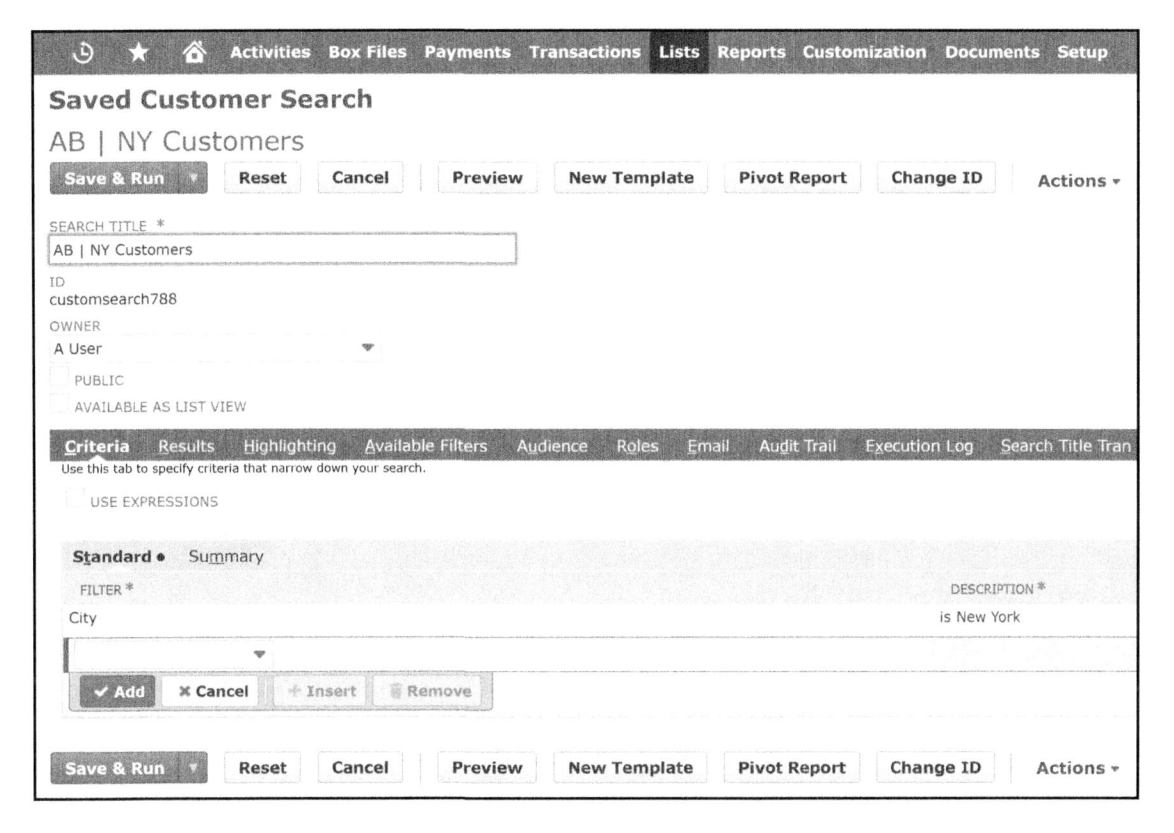

Setting up a filter in NetSuite Saved Searches

Analytics – Searches, Reports, and the Dashboard

The Excel custom filter option is equivalent to `Use Expressions` in NetSuite. This allows you to build extensive searches using AND as well as OR logic, in addition to parentheses. The parentheses must of course balance in order for the search to run properly:

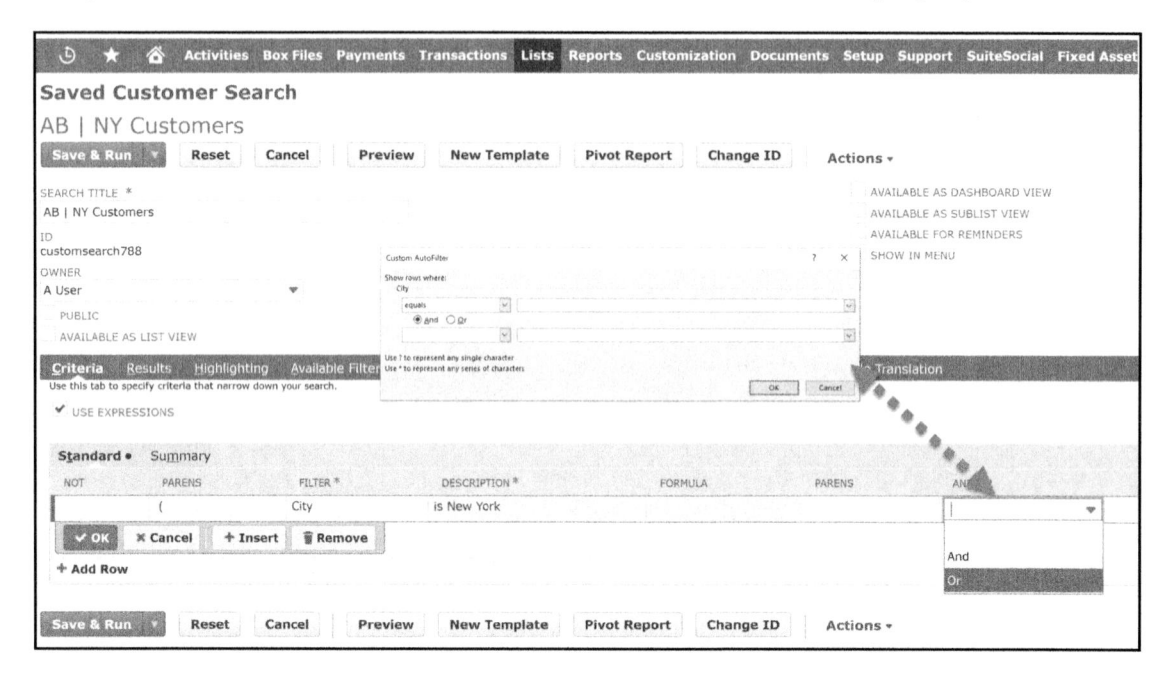

Comparison between Excel Filter and NetSuite Expressions

NetSuite also allows you to base queries on fields in other tables by clicking the filter button and scrolling down to the bottom of the list of filters. Fields on this table appear initially in the list and tables appear at the end of the list. We can distinguish fields from tables because tables are followed by an ellipsis sign. Clicking on that selection will allow you to select a field from the joined tables:

Link to joined tables represented by ellipses signs

Analytics – Searches, Reports, and the Dashboard

Formulas

NetSuite allows us to build searches based on formulas, in the same way that Excel does. To extend the standard criteria options by entering SQL formulas into the query, click the criteria drop-down and scroll down to the word **Formula** in the list. We will need to select the type of formula that will be used in this specific criteria, such as, **Formula Date**, **Formula Numeric**, and **Formula Text**. Selecting a formula option results in a popup window where we can select from the standard formula in the **FUNCTION** dropdown as well as selecting the NetSuite fields from the **FIELD** dropdown, in order to create the formula to be applied:

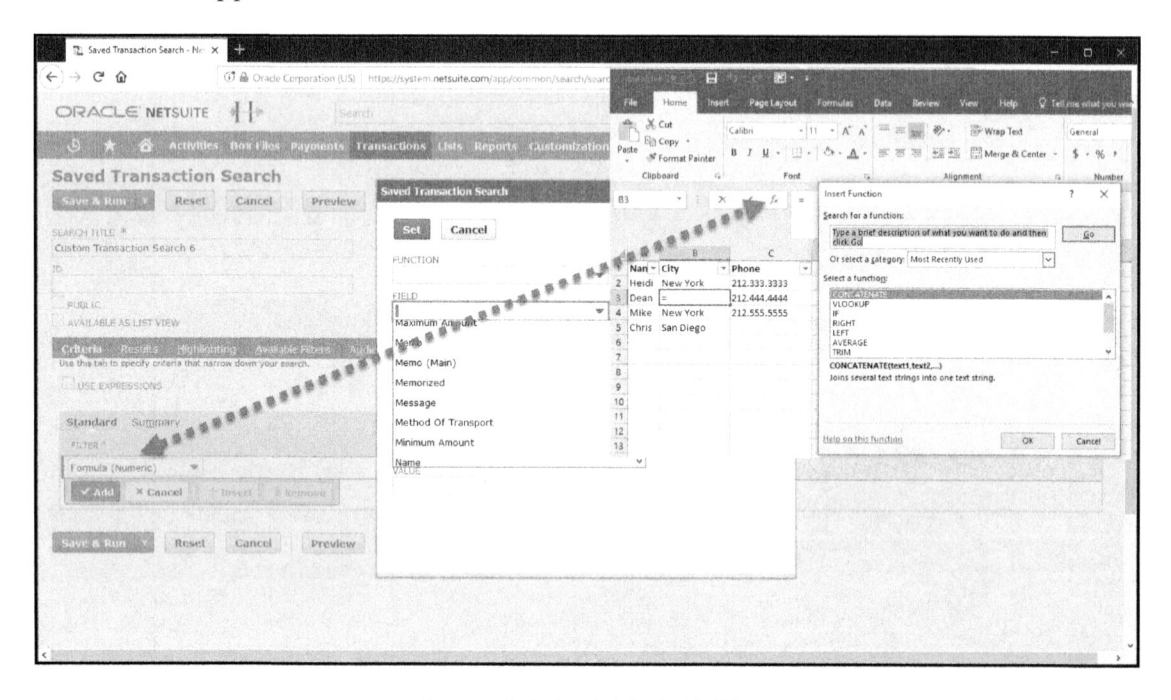

Comparison of using formulas in Excel and NetSuite

[228]

Standard versus summary criteria

There are two subtabs that appear on the criteria tab. We have been looking at the **Standard** Subtab but what is the **Summary** criteria subtab and how does it differ from the **Standard** subtab?

Let's illustrate this by using an example. Say the sales manager wants to analyze the transactions in the table and identifies customers have spent more than $10,000 last year:

Customer	Order Number	Amount
X	S123	$10,999
Y	S124	$9,999
Y	S125	$8,000
Y	S126	$4,000
Y	S127	$7,000
Z	S128	$9,000
X	S129	$400

If we were to apply the knowledge we have gained so far, we would simply add this query to our standard criteria, AMOUNT - TOTAL TRANSACTION> $10,000, which would return only one result, namely, Customer X. Customer Z would be excluded because they have one transaction which is less than the threshold. X would be returned because they have one transaction which is more than $10,000 on its own. Customer Y would be excluded from the results even though they have transactions amounting to $28,999 because none of their transactions meet the threshold on their own.

The result would be therefore misleading as it excludes our best customer from the results. We, therefore, need the system to perform a calculation (add up all the transactions by customer) prior to determining whether the total amount exceeds the threshold. We will find that option under the **Summary** criteria.

Go to **Lists** | **Search** | **Saved Search** | **New** and select **Transactions**:

1. Name the search.
2. Go to the **Criteria** tab:
    1. Add a filter of type = any of **Sales Order** and **Cash Sale**.
    2. Add the filter of date = within Last Year.
    3. Go to the **Summary** criteria subtab.
    4. Add a row, **Amount (Transaction Total)** and select **Sum** in the **SUMMARY TYPE** column. Then add the condition >10000:

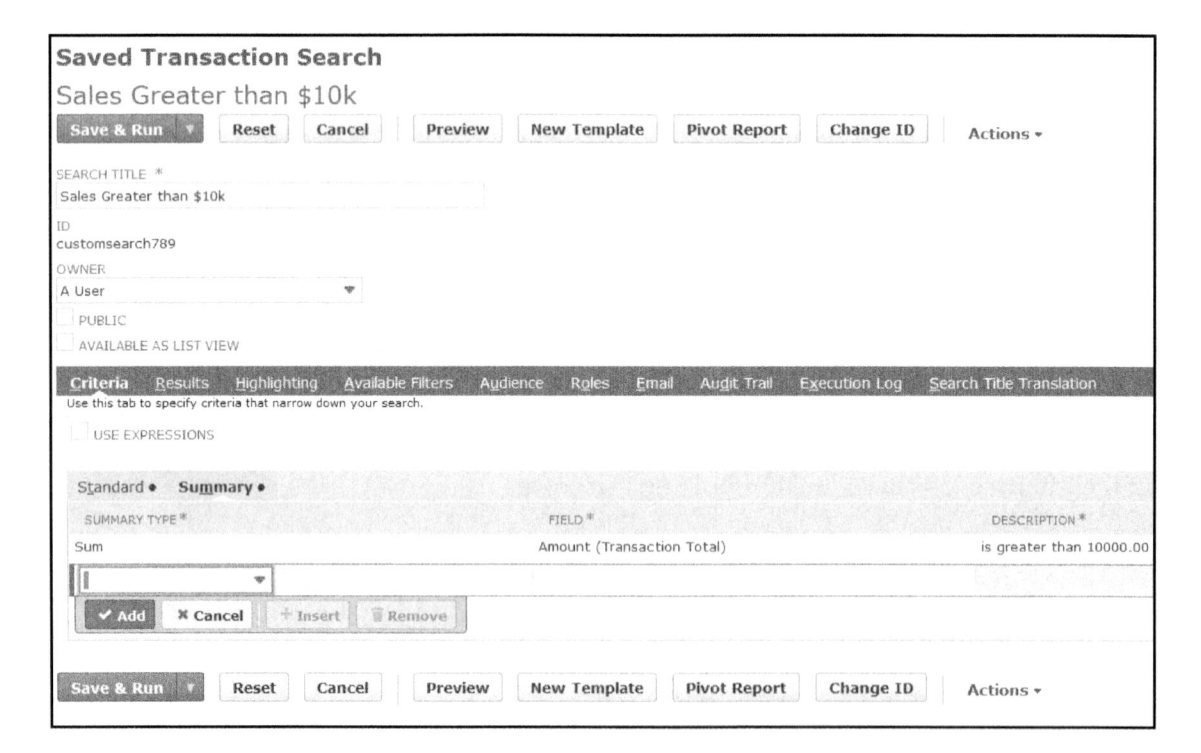

Performing a calculation in a Saved Search

The result will be to identify the customer who has spent more than $10,000 in total with the company last year.

Results tab

The **Results** tab is used to determine the columns that will be displayed in the results, such as **Name**, **City**, and **Phone**. We can simply add or remove rows in the **Results** tab to add or change the columns that will appear in the results. There is also a **Sort By** option on the **Results** tab which allows you to sort the data by any of the columns:

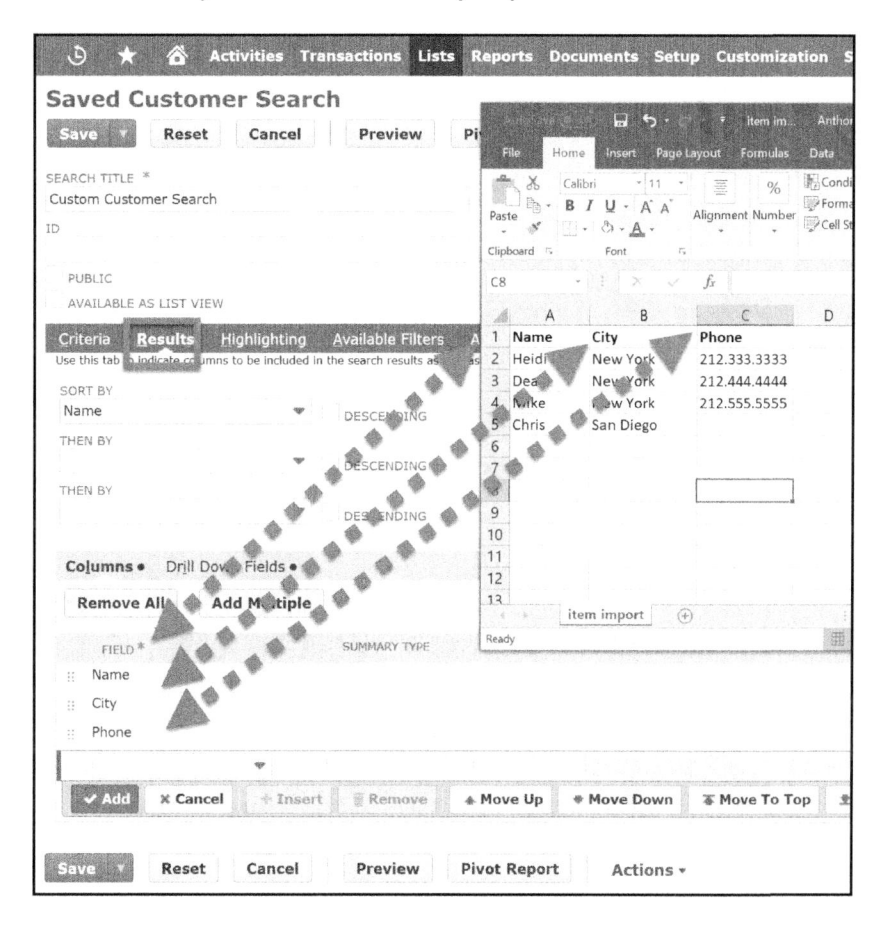

Comparison of columns in Excel and NetSuite

Summary column

The **Summary** column on the **Results** tab is used to perform calculations like an Excel pivot table. The **Summary** tab is used for this purpose, for instance, to count the number of records by city. The term *group* means "total by" in NetSuite. We group by the city and count by the name field to calculate the number of customers by city:

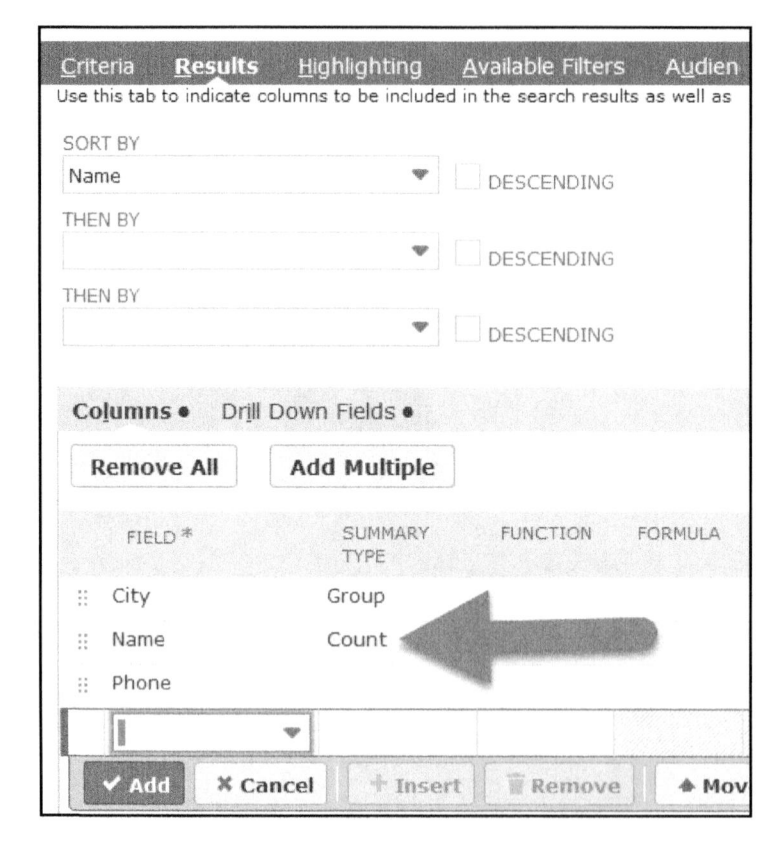

Totaling the number of customers by city

The choice of fields to use in the **Summary Type** column is crucial. A calculation based on a value in the time field within a time tracking search will error out. NetSuite provides an additional field, namely, time decimal, in order for you to create that calculation.

The result is a quasi-pivot table which displays the results of the calculation:

- The **Group** option is used to total the amount by the field in that row. So, for instance, using the group by sales rep with the sum by amount, will return a sales report by sales rep, adding up all the sales for each sales rep. It's possible to total by a number of different fields in the same search. Simply add an additional column and set the **Summary** type to Group for the the **City** field to create a sales by *Sales Rep* by **City** report. It is possible to flip the results to a Sales by City by Sales Rep report by simply switching the order of the group fields.

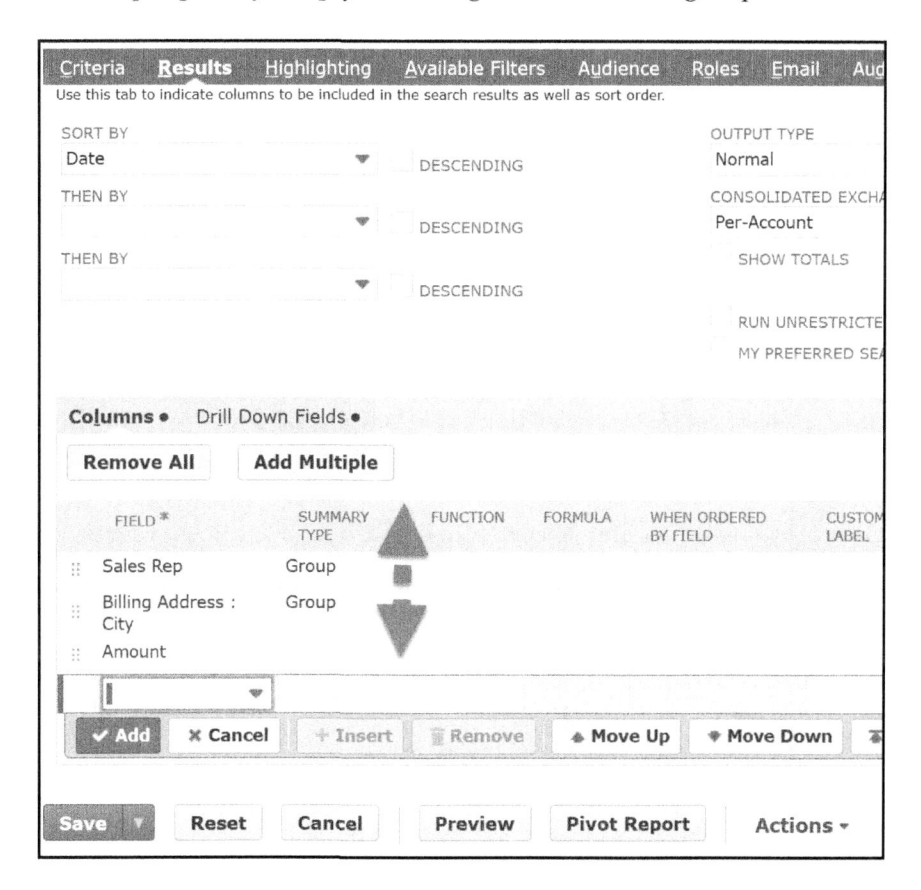

Pivot Results by changing the order of the group fields

- **Sum** is used in conjunction with **Group**, as you can see. **Sum** will add up value and is typically used when adding dollar values of transactions.

- **Count** is also used in conjunction with **Group**, but instead of adding the amounts of transactions, count adds the number of the transaction. Whereas the result of a sum search could be $10,000, the results of a count search would be 27 transactions.
- The **Average summary** type calculates the average of that field in that row.
- Maximum is the largest amount when applied to currency fields and the earliest date when applied to a date field. It is used in conjunction with the **When Ordered by Field** to change the sort based on the results of the maximum field.
- Minimum is the smallest amount when applied to currency fields and the latest date when applied to a date field. **When Order by also applies** to minimum.

Let's illustrate this with an example:

Transaction Date	Michael Mouse	Goofy	Donald Duck
Jan	100		
Feb	49	495	125
Mar	237		
Apr	295		28

- **Group by Customer**: Michael Mouse, Goofy, Donald Duck
- **Group by Customer** and **SUM by AMOUNT**: Michael Mouse *(100+49+237+295) = $681*; Goofy = 495; Donald Duck *(125+28)= $153*
- **Group by Customer** and **COUNT by AMOUNT**: Michael Mouse = *4*; Goofy = *1*; Donald Duck = *2*
- **Group by Customer** and **AVERAGE by AMOUNT**: Michael Mouse = *(100+49+237+295)/4 = $170.25*; Goofy = *495*; Donald Duck = *125+28/2 = 76.5*
- **Group by Customer** and **MINIMUM by AMOUNT**: Michael Mouse = *$49*; Goofy = *$495*; Donald Duck = *$28*
- **Group by Customer** and **MAXIMUM by AMOUNT**: Michael Mouse = *$295*; Goofy = *$495*; Donald Duck = *$125*
- **Group by Customer** and **MINIMUM by DATE**: Michael Mouse = Jan; Goofy = Feb; Donald Duck = Feb
- **Group by Customer** and **MAXIMUM by DATE**: Michael Mouse = Apr; Goofy = Feb; Donald Duck = Apr

Function column

The values selected in the **Function** column apply a specific format to a column in the search results. Options include the following:

- **ROUND**, **ROUND TO HUNDREDTHS**, and **ROUND TO TENTHS** will round a calculation so that results are easier to read than 0.2342456789943329. It applies to a numerical field—currency fields will round the amount by default.
- **YEAR, QUARTER, MONTH**, and so on returns the year, quarter, or month of a particular date, for instance, **Sales by Quarter by Customer**.
- **WEEK OF THE YEAR** converts the date in that row to the appropriate week of that year.
- **AGE in DAYS/MONTHS/YEARS** is used to calculate the time that has passed since a specific date.
- **% of Total** provides an additional metric to a **SUM**, a percentage of the total. Duplicate the amount field to make the result more meaningful.

Formula column

The formula column can be used to display the results of SQL formulas. They are accessed in the same way as formulas are selected on the **Criteria** tab. Click the criteria drop-down and scroll down to the word formula in the list. The **Results** tab has additional options such as **Formula Currency**, **Formula Date/Time**, and **Formula Percent**, in addition to **Formula Date, Formula Numeric**, and **Formula Text** found on the **Criteria** tab. Selecting a formula option results in a popup window where we can select from the standard formula in the **Function** drop-down, as well as selecting the NetSuite fields from the **Field** drop-down, in order to create the formula to be applied.

Custom label and summary label columns

These columns rename a field or summary field that will appear in the results. A summary field will automatically be displayed as **Sum of Amount**. Use the summary label to change that to TOTAL.

Analytics – Searches, Reports, and the Dashboard

Highlighting

The **Highlighting** tab formats the results if they comply with certain criteria, similar to the *Conditional Formatting* we would find in MS Excel.

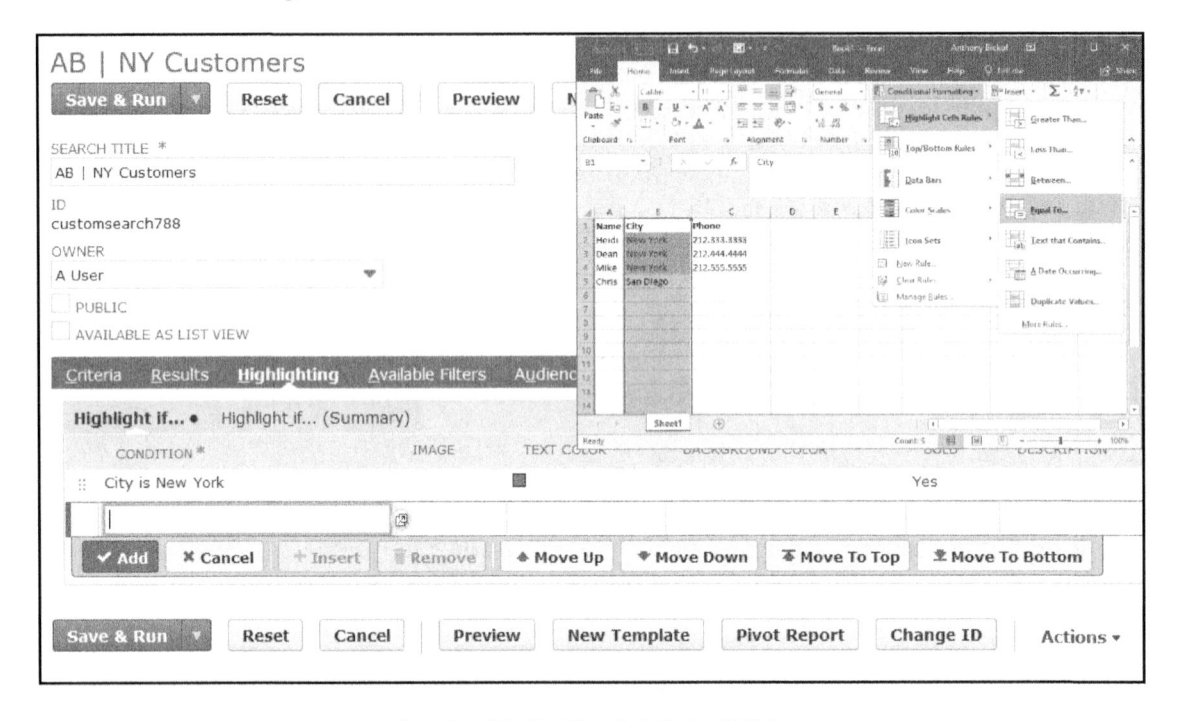

Comparison of Conditional Formatting in Excel and NetSuite

As an example, we could highlight all customers whose phone numbers start with 212 in a different color to the other records returned by the search:

1. Select the **Highlighting** condition and click **Set**.
2. Build the condition, for instance, phone number starts with 212.
3. Click **Set**.
4. Select the format you wish the highlighting to appear in, such as the text or background being in a different color or in bold.
5. Click **Save & Run**.

Highlighting has a summary option which works the same way as the summary criteria option discussed previously. It allows you to perform a calculation prior to evaluating whether the result meets the highlighting criteria.

Available filters

The **Available** filters tab appears next. It enables the user to pivot the data and is similar to the *Advanced Filters* in Excel. This is a great tool for administrators to create a search for users and lets them refine it as they need to, for instance, to build a search for all customers in California and to allow the user to refine the search for a specific city. One could, of course, build the city search as criteria instead—city = 'San Francisco' and city =' San Diego' and so on—but it is unmanageable because of the number of cities one would need to create individual searches for. Better to create the template for the user and allow them to execute their own city search based on their needs:

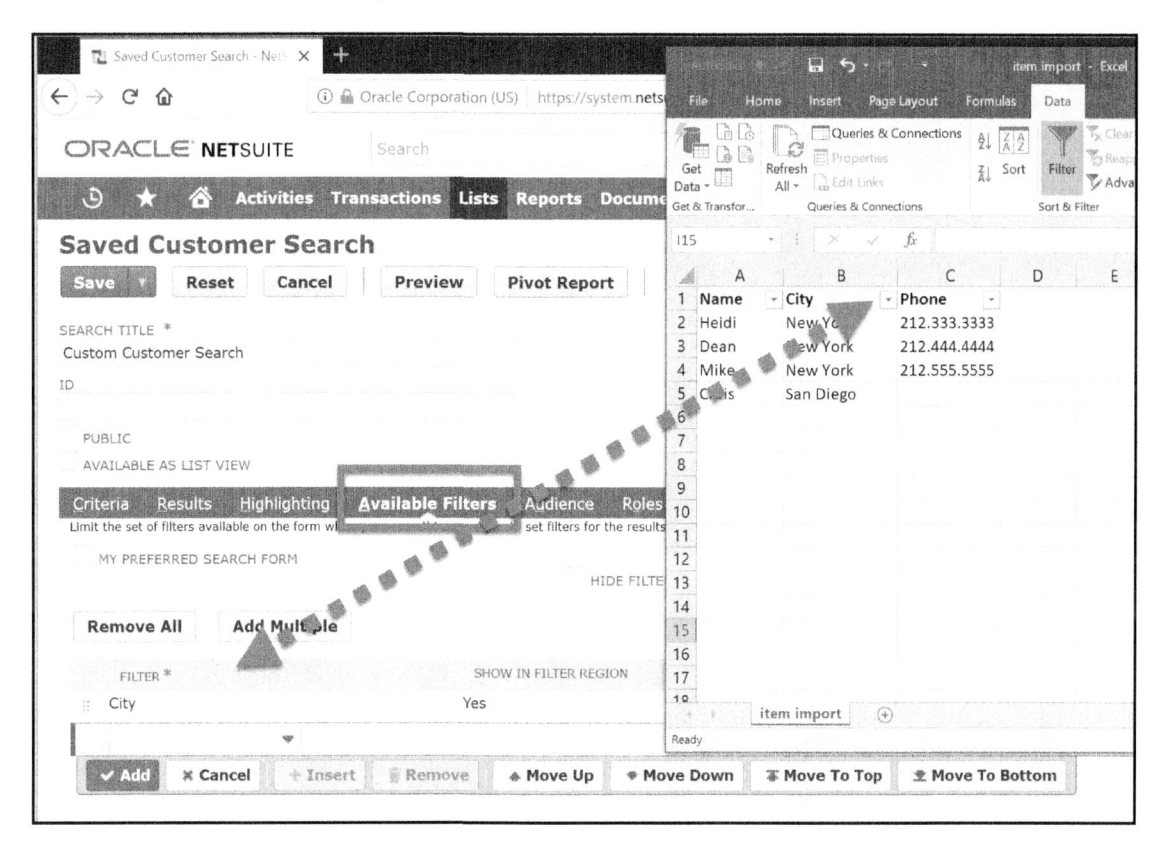

Comparison of Excel and NetSuite filters

Analytics – Searches, Reports, and the Dashboard

This allows the user to build their own searches, for instance, on the **Customer Search** screen:

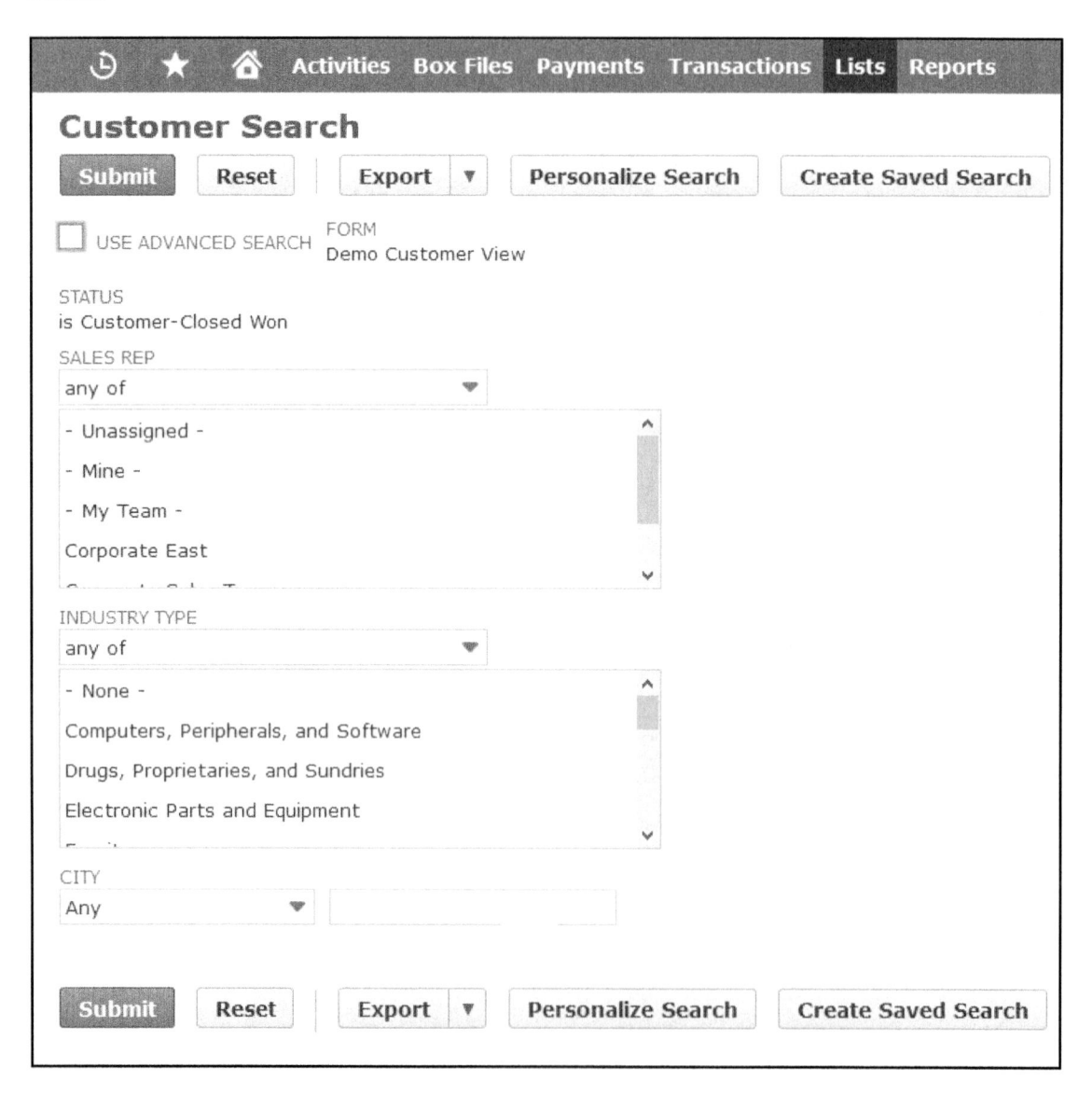

User advanced search form

Audience tab

We want to centralize the creation of searches and reports so that consumers of the information don't have to learn how to create the searches themselves. The **Audience** tab enables us to do this.

It provides us with more control than just checking the **PUBLIC** checkbox as the public checkbox opens the search to anyone with the permission to see the data. In the event that the majority of the searches in our database were set to public, the list of searches for each user would become unmanageable, making it difficult to find that search you created last month from a list of every search that was ever created:

Public search vs. specifying user access

Audience control, on the other hand, allows us to be more specific and determine exactly who needs to see this search and by implication, who doesn't. We can select specific employees, subsidiaries (for OneWorld users) departments, and roles.

Analytics – Searches, Reports, and the Dashboard

We can even choose to share the search with custom groups. Groups can be either static or dynamic. The members of a static group can be added manually to the group and may not have any data points in common. The dynamic group is made up of the results of running a search and the person needs to comply with the conditions of that search in order to appear in the results. The result is that the members of dynamic groups are constantly being updated as more records comply with the criteria. The corollary is also true. A member of the dynamic group is automatically removed from the group if the record no longer complies with the search criteria.

Let's illustrate the difference between static and dynamic groups by using the following example: assume the sales manager wants the results of a commissions search to be available to all the sales reps in her territory. We can create a group of those individuals and open the search to that group by selecting the group on the **Audience** tab of the saved search.

The type of group is an important determinant of the employees that will see the results of the commission's search. A static group would need to be updated when the territory changes. On the other hand, we can create a dynamic group of reps in that area and open the search to that group. Access to that search would change automatically as reps are added or removed from that territory.

By the way, the group itself is made up of a saved search. Create the saved search first and then go to **Lists** | **Relationships** | **Groups** | **New** and choose a dynamic group. Name the group and select the search referencing the employees in that territory and then save. Then return to the commission search you wish to share and select the group you just created from the list in the **Audience** group list.

The **Allow Audience to Edit** button is very significant because it gives the audience the ability to overwrite our search if we check off this box. It's therefore best practice to not provide the edit option and to leave the box unchecked. This allows the user to utilize the search as a template which they can modify but not overwrite. The user will be presented with an option to save the new search under a new name, as opposed to overwriting the administrator's search.

Email

Users are typically emailing search results around the company so NS gives us the ability to automate this using the **Email** tab. The email takes two possible forms, Scheduled Emails and Email Alerts.

Scheduled Emails

These are recurring emails containing the results of the search that is sent out to specific users on the schedule specified on the **Schedule** subtab. Check the **Send Emails According To Schedule** checkbox and set up the start date and time of the initial email. There is an option to summarize the results of the search, failing which, the recipient will receive individual emails for each result in the search. There is also an option to send if there are no results returned by that search at the scheduled time. We can also specify the recurrence schedule, for instance, whether this email be sent daily (to include or exclude weekends) or weekly, as well as whether there will be an end date or if this will go on indefinitely:

Scheduling a recurring email of search results

Scheduled emails are a good mechanism to keep management informed of the state of the business, such as sending an end-of-day report summarizing the sales generated during the day.

Email alerts

Email alerts are based on the occurrence of a specific event, as opposed to being sent at a specific time on a scheduled date. The saved search is transformed into the alert by checking the **SEND EMAIL ALERTS WHEN RECORDS ARE CREATED/UPDATED** checkbox in the **Email** tab. NetSuite will continually monitoring the database for the event and will generate an email the moment that the event takes place. The definition of the event may be broad, for instance, to email the sales manager whenever an opportunity record is created or updated. Alternatively, it even may be very specific such as generating that email only if a particular field has been changed. The field is specified in the **Updated Fields** subtab:

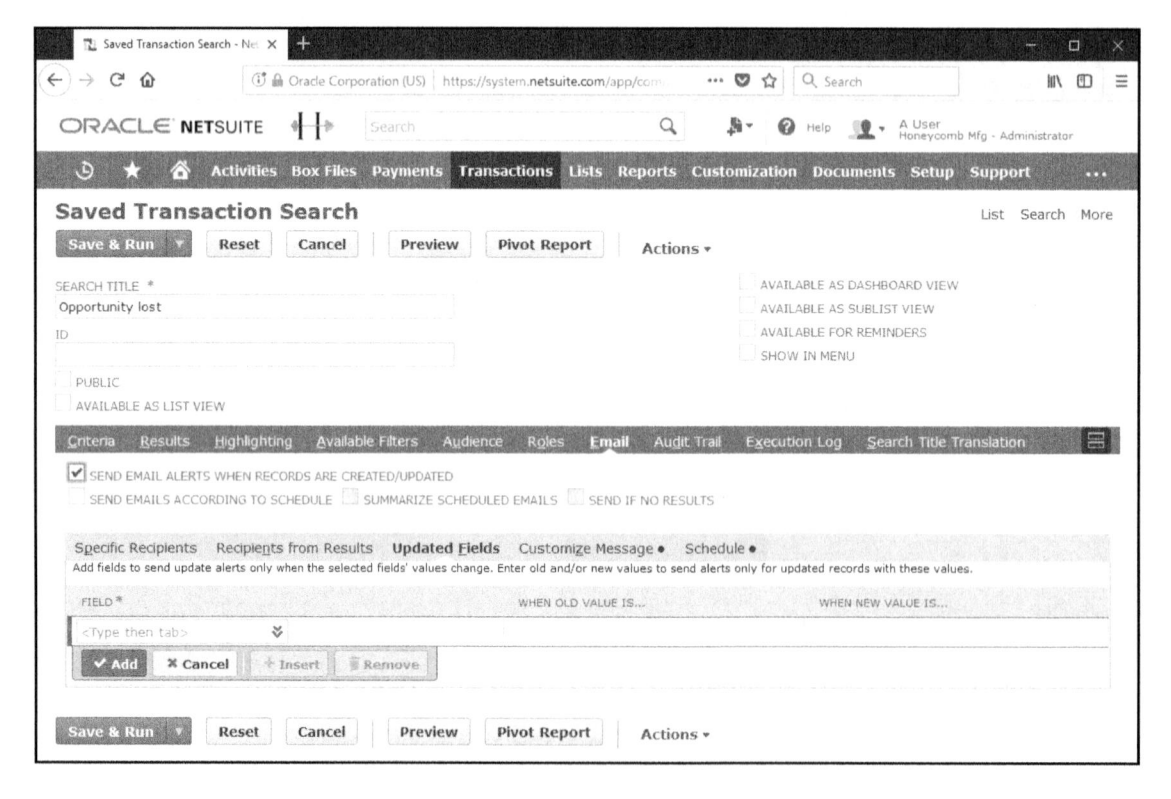

Saved Search email alerts

This is wonderful functionality and is not offered in reports. Build a search looking for that event and use this tab to alert someone that the event has happened. The use cases are endless. Send an email to the CEO if the CFO cuts a check in his own name. Send an email to the administrator if a bill from the LA Lakers is entered into the system, stating "someone has just purchased tickets to tonight's game" by using the fields on the **Customize Message** subtab.

The recipients of these emails can be specified individually or could be determined from the results of the search itself. The alert could therefore dynamically identify the sales manager responsible for that territory if a rep enters a sales order over $100,000. This feature can also be used to assist the collections department by sending an automatic email to customers whose invoices are overdue. Create a search looking for overdue invoices and include the email address of the customer in the results. Then, send the email alert when the event happens, choosing the recipients from the results, specifically the email address specified in the results.

Email alerts are extremely powerful yet, as they say, "with power comes responsibility." Be careful of overusing it because it has the potential of generating a lot of email for users and users will start to neglect those emails if there are too many received each day.

Roles

The **Roles** tab has the ability to specify the checkboxes found at the top of the screen on a per-role basis. We can determine the list and sublist option for each role that would apply as a default to their views of the data. That begs the question: what are those options and how do they work?

Analytics – Searches, Reports, and the Dashboard

Search settings

The search settings are found at the top of the screen. The title and ID should be filled out in order to easily identify this search in the future. The checkboxes at the top of the screen are also very useful:

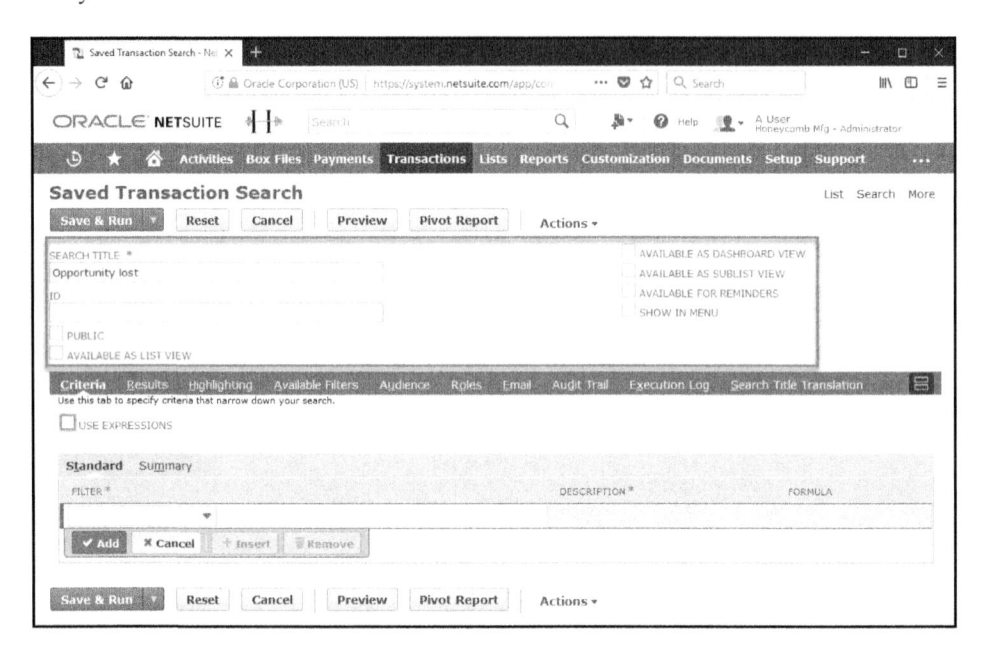

Saved Search settings

The PUBLIC checkbox

The **PUBLIC** checkbox enables us to create a search and makes it available to all of our users.

Available as List view

The **Available as List** view enables us to customize lists. Think of lists as searches without criteria. In other words, they are searches that return all of the records instead of filtering specific records out of the results. There are default lists of transactions (sales order, purchase orders, bills, invoices, and so on) and entities (customers, vendors, employees, and so on), for instance, **Transactions** | **Sales** | **Enter Sales Orders** | **List** or **Lists** | **Relationships** | **Customers**:

Chapter 8

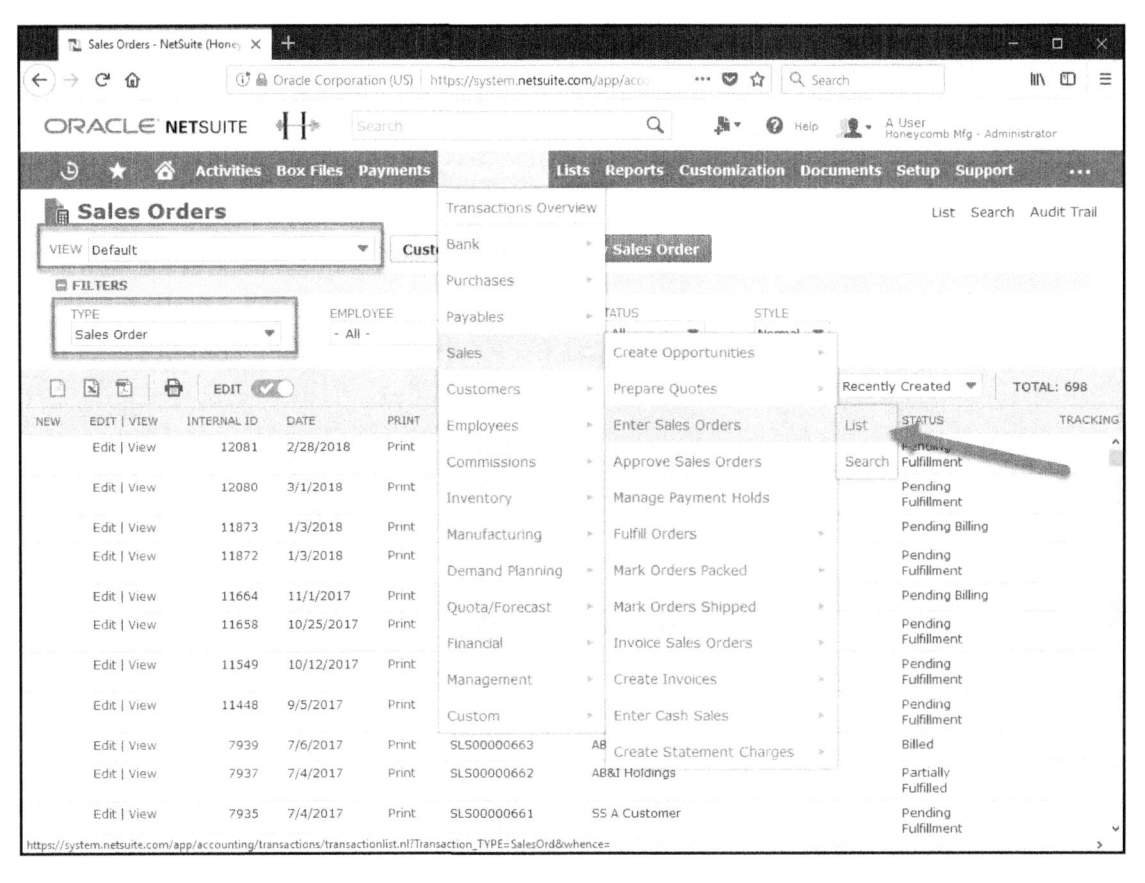

Available as list view

The list view is available in the drop-down at the top of the screen and will change the columns of data that are displayed for each record. There are a number of prebuilt lists such as default, all and financial, and so on. We can customize the columns being displayed by creating a saved search and clicking the list checkbox to make the search available in the view drop-down on that record type. We can add criteria to a list but I recommend not doing so. I have seen too many examples of users panicking that their records have disappeared because they have gone to a list which has filtered out their records. This becomes a huge problem until the administrator points out that the record is there and all the user needs to do is to change the list view!

Analytics – Searches, Reports, and the Dashboard

There is an easier way to edit those lists. Go to the list itself from the menu (for instance, **Lists | Relationships | Customers**) and click **Customize View**, which will open the saved search page for you to edit. Note that you can access to more options by clicking the **More Options** button, which will automatically check the **List** checkbox for you. Remember that all the other options we have learned about in saved search are available to be used in lists. We can, therefore, use highlighting as well as advanced filters to help our users work within a list. The **Available** filter appears as an option to filter the list, such as **Sales Rep** and **Stage**:

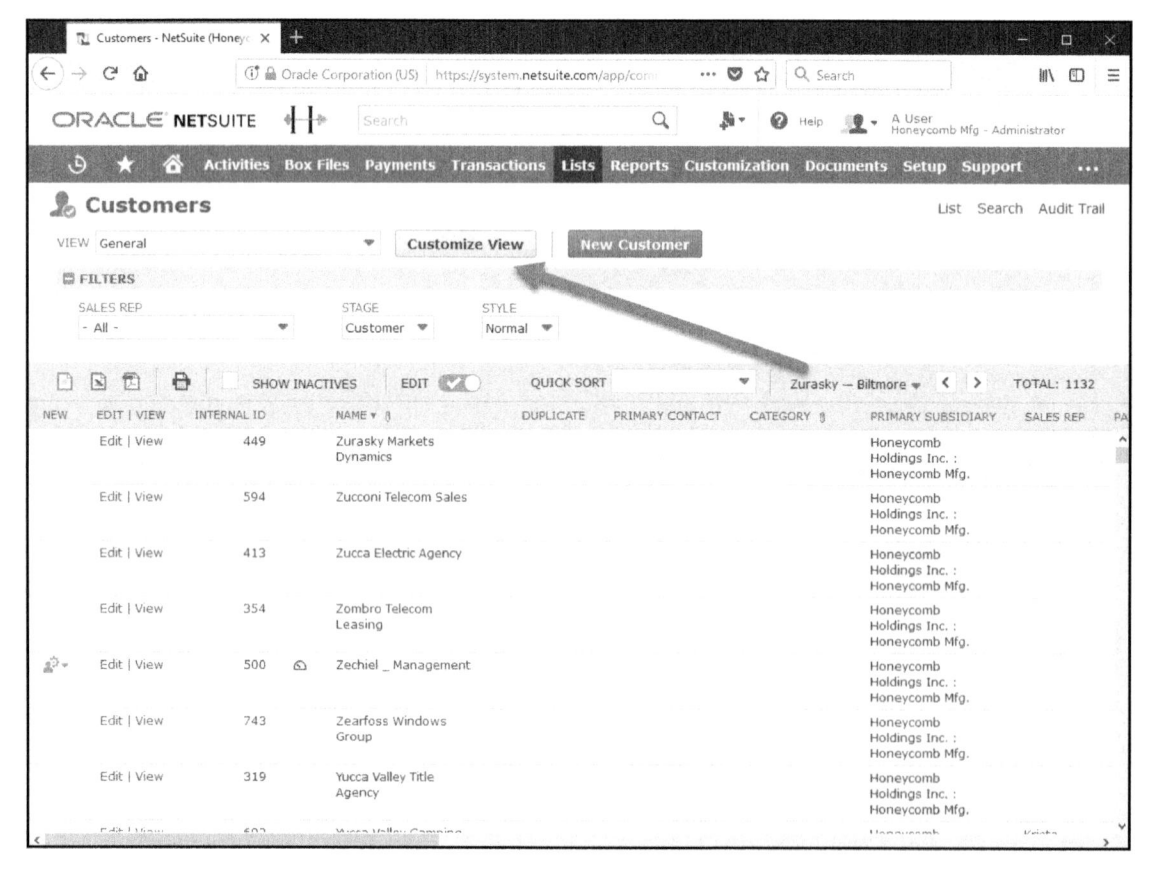

Customize a list view

[246]

Available as Dashboard view

The **Available as Dashboard** view is just that—it makes this search available to be chosen as a KPI, list or custom search on the dashboard.

Available as Sublist

The **Available as Sublist** view enables us to use our saved search skills to help users filter data on sublists. A sublist is similar to a list but appears in the tabs in a specific record:

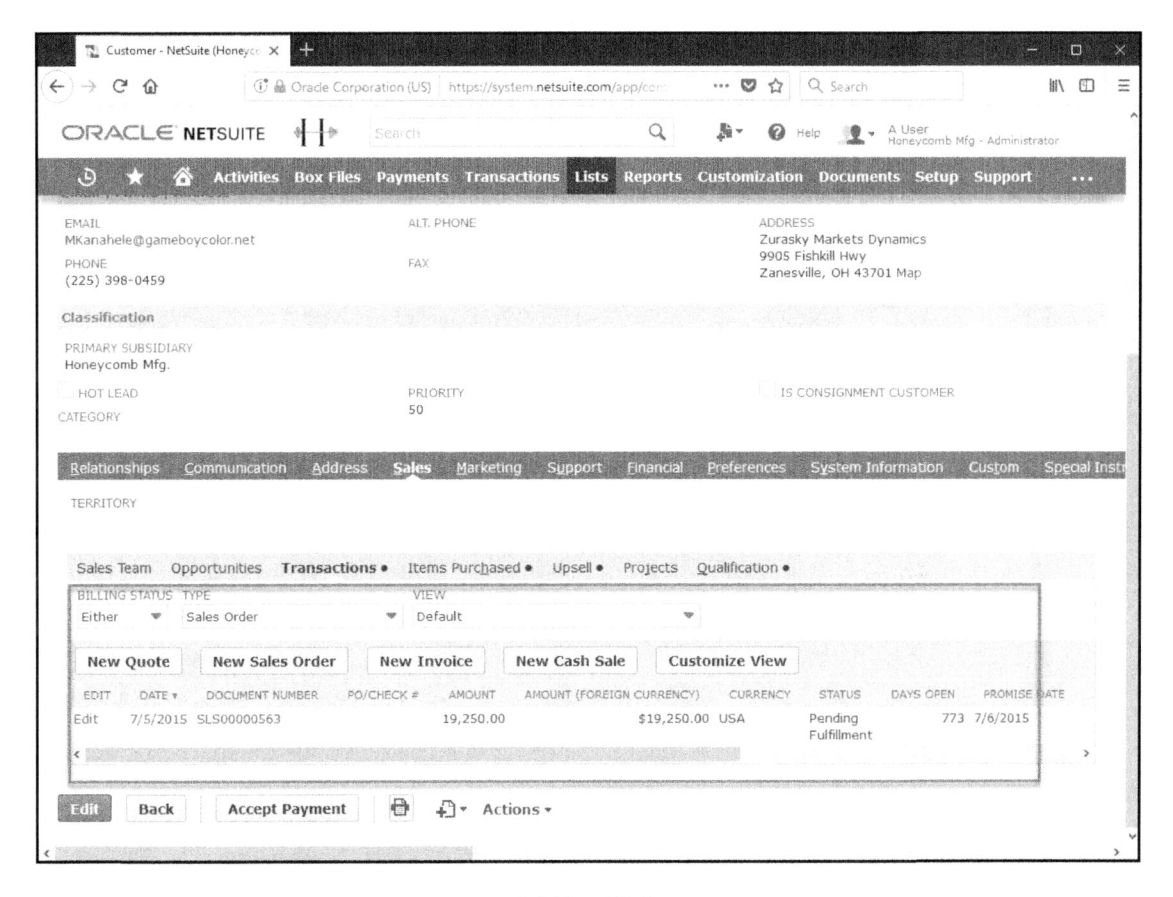

Available as sublist view

Analytics – Searches, Reports, and the Dashboard

Take the transactions sublist of a customer record as an example and assume that the accountant wants to view a specific field when looking at that view because clicking on each transaction to find that data is time-consuming and frustrating. Click the **Customize** button on the sublist and add that field to the results or even add a field to the available filters which will allow the user to toggle the data in that sublist on an individual record. Once again, the sublist checkbox will be automatically checked because we started to customize from the sublist itself.

Available for Reminders

NetSuite has a number of built-in reminders available for users to utilize as their task list of to-dos. There may be a need for additional reminders to be added based on your business or industry. **Available as Reminders** gives you the flexibility to add custom reminders to the dashboard by building a search looking for the event that needs to be attended and checking the **Available as Reminder** checkbox. The search will then be displayed as a custom reminder to be added to the reminders portlet on the dashboard. Custom reminders are displayed with a green C symbol in the **Select reminders** popup:

Available as Reminder

Examples

It's best to learn about saved searches in a practical way, so let's look at some examples. We will begin with an entity search and then move on to the more advanced transaction search.

Entity saved search example

We are required to build a search to identify customers in New York, sorted by customer name, with tier 1 customers appearing in red. Provide the user with the ability to refine the search by customer tier and make the search available to all sales reps so that they can place it on their dashboards:

1. Go to **Lists** | **Search** | **Saved Search** | **New** and select **Customer**.
2. Name the search with a descriptive name in accordance with a naming convention. There will be many searches created in your account and you want to be able to easily identify what the search does and who created it. I would recommend a naming convention beginning with the creator's initials. I will name my search `AB | Customers in NY`.
3. I can choose to make the search public by clicking the **Public** checkbox. This will make it available to all users who have access to that record, so it does not overwrite the permissions we set up in roles. The concern with **Public** is that it will appear in too many user search lists, especially if we make all our searches public. This makes it difficult for users to find their searches easily because of the sheer number of searches available, so it is something I tend to stay away from. I use the **Audience** tab instead to specify which users or groups or users need to see this search, instead of opening it to everybody by default.
4. There is also an option to make the search available on the dashboard by checking the **Available as dashboard view** checkbox. This would be used if I wanted to make this search available to individual contributors in the customer search portlet of their dashboards.
5. The search filters are built in the **Criteria** tab. Simply select the field from the dropdown and add in the Boolean search term, in this case, `City = New York`:
    1. There are many fields to choose from to build your search. Options include telephone numbers starting with `212` or a zip code such as `60611`. It all depends on the quality of your data. If the city field is not well populated or contains city names with a number of spelling mistakes, that field will not be the best one to use. There is no fuzzy logic in the saved search. If `New York` is misspelled as `New Uork`, that record will not be returned by our New York search.

Analytics – Searches, Reports, and the Dashboard

2. The use of multiple criteria, such as `City = New York, Phone number starts with 212,` or `zip code starts with 606` may initially return a limited set of results because the default setting in NetSuite is to use `AND` instead of `OR`. We need to check the **Use Expressions** checkbox to be able to make that change. Once checked, this opens up a choice between `AND/OR` that we can make on each row. It also allows us to use expressions to build even more advanced queries using the parentheses which is also available.
3. There are many options available when building the criteria such as city **CONTAINS, IS, IS EMPTY**, and so on, so be sure to choose the right one for the search you are trying to execute.
4. There are also dynamic filters available when searching by date fields, such as **TODAY YESTERDAY, THIS MONTH, LAST MONTH**, and so on. This allows you to reuse the search in the future as the system will automatically change the results if the search happens at midnight when Cinderella disappears and *tomorrow* becomes *today*.
5. There are options to create a search spanning multiple tables using fields that appear at the bottom of the list with an ellipses button next to them. This is a link to the joined table and allows you to return data based on the values in a field on the linked table. Simply select the table to be given the choice of fields to search within.
6. The **Results** tab is used to choose the columns that will be returned in our search. Simply select the field you want to add from the drop-down list.
7. We can also reorder the column by dragging and dropping them into a different order, as well as sorting the results by specific fields by selecting the field in the sort section at the top of the tab.
8. Always add the fields you've placed in your criteria into your results. This helps you identify errors pretty quickly by merely scanning the results. I know that something is wrong with my criteria if I see a CA customer in Toledo in my New York search and can start to troubleshoot the error before continuing.

9. I could use the highlighting tool to bring attention to a subset of in my results, such as my Tier 1 customers. Simply go to that tab and select the first row. You can then set up the highlighting condition, `tier = tier 1`, and then return to the initial screen where you can specify that those records should appear in red.
10. The available filter tab is used to help users create their own search results based on the template. You would simply add the **Tier** field to available filters and select the **Available as filter** checkbox. This will place the field at the top of the results of the search, which a user can utilize to see only one of the tiers in the results at a time. Note that you can add a multi-select for picklists when the user needs to see more than one tier at a time.
11. This search is private, as it stands. It can be opened to specific users by selecting those users in the **Audience** tab. The users can either be selected as an individual employee or by role.
12. Click **Save** to create the search.

These steps create the search that was requested, however, I would not perform all of these steps at once. I would save and run the search after each step in order to check that something hasn't gone wrong with that step. It's much easier to troubleshoot any mistakes when building the search in iterations, instead of in one step.

Once created, the search can also be used as a template for new searches. Simply edit the existing search name and make your changes, then click the **Save As** option instead of **Save**. This will save a brand new search under the new name while keeping the existing search intact.

Transaction search example

Build a *Sales by Customer* search. Calculate the total sales by customer and specify each customer's smallest and largest transaction.

Go to **Lists** | **Search** | **Saved Search** | **New** and select **Transactions**:

1. Name the search **Sales By Customer Search**.

2. Go to the **Criteria** tab:
    1. Add a filter of **Type** = **Invoice** and **Cash Sale**. The Type filter should always be the first filter that you add to a transaction search.
    2. The next filter to determine is the option for **Main Line**. This determines whether the transaction will be summarized in the result or whether it will return all line items in each transaction. So, this is a crucial decision. **Main Line** is set as **Yes** is the option to use when summarizing the entire transaction, whereas **Main Line** is set as **No** is used when looking at the line level of the transaction. Select **Main Line** and set it to **Yes**:

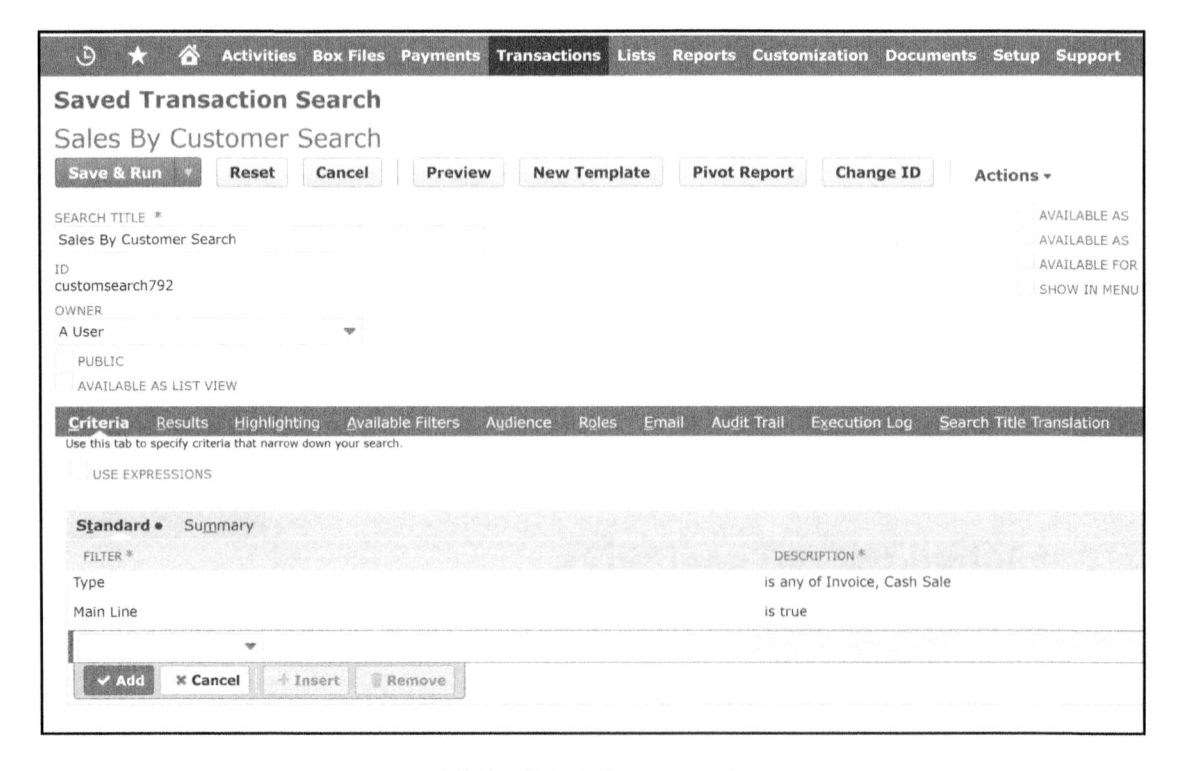

Main Line is 'Yes' setting for transaction search

3. Go to the **Results** tab and click the **Remove All** button.
4. Ensure that the name and amount fields appear in the results.
5. Click the **Summary** type of the row of the **Name** field and choose **Group**. Click the **Summary** type column of the row in the **Summary** field and select **SUM**.

6. Add an additional line and select **Amount**. Choose **Minimum** in the **Summary** type field.
7. Add an additional line and select **Amount**. Choose **Maximum** in the **Summary** type field.
8. Add an additional line and select **Amount**. Choose **Average** in the **Summary** type field:

Comparison of Maximum, Minimum and Average Summary types

9. Click **Save and Run**.

Reports

There are many similarities between searches and reports, as we discussed earlier. Many of the functions and searches are available in reports. You can add filters and choose the colors that you want to appear in the results. NetSuite has many built-in reports available to you, covering most records in the system.

[253]

Analytics – Searches, Reports, and the Dashboard

One of the key advantages of using reports is that you start customizing a report from a template. If you go to any report, you'll see a **Customize** option in the bottom left-hand corner of the screen which allows you to take the existing template and edit it to show just the information you need to see:

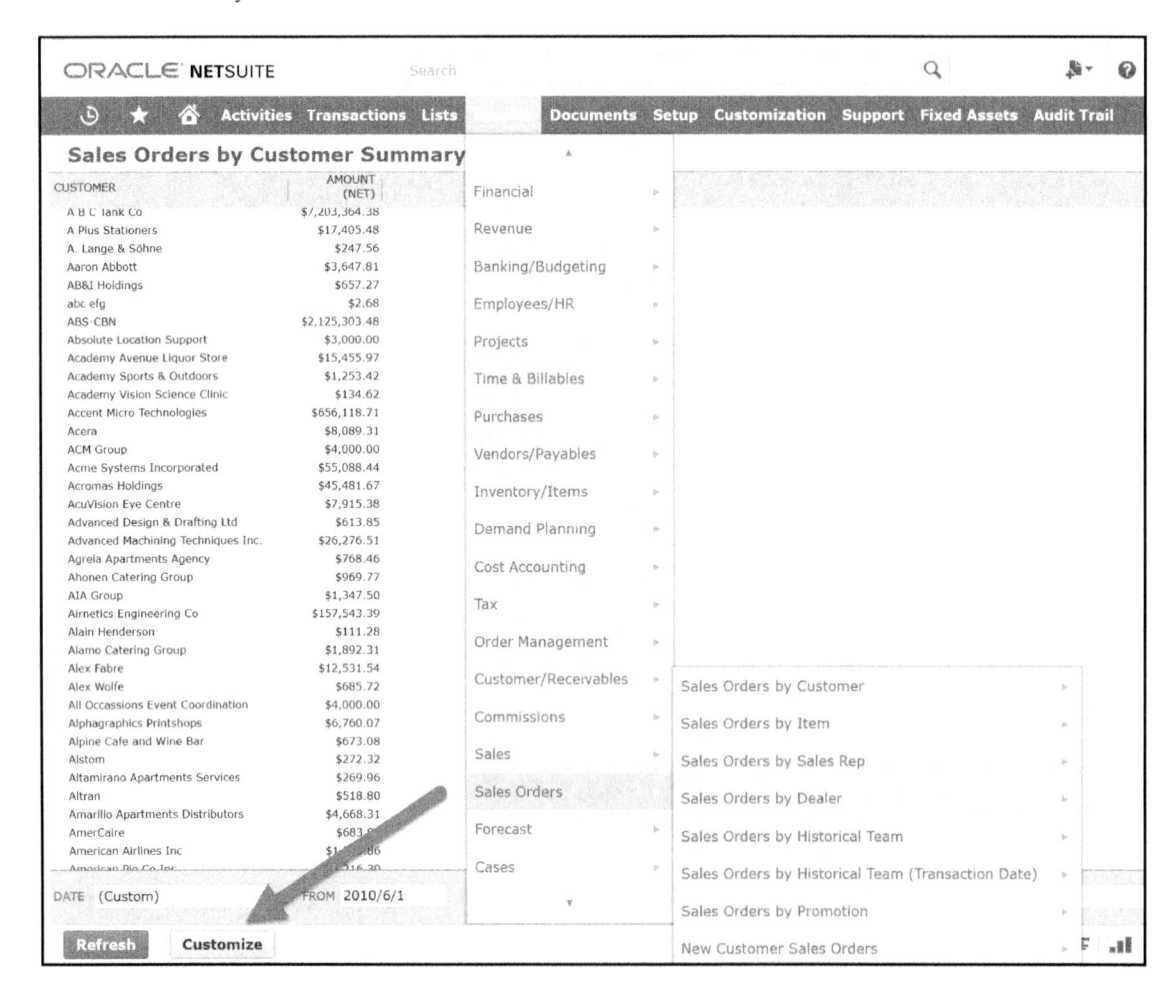

Customize standard report

But before we start customizing, let's review the options available out of the box. We'll illustrate this using a sales order report, however, most of the options we will be discussing apply to most of the other reports in NetSuite.

Let's start with the options in the bottom right-hand corner of the screen. You can export this report to Excel, CSV, MS Word, or to a PDF. You can email a report as well as set up a schedule report which will send a copy of this report to a particular person on a recurring basis. That person is usually an internal user but does not have to be internal. In fact, we could set up a specific report for a board member, for instance, and have that emailed to the board member every Monday morning. NetSuite gives you a powerful tool to share information but it is obviously a double-edged sword because you are exporting and emailing this data out of the system with no control over who can view it once it has been sent. There are also options to expand or collapse the details in the data and graph the report, if required:

Report options

Analytics – Searches, Reports, and the Dashboard

There are buttons at the bottom of the screen which are very useful when pivoting data. The obvious one is the date field, which lets you change the date range that you want to view the report within. There is an option to determine whether the report will be run by a certain time period or date range. This preference is set up in **Home | Set Preferences**, and the **Analytics** tab, where you can choose to report by period for **All Reports**, **Financials only**, or for neither:

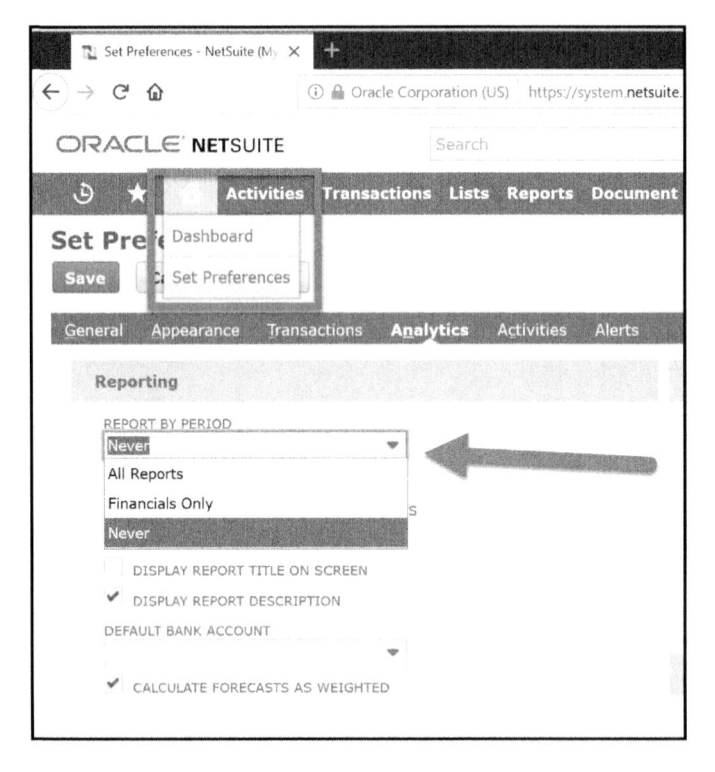

Setting Reporting user preferences

Note as well that the date ranges can be specified—you can detail specific dates where you'd like to run this report—or they can be dynamic and changing, for instance, this week or last year. As the date changes, the report parameters change with it.

Chapter 8

The **Columns** filter is a very powerful tool to pivot data. The default is to look at the totals, however, we can change that to break out the columns by subsidiary (for OneWorld users) or by the classifications of Department of Class and Location. This will expand the columns and show you the data for that specific category, in this case, sales orders by location. There are a number of different options in that dropdown and this is certainly an option you want to share with your users to give them the ability to pivot the data with ease:

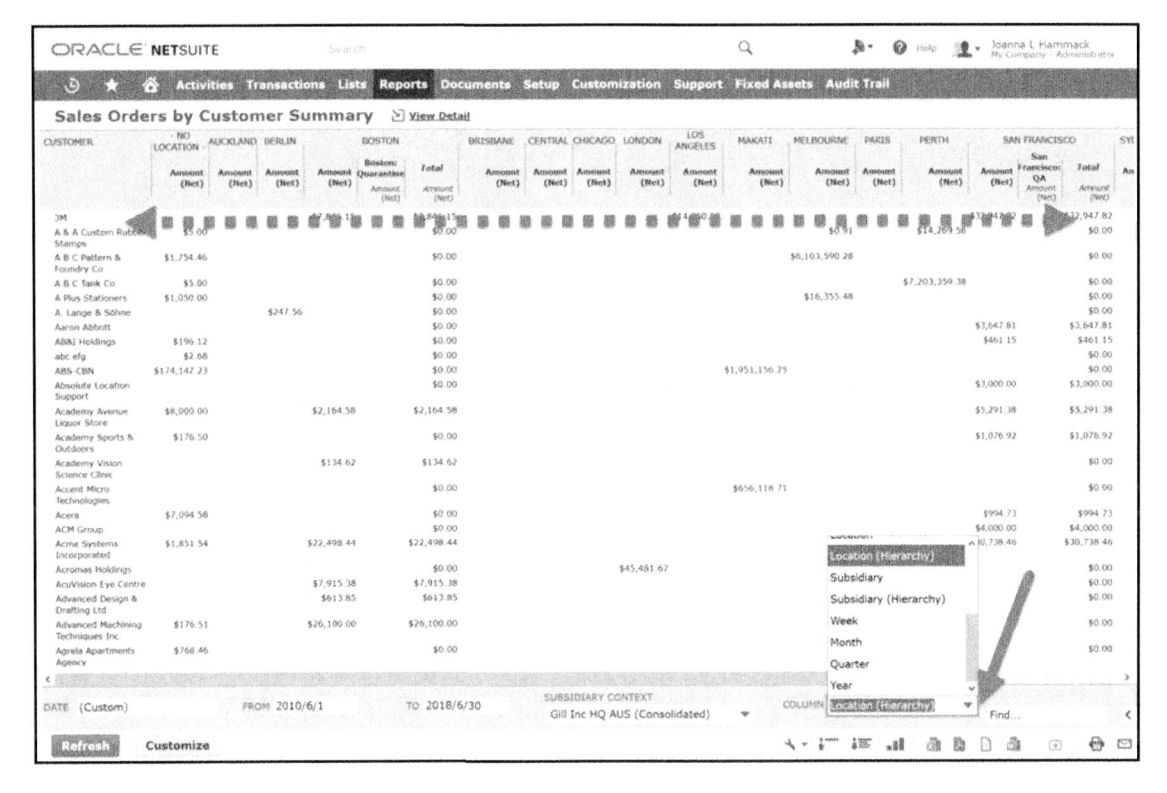

Pivoting data on standard reports

Analytics – Searches, Reports, and the Dashboard

There are additional options to compare the results of the report over time. Simply select the appropriate time range from the column's drop-down to pivot the data:

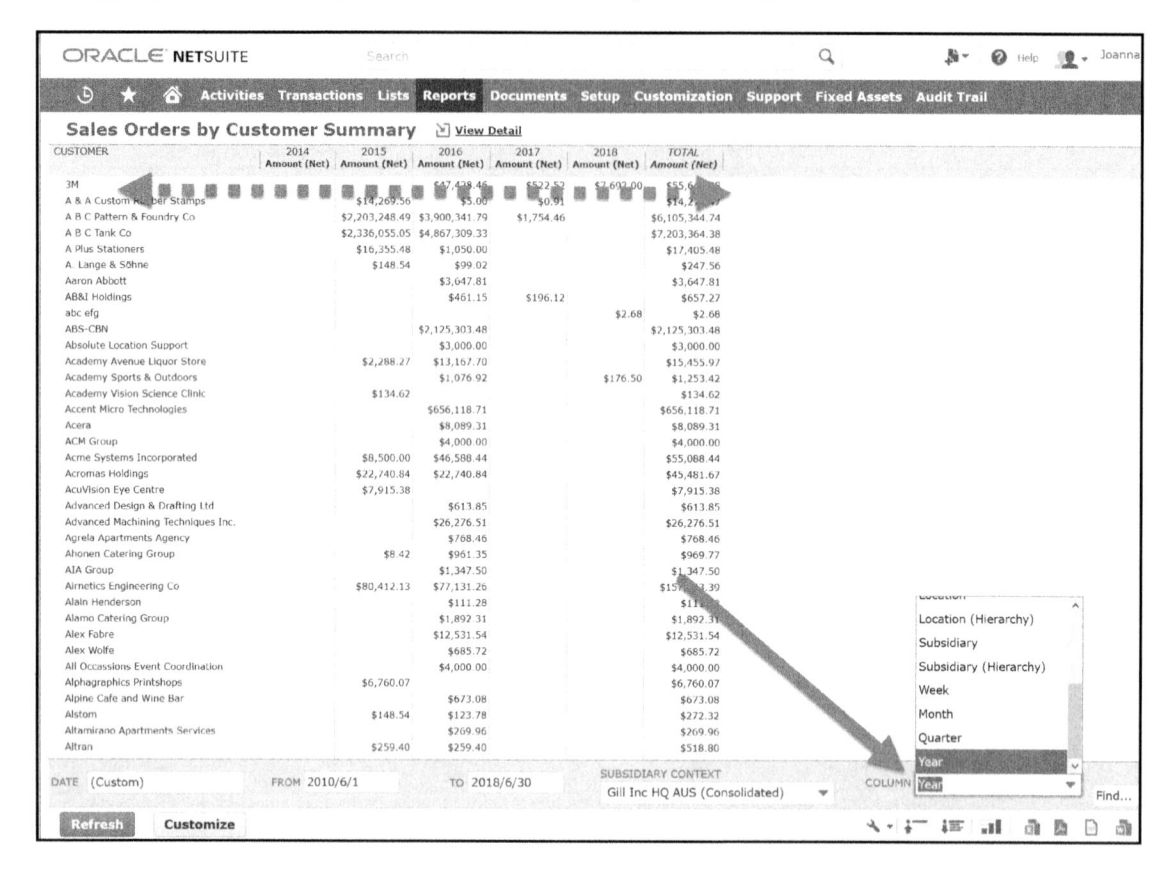

Pivot report data from the annual view

Remember that when you make a change to your filters in reports, you will need to click refresh for the change to be reflected in the data. This is unlike searches. In searches, the user just needs to click out of the filter in order for the page to refresh and the change to be reflected.

Standard reports

There are two types of reports in NetSuite, financial reports and other reports. Let's start customizing the standard report. Click the **Customize** button in the bottom left-hand corner of the screen. The customization options are very similar to those in saved searches. We can choose the columns that will appear in the results and on the second tab we get to choose the filters to add to the criteria. These are equivalent to the **Criteria** and **Results** tabs we saw in Saved Search, however, they are just in reverse order:

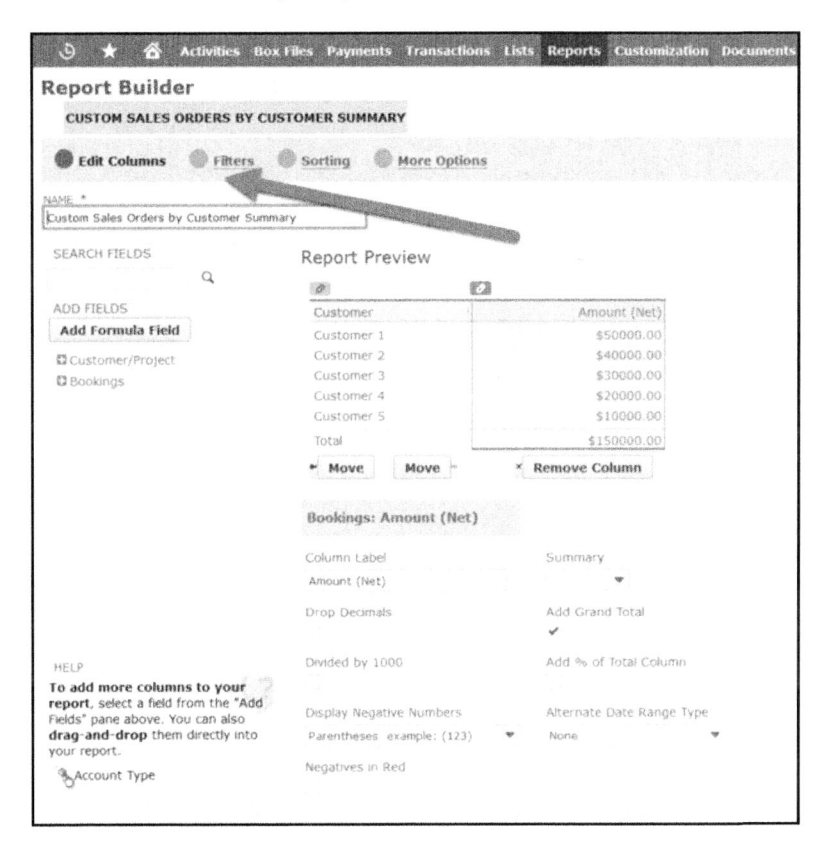

Comparing Report 'Edit Columns & Filters' to Saved Search 'Criteria & Results'

Report edit columns

If you want to change any aspect of the existing columns, select the column on the right-hand side of the screen and the options below that field. The options will change depending on the type of field you select. A dollar value field will give you the ability to set formatting options such as whether to divide by 1,000 or to format negative numbers in a certain way, such as in red or with a minus sign. We can change the label of the column and drop decimals if necessary. There are also options to perform calculations on that column using the **Summary** field, as well as adding a grand total and a percentage of the total into the results of that column:

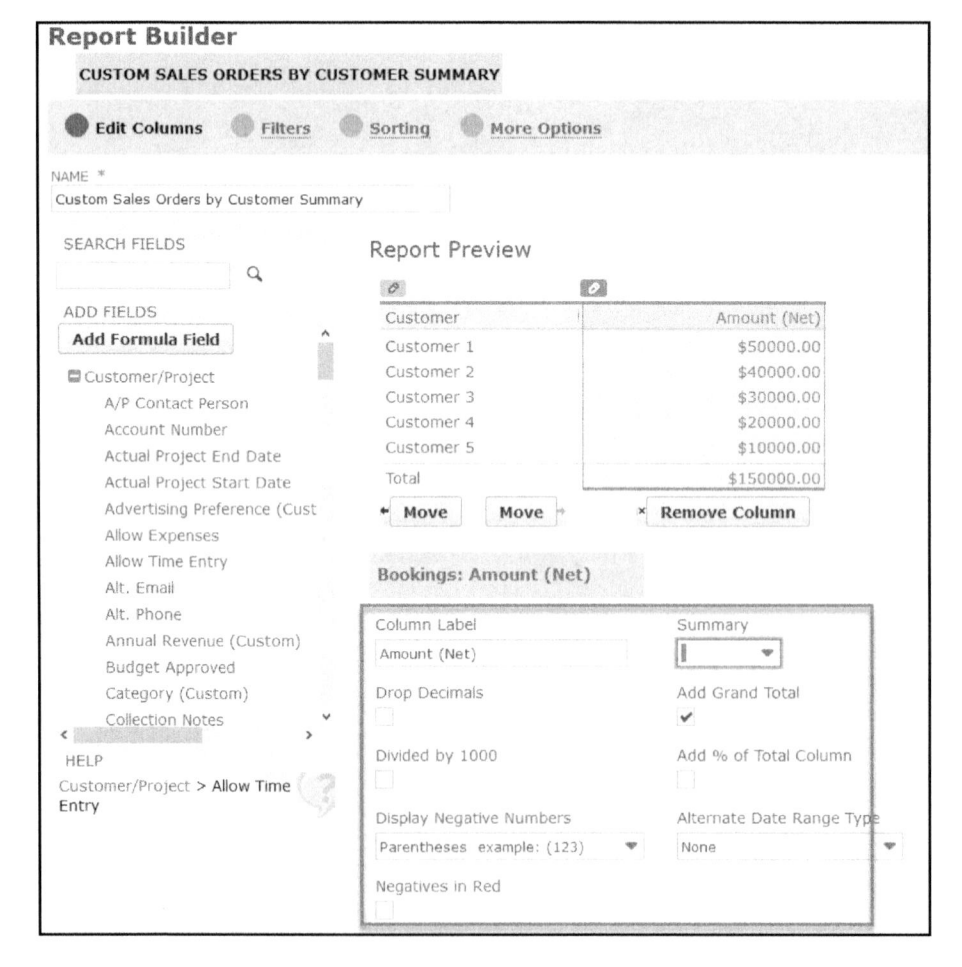

Formatting options by column

Chapter 8

There are also **Move** buttons available, in addition to a **Remove Column** button. Remove is self-explanatory yet **Move** does more than simply reorder the columns in the result. The **Move** left button is what we use to group columns in reports. Select the column and click **Move** to the left in order to group by that particular column (we can also drag and drop the column if preferred). If, for instance, we were asked to create a Sales Orders by Customer by Item report, we would go to **Reports** | **Sales Orders** | **Sales by Customer** and click customize. We would then add the item field to the columns by selecting it from the fields and folders in the list on the left-hand side of the screen:

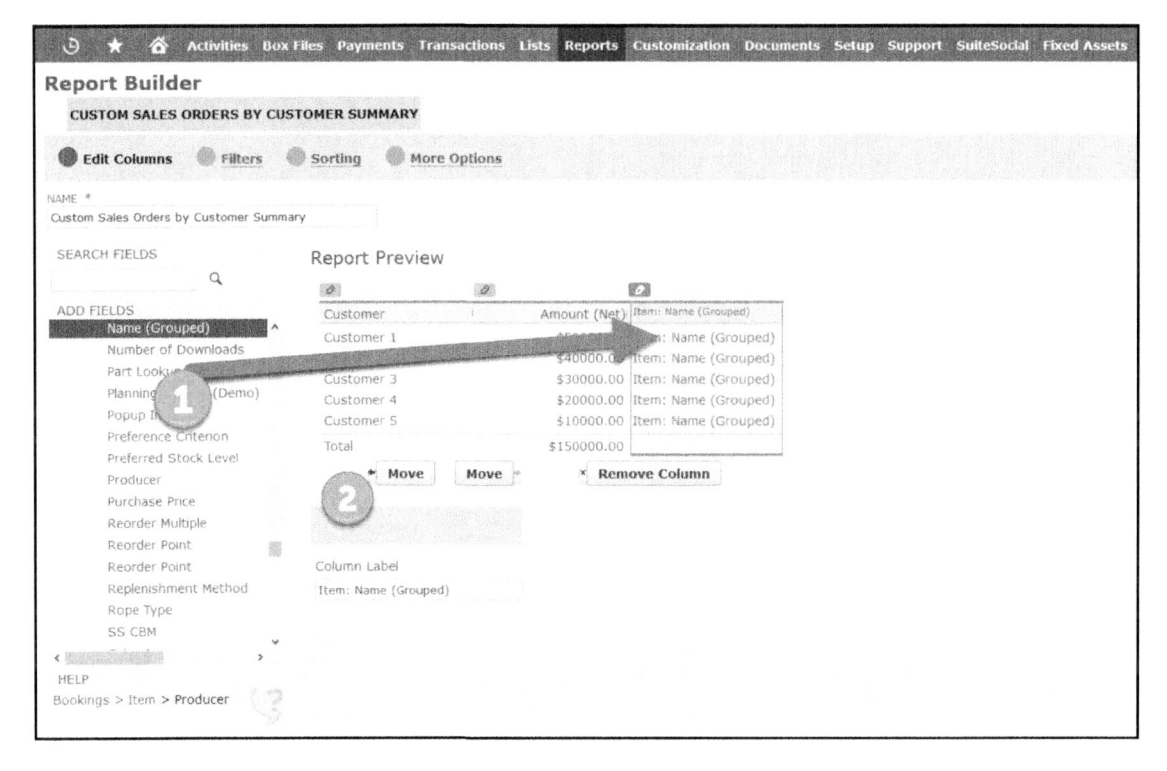

Add column to report

Analytics – Searches, Reports, and the Dashboard

Once we have added the item column, we will use the move left button to move it all the way over to the grouping area of the screen. The order of the columns is determined staring from the left, **Customer**, **Item**, and then the remaining fields. We will click the group previous checkbox in order to ensure that the customer is now grouped:

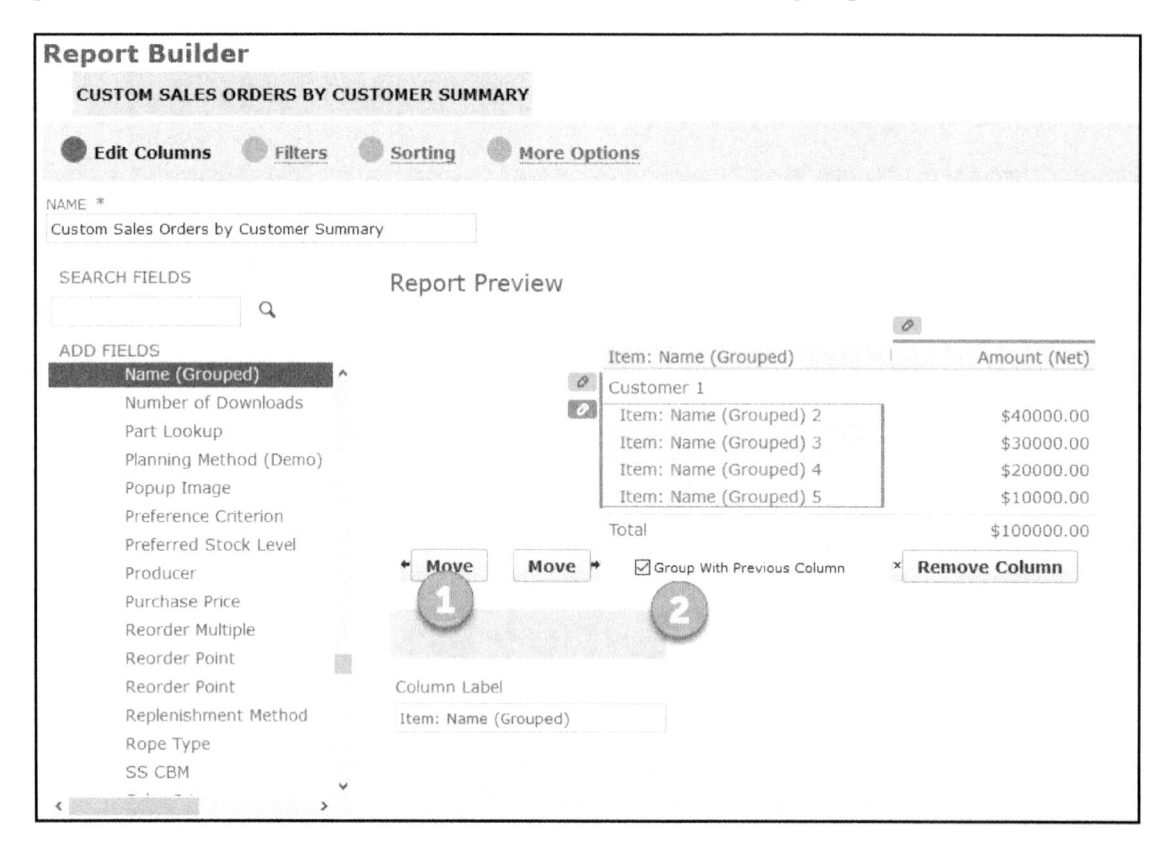

Group (Total by) a Field

[262]

Click **Preview** to show totals by Customer and then by Item:

Custom Sales Orders by Customer Summary	View Detail

Honeycomb Mfg
Honeycomb Holdings Inc. (Consolidated)
Custom Sales Orders by Customer Summary
January 1, 2008 - January 31, 2018
Options: Show Zeros

ITEM: NAME (GROUPED)	AMOUNT (NET)
Aaron Abbott	
CAN00003	$500.00
CAN00001	$799.00
Total - Aaron Abbott	$1,299.00
Alex Fabre	
CAN00001	$1,598.00
CAM00001	$1,000.00
CAN00002	$3,897.00
CAM00006	$3,300.00
Total - Alex Fabre	$9,795.00
Bennett Consulting	
KIN00001	$3,500.00
CHR00001	$4,485.00
Total - Bennett Consulting	$7,985.00
Fabre Enterprises	
KIN00001	$8,250.00
CHR00001	$18,750.00
Total - Fabre Enterprises	$27,000.00
Hahn & Associates	
CHR00001	$18,750.00
KIN00001	$4,950.00
Total - Hahn & Associates	$23,700.00
James McClure	
CAN00002	$1,299.00
Total - James McClure	$1,299.00
Jim Strong	
CAN00002	$1,645.90
Total - Jim Strong	$1,645.90
Justin Ramos	
CAN00001	$799.00
Total - Justin Ramos	$799.00
Kalinsky Consulting Group	
CHR00001	$6,875.00
KIN00001	$5,775.00

DATE (Custom)   FROM 1/1/2008   TO 1/31/2018   SUBSIDIARY CONTEXT Honey

Refresh   Return To Customization

Preview custom report

Analytics – Searches, Reports, and the Dashboard

On the other hand, if we wanted to reverse it and look at the report as a sales by Item by Customer report, we could edit the **Sales by Item** report and add the **Customer** column and then of course group by customer. We could also use our existing report and simply switch the order of the item and customer fields by selecting the item column and clicking move left, which would give us the same result as if we started with the **Sales by Item** report:

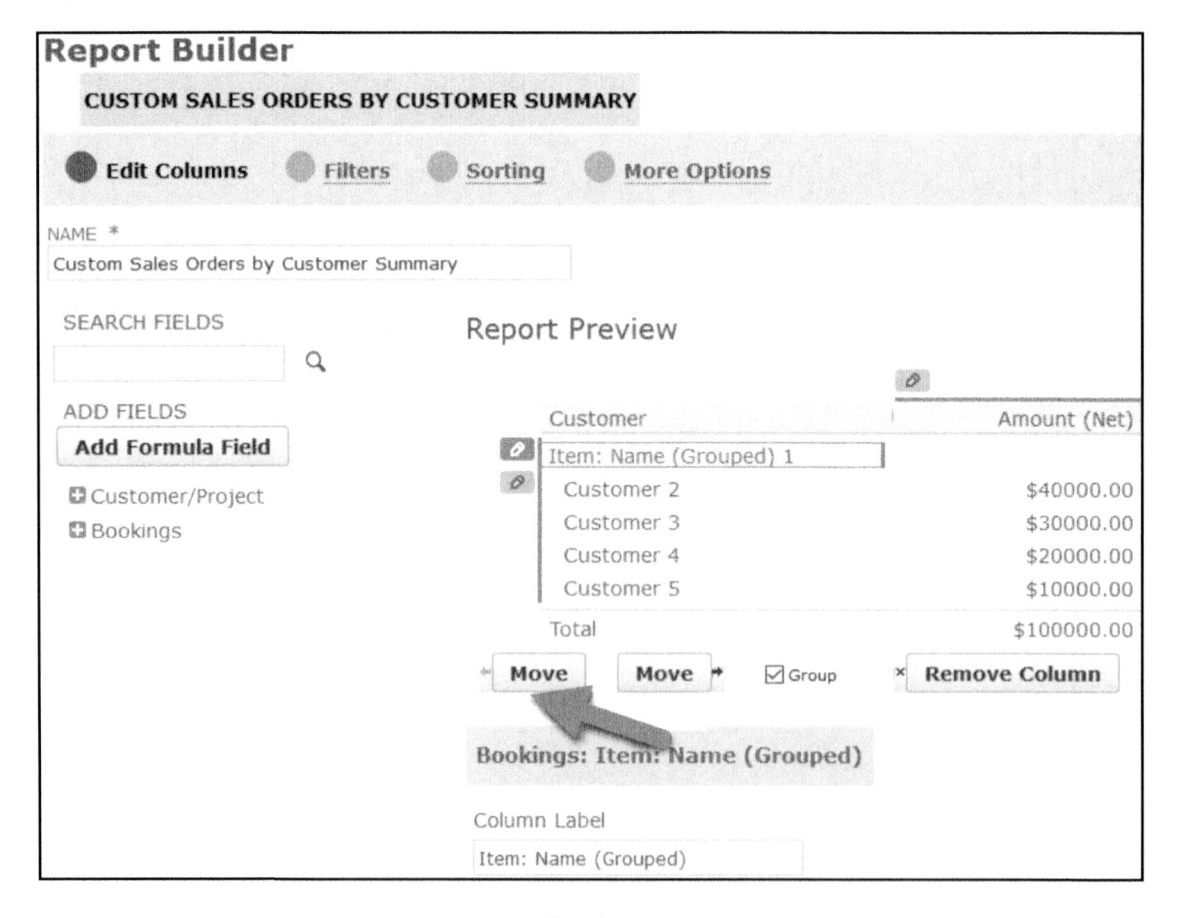

Report Builder

CUSTOM SALES ORDERS BY CUSTOMER SUMMARY

● **Edit Columns**   ● Filters   ● Sorting   ● More Options

NAME *
Custom Sales Orders by Customer Summary

SEARCH FIELDS

ADD FIELDS

Add Formula Field

➕ Customer/Project
➕ Bookings

Report Preview

Customer	Amount (Net)
Item: Name (Grouped) 1	
Customer 2	$40000.00
Customer 3	$30000.00
Customer 4	$20000.00
Customer 5	$10000.00
Total	$100000.00

← **Move**   **Move** →   ☑ Group   ✕ **Remove Column**

Bookings: Item: Name (Grouped)

Column Label
Item: Name (Grouped)

Move column

All of the fields that are available can be found in the folders on the left-hand side of the screen. Simply expand the folders to find the field that you are looking for. If you find that field, you can use the search box to search through the fields to find your search term:

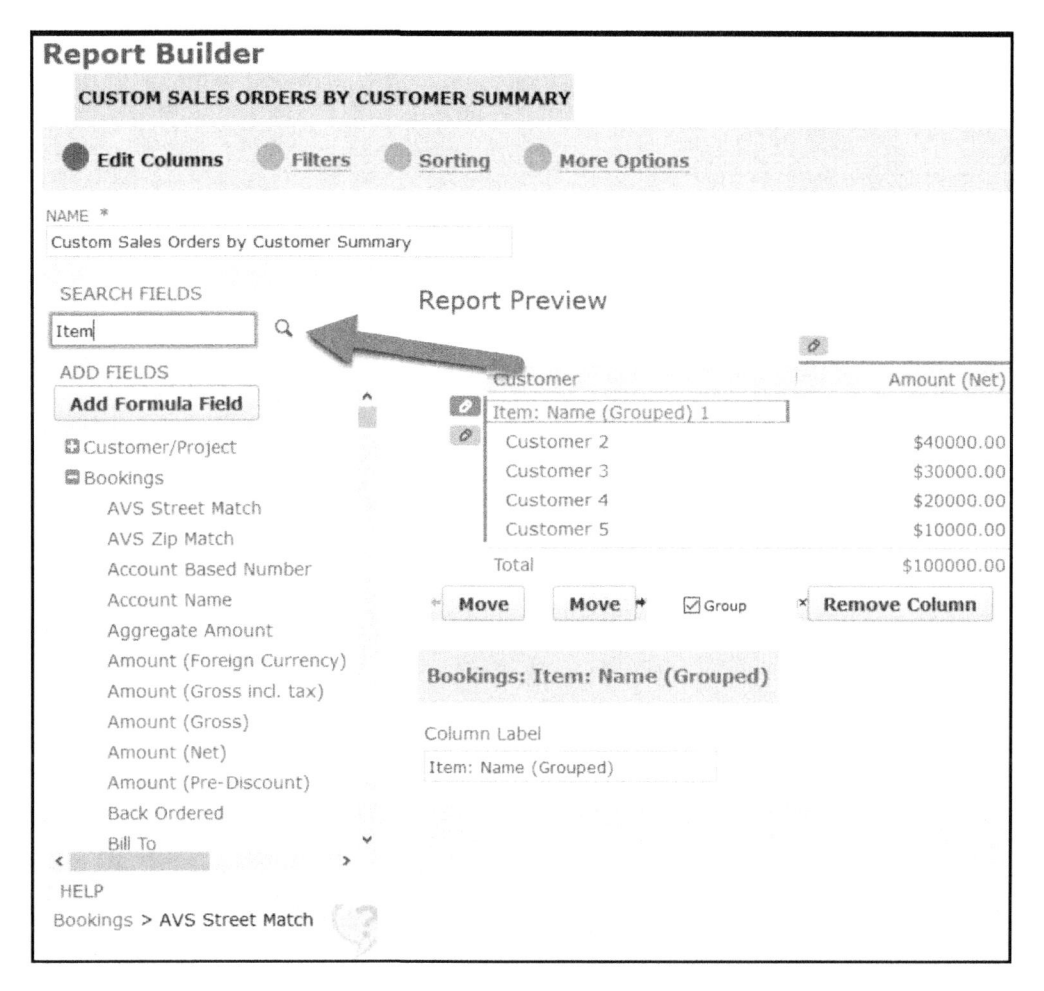

Search for fields to add to report

The **Name** field on the **Edit Columns** screen is used to rename the report to something more meaningful. We should use a naming convention like we discussed in earlier in this chapter then we discussed the naming of Saved Searches to ensure that we can recognize this report easily. There is also a formula button that can be added to the columns to perform simple calculations. Once added, we can determine the calculation that needs to be run. The options are very limited, however:

- Addition [Sum x+y]
- Subtraction [Difference x-y]
- Percent difference of X [((x-y)/x*100]

Analytics – Searches, Reports, and the Dashboard

- Percent difference Y [((x-y)/y*100]
- Ratio [x/y]
- Percent ratio (x/y*100]
- Multiplication [x*y]

Select the columns you wish to represent x and y and choose the appropriate formula from the list:

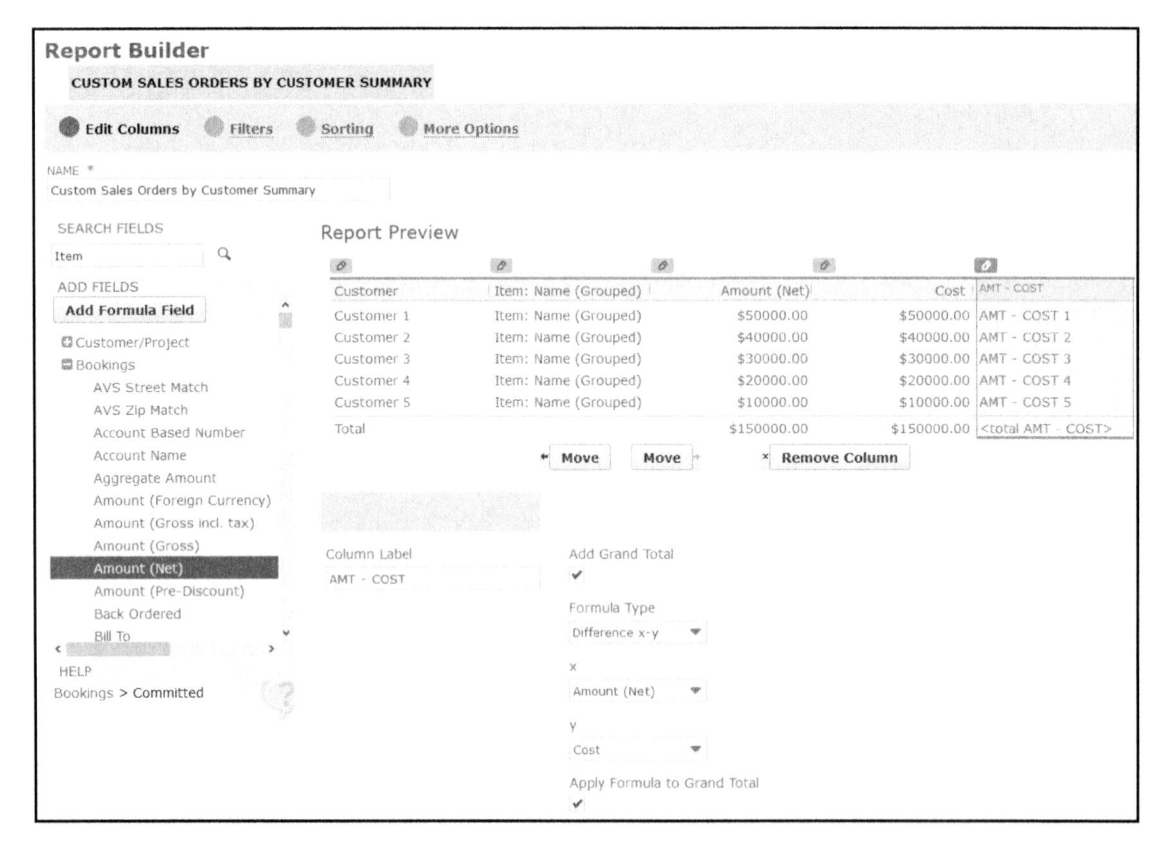

Perform calculations using the Formula field

There is an important option available to create comparative reports, comparing values from a current period to a previous period in one report:

[266]

Illustration of comparison report by Alternate Date Range

This is achieved by adding a duplicate amount field into your columns and choosing **Alternate Date Range Type** from the options. The alternate date range for that column is either **Relative to report date** or **Relative to today's date**. The **Relative to report date** is typically used because it has greater flexibility to report accurately on different date ranges. Once selected, we choose the alternate date range parameters from the many date ranges on offer, such as yesterday, last week, last month, and so on:

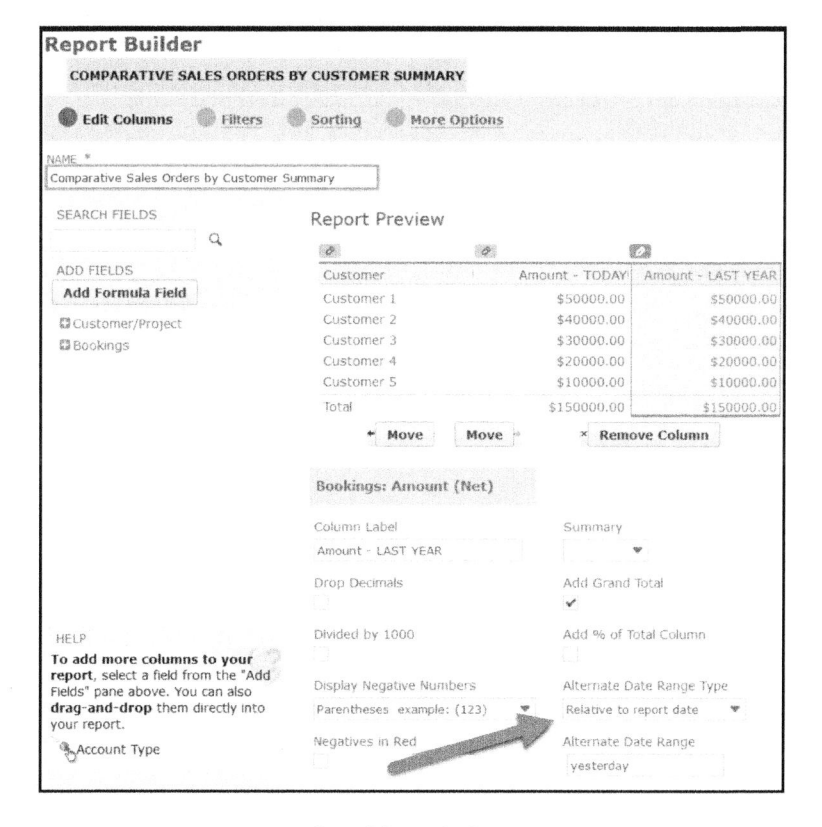

Set up of Alternate date Range

Analytics – Searches, Reports, and the Dashboard

Report filters

The filter tab enables us to filter out data from our results. Simply add the field from the left-hand side containing the folders and fields and then set the criteria for this report, such as this Business to Consumer sales report, which filters out all customers who are not individuals:

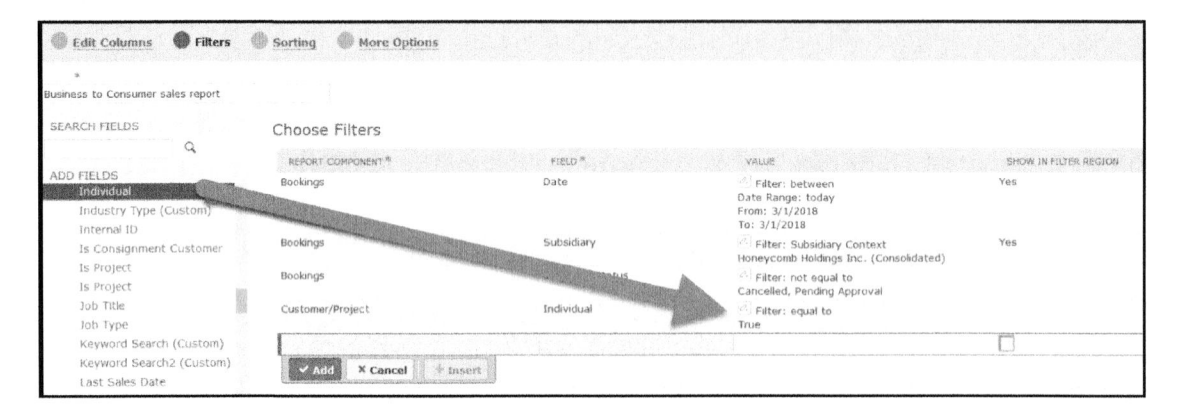

Add a Report Filter

The fields are added in the same way as they were on the **Edit Column** screen, and there is also a search box to search for a field if it is not easy to find using the folder structure. Notice as well that you can add the filter and check the **Show in Filter** column which adds it as an available filter in the report results:

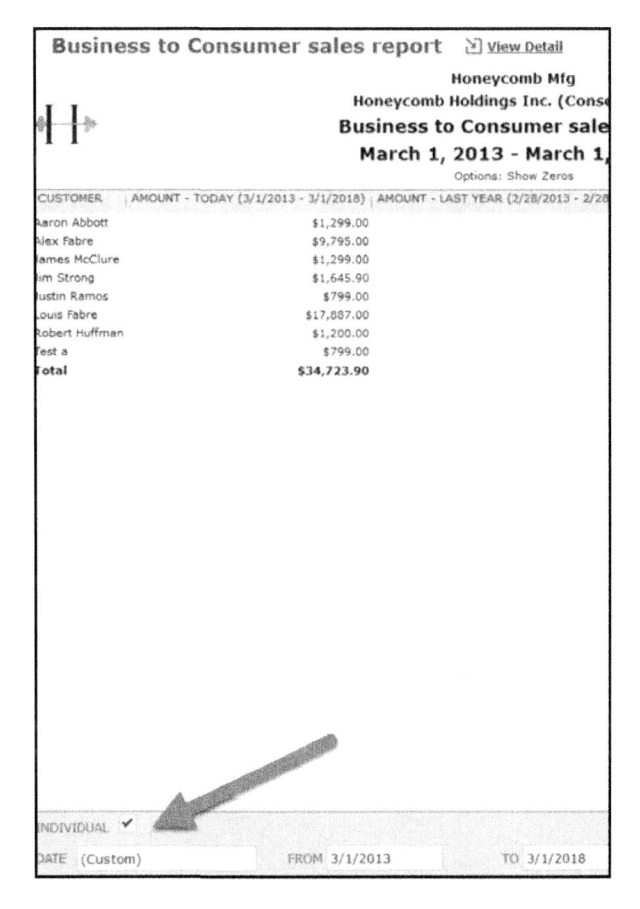

Enabling User to pivot results based on custom filter

Report sorting

We can sort the result by any number of fields. Select the field from the add fields column on the left of the screen and determine the sort order, either ascending or descending order.

Analytics – Searches, Reports, and the Dashboard

Report – More options

The options tab has some interesting variations compared to what we would see under save searches. There is an **Audience** tab and an **Access** tab which seems to be duplications:

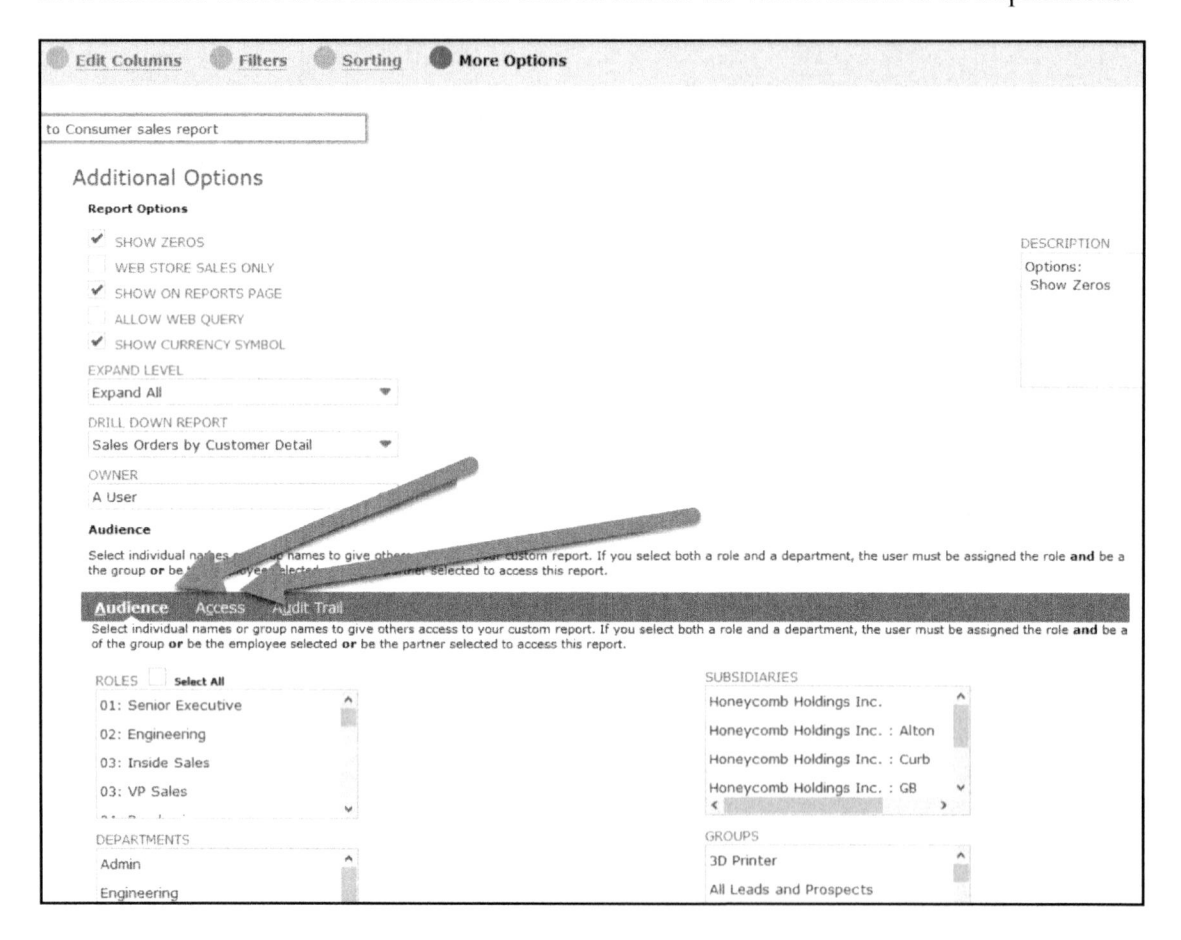

Set user access based on audience and access control

They are not. Audience control works the same way as it does within saved search. It opens this report to users provided that those users have permissions to view this information in their role. What if the user lacks those permissions in their role? Well, that's what the **Access** tab is for. It is an override which gives the user selected on that tab access to this report, whether or not they have access to this data based on the permissions of their role.

There is also a checkbox called web query. This creates an additional export option once you've customized and saved this report:

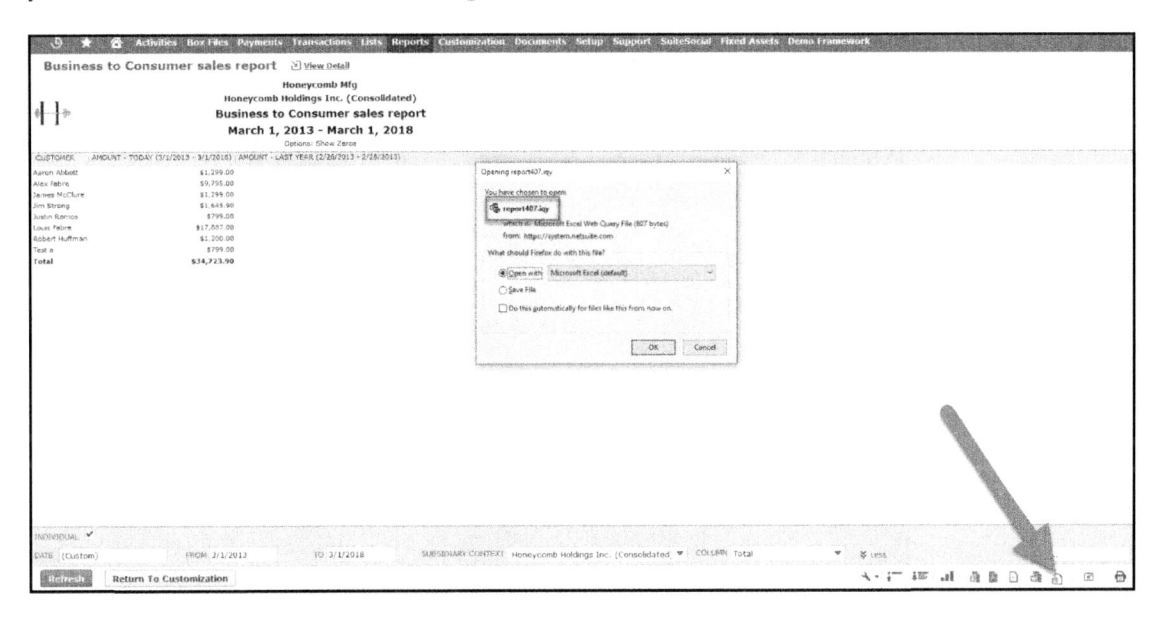

Exporting an Excel web query

Analytics – Searches, Reports, and the Dashboard

The export to Excel web query that is created by this checkbox creates a built-in link to the data in the report from within the MS Excel application. This makes the exported version dynamic instead of simply a static version of the report based on the date and time that the report was run. Users can click the **Refresh** button in Excel to refresh the information that is returned by the report. This is another option that enables external users to review your NetSuite data. No NetSuite license is required to see the information in Excel. All that is required is a NetSuite user email address to open and refresh the information. This obviously has its risks as it provides access to data without any ability to control that access, other than removing that access via the web query and thereby breaking the link with the report. Web query can be very useful but must be used with extreme care, especially when dealing with sensitive data:

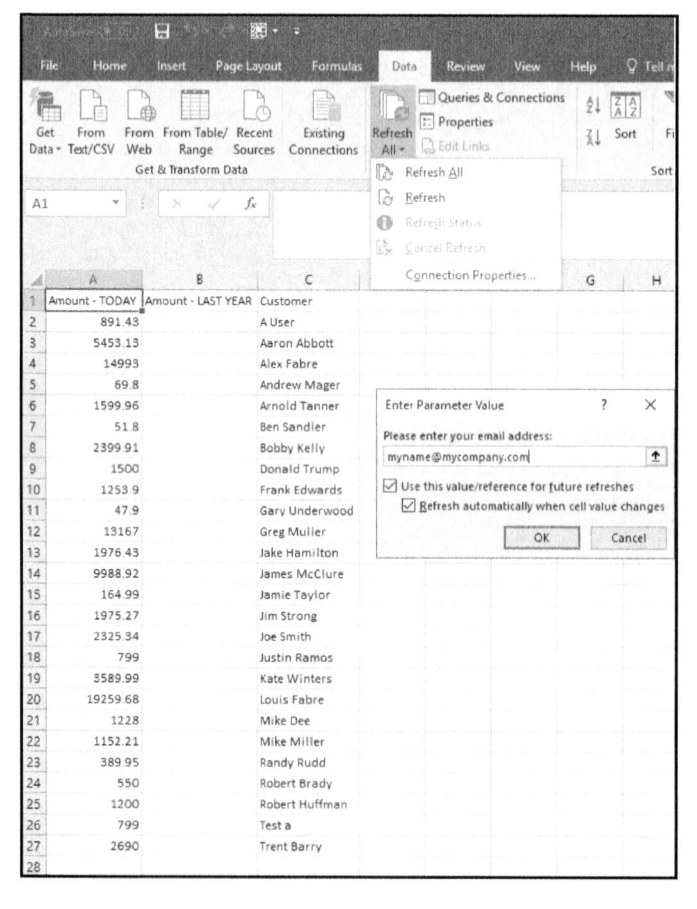

Execute Web Query in Excel

Financial Report Builder

The accountant may require different layouts of the financial statements for different audiences. The bank may require a different format of the financial statements, as an example. The financial report builder is used to create customized financial statements, as the name suggests. The main difference between financial reports and standard reports is the additional control we are given over the layout of financial reports in the **Edit Layout** tab. Go to **Reports** | **Financial** | **Income Statement** | **Customize**:

Edit layout tab for a customized financial statement

The layout is made up of multiple sections, made up of a header row, the account rows, and the total of that section. We will analyze the different components of the layout by superimposing the actual report on the layout section:

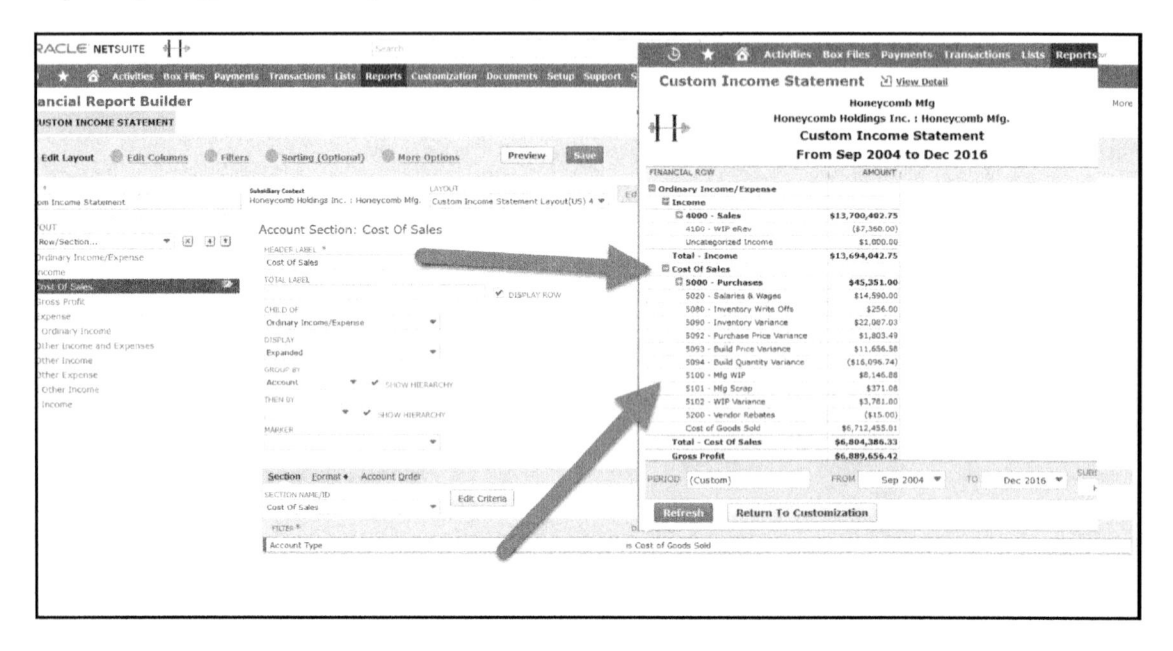

Compare financial report customization with result

The header label determines the name of that section and the child of determines where this section will appear in the hierarchy of the report. The components of that section are determined by the criteria, which is entered at the bottom of the screen. The criteria in this example is the **Account Type is Cost of Goods Sold**. The **Accounts Type** is a function of the chart of accounts setup where we select the **Account Type** as we create the **Account**. Go to **Lists | Accounts | Chart of Accounts | New** and review the **Type** field:

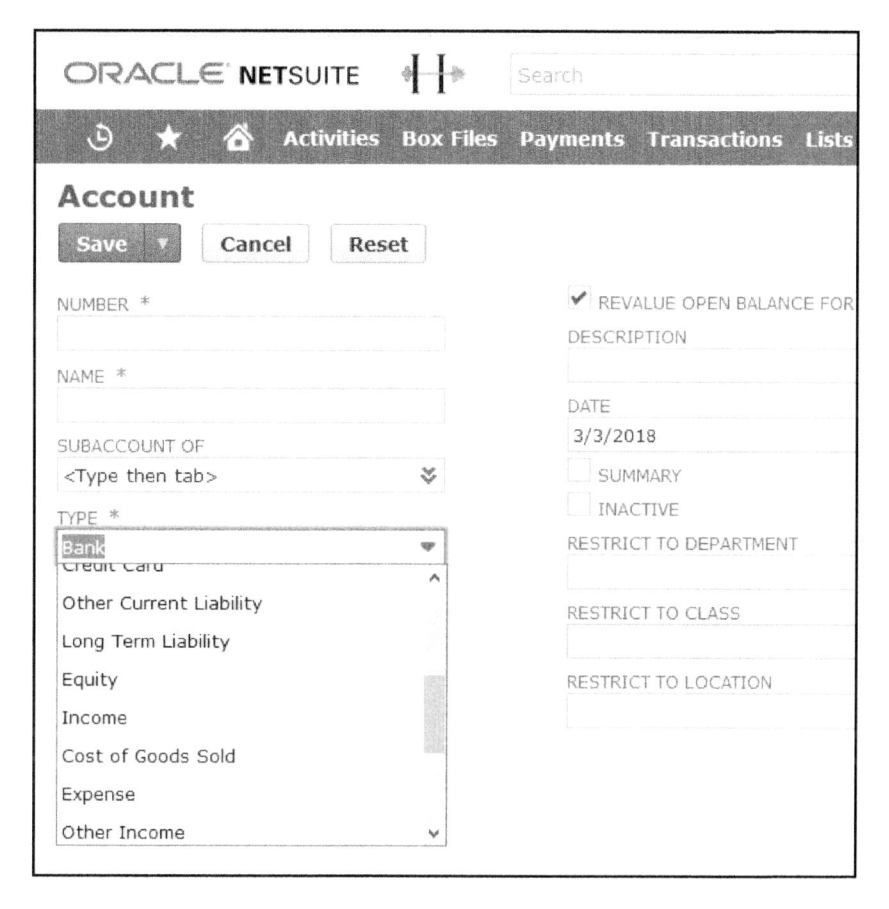

Account setup in chart of accounts

We can change the components of that section by changing the criteria. Click the **Edit Criteria** button to create different filters to place different Accounts into that section. Alternatively, click the **Add Row/Section** button to add an additional section made up of different accounts.

Analytics – Searches, Reports, and the Dashboard

We can use header rows in the hierarchy. The Header Row performs a calculation based on the sections within it, thereby summarizing the values of the accounts within it. The calculation can be either dynamically generated by adding together all the rows within the header or based on a specific formula which we determine. We have additional options available to format the header row including different fonts and colors:

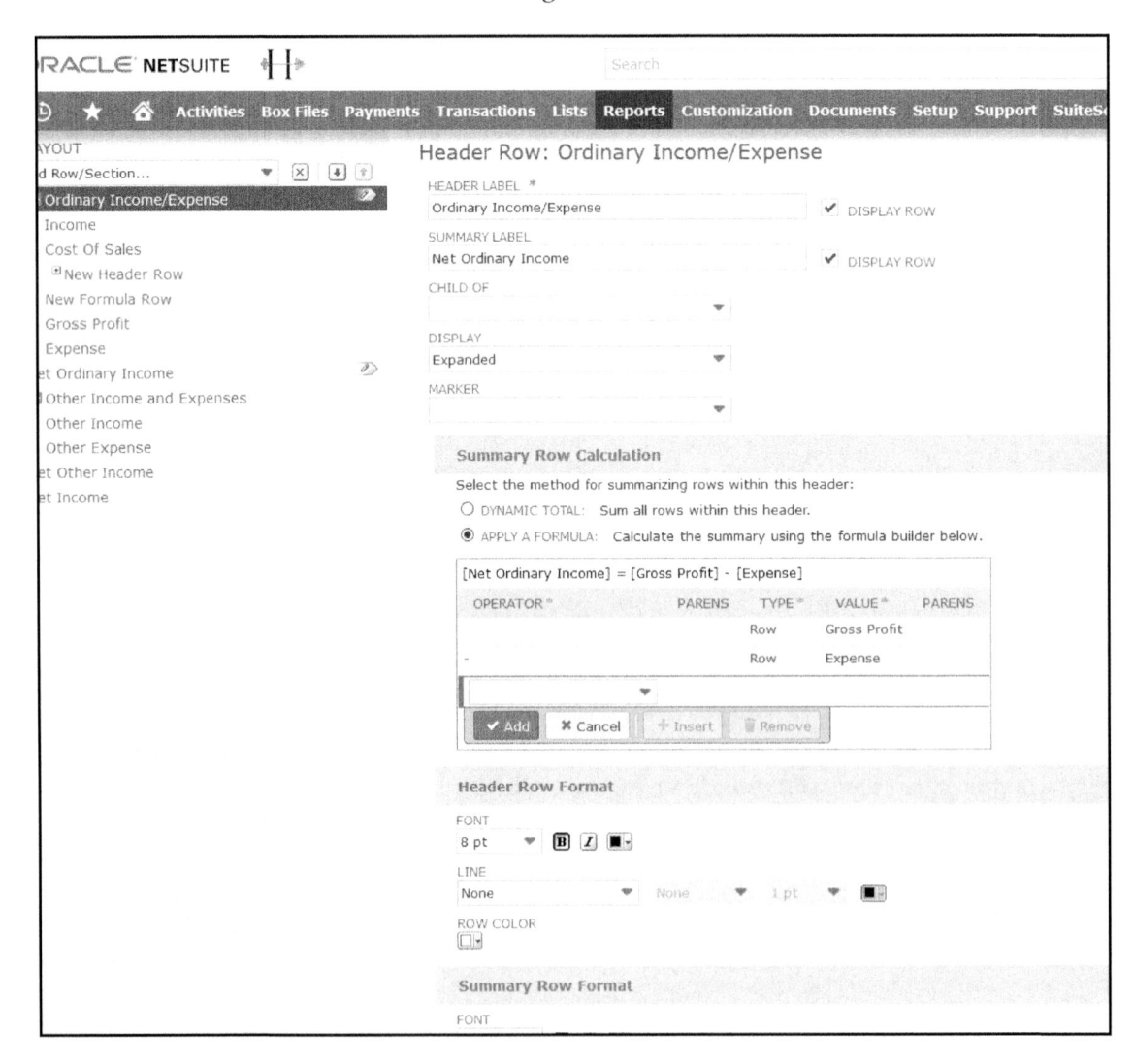

Building a financial report formula

We can amend the existing layout of the pre-built templates by removing a line using the **x** remove button, changing the order using the up and down arrows, or adding our own lines by clicking the *add* dropdown. This gives us the power to completely revamp the layout to change the sections, the accounts combined with each section, additional calculations using formula rows, and additional descriptions by adding text rows:

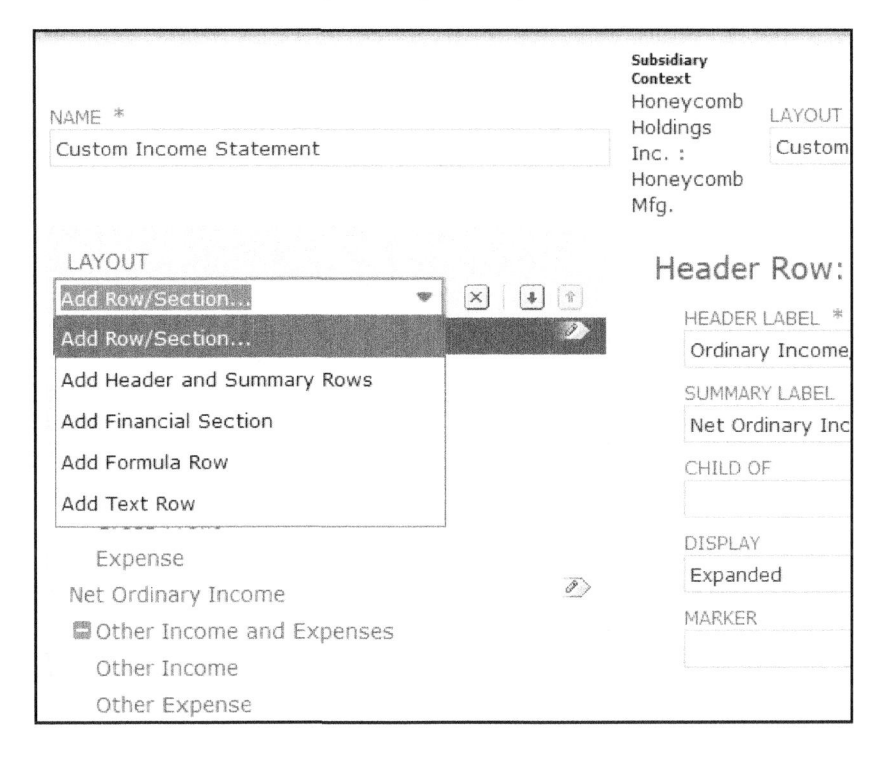

Add a Section/ Row

Dashboard

We have spoken about the power of the dashboard, but how do we get information onto the dashboard? How do we get custom search and reports onto the dashboard for our users to view? The saved search has more applicability compared to the dashboard because it is the basis for all custom KPIs, Custom Searches, Custom Lists, and KPI Scorecards. Custom search results are the easiest because all that is required is for the Saved Search to have the **Available on Dashboard View** checked off. The user can then add the saved search or list to their dashboard view with ease.

Custom KPIs and KPI Scorecards

The Custom KPIs and KPI Scorecards are a little more complicated. They also rely on Saved Searches and are typically searches that perform a calculation using the summary column on the saved search page. We can use the same saved searches for both KPIs and KPI Scorecards.

KPI

The key to creating a saved search that appears on the dashboard as a KPI is to ensure that there are no date filters on the **Criteria** tab of that KPI. The reason is very logical. KPIs allow you to view data over time, whether looking at the current period or the previous comparative range. KPIs are also linked to trend graphs, which analyze a trend over time. Adding a date filter on the criteria would break the entire timeline and restrict us to the dates within that date filter.

The other important aspect is to ensure that a date field appears in the available filters. Without it, you will only see the present value and will not be able to use the comparative date range option.

Custom KPI example

Build a Custom KPI analyzing the number of shipments completed by the San Francisco location over time.

Go to **Lists** | **Search** | **Saved Search** | **New** and select **Transactions**:

1. Name the search `Shipments by SFO`.
2. Check the **Available as Dashboard View** checkbox.
3. Go to the **Criteria** tab:
    1. Add a filter of **Type** = **Item Shipment**. The **Type** filter should always be the first filter that you add to a transaction search.
    2. Add a filter of **Location** = **San Francisco**:

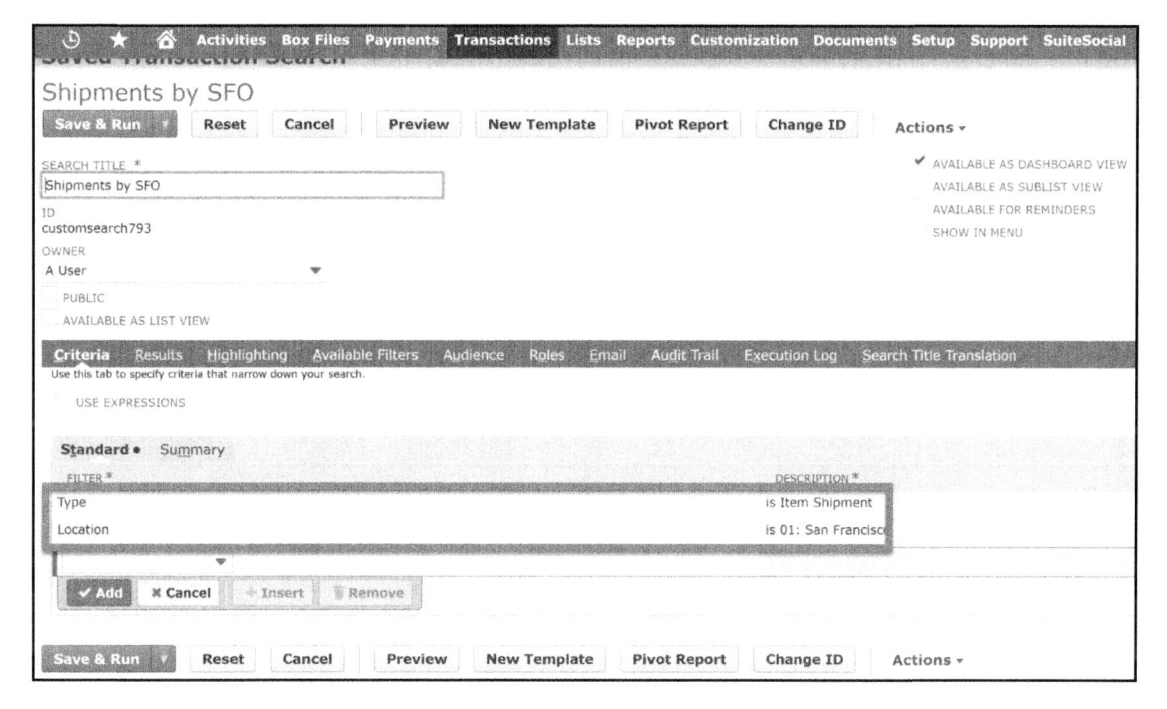

Saved Search criteria

3. Go to **Results**.

Analytics – Searches, Reports, and the Dashboard

4. Add the **Document Number** field with a summary **Type** of **Count**:

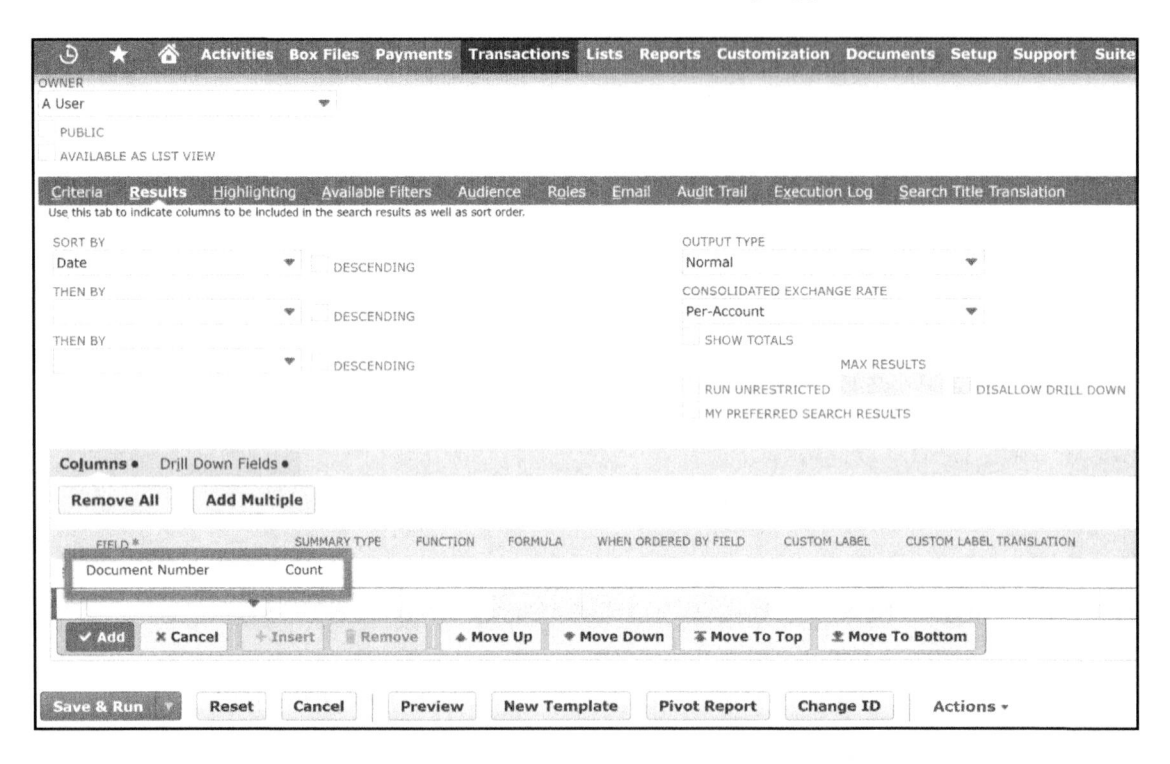

Saved Search results tab

5. Go to **Available Filters** and select **Date**.
6. Click **Save & Run**.
7. Go to the **Key Performance Indicators** portlet on the home dashboard.
8. Click **Setup**.
9. Add a custom KPI and select this report for the list of saved searches.
10. Add a date range and comparative range. Click **Save**:

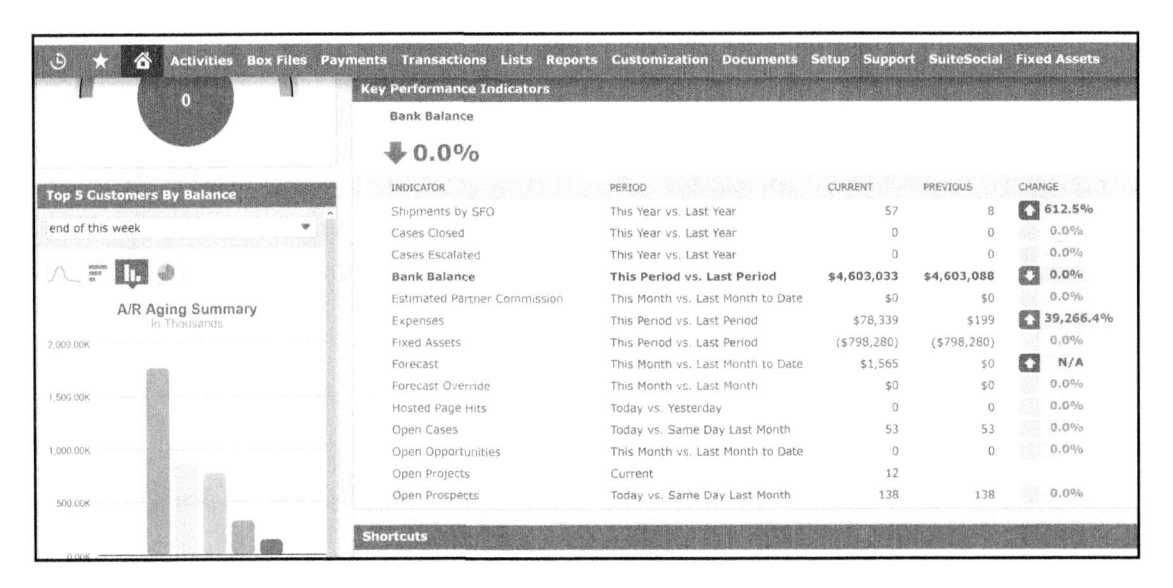

KPI Results on the dashboard

KPI Scorecard

KPI Scorecards need to be enabled in **Setup | Company | Enable Features** to be available in the system. Go to **Customization | Centers and Tabs | KPI Scorecards** to view your list of existing scorecards. We can add additional scorecards by clicking New.

Name the new KPI Scorecard and provide a description. We then choose the searches that will form the basis of the KPI Scorecard. These may be existing pre-built standard reports or can be custom KPIs, as you can see from the list options. You will, however, need to go to the **Custom** tab in order to select the custom KPI searches that will be represented on the front page. Once we've selected the search, we can view the results of the search or even perform calculations based on the results of the search.

We can compare KPIs or custom KPIs to each other, such as such comparing one KPI as a percentage of the other or subtracted from another KPI. We will use the label column to **Label** the Custom KPI in order to identify the metric properly on the user's dashboard. As you can see, we can add any number of KPIs or calculations, however, there is a restriction to only 10 custom KPIs per scorecard.

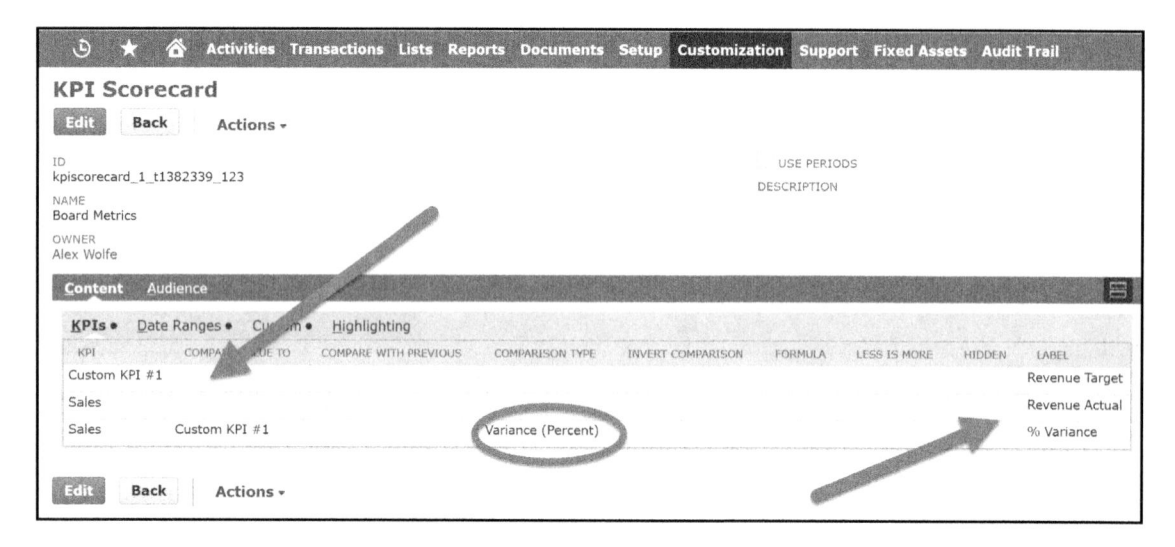

KPI Scorecard Setup KPIs

Once you've selected the KPIs that will be displayed, you can go to the **Date** tab to select the date ranges you want to appear in the KPI scorecard. Those dates ranges are dynamic, as we've come to expect, and you can add any number of dynamic ranges to the KPI Scorecard. You can then save the KPI Scorecard and go to the dashboard to test it.

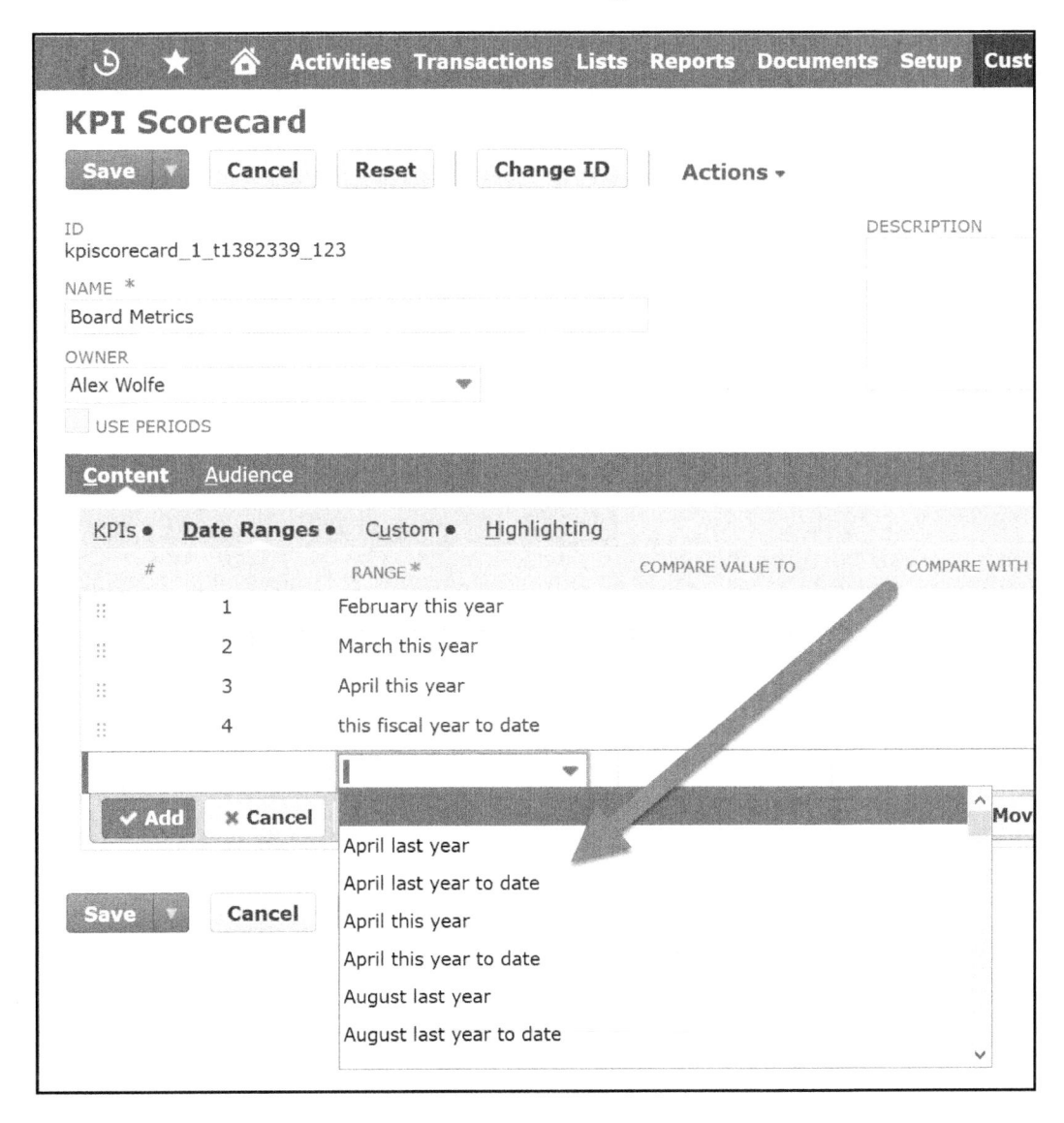

Setup Date Ranges on KPI Scorecard

Analytics – Searches, Reports, and the Dashboard

Open the KPI scorecard and choose setup; select the scorecard you just created. You can choose whether to have the KPIs appearing as rows and the date ranges as columns or the opposite, namely, date ranges as rows and KPIs as columns. Once the KPI scorecard is working as designed, you can go back to the scorecard itself by clicking on the ellipsis button and selecting edit.

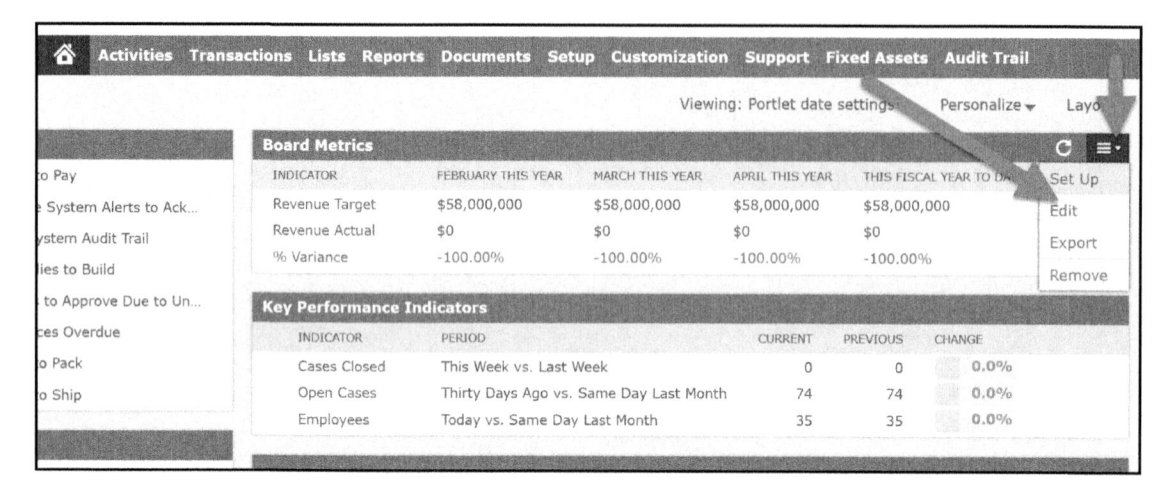

Edit the KPI Scorecard directly from the Dashboard

You can then open the Scorecard to a specific audience by selecting the audience control tab. Click **Save** to publish that scorecard to those users.

KPI scorecard example

Let's build on our previous example and create a KPI Scorecard comparing the number of shipments of the San Francisco location to all the shipments completed by the company:

1. We already built the search for San Francisco, so we'll start there. Do a *global search* for `sea: Shipments by SFO`.
2. Edit the search.
3. Remove the **Location** criteria.
4. Rename the search to `Shipments`.
5. Click **Save As**.

6. Go to **Customization** | **Centers and Tabs** | **KPI Scorecards** | **New**.
7. Name the scorecard **Shipment Analysis**.
8. Go to the **Custom** tab and set the San Francisco search as **Custom KPI #1** and the **Shipments** search as **Custom KPI #2**:

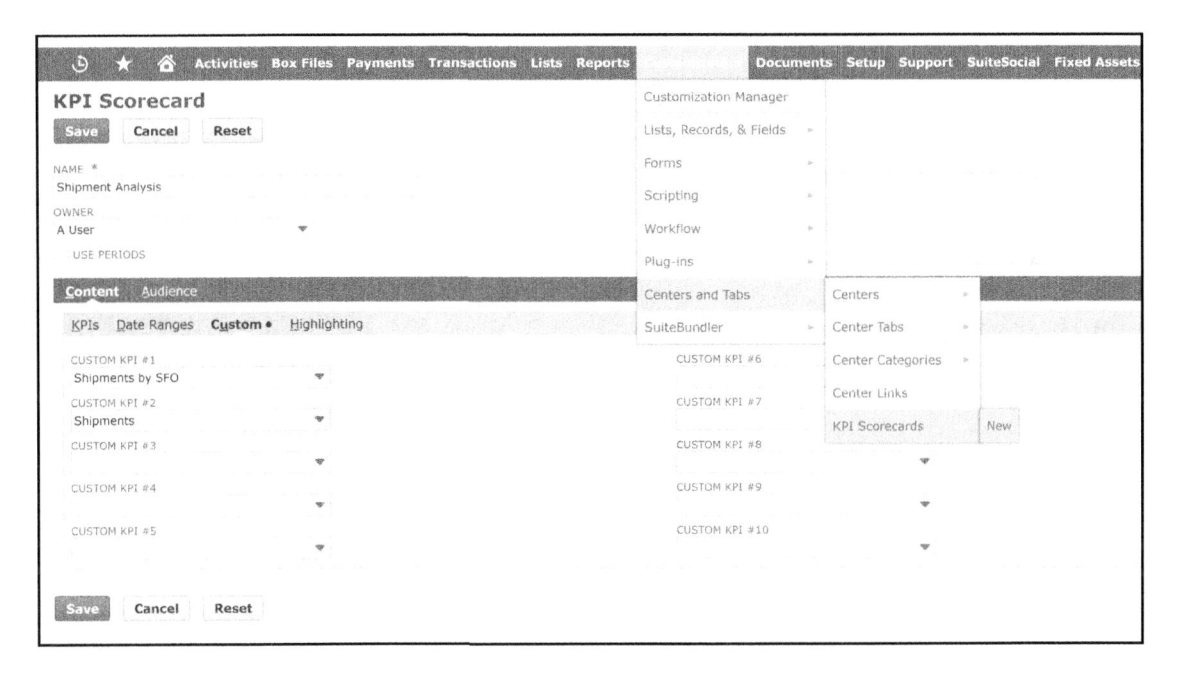

Add New KPI Scorecard

9. Go to the **KPIs** tab and select **Custom KPI #1** in the first line and add SFO in the label.
10. Select **KPI 2** in the second line and add `All Locations` in the label.
11. Select **Custom KPI #1** in line three and select **Custom KPI 2** in the **Compare Value to** column.

[285]

Analytics – Searches, Reports, and the Dashboard

12. Choose **Variance (Percent)** in the **COMPARISON TYPE** column:

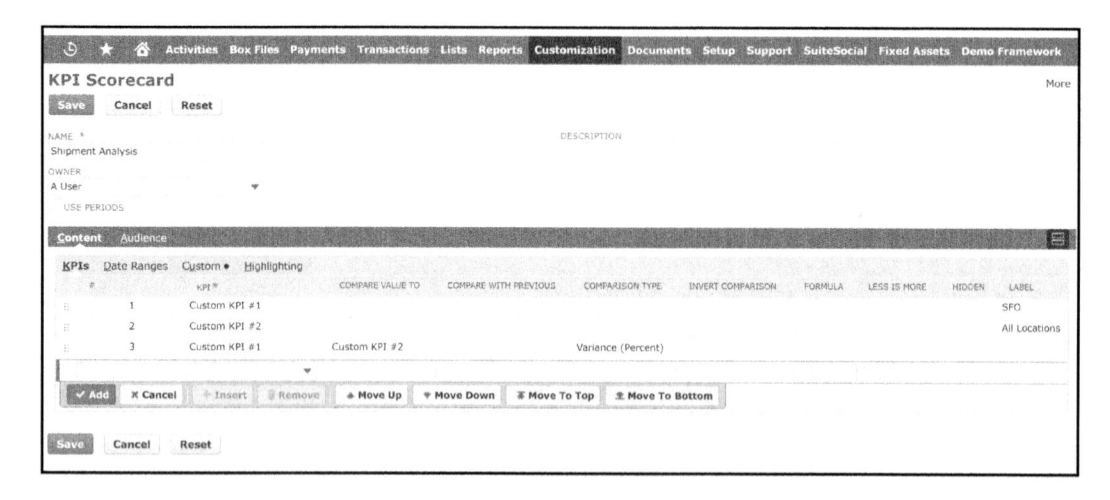

Comparison Type of Percent Variance

13. Go to the **Date Ranges** tab and select the **Date Ranges** you wish to analyze:

Data Ranges tab for the KPI Scorecard

14. Click **Save**.
15. Return to the home dashboard.
16. Choose **Setup** on the **KPI Scorecard** portlet.
17. Select the **Shipments Analysis** scorecard from the list of available scorecards.
18. Click **Save**:

Shipment Analysis		
INDICATOR	LAST FISCAL YEAR	THIS FISCAL YEAR
SFO	8	57
All Locations	16	58
Shipments by SFO vs. Shipments	-50.00%	-1.72%

KPI Scorecard on Dashboard

Summary

In this chapter, we looked at the business intelligence tools that NetSuite offers and showed how you can use these tools to have an immediate impact on your company. Start by setting up the standard dashboard portlets for your users and selecting the standard reporting options that are on offer. Teach your users how to manipulate the reports using the standard functions that we demonstrated in this chapter, in order for them to gain a better understanding of the health of the business.

That alone should impress your users, however, you can use the tools we described in the **Saved Search** section to take it even further. You can build complex searches covering multiple data tables using the filters on the **Criteria** tab. Furthermore, you can add columns to the results of the search on the **Results** tab, as well as perform calculations to change the data into valuable insights. We showed how you can highlight metrics when they are at risk of falling short or have achieved specific goals using the **Highlighting** tab. We also showed you how the available filters can be used to enable your users to build their own searches based on your initial template, as well as create alerts that will generate emails upon the occurrence of a specified event.

We then turned our attention to reports and showed you a similar functionality: the ability to filter, set columns, and perform calculations on those columns to provide users with additional insight into the state of the business.

Lastly, we turned our attention back to the dashboard, demonstrating how we could leverage our knowledge of saved searches to summarize the data onto the dashboard using Key Performance Indicators and KPI Scorecards.

You now have the knowledge to provide your users with incredible insights, which they can access by simply clicking on the dashboard button, enabling them to keep track of strategic goals while executing tactical tasks on a day-to-day basis.

We will now shift our attention to a fundamental question, which you will likely be faced with as a NetSuite administrator. Can NetSuite run the entire business or should we use specialist software to automate a particular department?

9
Workflows

As we have seen, NetSuite packs in a lot of tools to standardize and automate processes across an entire company, yet it may not automate all the processes that your company requires. What do we do then?

Scripting is always an option, but that can be costly and time-consuming, so NetSuite has included a point-and-click automation builder called SuiteFlow.

SuiteFlow is very powerful but does have its limitations. It can, however, automate a number of tasks, such as approval routing, automating the inputting of data, and normalizing data, and it can even create completely new records based on certain criteria. This chapter includes the following:

- Approval routing and implementing complex approval routing for purchase orders based on multiple criteria, such as department, location, and class, as well as employee hierarchy
- Automating the inputting of data
- Normalizing data
- Creating new records and automatically invoicing certain sales orders once fulfilled

This is an introductory chapter on SuiteFlow and is designed to give you the tools to start using it. This chapter is not meant to be an extensive review on SuiteFlow, which could comprise a whole book in and of itself. We will look at the functions within SuiteFlow and demonstrate how they work by means of a use case.

Workflows

SuiteFlow

A workflow is made up of different states, which follow each other sequentially. Each state is made up of different actions that occur within the state, and of course, we can determine the order in which the actions take place so this becomes like a sequential decision tree. The workflow starts in state 1 and will only move to the next state once all of the appropriate actions in that state have been completed. We can build logic into these states and actions so that the workflow can skip a state or an action depending on the criteria that we set:

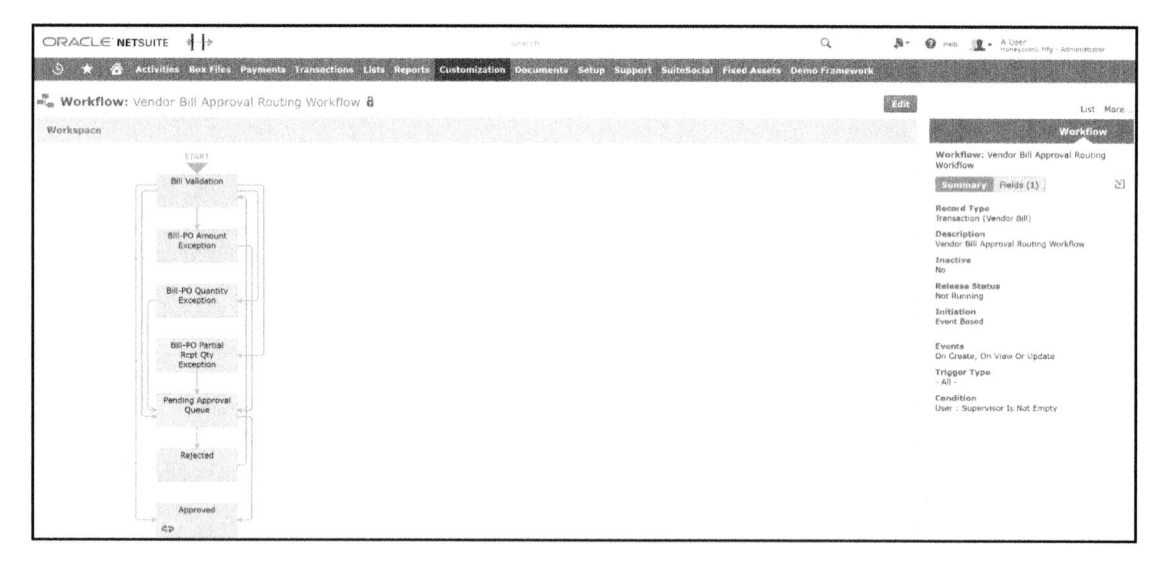

Workflow represented in sequential order

Drip marketing is a great example of this. Marketing is used to communicate with leads and customers continually over time. Each communication is like the drip of a drop of water as it hits the surface. Each drop of water does not have any specific effect, however, the continual dripping is what causes the surface to break down. This is obviously a difficult task to achieve as we need multiple drops to have any effect and that is almost impossible to do without automation.

In our example, let's assume we want to send leads to a trade show and send an email thanking them for visiting our booth, inviting them to fill out a survey just like the one we created in `Chapter 6`, *Customization*. If the email bounces, we want to remove that person from the database. If, however, the email is received, read, and acted upon, we want to automatically schedule a phone call from a sales rep who will contact the lead. On the other hand, if the customer does not respond to the email, we will want to send a follow-up email in 2 weeks' time using a different template, and so on and so forth.

Now, this would obviously be very difficult to manage if we were doing it manually, however, and workflow can provide this function so that it's automated. It can identify leads to send the email to, as well as the time to send the email and which leads need to be followed up with a phone call and which with an email.

To understand how workflows works, we will start by asking five questions: which, when, why, what, and how.

Which record will be affected?

Which records will the workflow be running on? Will it be a customer record or based on transactions? And if so, which specific transactions will it base the actions upon?

Workflows

The **RECORD TYPE** and **SUB TYPES** are determined in the **Basic Information** entered when we create the workflow at **Customization** | **Workflow** | **Workflows** | **New**:

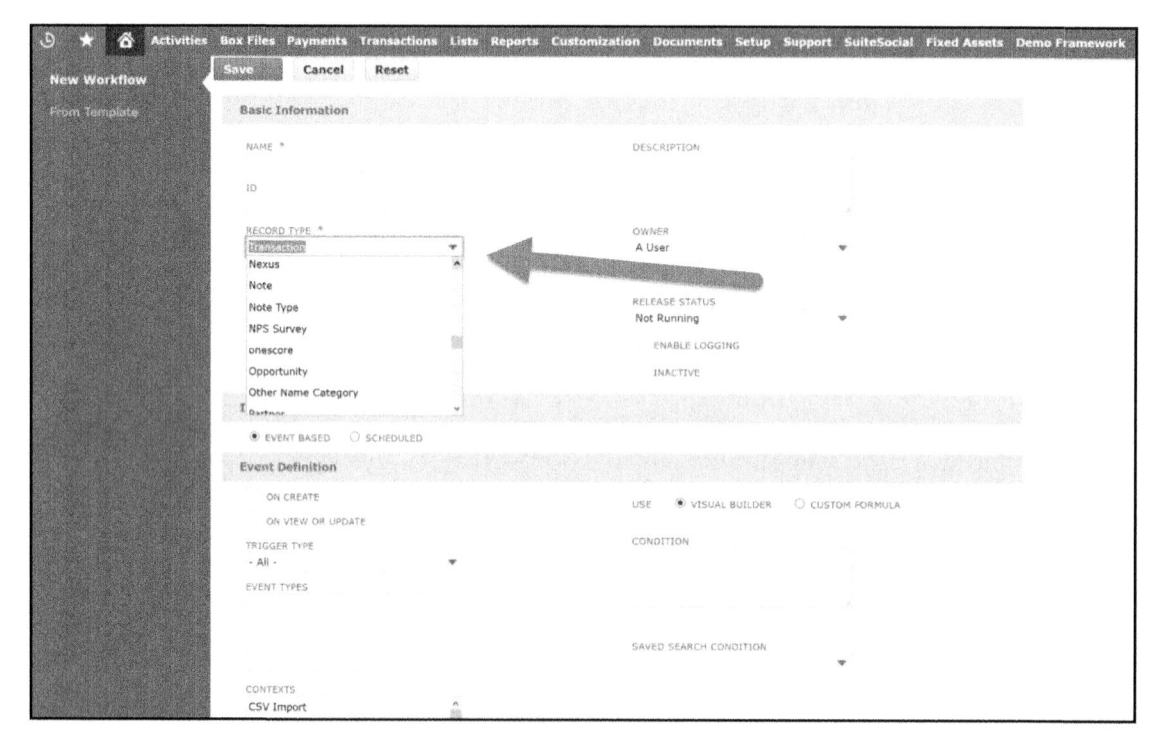

Workflow record type

Workflows can be created for any record, including custom records, such as the NPS survey custom record we created in an earlier `Chapter 6`, *Customization*:

Chapter 9

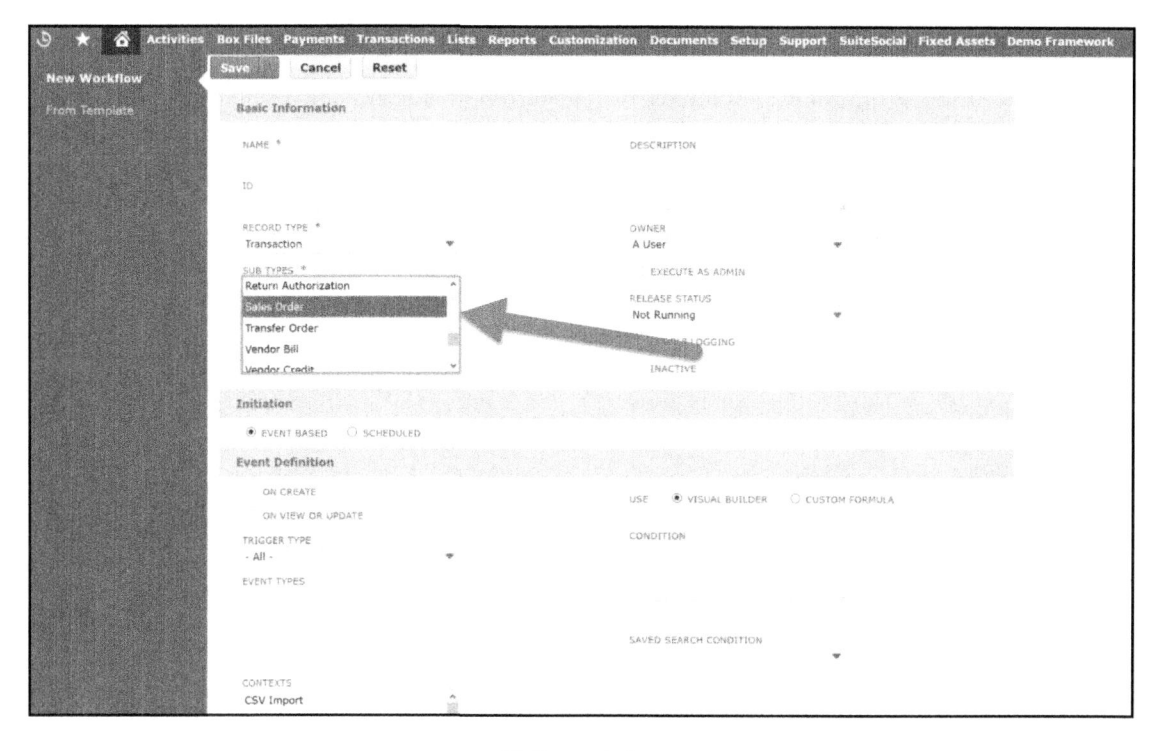

Workflow record subtype

We can go further than type and subtype to specify the records that need to be updated by restricting the workflow to operate only on records returned by a specific saved search. We can see that option in the **Event Definition** section of the screen. Alternatively, we can restrict this instead using a formula entered into the condition field of that tab.

When will the automation be activated?

When will actions in the workflow take place? This question is made up of two parts:

- When will the workflow be initiated?
- What is the order of the steps that are taken in the workflow?

[293]

Workflows

Initiation

Workflows can be scheduled or event based. Scheduled workflows run on a particular schedule, for instance, the drip marketing campaign could run every Monday morning, determining the next step for all the leads in that funnel. For that reason, schedule workflows tend to be server-side. Alternatively, the workload could be events driven. The action is taken as soon as a user creates a new record, which is a client-side workflow.

The selection of event-based and scheduled workflows is made in the **Initiation** tab when we create the workflow in **Customization | Workflow | Workflows | New**:

Customization | Workflow | Workflows | New

[294]

Order

The workflow is subdivided into states which take place in a sequential order, such as the workflow in the following screenshot. The **New Customer Promotion** state is preceded by the **Spring Sales** state and followed by the **15% Discount** state, and lastly the **Spring Catalog** state. On the other hand, the flowchart also shows that the records can skip states, such the **Spring Sales** and **New Customer Promotion** states, and go directly to the last state, depending on the lead's response to the campaign:

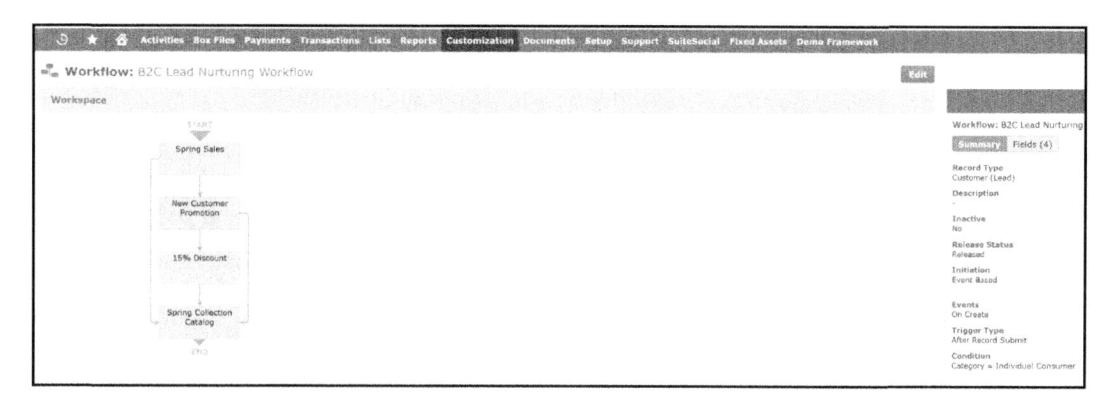

Sample Workflow with multiple states

We can also determine the order of actions within each state. If we click on the **Spring Sales** state, we see the actions that will be executed in that state appear on the right-hand side of the screen:

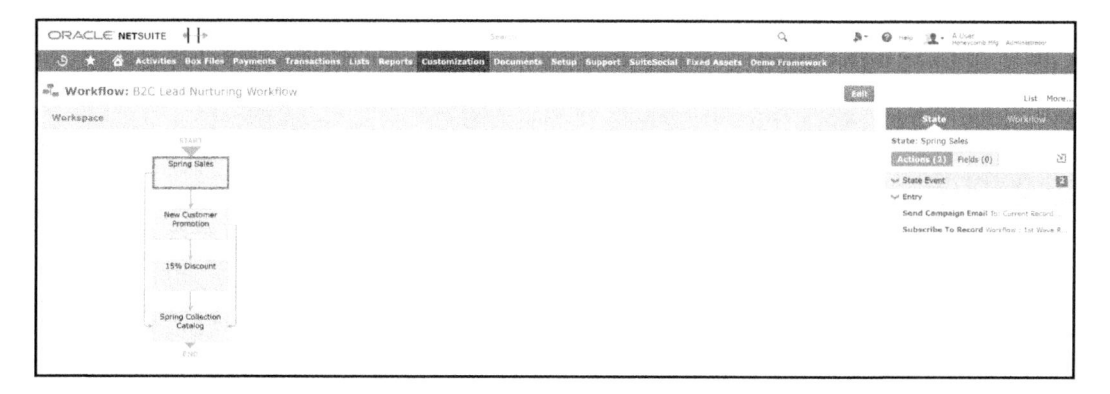

Actions executed while in a state

In this case, there are two actions that can be taken in this state, the first being to **Send Campaign Email** and the second to **Subscribe To Record**.

[295]

Workflows

Triggers

An action can be triggered by a number of events, such as the following:

- Before record load, for instance, manipulating data when the user comes to the page
- Before record submit, for instance, performing validation of the data inserted into the record prior to saving
- After record submit, for instance, performing an action such as creating an associated record as soon as the record is created

The trigger is selected for each action in the **Trigger on** field:

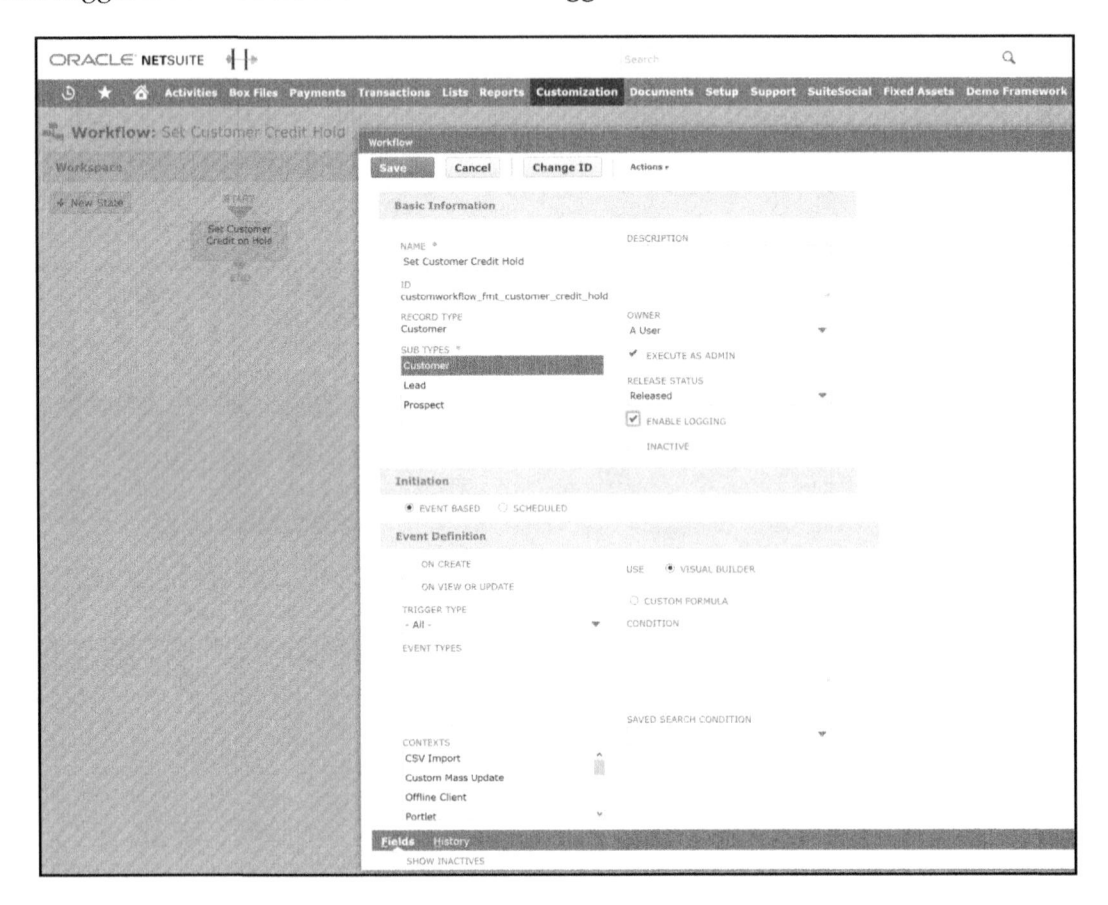

What will be automated?

What do we need the workflow to do? What action should it take?

We find those options in the **Actions** themselves. These are the options we get when we create a **New Action**:

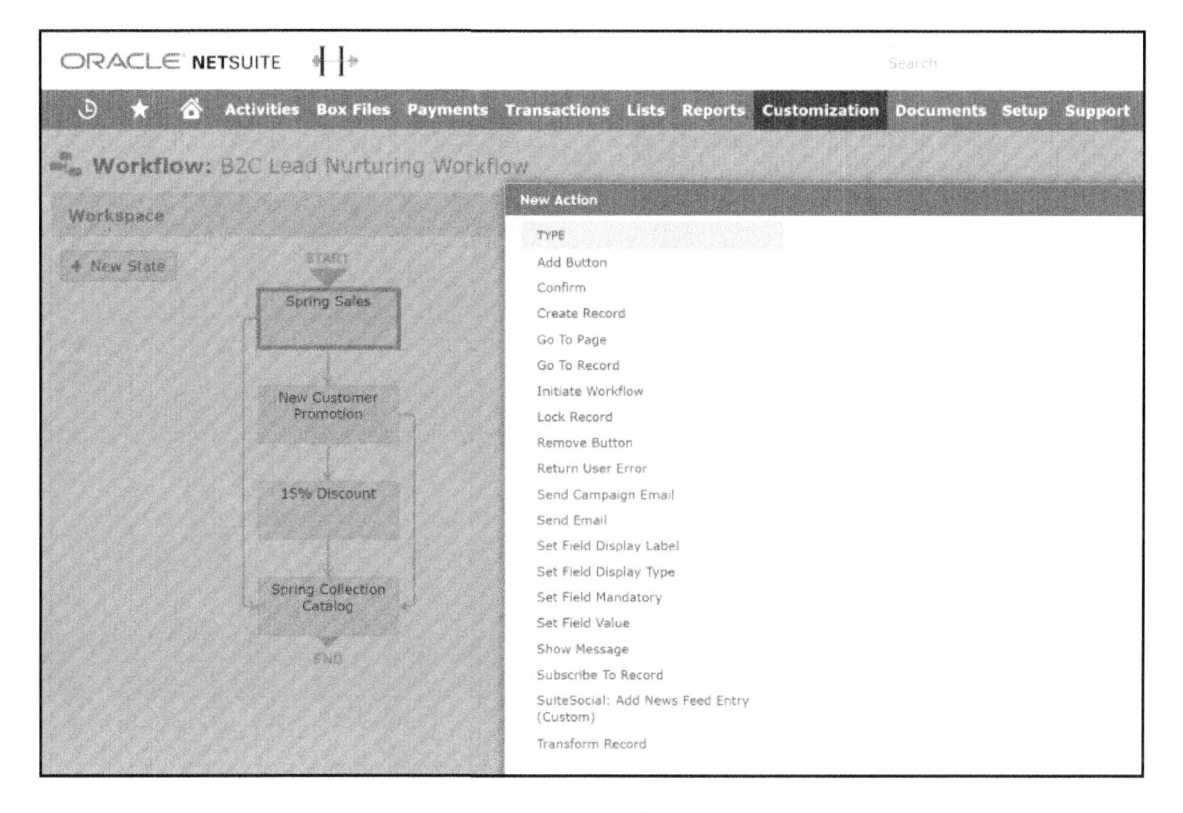

Types of actions available

You can do the following:

- **Add Button** to the UI and associate it with additional functionality, such as navigating to another record or to a new state in the workflow
- Add a **Confirm**; this creates a popup message box with customizable text and the options to click **OK** or **Cancel**

- **Create Record**, for instance, automatically create the fulfillment when the sales order is entered
- **Go To Page**
- **Go To Record**; this creates a hyperlink to a specific record in NetSuite
- **Initiate Workflow**
- **Lock Record**; this removes the edit button from a record, ensuring that it can no longer be edited
- **Remove Button** that is otherwise available to the user on that record
- **Return User Error** for data validation, such as customer credit limit is too high
- **Send Campaign Email**
- **Send Email**; this can also be accomplished using the saved search email functionality without the need to create a workflow
- **Set Field Display Label** to change the label of a specific field, if needs be
- **Set Field Display Type** to change the type of data that can be entered into that field
- **Set Field Mandatory**
- **Set Field Value**, for instance, set a specific currency based on the country of the customer
- **Show Message**
- **Subscribe To Record**
- **Transform Record**

How do we set up a workflow?

Now that we know what we need to do, the next question is how to do it. Let's look at creating a workflow consisting of states and actions.

Creating a new workflow

Start by creating the workflow itself by going to **Customization** | **Workflow** | **Workflows** | **New**:

1. Give it a name and select the record and **SUB TYPE** that the workflow will run on. This is a multi-select option.

Chapter 9

2. Select a **Release Status**. There are three possible statuses for a workflow, **Not Released**, **Released**, and **Testing**:
    - **Not Released**: It is equivalent to inactive. The workflow will not function, whether for testing purposes or to actually run.
    - **Released**: It means that the workflow is running and will work for any user or record that complies with the criteria of the workflow.
    - **Testing**: It restricts the use of the workflow to the author of the workflow, for instance, a workflow designed to execute on the creation of a sales order will only execute when the author creates the sales order. If any other user were to create the sales order, the workflow would not execute at all.
4. Naturally, we will be testing and troubleshooting our workflows by setting the **Release Status** to **Testing.**
5. Choose whether the workflow will be scheduled or the event driven in the **Initiation** section.
6. We can further restrict the circumstances that will trigger the workflow in the **Event Definition** section.
7. Select whether the workflow will apply when creating new records or when viewing and updating a new record; alternatively, it can apply in all cases.
8. Select the **Trigger** type.
9. Select the **Event** types; this will apply to such **Copy** vs. **Create** vs. **Edit**. This is a multi-select option.
10. We have the choice of further restricting the workflow to a certain context where, for instance, we need the workflow to apply CSV import actions but not **MASS UPDATES**.
11. We can further restrict the workflow by building a search and restricting the workflow to run on records returned by that search.
12. Save the workflow.

[299]

Workflows

Creating states

Let's see how to create states:

1. Add a state to the initial **State** by clicking the **New State** button.

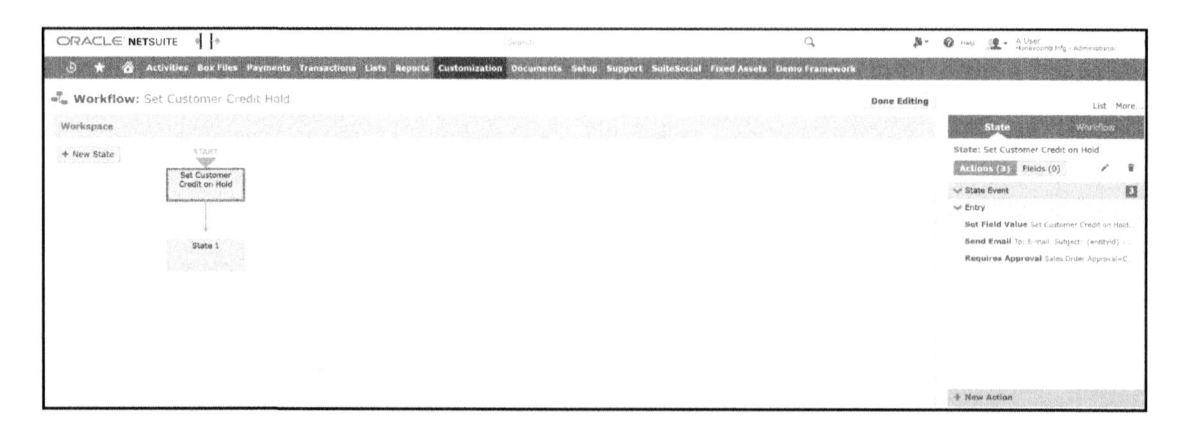

1. The state is configured by highlighting the state and clicking the pencil icon on the right of the screen:

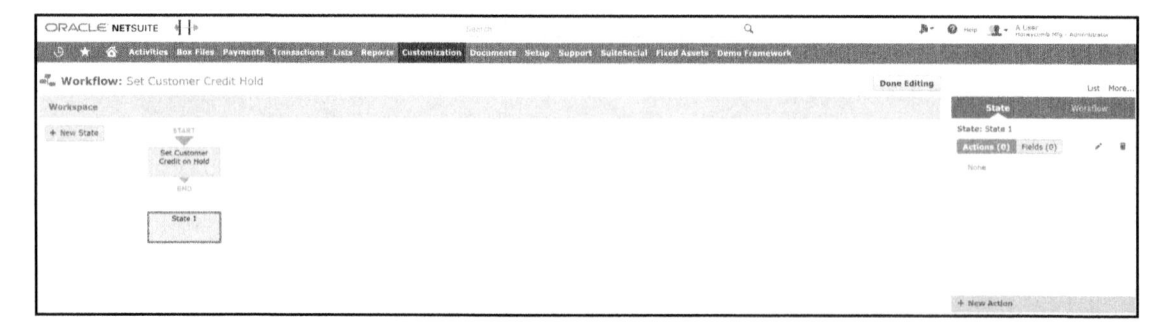

Add a State to the Workflow

3. The **State** popup appears, enabling us to rename and configure the state.
4. We add the **State** to the sequence by selecting the arrow below the previous state. This becomes a semi-circle and we can drag and drop it onto our new state to join the two together:

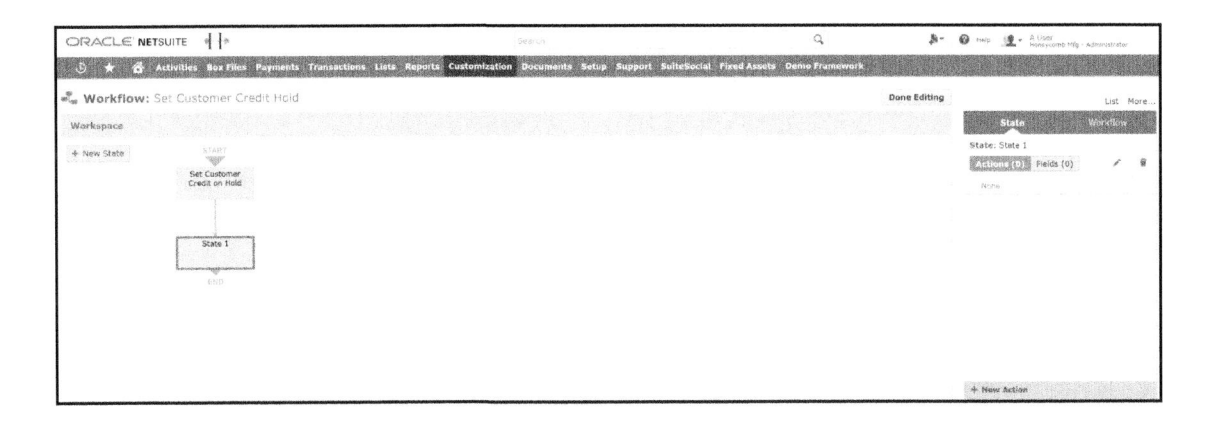

Creating Actions

Actions are added as follows:

1. Select the **State** and click on the **New Action** button on the right side of the screen. This brings up the **New Action** selection:
2. Choose the type of action that is needed and configure it appropriately:

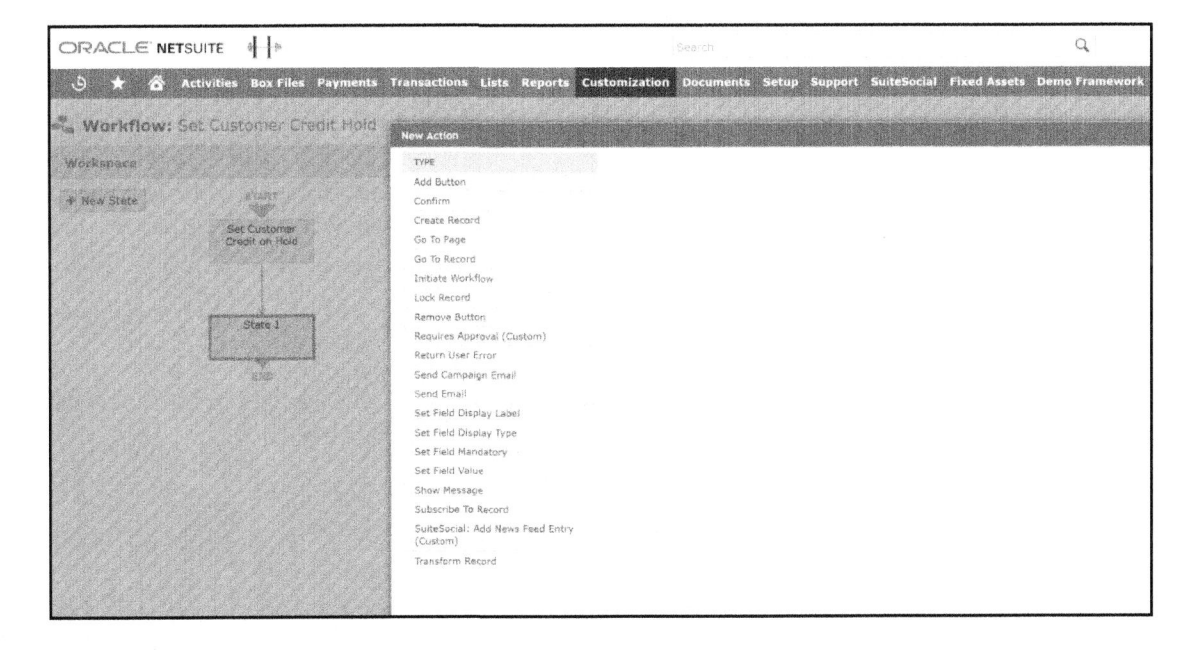

3. Each action has its own configuration options, however, the possible actions span the length and breadth of the system. Options include the following:
    - **Add Button,** which can be used to assist in navigation or even to add an approval or rejection step into a process.
    - The **Confirm** action creates a popup for the user to confirm an action and can be used to alert a user of a potential problem, such as creating an order for a free item.
    - **Go To Page** to take the user to the page containing the next step in the process.
    - **Send Email** to alert a user, such as a manager, when a particular event occurs. Note that this can also be achieved using a saved search alert.
    - **Set Field Mandatory** may seem like a duplication as we have a similar option available in form customization, however, it has an advantage. The field can be set to mandatory depending on factors contained in a saved search, for instance, only when communicating with tier 1 customers.
    - **Set Field Value** is used very often to automate the inputting of data.
    - **Transform Record** can automate a process, for instance, automatically creating a bill from a purchase order as opposed to doing it manually.
4. Click **Done Editing** once all the steps in the workflow have been completed.

Troubleshooting workflows

Thomas Edison observed: *I have not failed. I've just found 10,000 ways that won't work.* While we recognize that we are likely to fail before we succeed, how can we minimize the number of tries we take to find the right answer?

Workflows have a built-in execution log that is initiated by checking the **ENABLE LOGGING** checkbox:

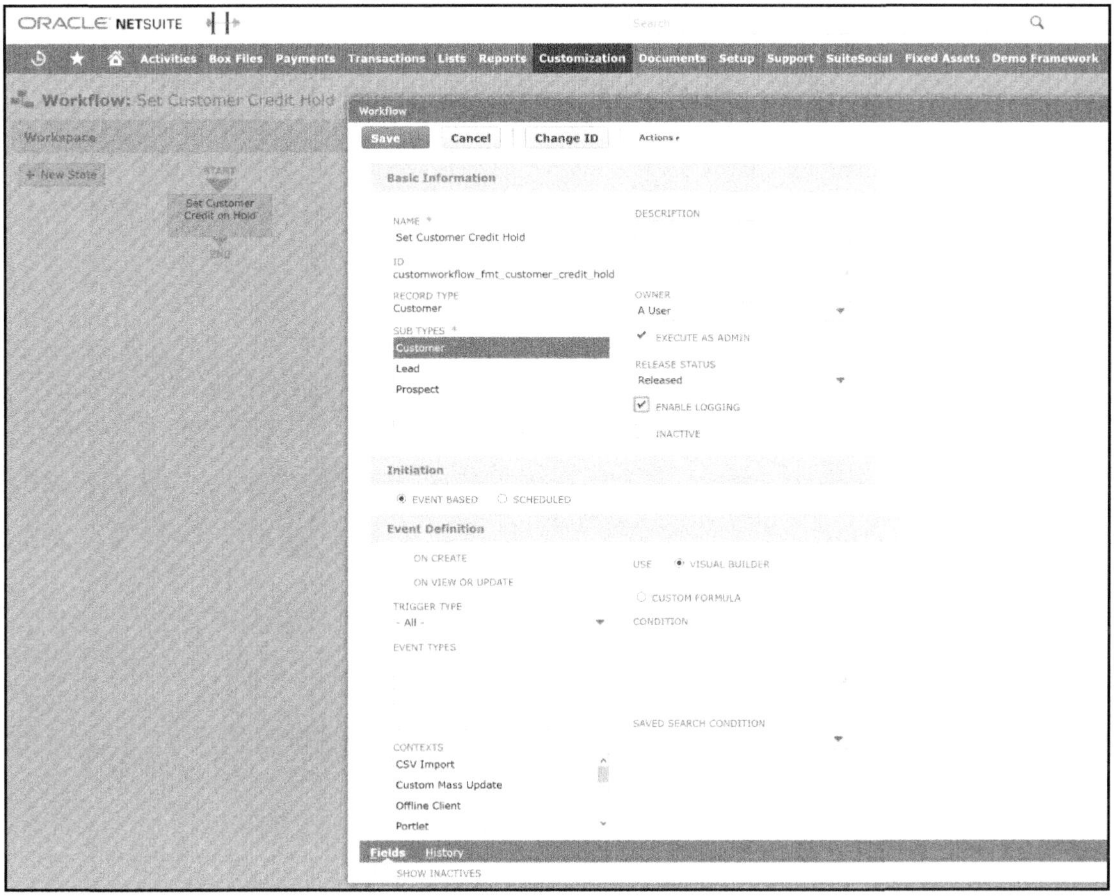
ORACLE NETSUITE
Activities Box Files Payments Transactions Lists Reports Customization Documents Setup Support SuiteSocial Fixed Assets Demo Framework
Workflow: Set Customer Credit Hold
Workflow
Save
Cancel
Change ID
Actions
Basic Information
NAME *
Set Customer Credit Hold
DESCRIPTION
ID
customworkflow_fmt_customer_credit_hold
RECORD TYPE
Customer
OWNER
A User
SUB TYPES *
Customer
Lead
Prospect
EXECUTE AS ADMIN
RELEASE STATUS
Released
ENABLE LOGGING
INACTIVE
Initiation
EVENT BASED
SCHEDULED
Event Definition
ON CREATE
ON VIEW OR UPDATE
USE
VISUAL BUILDER
CUSTOM FORMULA
TRIGGER TYPE
- All -
CONDITION
EVENT TYPES
SAVED SEARCH CONDITION
CONTEXTS
CSV Import
Custom Mass Update
Offline Client
Portlet
Fields
History
SHOW INACTIVES

Workflows

Once enabled, the execution log is generated and is found in the **Workflow History** subtab of the **System Information** tab of the record or transaction on which the workflow is running:

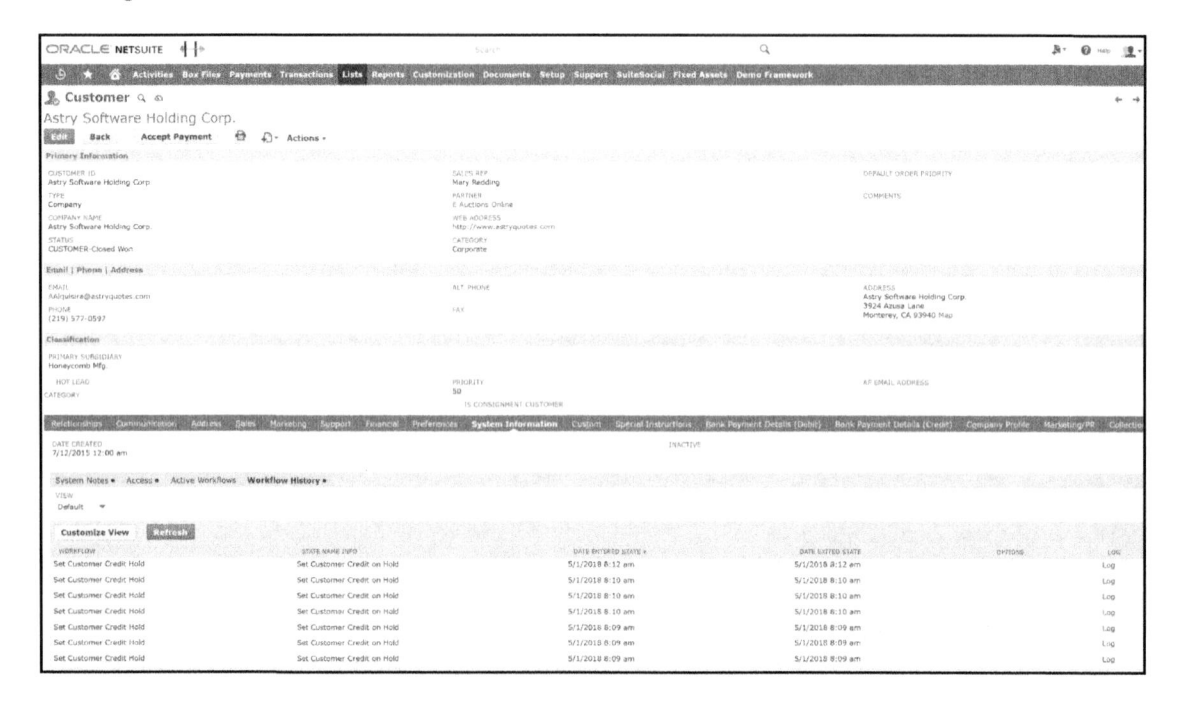

We can also see whether the workflow is active on this record by selecting the **Active Workflows** subtab in the **System Information** tab on the record or transaction on which the workflow is running.

Use case

Accounting wants to create a specific email address for the AP department on each customer record. We are then required to send any invoices to the AP email address if an email address is entered on the customer record.

There are three parts to this use case:

- Create the AP email custom field.
- Create a saved search to limit the workflow to execute only on transactions for those customers who have an AP address on their customer record.
- Create a workflow to email the transaction to that email address.

Creating the custom field

Go to a customer record and click the **Customize** button in the top right-hand corner of the screen. Select **New Field**:

1. Name the field **AP email Address**
2. Enter the field ID as `_apemail`
3. Select email address from the **Type** dropdown
4. Go to the **Display** tab and select the subtab **Main**
5. Click **Save**

Saved search

Start by creating the saved search to determine the specific records that will be affected

1. Go to **Lists** | **Search** | **Saved Search** | **New**
2. Select **Transaction**
3. Name the search **Customer Has AP email**
4. Add criterion by going to the **Customer (Main Fields)** in the dropdown list
5. Select **AP email Address is not Empty**

Workflow

Now we will setup the **Workflow** and incorporate the **Saved Search**:

1. Go to **Customization** | **Workflow** | **Workflows** | **New**
2. Name the workflow **Send Invoice to AP email address**
3. Provide an ID: `_sendapemail`
4. Set **RECORD TYPE** as **Transaction**

5. Set **RECORD SUBTYPE** as **Invoice**
6. Click **Execute as Admin**
7. Set **Release Status** as **Testing**
8. Click **Enable Logging**
9. Go to **Event Definition** and select **On Create**
10. Select **State 1** and click **New Action**
11. Choose **Send Email**
12. Go to the **Saved Search Condition** field and select the **Customer Has AP email** search
13. Go to the **Send** section and choose **From Field: Current Record: Employee**
14. Go to the **Recipient** section
15. Choose **Customer** from the **Record Join Field**
16. Select the **AP email address** from the **Field** below it
17. Go to the **Content** section and select an appropriate template from the **Template** field
18. Go to the **Attachment** section and check the **Include Transaction** checkbox
19. Select the **Type** as **Inline Text**
20. Click **Save**
21. Click **Done Editing**

Summary

Workflows give us the ability to automate and standardize almost any process. With it, we can transform data, send emails, communicate with the user, and so on. It is an extremely useful tool we can leverage for functions where NetSuite lacks the automation we require out of the box.

The NetSuite functionality is improving all the time as they introduce richer features with every new release. Yet, how does this release cycle work? How do we know whether the new version includes functionality that we desperately need and are looking to build using a custom workflow? And, more importantly, how can we be sure that the new version will not break any customizations, integration, and workflows? That's the topic of the next chapter, *New Releases*.

10
Integration

Salesforce.com, Magenta, and Shipstation. These are all specialist software with deep, rich functionalities. On the other hand, NetSuite is an ERP and CRM suite and, being a generalist, offers deep functionalities over a large breadth of departments. Specialist tools, on the other hand, have a narrower focus but go much deeper into functionality. Should this be implemented in NetSuite or alternatively set up in a specialist product that is then integrated with NetSuite?

This is a question that has either come up or will come up in your deployment. I guarantee it. In this chapter, we want to focus on this question and develop a framework for answering these types of questions.

This chapter will cover:

- The suite versus best of breed
- The framework

The suite versus best of breed

In a sense, this conundrum is an argument between breadth and depth. Do we want a system that has great of breadth in that it automates many different processes spanning the entire company? Alternatively, do we need the depth of best of breed products, which have the deepest functionalities in their respective specialties?

The suite

The NetSuite value proposition is that the whole is greater than the sum of its parts. As we have seen, consolidating everything into one system provides a number of unique benefits.

Integration

The benefit of the suite is not just that we can execute sales operations, marketing, fulfillment and receiving, invoicing, payment, processing, and so on in one convenient system. The system relates all of these activities to the individual customers and vendors that we interact with. We can, therefore, get the proverbial 360-degree view of the customer, including sales operations, marketing, fulfillment and receiving, invoicing, and payment processing performed for each individual customer.

It also provides analysis by vendor partner and even by item, where NetSuite shows a complete history of purchasing and selling transactions for each individual item record. And of course, the suite automates the entire company whereas the best of breed automates individual departments instead.

Best of breed

Best of breed has the deepest functionality in that specific department. The challenge, however, is to exchange the knowledge contained therein with the other business systems. Doing this manually is inefficient and error-prone. If there is an inconsistency between the data in two different systems, we are always left with the nagging question of which system is the most up to date.

Integration can solve this problem by consistently synchronizing the data between these systems, however, it is complex and therefore costly to do so. The rise of cloud services has ameliorated this problem to some extent in that it is usually easier to integrate cloud systems than it is client-server databases. Nonetheless, integration does add complexity to the management of business systems.

The framework

Let's perform a thought experiment in an effort to develop a framework to decide whether to use the suite or a best of breed which is integrated with NetSuite. If you are inclined to use best of breed systems. you need to decide which modules should be replaced by the best of breed.

Let's take an analogy and pose this question: when buying a new computer, should I purchase Microsoft Office or use Google Docs instead? MS Office will cost me $500 whereas Google Docs is free.

We can look at the question from a different perspective: how can Microsoft justify charging $500 when a competing product is available for free?

The answer is that Word, Excel, and so on have much deeper functionalities than Google Docs, as we can see by just comparing the relative menu items for each product. In a sense, we could say that Google Docs is for the basic user whereas Office is for the power user.

So, which should we choose?

Well, if you're a power user then your extensive use may justify the cost of MS Office. If, on the other hand, you'll be using the only basic functions, then Google Docs may be sufficient.

There are of course other factors that come into the decision, such as the fact that Word is the standard in word processing and so everyone is already trained in it. I will be more efficient initially using Word because I already know it so well. (Incidentally, that is the same reason why we all continue to use the QWERTY keyboard even though it was originally designed by typewriter manufacturers to slow down typing, which would jam up early typewriters if the keys were pressed too quickly. We continue to use the theoretically slowest combination of keys to this day because it is the standard and everyone now knows it so well.)

Lessons learned

What do we learn from this analogy? Firstly, that one can make a lot of money selling something that is also offered for free—just ask the bottled water industry!

Salesforce.com may be the standard in sales force automation and there are countless sales reps and sales managers who already know it well. Being a specialist, it has deeper functionality than NetSuite but the key question is how extensively will you be using that functionality?

We can also see that the key question is how much of that deep functionality are you going to take advantage of when opting for a best of breed? Do you really need that extra automation provided by that module? If so, it may be best to opt for the best of breed and integrate. If, on the other hand, the functionality that you will be using is a simple, standard functionality, it's probably not worth the cost and hassle of integration.

The caveat here is training and adoption. Salesforce.com is the standard for Salesforce automation software. so it may be easier to hire sales reps with that experience. It is just one of the factors to take into consideration when deciding whether to use NetSuite's built-in functionality or to move on to a best-of-breed alternative.

Summary

Every situation is unique and you will need to decide whether to opt for the suite as a whole or the suite plus best of breed. We can see, though, that there needs to be compelling reasons to opt for best of breed. It is not just a matter of preference; you need to use the depth of the functionality to justify the cost and complexity of integrating the new software.

NetSuite is always building new functionality into each new version so the hope is that a new version will include important processes that you may be missing. Where do look to find the details about forthcoming NetSuite version? That is the subject of our new chapter on New Releases.

11
New Releases

One of the advantages of using NetSuite is that you are always on the latest release, so can take advantage of the latest features and functions. On the other hand, we need to know how to prepare for upgrades in a scenario where there are constant upgrades.

In this chapter, I will explain the upgrade process and outline the tools available for you to plan and test to ensure a trouble-free upgrade cycle.

In this chapter, we will focus on the Semi-Annual Release Cycle while specifically discussing:

- Major releases
- Release Preview
- Preparing for the upgrade
- Training videos
- Test plan
- Sandbox

Major releases

NetSuite has two major releases per year. The precise schedule changes each year but you can expect the first release in or around April and the second in August, give or take. The releases are usually designated the format of *release year.1* and *release year.2*.

It would be pretty difficult to upgrade each and every NetSuite database on the same day, not to mention risky, so NetSuite phases a release over a period of a few weeks. This enables them to upgrade customers over that period of time. Think of it as NetSuite upgrading 20 percent of customer databases every weekend for 5 weeks. The actual schedule differs each year.

New Releases

What release am I on?

The easiest way to tell the precise release that you are working on is to check out the bottom of the home dashboard:

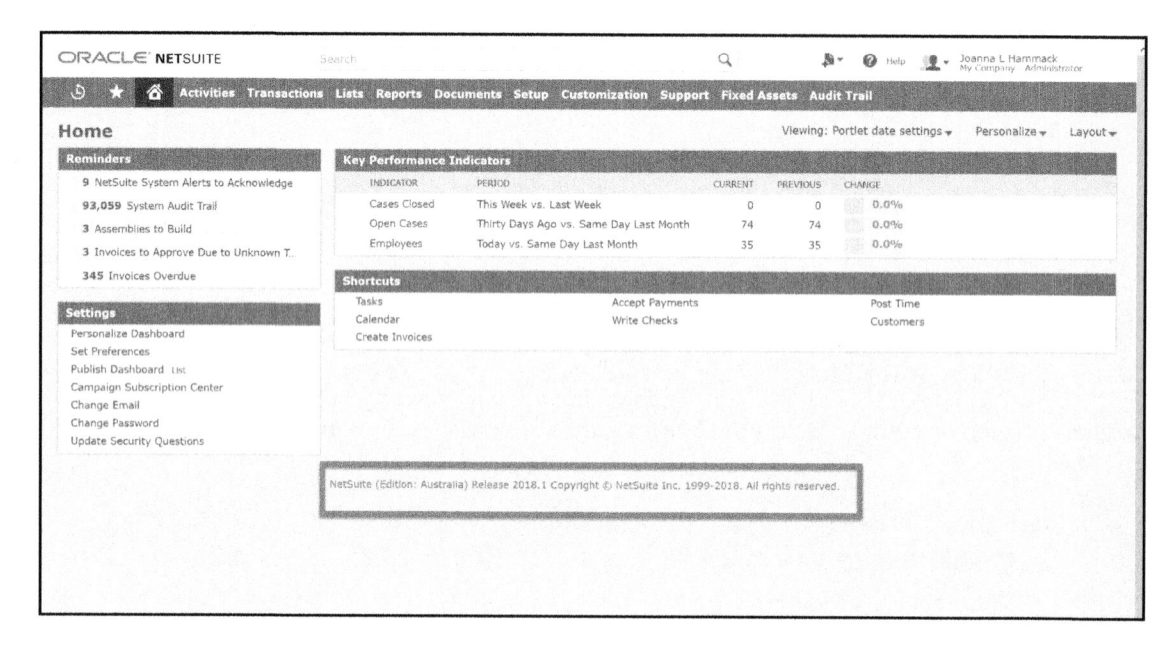

This database is on the 2018.2 release

Notifications

You must be thinking: how will I be notified of a new release?

NetSuite will send the primary contact notifications of upcoming releases. In addition, the administrator can specify other users who should be receiving notifications in the Release and Sandbox section under **Setup** | **Company** | **Email Preferences**:

Chapter 11

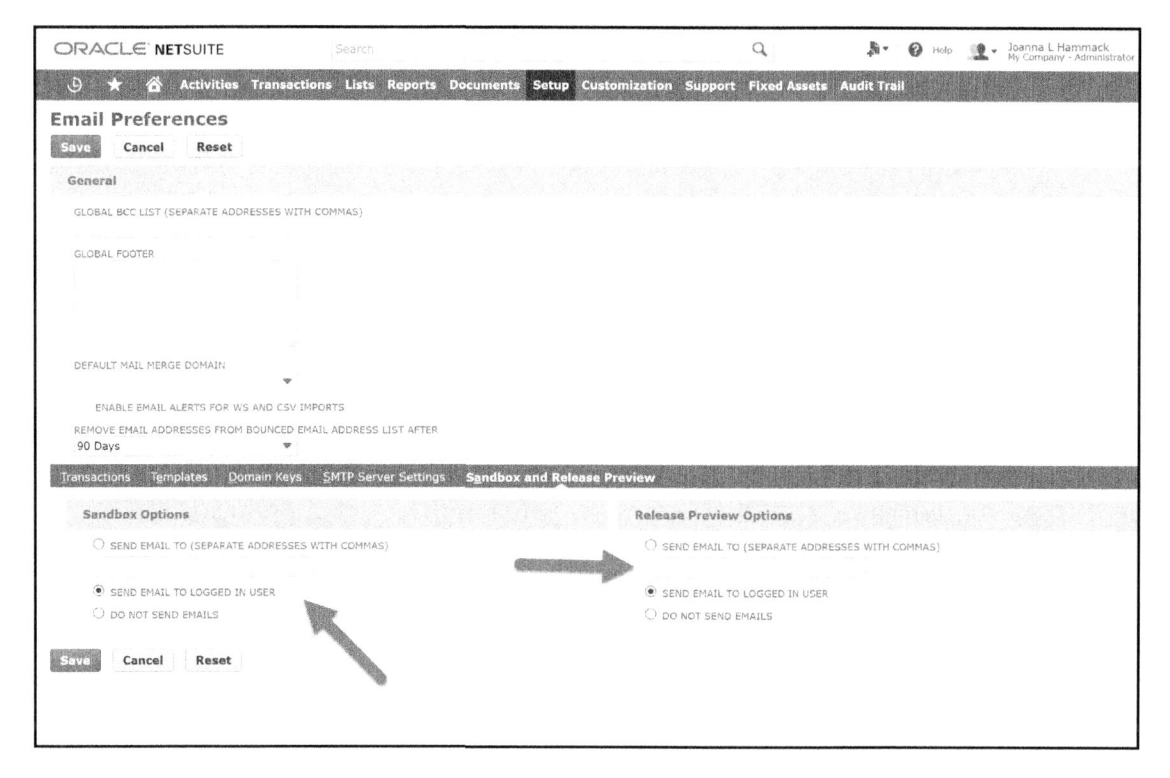

Email preferences setting

Furthermore, NetSuite will push a new portlet onto your home dashboard by default, aptly titled New Release Portlet. It contains details on the new release, including links to the Sneak Peeks, which document the new functionality contained in the new release. This portlet will also display the dates of your scheduled upgrade.

I suggest minimizing the portlet by clicking the Header so that it does not interrupt your daily tasks. You can then maximize it by clicking the Header once again when you are ready to explore the information contained therein.

Important dates

There are two important dates to take note of in the New Release Portlet:

- The upgrade of your production account, which determines the specific date that your account will be upgraded within the timeline of the general release
- The date on which you can access the **Release Preview**

Release Preview

The **Release Preview** account is a temporary test account that is a replica of your live database. It is provided free of charge to you to test the new functionality prior to the release. This account has no interaction with your live account after being provisioned, so don't expect any additional data to synchronize between the two. It's always wise to perform some testing prior to the actual release, the **Release Preview** account is the perfect place to perform this testing.

We access the **Release Preview** database by logging into NetSuite in the normal way and selecting the change role button. The link to the Release Preview will appear there.

Preparing for the upgrade

NetSuite provides us with a number of tools to help us prepare for the release.

Sneak peeks and release notes

NetSuite provides documentation detailing the new functionality in the new release. We can access those documents from the New Release Portlet or from Suite Answers:

1. Click **Help**.
2. Click **SuiteAnswers**.
3. Find the **New Release** section at the bottom-left corner of the screen for links to the release notes and sneak peeks:

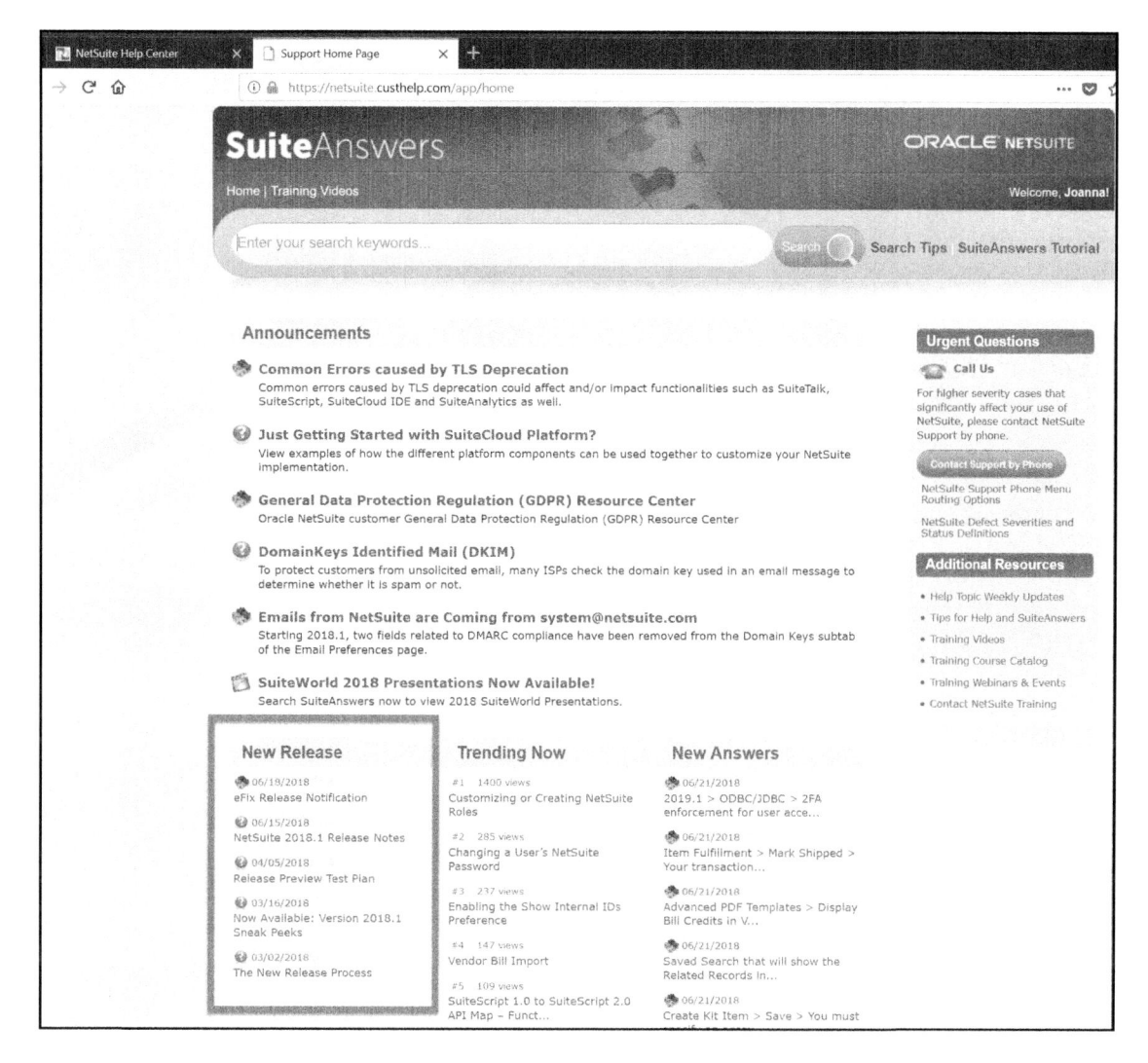

New Release options in Suite Answers

Training videos

NetSuite also provides training on the new functionality, which is also available in **SuiteAnswers**. This training becomes available the closer we get to the release dates, so don't expect to be able to watch it as soon as you see the New Release Portlet appear.

New Releases

There will be a link to the training provided in the New Release Portlet. It is also housed in **SuiteAnswers** and can be found by selecting training videos in **SuiteAnswers** and choosing the **New Features Training** section:

New Features training videos in SuiteAnswers

Test plan

We will need a plan before we can start testing, and NetSuite provides a test plan template for us to document our business process that requires testing. We can access that template in the NetSuite Help center:

1. Click **Help** to access the **Help Center**
2. Go to the **New Release** section and download the test plan:

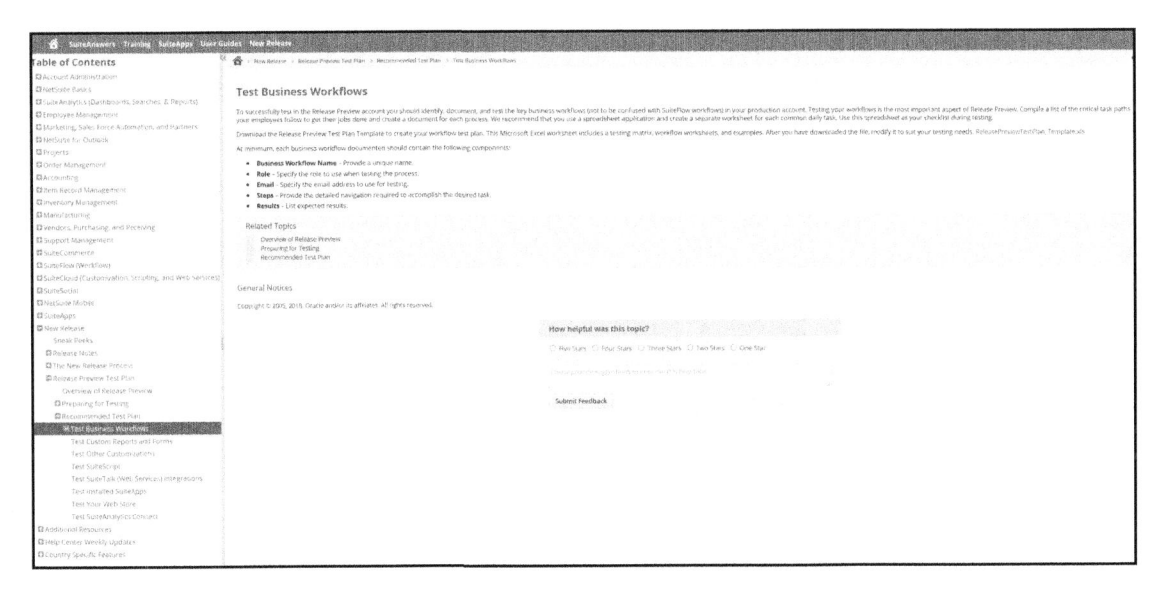

Test Release Plan download screen

It is a basic template providing a format to help you detail your processes. While this can be a time-consuming task, remember that you can reuse the document to test in future releases.

Sandbox

If you've purchased a sandbox account for testing, you'll want to know the upgrade date for the sandbox, which once again, you'll find in the New Release Portlet. Sandbox accounts usually undergo the upgrade after the production accounts have been upgraded. If you have purchased Premier Tier service, however, you can request that the sandbox is upgraded before production.

Summary

There is no need to be concerned with the update schedule, as NetSuite provides us with a demo environment to test on, as well as a test-plan template to ensure that all goes well with the upgrade. There is also comprehensive documentation proved, as well as training on the new features that will be introduced so that we can fully prepare for the semi-annual upgrades.

While more and more functionality is being built into the product, it is possible that it does not work as advertised. How do you troubleshoot issues that may arise in a new version? In fact, how do you troubleshoot issues that may arise in general? That is the focus of our next chapter called Troubleshooting Tips.

12
Troubleshooting Tips

What do you do when something goes wrong? Luckily, NetSuite has a bunch of tools that can help us troubleshoot issues. This chapter will be looking at those tools, as well as providing a framework for how to handle and troubleshoot any issues that may arise.

In this chapter, we will focus on the NetSuite documentation, help center, SuiteAnswers, and the NetSuite user group. Then, we'll look at a logical approach on how to think about these issues. This will provide us with insight into the following:

- Database uptime
  Documentation
- Help center
- SuiteAnswers
- NetSuite user group
- A methodology for troubleshooting

Database uptime

The NetSuite website is very unlikely to go down, but it does happen. What do you do when your company cannot access the NetSuite database?

NetSuite operates a separate website, which provides the status of database access. The website can be found at `https://status.netsuite.com/`.

Troubleshooting Tips

Documentation

NetSuite has a full set of documentation and user guides that are available within the NetSuite help center. These are PDF documents, which are very comprehensive but unfortunately also very long, and can be tedious to read through. To access these documents, go to **Help** and select the **UserGuides**, which you can find as a tab at the top of the screen:

User Guides available in Help

Help center

NetSuite also has a comprehensive help knowledge base, which is accessed by clicking on the **Help** button in the top-right corner of the user interface. The help database is searchable, as you can see from the search bar. It also contains a table of contents, listing all the topics by module:

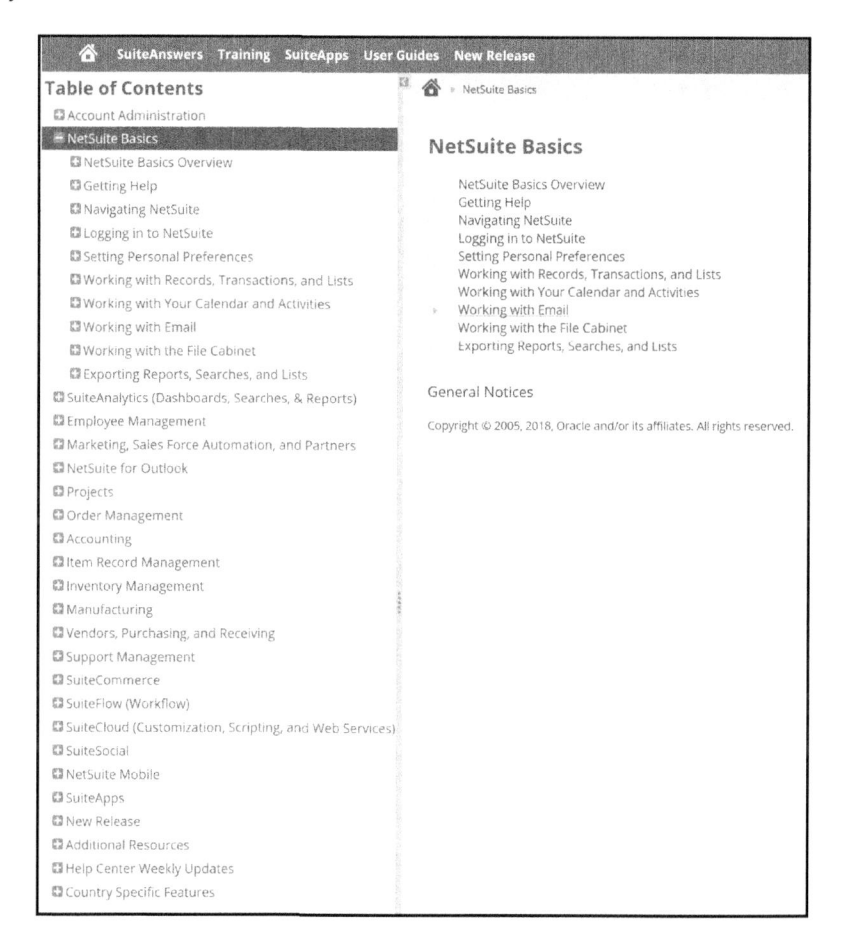

NetSuite Help Center

The articles in the help center are pretty theoretical, giving you the specifics of the features and functions as documented by the NetSuite product management and documentation teams. It can be very useful when learning about new features, but lacks the practical tips and real-world examples you may be looking for. You can find that information in the **SuiteAnswers** database.

Troubleshooting Tips

SuiteAnswers

You access **SuiteAnswers** from within the help center by clicking the **SuiteAnswers** tab. **SuiteAnswers** comprises the help documentation as well as practical tips by the NetSuite support organization based on real questions that they have answered in the past. It is, therefore, more useful than Help itself, however, the number of results that are returned by a search can be a little overwhelming. Let's take a simple search for *Advanced Revenue Management* as an example. You'll see that some of the results of the search come from the help center, while others come from the **SuiteAnswers** knowledge base. If we drill down into a **SuiteAnswers** article, you'll see that it contains very practical information and specific tips to replicate in your own database:

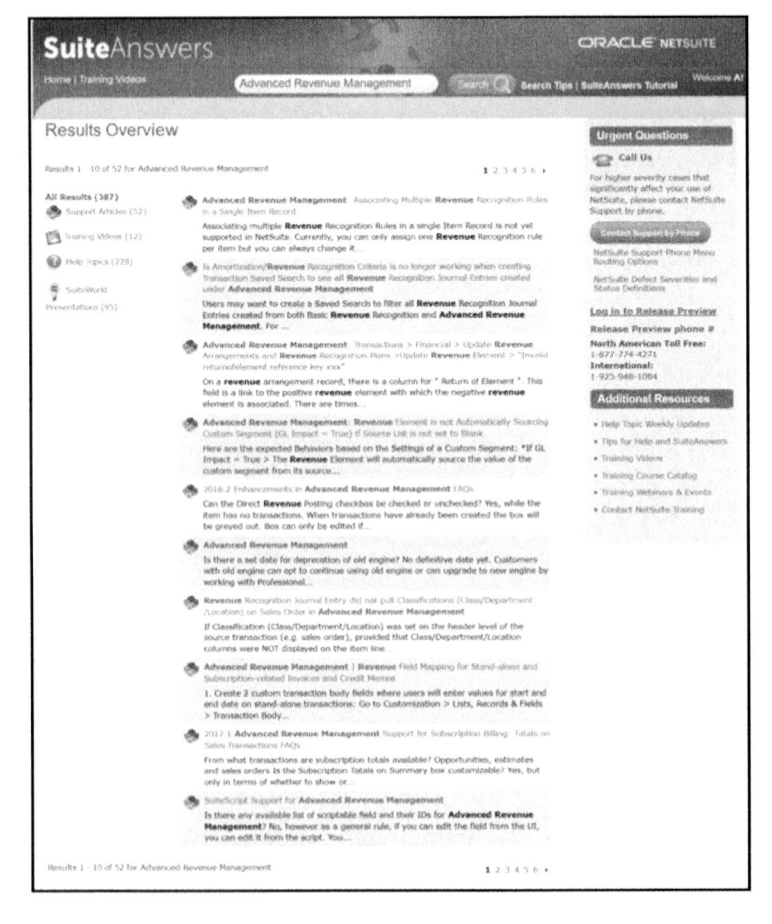

SuiteAnswers

Training videos

SuiteAnswers also has a number of training videos available, which demonstrate the functionality of the product itself. Just click on the trading videos link and view the various categories of videos available, which are sorted by module:

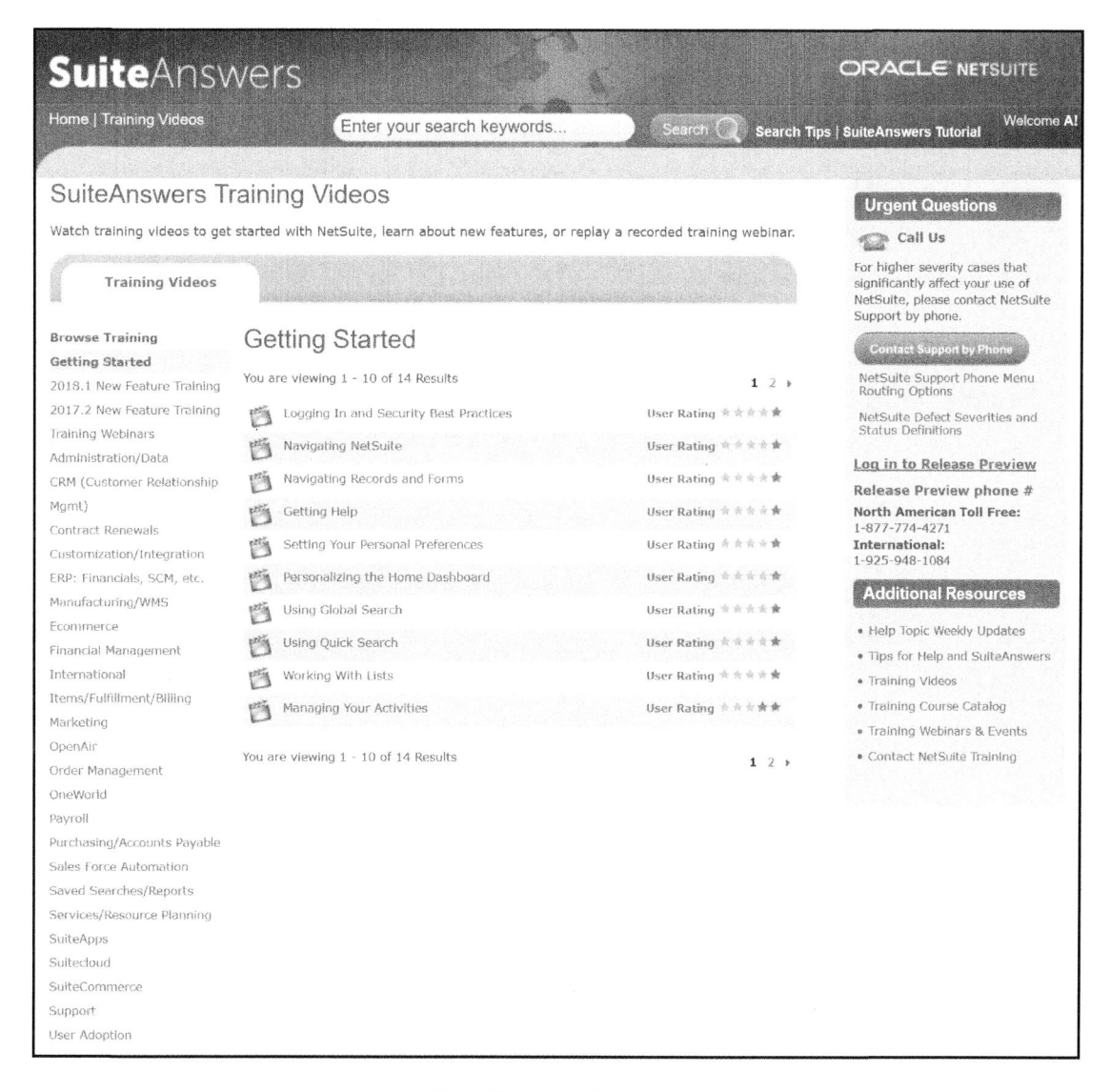

Training Video section in Suite Answers

Troubleshooting Tips

NetSuite user group

In addition to this built-in information, you can also join the NetSuite user group. This is a user group made up of users like yourself who post and answer questions based on their experiences. It can be very useful for answering questions that are not completely unanswered in **SuiteAnswers**. It is very practical, with people giving their honest opinion and assessment about the various NetSuite functionalities. Access the user group at https://usergroup.netsuite.com/users:

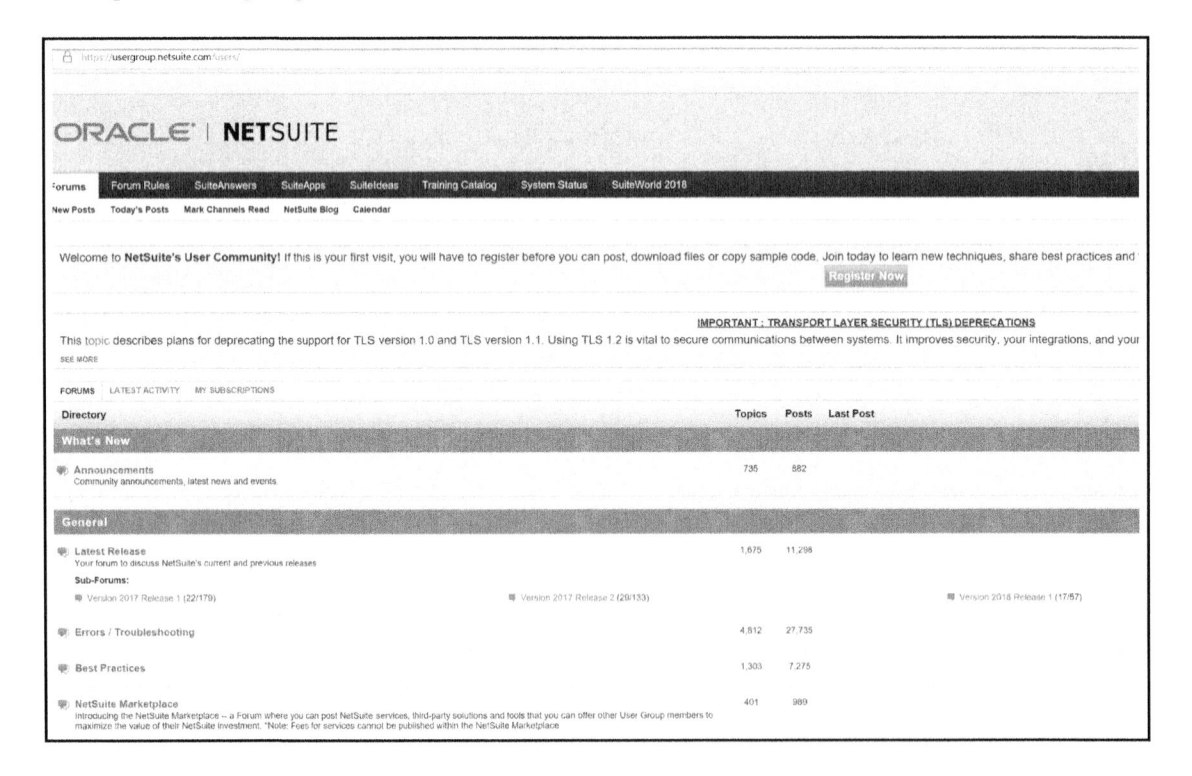

A methodology for troubleshooting

I like to divide issues into one of two categories:

- Errors, such as, "I expect outcome 'A' but am receiving outcome 'B'."
- New functionality, such as, "It would be great if the system could ..."

Troubleshooting errors

Here are some tips to use when troubleshooting errors:

1. Test to see whether the issue is unique to this user by logging in as a different user with the same role. If the second user does not receive the error, it was likely caused by the user's profile.
2. Test to see whether the issue is unique to this role. Try to access that feature in the administrator role. If the Administrator can access the feature, it's possible that the issue stems from the role. Review the permissions on the role. If you are unsure of the permission that needs to be added, use this trick:
    1. Assign yourself that user's role.
    2. Copy the URL of the feature as you access it in the administrator role.
    3. Change your role to the user's role, and paste the URL into the browser address bar. This will likely result in a permissions error, however, the actual error message will show you the permission that is missing on the user's role. You then have the option of adding the permission to the user's roll or adding it in the specific employee's global permissions in order for them to access that function.
3. If you get the same error as the user while logged in as the administrator, change the form to a different form and retest. If you no longer receive the error, the problem is to be found on that form.
4. If the error persists while logged in as the administrator, check the relevant preceding record to see whether an incorrect value has been sourced in from that record. For instance, check the customer record, item, shipping item, and sales tax item when troubleshooting an error on a sales order to ensure that the correct information is sourcing in from those records.
5. If the error persists, go to the **Workflow History** tab on the record and check whether a workflow has been triggered causing the error.
6. If the error persists, start researching the knowledge base, **SuiteAnswers**, and the user group for a solution.
7. As a last resort, submit a case to NetSuite Support.

New functionality

There will come a time when management asks you for specific functionality. It may be a new process or a tweak to an existing process. Let's look at the steps you can take to implement that functionality.

Troubleshooting Tips

Enabling features

Go to **Setup** | **Company** | **Enable Features** and look through the various options available there. Remember that NetSuite could have a different name for the function that you are looking for, so be sure to check the field-level help by clicking the label of each feature to see whether it applies to your problem:

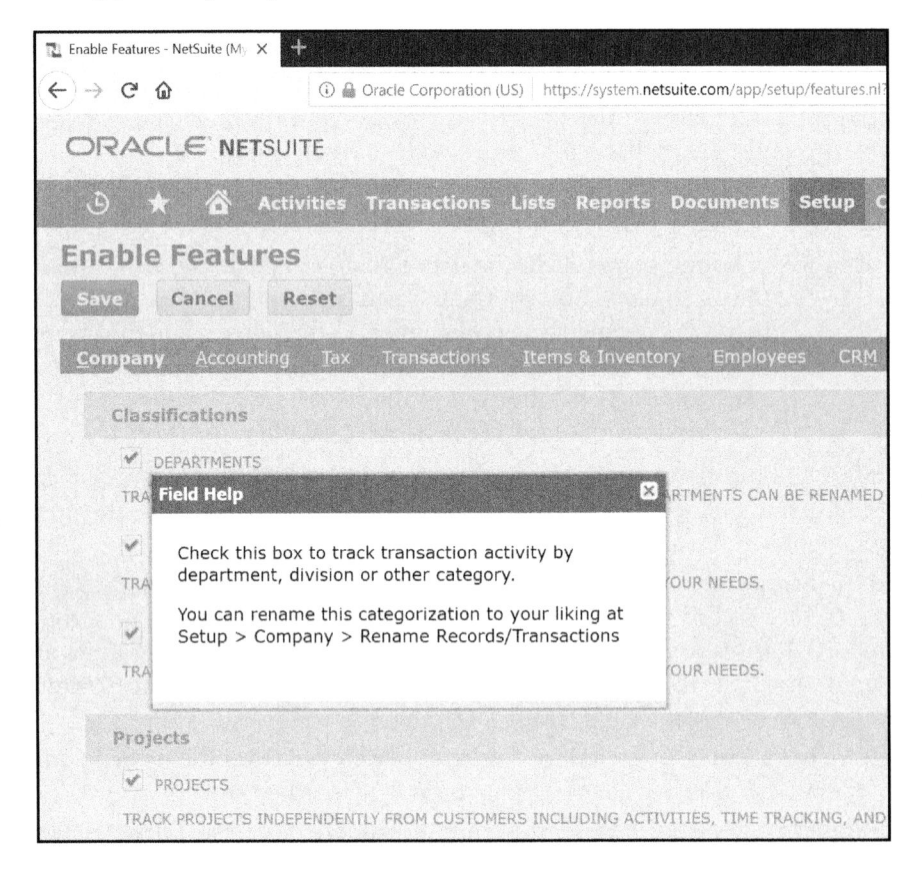

Field-Level Help on the Enable Features screen

Accounting preferences

Go to **Setup** | **Accounting** | **Accounting Preferences**. This is the heart of the ERP and if NetSuite provides that functionality, any tweaks to the configuration will likely be found here. Look through the list of options within **Accounting Preferences** to see whether any of those selections can solve your problem.

Chapter 12

Setup manager

If you are still baffled, click in the **Setup** tab to be taken to the **Setup Manager**. This provides us with a search box to search the entire Setup menu for your search term. If it is found, NetSuite includes hyperlinks to those pages and the search term will appear highlighted in red for you to easily find it:

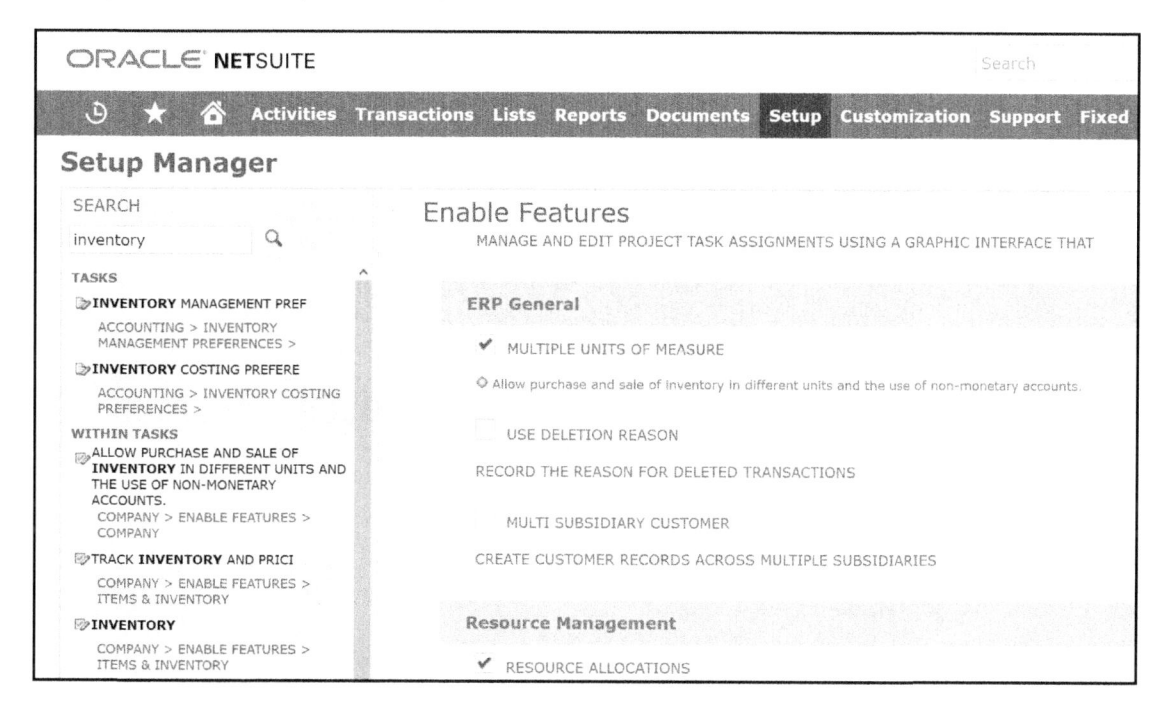

Search Function in Setup Manager

Help Center

NetSuite hides any features that have not been purchased from the UI, so we may need to go outside of the database to determine whether the feature indeed exists.

[327]

Troubleshooting Tips

Access the help center by clicking on the Help button and performing a search for this functionality. The results of the query can tell you not just whether it exists, but whether a feature is available in your account, as we can see from the highlighted text within the result of the search, in the following screenshot:

Results of Help Center search

A philosophical approach

If you still come up empty, I'd encourage you to take a philosophical approach to the question. Ask yourself whether this request seems fairly typical in your industry or somewhat unique. Selling on consignment is a typical process in warehouse distribution and retail companies, whereas a script to automatically open a bottle of champagne when a $1,000,000 deal is signed seems a little more custom. The first question is so typical that you can be sure it's come up before among the thousands of NetSuite customers out there, so there must be some solution. It may not be the optimal solution to the problem, but it is a starting point. The second question is likely unique and may require a completely custom approach. To take a medical analogy, the second problem is so specialized and uncommon that it might require a brain surgeon to fix. The first problem, on the other hand, is as typical as the common cold and can be solved at a lower cost by a visit to the pharmacist.

The point is that there is no need to reinvent the wheel. If you are looking for functionality that should be standard, don't solve the problem on your own. Instead, find the answers that others have come up with to solve that problem. Go to **SuiteAnswers** and the user group, or even do a Google search. It's likely that the answer is out there somewhere. You just need to find it!

Summary

I spoke to a frustrated accounting manager on a recent phone call. He was exasperated by the various issues his company was encountering with their NetSuite system and the thought of the thousands of dollars it would take to fix the problems. Without him even going into the minute details of each specific problem, I was able to reassure him. His challenges were typical for businesses in his industry, so there must be answers out there.

NetSuite has a vibrant community of customers and partners. Issues are constantly being funneled back to NetSuite and solutions are documented in the help center, **SuiteAnswers**, and on the user group. There is no need to solve all these problems on your own. Join the community and access its resources to help you find solutions to the problems you encounter.

In this chapter, we focused on solving problems. In the next chapter, we will look at a checklist you can use to perform periodic maintenance in order to reduce the number of issues that may arise.

13
An Ongoing Maintenance Checklist

Einstein observed that 'Intellectuals solve problems, geniuses prevent them'. How do we prevent problems? In this chapter, we will focus on a system maintenance checklist that can be used to prevent problems.

In this chapter, we will focus on tasks you can perform periodically to:

- Create backups
- Review Administrative Notifications
- Review administrative confirmations
- Review the Login audit trail
- Detect Duplicate records

Checklist

Now let's create a list of monthly activities that an administrator would undertake, starting with backups.

Backups

There was a time when a help desk would solve 80% of user problems with 2 solutions, reboot Windows or restore from backup!

We needed onsite backups, offsite backups, on-premise, on the cloud. Backups and backups of backups. We needed copies of our data in multiple different locations just in case something went wrong with a database server.

An Ongoing Maintenance Checklist

A few years ago, a colleague got a phone call from the CEO of a medium-sized company asking how long it would take to be implemented on NetSuite. My friend replied that a six-month timeline was reasonable for a company of that size. The CEO interjected: *You don't understand*, he exclaimed *the server housing my on-premise ERP system just failed and we've just realized that our backups weren't running properly. If I'm not up and running on a new ERP by next Tuesday, I'll be out of business!*

We are lucky that our ERP is in the cloud, so the responsibility to manage backups rests with NetSuite. While backups are not necessary, there are is an option to back up your data locally if you choose:

1. Go to **Setup** | **Import/Export** | **Full CSV Backup**
2. Click **Submit**:

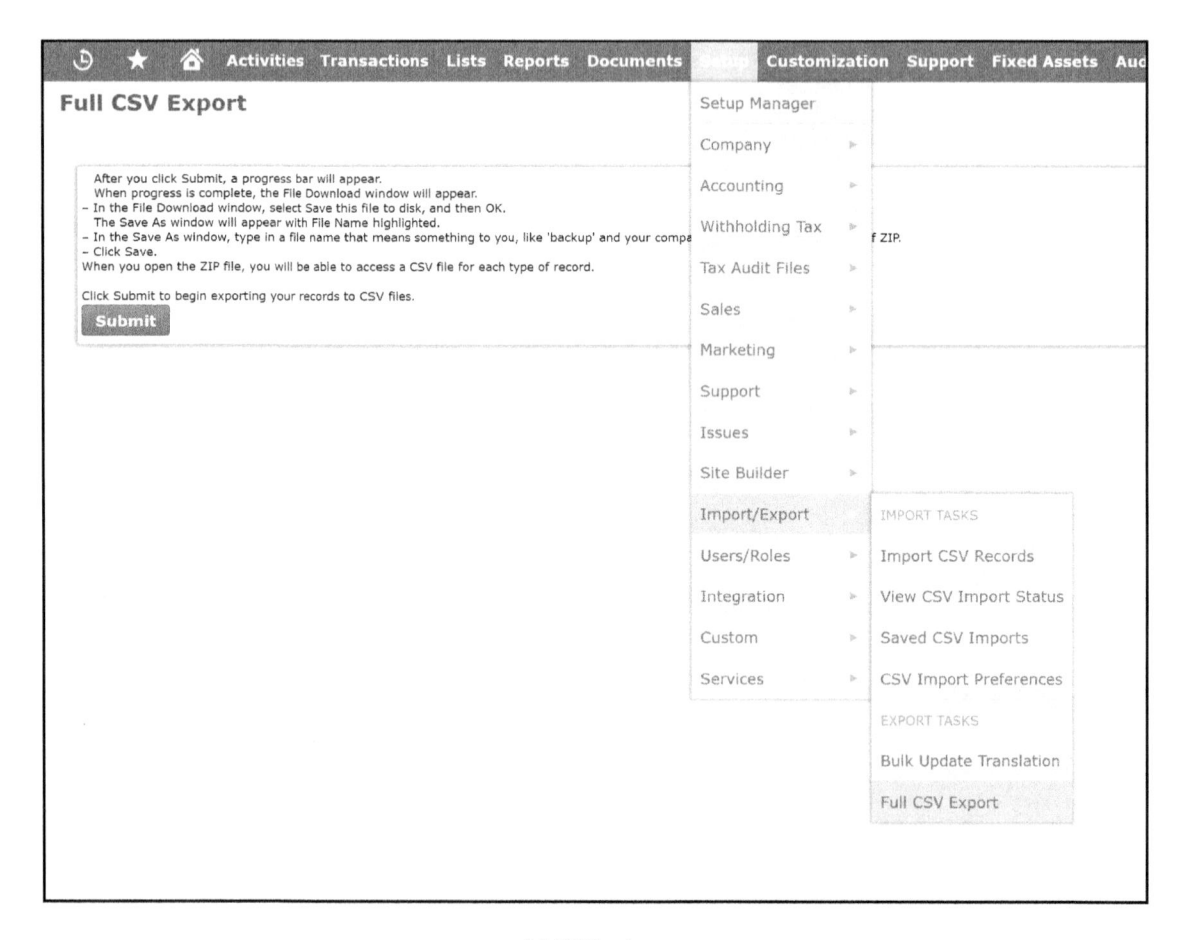

Full CSV Export page

[332]

Chapter 13

This is a manual process. If, on the other hand, you'd like to automate backups, you can use the Send Recurring Emails option in both reports and saved searches, which we discussed in `Chapter 8`, *Analytics – Searches, Reports, and the Dashboard*. The exported data will be limited to the records contained in the report or search. Furthermore, it also requires you to set up the custom report or search to select all the fields you wish to export:

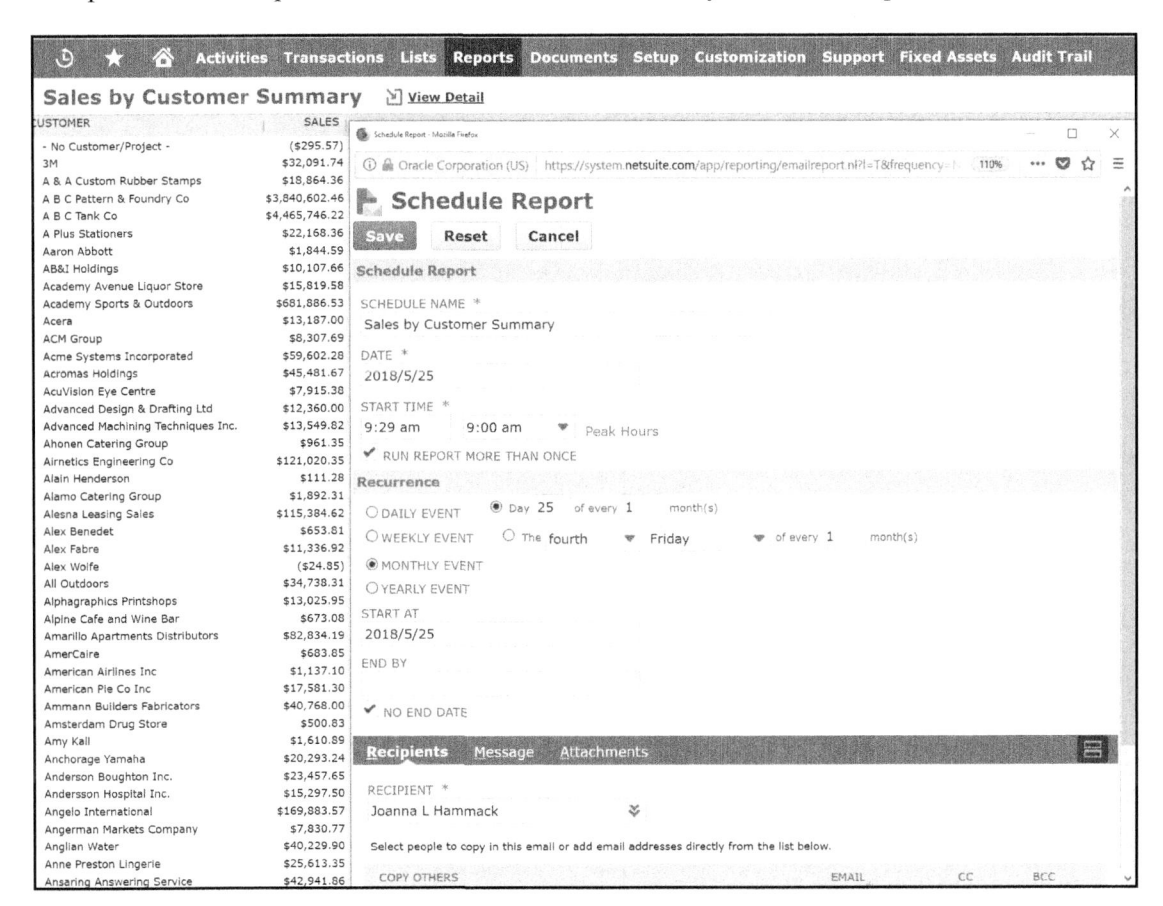

An Ongoing Maintenance Checklist

Review administrative confirmations

Administrative notifications, such as scheduled maintenance notifications, appear intermittently when you log into the system. They can also be emailed to you if you prefer. You can also review them at **Setup | Company | Administrative Notifications** on the **Confirmed** and **Pending Confirmation** screens:

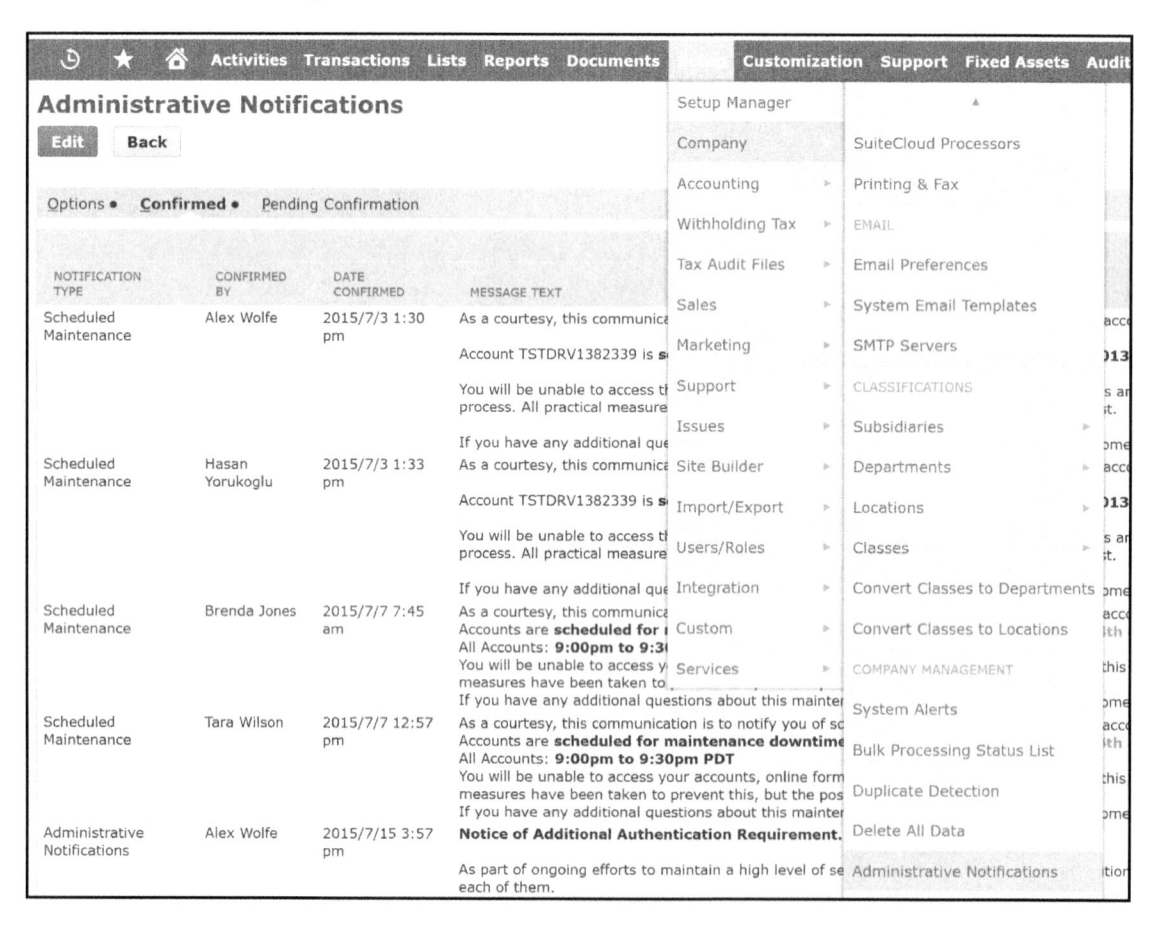

List of Administrative Notifications

[334]

These notifications contain important information, such as legal, maintenance, billing, and service release information, and should be reviewed to ensure that there are no surprises in your future.

System alerts

System Alerts advise you of issues NetSuite has run into when processing transactions, such as the failure to create an integrated shipping label for an order. The **System Alerts** page is found at **Setup** | **Company** | **System Alerts**. Click an alert to get more information on the reason for the failure:

A system alert detail message

There is also a handy **System Alert** dashboard reminder that you can enable to keep track of this information on a real-time basis:

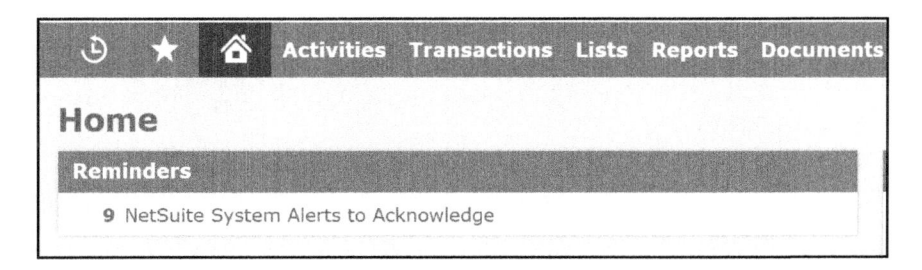

System Alerts Reminder

An Ongoing Maintenance Checklist

Login audit trail

Are you concerned that an unauthorized person is trying to log into your account using a stolen password? The login audit trail can tell you who logged in and from what IP address. Go to **Setup** | **Users/Roles** | **Login Audit Trail**.

NetSuite has built a search to review this information. We can filter the search by user, date, role, and even IP address. The results can also be filtered to login failures or failures on the security questions. Simply click **Submit**:

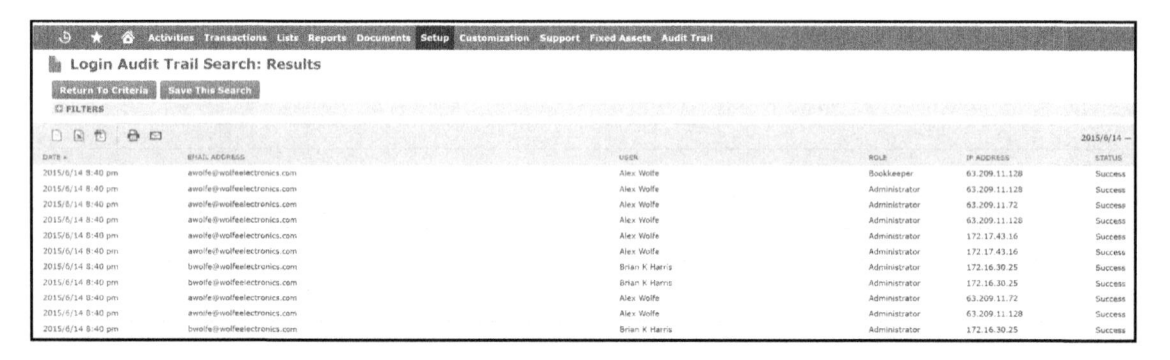

Login Audit Trail Search: Results

Billing information

NetSuite has a **Billing Information** page to help you keep track of the licenses that you have purchased, as well as the amount that you are using. It is found at **Setup** | **Company** | **View Billing Information**:

Chapter 13

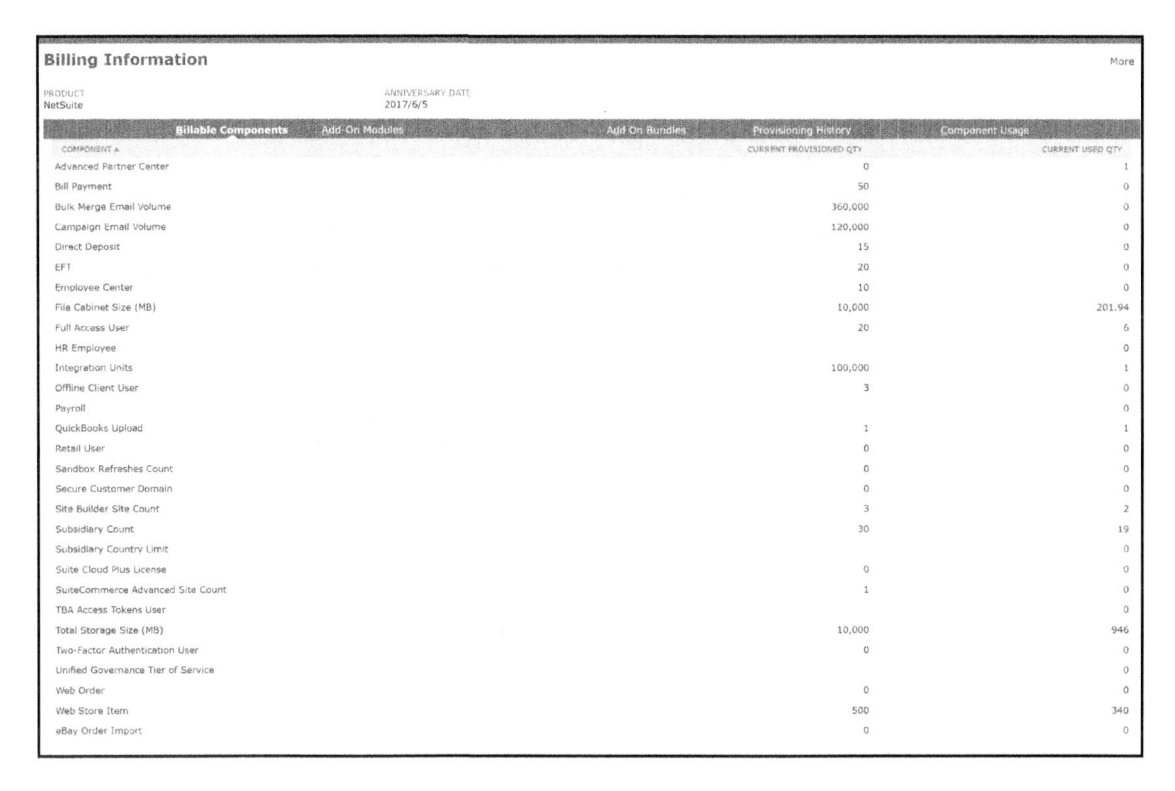

Billing Information				More
PRODUCT: NetSuite	ANNIVERSARY DATE: 2017/6/5			

Billable Components	Add-On Modules	Add On Bundles	Provisioning History	Component Usage
COMPONENT ▲			CURRENT PROVISIONED QTY	CURRENT USED QTY
Advanced Partner Center			0	1
Bill Payment			50	0
Bulk Merge Email Volume			360,000	0
Campaign Email Volume			120,000	0
Direct Deposit			15	0
EFT			20	0
Employee Center			10	0
File Cabinet Size (MB)			10,000	201.94
Full Access User			20	6
HR Employee				0
Integration Units			100,000	1
Offline Client User			3	0
Payroll				0
QuickBooks Upload			1	1
Retail User			0	0
Sandbox Refreshes Count			0	0
Secure Customer Domain			0	0
Site Builder Site Count			3	2
Subsidiary Count			30	19
Subsidiary Country Limit				0
Suite Cloud Plus License			0	0
SuiteCommerce Advanced Site Count			1	0
TBA Access Tokens User				0
Total Storage Size (MB)			10,000	946
Two-Factor Authentication User			0	0
Unified Governance Tier of Service				0
Web Order			0	0
Web Store Item			500	340
eBay Order Import			0	0

Billing Information page

The number of **Full Access Users** is very important and it shows you how many more users can be added before you'll need to purchase more user space. Keep track of the **File Cabinet Size (MB)** usage in addition to **Bulk Merge Email Volume** and **Campaign Email Volume**, as you will need to purchase more volume if you expect to exceed the provisioned limits.

Duplicate detection

Duplicates happen, so NetSuite has a duplicate detection tool to help us merge duplicate records. We discussed this at length in `Chapter 2`, *Exploring NetSuite Tools*. The tool can be found at **Lists | Mass Updates | Entity Duplicate Detection**:

[337]

An Ongoing Maintenance Checklist

Duplicate Detection page

It identifies duplicates based on the settings in **Setup | Company | Duplicate Detection** and enables you to merge duplicate records into one master record. Detecting duplicates can be a difficult task as one value in a field can result in a duplicate being incorrectly categorized. It is, therefore, worthwhile to change the detection criteria and see whether this identifies any additional duplicates to be merged.

Summary

The advantage of operating in the cloud is that so many traditional administrative steps are handled for us by NetSuite. This reduces our technical responsibilities and enables us to spend more time helping our users get the most out of this application.

If you've made it this far, you've seen the impact a good administrator can have by understanding this application. We've discussed how NetSuite can automate virtually all the processes in your company. We've demonstrated the main processes and shown you the levers you can use to tweak a process. We've also explored the pages you need to look at when you need to implement new processes. You now have the knowledge to tighten the security of the application as well as customize it for your industry. You can import and manipulate data, as well as being able to leverage the business analytics so that your users can monitor the performance of the business. You know how to prepare for new releases and what to do when things go wrong.

In short, you have the tools and the knowledge to support your users from both a business and a technical perspective. My hope is that you can start using these tools right away and make yourself an invaluable asset who can provide the day-to-day support and the strategic direction every company needs.

Other Books You May Enjoy

If you enjoyed this book, you may be interested in these other books by Packt:

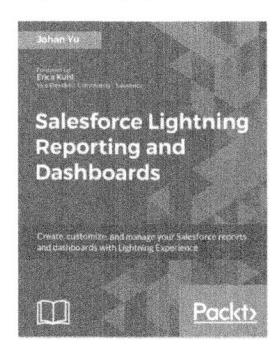

Salesforce Lightning Reporting and Dashboards
Johan Yu

ISBN: 9781788297387

- Navigate in Salesforce.com within the Lightning Experience User Interface
- Secure and share your reports and dashboards with other users
- Create, manage, and maintain reports using Report Builder
- Learn how the report type can affect the report generated
- Explore the report and dashboard folder and the sharing model
- Create reports with multiple formats and custom report types
- Explore various dashboard features in Lightning Experience
- Use Salesforce1, including accessing reports and dashboards

Other Books You May Enjoy

Learning Salesforce Einstein
Mohith Shrivastava

ISBN: 9781787126893

- Get introduced to AI and its role in CRM and cloud applications
- Understand how Einstein works for the sales, service, marketing, community, and commerce clouds
- Gain a deep understanding of how to use Einstein for the analytics cloud
- Build predictive apps on Heroku using PredictionIO, and work with Einstein Predictive Vision Services
- Incorporate Einstein in the IoT cloud
- Test the accuracy of Einstein through Salesforce reporting and Wave analytics

Leave a review - let other readers know what you think

Please share your thoughts on this book with others by leaving a review on the site that you bought it from. If you purchased the book from Amazon, please leave us an honest review on this book's Amazon page. This is vital so that other potential readers can see and use your unbiased opinion to make purchasing decisions, we can understand what our customers think about our products, and our authors can see your feedback on the title that they have worked with Packt to create. It will only take a few minutes of your time, but is valuable to other potential customers, our authors, and Packt. Thank you!

Index

A

administrative confirmations
  reviewing 334
  system alerts 335
administrator supporting features, Netsuite
  dashboards, publishing 33
  Duplicate Detection 29, 30
  password policy 30, 32
  searches, building 33
  workflow manager, used for automating tasks 35
audience tab 239
audit trail
  about 122, 126
  Saved Search Execution Log 127
  System Notes 124
  View Login Audit Trail 122
authentication
  about 108
  IP address rules 109
  login URL 109
  security questions 109
  username and password 108
available filters tab 237

B

best of breed
  about 308
  versus suite 307
building blocks, order-to-cash process
  about 95
  customer 96
  item record 97
  shipping items 98
building blocks, procure-to-pay process
  about 72
  employees 73
  item record 75
  vendors 74

C

characteristics, customization
  custom field, creating 141
checklist
  about 331
  backups 331
criteria tab
  about 224, 226
  formulas 228
  standard criteria, versus summary criteria 229
CSV import wizard 178, 179, 181
custom entity field 143
custom KPI
  about 278
  example 278, 280
custom records
  about 151
  example 152, 155, 159
  online form example 160, 162, 165
  online forms 152
  reporting 160
custom reports
  about 128
  access sub tab 130
  audience sub-tab 129
  file cabinet 131
customer import
  about 185
  use case, example 188, 190, 192
customization
  about 135
  characteristics 141
  options 136

tips 137, 139
tricks 137, 139
customizing forms
  about 165
  main screen 166, 169

D

dashboard
  about 277
  custom KPI 278
  KPI scorecard 278
  overview 214, 216, 217, 219, 220, 222
defaults and preferences, order-to-cash process
  accounting preferences 91, 93
  accounts receivable, in accounting preferences 94
  configuring 89
  sales and pricing section, in accounting preferences 94
  shipping and tax 90
defaults and preferences, procure-to-pay process
  approval routing 72
  configuring 67
  general tab 68
  items/transactions tab 68
  order management 69, 71, 72

E

edge cases
  about 205
  CSV import, extending 208
  transaction form, changing via import 206
email tab
  about 240
  email alerts 242
  scheduled emails 241
employee field
  use case 145, 148, 150
Enterprise Resource Planning
  about 7, 10, 12, 14
  need for 7, 10, 12, 14

F

financial report builder 273, 275
forms 112
framework
  about 308
  learning 309
functionality, troubleshooting
  features, enabling 326
  help center 327
  philosophical approach 328
  preferences, accounting 326
  setup manager 327

H

highlighting tab 236
HTML layouts 170, 172, 175

I

imports
  best practices 182
  internal IDs 182
  source data 184
  tips 184
  troubleshooting 209
item import
  about 193
  inventory import 194
  kit import 196, 198

K

Key Performance Indicators (KPIs) 40
KPI meters 41
KPI scorecard
  about 278, 281, 284
  example 284, 286
KPI scorecards 42

L

list records
  about 56
  accounts chart 60
  customers 56
  employees 60

items 59
transactions 61
vendor 58
login audit trail
  about 336
  billing information 336
  duplicate detection 337

N

Net Promoter Score (NPS) 152
NetSuite
  about 14, 16
  administrator, supporting features 24, 26, 28
  business, supporting features 18, 19, 23
  database uptime 319
  documentation 320
  help center 321
  notifications 312
  release 311, 312
  release notes 314
  release preview 314
  release, dates 314
  sandbox 317
  sneak peaks 314
  SuiteAnswers 322
  test plan 317
  upgrade, preparing 314
  user group 324
  user, supporting features 36, 38
  videos, training 315, 323

O

order-to-cash process
  about 86
  features, enabling 86

P

PDF layouts 170, 172, 175
permissions 111, 112, 113
procure-to-pay process
  about 65
  feature, enabling 66

R

reports
  about 253, 256, 258
  advantages 223
  financial report builder 273, 275
  standard reports 259
  versus searches 223
restrictions
  about 112, 114
  access, to records 116
  by segment 116
  forms 118
results tab
  about 231
  custom label columns 235
  formula column 235
  function column 235
  summary column 232, 234
  summary label columns 235
roles
  about 111, 243
  center 112
  differences, identifying 120
  global permissions 121
  user roles 119

S

saved searches
  about 224
  audience tab 239
  available filters tab 237
  criteria tab 224, 226
  email tab 240
  entity saved search example 249
  examples 249
  highlighting tab 236
  results tab 231
  roles 243
  search settings tab 244
  transaction search example 251
search settings tab
  about 244
  dashboard view 247
  for reminders 248

list view 244
public checkbox 244
sublist view 247
searches
　advantages 223
　saved searches 223
　versus reports 223
standard reports
　about 259
　edit columns 260, 262, 264, 265, 267
　filters 268
　more options 270, 272
　sorting 269
subsidiary hierarchy
　setting up 54, 55
suite
　about 307
　versus best of breed 307
SuiteFlow
　about 290
　actions, creating 301
　automating 297
　automation, activating 293
　initiation 294
　order 295
　record, affecting 291
　states, creating 300
　triggers 296
　workflow, creating 298
　workflow, setting up 298
　workflow, troubleshooting 302

T

transaction field
　use case 145, 148, 150
transaction import 199, 202, 204
transactions, list records
　advanced intercompany journals 62
　intercompany journal entries 62
transactions, order-to-cash process 100, 101, 104
transactions, procure-to-pay process 76, 78, 81, 83, 85
troubleshooting
　errors 325
　functionality 325
　methodology 324

U

use case
　about 304
　custom field, creating 305
　saved search 305
　workflow 305
user supporting features, NetSuite
　data, pivoting on dashboard 47, 48
　Global search 49, 50
　Key Performance Indicators (KPIs) 40
　KPI meters 41
　KPI scorecards 42
　list portlet 43
　memorized transaction 50
　reminders 39
　report snapshots 46
　Saved Search portlet 44
　Trend Graph 45